The World Jewish Congress
1936—2016

The World Jewish Congress
1936—2016

Foreword by
Ambassador Ronald S. Lauder

Edited by
Menachem Z. Rosensaft

WORLD JEWISH CONGRESS

New York • Jerusalem • Geneva • Brussels • Buenos Aires • Vilnius • Zagreb

ISBN: 978-0-996-9361-1-8

Library of Congress Cataloging-in-Publication Data

Names: World Jewish Congress. | Rosensaft, Menachem Z., 1948- editor. |
  Lauder, Ronald S., writer of foreword.
Title: The World Jewish Congress, 1936-2016 / edited by Menachem Z. Rosensaft;
  foreword by Ambassador Ronald S. Lauder.
Description: First edition. | New York : World Jewish Congress, [2017] |
  Includes bibliographical references and index.
Identifiers: LCCN 2016050516 | ISBN 9780996936118 (hardcover : alk. paper)
Subjects: LCSH: World Jewish Congress--History. | World Jewish
  Congress—Political activity. | Judaism—Relations—Catholic Church. |
  Banks and banking, Swiss—Corrupt practices. | Holocaust, Jewish
  (1939-1945)—Reparations.
Classification: LCC DS101 .W636 2017 | DDC 305.892/400601—dc23
LC record available at https://lccn.loc.gov/2016050516

COMPOSITION BY MILES B. COHEN
MANUFACTURED IN THE UNITED STATES OF AMERICA
BY G & H SOHO, INC.
www.ghsoho.com

Contents

List of Abbreviations

ADL	Anti-Defamation League
AJA	American Jewish Archives
AJCSJ	American Jewish Conference on Soviet Jewry
AMIA	Asociación Mutual Israelita Argentina (Argentine Israelite Mutual Association)
BDS	Boycott, Divestment, and Sanctions
COJO	World Conference of Jewish Organizations
CPA	Communist Party of Australia
CPSU	Communist Party of the Soviet Union
CRIF	Conseil Représentatif des Juifs de France
CRRC	Commission for Religious Relations with the Jews
CZA	Central Zionist Archives
DAIA	Delegación de Asociaciones Israelitas Argentinas (Delegation of Argentine Jewish Associations)
DP	Displaced Persons
ECAJ	Executive Council of Australian Jewry
ECOSOC	UN Economic and Social Council

FIFA	Fédération Internationale de Football Association
FLN	Front de Libération Nationale (National Liberation Front; Algerian socialist political party and nationalist movement)
GDR	German Democratic Republic
ICFR	Israel Council on Foreign Relations
ICRC	International Committee of the Red Cross
ICJP	International Council of Jewish Parliamentarians
IDC	Interdisciplinary Center Herzliya
IDF	Israel Defense Forces
ICJ	International Court of Justice
IJA	Institute of Jewish Affairs
IJCIC	International Jewish Committee on Interreligious Consultations
ILC	International Catholic-Jewish Liaison Committee
IMCS	International Movement of Catholic Students
IMT	International Military Tribunal at Nuremberg (1945–1946)
IPU	Inter-Parliamentary Union
JDC	American Jewish Joint Distribution Committee
JDCorps	Jewish Diplomatic Corps
JTA	Jewish Telegraphic Agency
LAJC	Latin American Jewish Congress
MOU	memorandum of understanding
NAA	National Archives of Australia
NCDF	National Community Directors' Forum
NGO	non-governmental organization
OSI	Office of Special Investigations
OSS	Office of Special Services
ÖVP	Österreichische Volkspartei (Austrian People's Party)
PDI	Parti Démocratique pour l'Independence (Democratic Independence Party; Morocco)
PLO	Palestinian Liberation Organization
SACC	Security and Crisis Centre

SBA	Swiss Bankers Association
SBC	Swiss Bank Corporation
SFJC	Swiss Federation of Jewish Communities
SPÖ	Sozialistische Partei Österreichs (Austrian Socialist party; in 1991 renamed: Sozialdemokratische Partei Österreichs)
TSKŻ	Jewish Social Cultural Organization (Poland)
UBS	Union Bank of Switzerland
UNCHR	UN Commission on Human Rights
UNESCO	UN Educational, Scientific and Cultural Organization
UNHCHR	UN High Commissioner for Human Rights
UNHRC	UN Human Rights Council
UNICEF	UN International Children's Emergency Fund
UNRRA	UN Relief and Rehabilitation Administration
UNWCC	UN War Crimes Commission
USSR	Union of Soviet Socialist Republics or Soviet Union
WIZO	Women's International Zionist Organization
WJRO	World Jewish Restitution Organization
WZO	World Zionist Organization
ŻIH	Jewish Historical Institute (Warsaw, Poland)

Foreword

Ambassador Ronald S. Lauder

In August of 1942, a man named Gerhart Riegner tried to alert the world
to the atrocities that were being perpetrated against Jews in Poland and
that these crimes against humanity were part of Hitler's plan to annihilate
all of the Jewish people. Many of us know that Dr. Riegner headed the
Geneva office of the World Jewish Congress at that time, and some of us
know that he later served for many years with great distinction as the
WJC's secretary-general. But did you know that Gerhart Riegner also
was largely responsible for the remarkable change in the Catholic-Jewish
dialogue that altered the Vatican's attitude toward Jews after two thousand
years of anti-Semitic hatred? And did you know it was the Swedish Section
of the WJC that brought about Raoul Wallenberg's heroic mission to
Budapest during the Holocaust, which prevented the deportation of tens
of thousands of Hungarian Jews to what would have been an almost certain
death?

We know that it was the WJC that exposed Kurt Waldheim's sordid
Nazi past before he was elected president of Austria in 1986—I was the
US Ambassador to Vienna at that time—but did you know that the WJC

Ambassador Ronald S. Lauder is President of the World Jewish Congress.

negotiated with North African governments during the 1950s to enable Jews from Morocco, Tunisia, and Algeria to leave for Israel, France, and elsewhere? Did you know that a senior WJC official advised Justice Robert H. Jackson at the post–World War II trial of Nazi war criminals at Nuremberg? And did you know that under the indefatigable leadership of CEO Robert Singer, the WJC today has developed and is implementing an unprecedented agenda of ambitious and far reaching programs and activities on behalf of the Jewish people? These are only some of the WJC's dramatic accomplishments that are described with great eloquence in the book you hold in your hands. I am deeply grateful to my longtime friend Menachem Rosensaft for compiling and editing this truly magnificent account of the WJC's history since its founding in 1936. The authors whom Menachem brought together remind us not only what the WJC did in the past, but why the Jewish people need this vital organization now more than ever and will continue to need it in the future.

The World Jewish Congress has always been unique, different from other Jewish organizations because it is truly a democratic global body made up of more than one hundred communities around the world. The WJC was created on the eve of the Holocaust in 1936, just three years after the Nazi rise to power, out of the need to organize in the face of the dangerous anti-Semitism sweeping across Europe. As Menachem writes in his introduction, not only did no international Jewish organization exist in 1936, but the WJC's founders faced tremendous opposition from other Jewish leaders and groups who did not want an organization advocating politically for Jewish rights. Our mission has not changed. It is the same today as it was then: to give the Jewish people a voice in the international arena, to protect Jews against anti-Semitism and violence, to defend Jewish values and interests anywhere and everywhere in the world, and—since 1948—to support and defend the Jewish state of Israel against its enemies and detractors.

The WJC's overriding goal is to protect Jewish communities across the globe and to allow Jews everywhere to live freely as Jews, without discrimination or the threat of persecution. While there is no doubt that Jews currently are in a better and safer position than they were in 1936, much work remains to be done. It is true that today there is a prevalence of democratic governments that are strongly supportive of Jewish concerns and with which the WJC regularly interacts. But anti-Semitism is on the rise again all over the world, and coupled with the frighteningly fast-growing threat of global terrorism, our Jewish communities face enormous danger and pressure. Over the last decade, we have witnessed unfathomable acts of violence against Jews in Israel, in Europe, and even in the United States. Jewish communities in many parts of this world have no choice but to instate heavy security apparatuses to protect their institutions. In Europe, Jews are faced with the double threat of growing far-right movements and violent instances of Islamic jihadism. In the United Nations and many of its bodies and agencies, an anti-Israel bias has become a frightening phenomenon.

The WJC protects Jews everywhere and constantly defends the State of Israel against these threats through direct contact with the world's leaders. Over the last decade, I have visited scores of communities and met with presidents, prime ministers, foreign ministers, and local officials, conveying the concerns of our communities and representing their interests.

The WJC is the official representative of the Jewish world. We are exceedingly well-coordinated and have strong contacts with governmental and international institutions and personnel on all levels. We are well positioned to carry out the critical work of protecting and defending Jewish interests and the State of Israel because we are the centralized body of the global Jewish community. In some ways, the WJC can be seen as the world government of the Jewish people—a democratically organized body convening communities from across the world to work together for our collective vision of a safer today and a better tomorrow. As in all other governments, our affiliated communities may not always agree with each other, but thanks to the WJC, they have a platform for global discussion and know that the WJC stands up for them in the international arena and, when necessary, to their own governments back home. Due in large part to the strength of the State of Israel and the existence of the WJC, as well as other Jewish organizations, the Jewish world no longer fears another Holocaust. Like the founders of the WJC who gathered in Geneva in August 1936, we are determined to defeat our enemies; and perhaps most important, thanks to the WJC, Jews around the world know that they are not alone.

Introduction

Menachem Z. Rosensaft

On June 7, 2007, when Ambassador Ronald S. Lauder succeeded Edgar M. Bronfman as president of the World Jewish Congress, he took over a venerable organization that was in a state of reputational chaos and dire financial straits. Just prior to announcing his resignation in March of that year, Bronfman fired Israel Singer—the WJC's former secretary-general, who had been made chairman of the organization's Policy Council— accusing Singer of serious financial misconduct. A highly publicized investigation by the New York attorney general into the WJC's financial operations and absence of meaningful governance procedures placed the then seventy-one-year-old, Geneva-based organization under a cloud and adversely affected its fundraising. The costly retention of two major New York law firms in connection with the attorney general's investigation, as well as a number of controversial, not to say ill-advised, attempts at legal maneuvering—including a defamation lawsuit (which was ultimately withdrawn) against the veteran WJC leader Isi Leibler, who had blown the whistle on Israel Singer's activities in the first place—severely depleted the WJC's reserves to the point of virtual insolvency.[1] Quite a few of

Menachem Z. Rosensaft is general counsel of the World Jewish Congress.

Ambassador Lauder's friends and associates wondered why he would want to take on the not inconsiderable burden of trying to restore the WJC to its erstwhile glory and prominence. For many, what was commonly referred to as the Israel Singer scandal overshadowed the WJC's many important accomplishments.

Ten years later, the WJC is widely recognized as one of the most influential international Jewish organizations—perhaps the most important—with the 2004–2007 scandal a distant memory, if that. Under Ambassador Lauder's leadership, and thanks to his vision and personal generosity, the WJC has regained both respectability and credibility, no small achievement.

Shortly after taking office, Ambassador Lauder engaged the legendary Jewish professional leader, Michael Schneider, as the WJC's secretary-general. Schneider had been executive vice-president and chief executive officer of the American Jewish Joint Distribution Committee (JDC) and for years has been universally revered for rescuing Jews in Iran, Ethiopia, Yugoslavia, and elsewhere, often under the most challenging and daunting conditions. Schneider's immediate task was to restore luster to the WJC's internal operations, something he accomplished in large part as a result of his own impeccable reputation for integrity.

To a certain extent, and prodded in large part by the requirements of the New York State attorney general, Schneider's predecessor, Stephen Herbits, had already begun the process of instituting much-needed governance reforms at the WJC by the time Ambassador Lauder and Schneider took charge of the organization. A new director of finance, Chaim Reiss (now chief financial officer), had established financial controls and personnel procedures in place of a previously haphazard and often erratic modus operandi. At the same time, however, Herbits defended Israel Singer assiduously for two years against charges that he had engaged in self-serving financial improprieties.[2] Eventually, Herbits turned on Israel Singer with a vengeance. At the end of Herbits's tenure at the WJC, he unsuccessfully urged the New York State attorney general to reopen the office's investigation into Singer's actions.[3]

Schneider succeeded in calming the waters. He restored morale and a sense of purpose among the WJC staff with his decency, intelligence, lack of ego, sincerity, and, not least, humor. The state of perpetual tension and paranoia that had existed with the mercurial Herbits at the helm was replaced with a calm, professional, and emotionally stable atmosphere. Schneider also resolved numerous controversial litigations and other disputes that were taking up the WJC's time and resources, often needlessly and as the result of pique rather than logic. Throughout this period, the late and much beloved Hella Moritz provided a welcome sense of imperturbability, steadfastness, and institutional continuity.

Also, efforts to revise the WJC constitution had stalled during the Herbits regime. Ensuring transparent and democratic governance through a state-of-the-art constitution was one of Ambassador Lauder's priorities. In the fall of 2007, he retained me to draft a new constitution for the organization, a task I was able to accomplish in large part with the assistance of the WJC's chief operations officer John Malkinson and with the input, counsel, and support of a lay constitutional committee that included the late Mervyn Smith of South Africa, one of the heroes of that country's anti-apartheid movement, and Robert Goot of Australia. After the adoption of the new constitution at the January 2009 WJC plenary assembly, I was appointed the organization's general counsel.

On the political side, Ambassador Lauder refurbished and enhanced the WJC's image and impact by taking his defense of Jewish rights and the State of Israel to the corridors of power across the globe. In meetings with world leaders ranging from Barack Obama, Joe Biden, John Kerry, Angela Merkel, François Hollande, and Vladimir Putin to Popes Benedict XVI and Francis, to Venezuela's Hugo Chavez, Egyptian President Abdel Fattah el-Sisi, the Palestinian Authority's Mahmoud Abbas, and King Abdullah of Jordan, among many others, not to mention virtually every Israeli government and political leader, he established beyond doubt that Jewish communities and individual Jews threatened by anti-Semitism and worse once again had a formidable champion in the WJC.

In May of 2013, Robert Singer became the senior professional at the WJC, with the new title of CEO and Executive Vice President. He had previously spent more than fourteen years at the helm of World ORT, the largest Jewish education and vocational training non-governmental organization in the world with more than three hundred thousand students in thirty-seven countries. Since then, Ambassador Lauder and Robert Singer (no relation to Israel Singer) have taken the organization to unprecedented heights, as described in detail in Robert Singer's chapter in this book.

The purpose of *The World Jewish Congress, 1936–2016* is to provide a retrospective overview of some of the major highlights in the WJC's eighty-year history. To a considerable extent, the present volume is a successor to and continuation of a previous book, *Unity in Dispersion: A History of the World Jewish Congress*, published by the WJC in June of 1948, on the occasion of its second plenary assembly in Montreux, Switzerland. That plenary assembly was held less than two months after the proclamation of the State of Israel, one of the two watershed events of the twentieth century for the Jewish people, the other being the Holocaust. Calling *Unity in Dispersion* "a candid answer to the summons of history," then WJC Secretary-General A. Leon Kubowitzki wrote in his preface:

> On the eve of a new epoch in Jewish history, it was keenly felt that the experiences not only of the Congress but also of its predecessor, the Comité des Délégations Juives, ought to be committed to print. The realities of Jewish life are rapidly shifting before our very eyes, and soon a new generation will arise which knows not our problems and to which many of our controversies will be incomprehensible. . . . For the last thirty years the activities of the Comité des Délégations and the Congress have been woven into the woof and warp of Jewish history and their record cannot be written down without Jewish history being written at the same time.[4]

A similar imperative was the catalyst for *The World Jewish Congress, 1936–2016*. The WJC has been a major—sometimes the only—protagonist in many of the geopolitical dramas affecting world Jewry since the organization's founding in August 1936 in Geneva, and especially since the 1948 Montreux plenary assembly. It was felt that a chronicle of the WJC's accomplishments over the course of these eight decades would be a valuable resource to scholars, educators, present and future activists in Jewish and human-rights oriented endeavors, and interested observers generally.

We chose not to commission a historian to write an all-inclusive, chronological account, but instead opted for a thematic mosaic that enabled us to bring together the perspectives of historians as well as a number of actual participants in the events they describe. First, we believed that organizations—much like individuals—have distinct, sometimes even multi-faceted personalities, and it was our hope that our chosen format enables the WJC's personality, and those of some of its leaders over the past eighty years, to come to the fore. Second, we were confronted with the reality that not all WJC archives located in different parts of the world are readily accessible.

In 1982, the WJC donated the entire archive of its New York office to the American Jewish Archives (AJA) in Cincinnati, Ohio. This archive, which has been meticulously digitized and catalogued by the AJA, consists of approximately 1.2 million documents and spans the period from before the organization's founding in 1936 until 1980. It includes, among many other critically important documents, correspondence from the WJC's Geneva office in the 1930s, the full records of the early WJC plenary assemblies, submissions by the WJC to the League of Nations and the United Nations, and publications of the WJC's Institute of Jewish Affairs. This archive is meticulously maintained in accordance with the highest standards, and it is a genuine pleasure to work with the AJA staff, in particular Kevin Proffitt, Senior Archivist for Research and Collections and director of AJA's Fellowship Programs, and AJA Executive Director Dr. Gary P. Zola.

Subsequently, 4.5 million documents from ten different WJC offices were placed with the Central Zionist Archives in Jerusalem. However, the majority of these documents have not yet been digitized and catalogued, making them neither easily nor readily accessible. In addition, other WJC archives, as well as the papers of a number of WJC leaders, are located at the Institute of Contemporary History and Wiener Library in London, the University of Southampton, Yad Vashem, the US Holocaust Memorial Museum, the Alex Dworkin Canadian Jewish Archives (formerly, the Canadian Jewish Congress Charities Committee National Archives), and at other institutions. Thus, the research required for an authoritative, comprehensive history of the WJC would constitute a daunting if not impossible undertaking at the present time.

The composition of *The World Jewish Congress, 1936–2016* was guided to a considerable extent by the Talmudic adage (*Ḥagigah* 17a) תפשת מרובה לא תפשת *tafasta meruba lo tafasta*, which translates liberally as, if you try to do too much, you end up with nothing, or at least with far less than the desired result. It was clear to us from the outset that the book could not cover all of the WJC's activities, programs, diplomatic initiatives, diverse lay and professional personalities, and internal deliberations between 1936 and 2016, or even between 1948, when *Unity in Dispersion* was published, and the present time. Instead, we have based the format of our new book on a number of what we deem to be compelling considerations. First, we felt that a fresh look at and an appreciation of the WJC's role and record during the years of the Holocaust was important in order to understand the organization's subsequent priorities and chosen directions. Second, we decided to focus in depth and detail on the following thirteen principal areas of the WJC's activities and agenda since the end of World War II:

- The WJC's contribution to the International Military Tribunal at Nuremberg
- The postwar attitudes to, and relationship with, Jews living in Germany
- The WJC's relationship and interaction with the State of Israel
- The WJC's presence and impact at the United Nations
- Diplomatic efforts on behalf of North African Jewry
- Memorialization of the Holocaust at Auschwitz-Birkenau
- Gerhart Riegner's groundbreaking role in launching the Jewish-Vatican dialogue
- Quiet diplomacy versus public activism in advocating for Soviet Jewry
- The campaign to repeal the UN's "Zionism is racism" resolution
- The fight to force Swiss banks to disgorge Holocaust-era assets belonging to Jews
- The Kurt Waldheim Affair
- The complex and sensitive efforts to manage relations with Communist countries
- Efforts to bring the perpetrators of the Buenos Aires terrorist bombings to justice

Third, we include a significant speech by each of the Jewish leaders who held the WJC presidency in the past to highlight their strikingly different personalities. Finally, the WJC today is very much a reflection of both the personality of its president, Ambassador Ronald S. Lauder, and the course he has charted, and continues to chart, for the organization.

Since 2013, the implementation of that course has been in the hands and under the direction of the WJC's CEO and executive vice president Robert Singer. Their concluding chapters, therefore, focus on the present and the future. Our hope is that the combination of all these elements gives the reader an understanding of the role the WJC has played and what it has accomplished over the past eighty years, its broad range of programs and activities today, and insights into its likely trajectories in the future.

It should be noted that we deliberately opted not to highlight numerous episodes and events commonly associated with the WJC. For instance, we do not devote a chapter to German-Jewish reparations, primarily because although the WJC was a key participant in the early process that culminated in the historic Luxemburg Agreements of 1952, the organization as such was neither the catalyst nor a principal protagonist in the negotiations themselves or in the subsequent implementation of these agreements. In October 1944, the delegates at the WJC's War Emergency Conference in Atlantic City, New Jersey, adopted a resolution calling for both restitution and compensation to individual Jewish victims of Nazi persecution,[5] and that same year Dr. Nehemiah Robinson of the WJC Institute of Jewish Affairs published a monograph laying forth the legal rationale for not just individual compensation, but also collective compensation by Germany to the Jewish people as a whole.[6] Thereafter, Dr. Noah Barou, one of the founders of both the WJC and its influential British Section, and the long-time chairman of the WJC's European Executive, was a mostly unsung advocate for pressing the new West German government to provide reparations. Indeed, following Barou's death in 1955, Nahum Goldmann wrote that, "I am not at all sure whether the great chapter in Jewish history which we call the reparations agreement with Germany . . . would have come about if it had not been for Noah Barou."[7] On the other hand, Goldmann's own central role in the reparations negotiations was not in his capacity as WJC president, but rather as head of the Conference on Jewish Material Claims Against Germany, commonly referred to as the Claims Conference; and while the WJC is a founding agency of that organization, Goldmann convened the Claims Conference in 1951, at the request of Israeli Foreign Minister Moshe Sharett, in Goldmann's capacity as co-chairman of the Jewish Agency for Israel.[8]

Unfortunately, we did not have the space to feature the many important accomplishments of the different sections of the WJC in the United Kingdom, France, Sweden, and elsewhere. The WJC's British Section in particular, headed between 1945 and 1950 by the Marchioness of Reading, Member of Parliament Sidney Silverman, Dr. Barou, and Alex Easterman, among others, provided critical political assistance and support to the Holocaust survivors in the Displaced Persons (DP) camp of Bergen-Belsen that enabled the leaders of the Jewish DPs to prevail in a succession of confrontations with the military authorities in the British Zone of Germany. Also, Natan Lerner's insightful reminiscence covers only the WJC's role and activities in Israel through the early 1980s. Consequently, the book does not make reference to the Hebrew-language Jewish-affairs journal *Gesher*, edited for many years by the late Dr. Shlomo Shafir, or to the WJC Research Institute, established in Jerusalem in the 1990s, which published more than 150 research studies and policy papers during its fifteen-year existence.

To fully grasp the significance of the WJC's place and role in contemporary Jewish and world history, a brief review of the organization's origins and early years provides an explanatory context.

The WJC's roots lie in an ad hoc body called the Comité des Délégations Juives auprès de la Conférence de la Paix (Committee of Jewish Delegations at the Peace Conference) that was formed in 1919 to advocate "for the protection of the Jewish population of Bulgaria, Esthonia, Finland, Greece, Lithuania, Poland, Rumania, Russia, Czechoslovakia, Ukrainia, Jugo-Slavia, and other East and Central European lands" before the Versailles Peace Conference.[9] The Comité des Délégations Juives was comprised of Jewish representative bodies from the United States (the American Jewish Congress, which had come into being one year earlier), Canada (the Canadian Jewish Congress), Eastern Galicia, Italy, Palestine, Poland, Romania, Russia, Czechoslovakia, Ukraine "by written mandate," Greece (Thessaloniki), Transylvania, and Bukovina, as well as the American Jewish Committee, B'nai Brith, and the World Zionist Organization. This composition in and of itself was revolutionary: it constituted the first organized international endeavor by Jewish organizations and communal groups in the face of "pogroms which have been carried out in some of the East European countries against the peaceful Jewish inhabitants," and that "have revolted the conscience of the world."[10] The president of the Comité des Délégations Juives was US Circuit Court Judge Julian W. Mack of the American Jewish Congress, who had also been one of the founders of the American Jewish Committee in 1906; one of its vice presidents was Louis Marshall of the American Jewish Committee; and its secretary general was the Zionist leader Leo Motzkin, originally from Russia but at the time based in Paris.

The fact that the American Jewish Committee joined the Comité des Délégations Juives was especially noteworthy because it had vehemently opposed the formation of a broad-based representative body for American Jewry, and subsequently would be equally opposed to the very concept of a world Jewish congress, something which the founders of the American Jewish Congress, in particular Rabbi Stephen S. Wise, advocated from the outset. On the other hand, the prior several decades had seen a dramatic increase in anti-Semitic incidents and manifestations, from the Dreyfus Affair in France to pogroms in Kishinev and other parts of Eastern Europe, to the Beilis blood libel trial in Russia, all of which had been widely covered in the press.[11] In fact, the American Jewish Committee itself had been founded in 1906 following the Kishinev and other pogroms "to prevent the infraction of the civil and religious rights of the Jews throughout the world."[12] Thus, Louis Marshall, who succeeded Judge Mack as head of the Comité des Délégations Juives after the latter's return to the United States, declared that

> [t]he purpose of our mission to Paris was to co-operate with organiza-
> tions from all parts of Europe to secure full civil, religious, and polit-
> ical rights for the racial, religious, and linguistic minorities of Eastern
> Europe.... They have been deprived of the most elementary rights such
> as are guaranteed to all citizens of the United States, of England, of
> France, and of Italy.[13]

Following the end of the Peace Conference, the Comité des Délégations Juives remained in existence, under Motzkin's leadership, albeit without the participation of some of the organizations that opposed any permanent international Jewish representative body. Over the years, it made representations on behalf of Jews threatened by anti-Semitic discrimination or worse in various Eastern European countries,[14] and in 1933, it helped score an impressive victory against the new Hitler government by forcing the temporary nullification of anti-Semitic laws in German Upper Silesia.[15]

Simultaneously, both Motzkin in Europe and Rabbi Stephen S. Wise in the United States, among others, wanted to form an international body to advocate and act on behalf of Jews and Jewish communities across the globe. As early as December 17, 1918, the delegates to the inaugural session of the American Jewish Congress in Philadelphia adopted a resolution instructing its European delegation, "as soon as peace is declared among the warring nations . . . to take the necessary and effective steps in co-operation with the representative Jewish bodies in other countries for the convening of a World Jewish Congress."[16] In May of 1923, Motzkin called for a World Conference of Jews to address issues of Jewish concern, especially in light of the violation of Jewish minority rights in various European countries.[17]

The first concrete development on the road to establishing such a world body took place August 17–19, 1927, when sixty delegates from the United States, twelve other countries, and Palestine gathered in Zurich for the World's Conference on Jewish Rights. Simon Dubnow, widely recognized as the greatest living Jewish historian, gave an overview of Jewish emancipation since the French revolution. Calling minority rights for Jews "the culmination of their national freedom,"[18] he stressed the need for an organization that would be "a seeing eye and a hearing ear."[19] Motzkin, meanwhile, called for the creation of a committee to coordinate the activities of the various Jewish agencies that were making efforts on behalf of Jewish minorities,[20] and such a body, called the Council on the Rights of Jewish Minorities, was formed.[21]

The next four years saw Nazism on the rise in Germany and an intensification of the increasing anti-Semitic manifestations in other Eastern and Central European countries. Nevertheless, in 1931 when Wise took further steps in the direction of convening a world Jewish congress, he met with considerable opposition. Confronting his critics at the annual session of the American Jewish Congress, he said:

> I refuse to believe that we may never summon the representatives of world Jewry together for wise and considered action with respect to their common problems because of the danger of allegations being made

such as those that are to be found in the protocols of the elders of Zion. There is only one problem before us with respect to a world Jewish congress: Can it help? Will it serve the highest interest of the Jewish people?[22]

One year later, as anti-Semitism posed an ever greater threat and the Nazi Party was becoming dramatically stronger, the American Jewish Congress voted to convene another world conference of Jews in Geneva. Wise explained to the delegates why a world Jewish congress had become an urgent necessity:

> In the Zurich conference which met five years ago we thought things were serious and grave, but 1927 is the Messianic year compared with 1932. At that time Hitlerism was unknown—that Austrian adventurer who made a few speeches. No one took him seriously.[23]

In response, Dr. Cyrus Adler, the president of the American Jewish Committee, went public with his harsh opposition to Wise's initiative. In an article published in the *American Hebrew and Jewish Tribune,* Adler denounced the convening of both a world Jewish congress and a preparatory conference as "a sensational blunder—perhaps one of the most colossal mistakes in the history of the Jewish people." As far as Adler was concerned,

> For a congress of persons from many parts of the world to discuss the peculiar economic, political, and social conditions affecting the Jews in the various countries would be to furnish a spectacle that would be ludicrous and possibly tragic. . . . The enemies of the Jews in every country, and especially in Germany, would seize upon the congress as an alleged justification of their charges.[24]

Wise's reaction, in the form of a statement signed by himself and two other leaders of the American Jewish Congress, was swift and equally direct:

> Dr. Adler and his associates of the American Jewish Committee are evidently governed by the fear that a Jewish conference and ultimately a world Jewish congress will lead the world to suspect that Jews are united in defense of their imperiled or impaired rights. The call for

this conference has already met with an eager response by leaders of European and American Jewry, conscious of the need of united consideration and common action on the vast complex of Jewish problems.[25]

From August 14 to 17, 1932, the first of three World Jewish Conferences that preceded the formal founding of the WJC was held in Geneva. Ninety-four delegates from seventeen countries participated, but the American Jewish Committee, the Board of Deputies of British Jews, and the Hilfverein der deutschen Juden in Germany were among the communal bodies that chose not to attend. The American Jewish Congress had invited a young Zionist leader from Germany, Dr. Nahum Goldmann, to organize this event. It was the beginning of his lifelong leadership role on behalf of world Jewry. A compelling orator, he explained the purpose of a world Jewish congress to the delegates:

> It is to establish the permanent address of the Jewish people; amidst the fragmentation and atomization of Jewish life and of the Jewish community, it is to establish a real, legitimate, collective representation of Jewry which will be entitled to speak in the name of the 16 million Jews to the nations and governments of the world, as well as to the Jews themselves.[26]

This conference decided to convene a world Jewish congress based on the then quite controversial proposition that the Jewish people constituted a national entity; and the delegates elected an Executive Committee, including Wise and Goldmann, to bring the congress into being.

Goldmann's rapid rise to the upper echelons of the group that spearheaded the creation of a world Jewish congress underscored the close relationship of the WJC's founders with the Zionist movement. In 1931, at the Seventeenth Zionist Congress, he had been one of the engineers of the removal of Chaim Weizmann from the presidency of the World Zionist Organization (WZO);[27] and he became close to Stephen Wise, who was another of Weizmann's opponents on that occasion.[28] It is significant that numerous other Zionist leaders and personalities such as Motzkin; Nahum Sokolow, Weizmann's successor as president of the WZO; Joseph Sprinzak, the future speaker of the Knesset (Israeli parliament); and

Yitzhak Gruenbaum actively participated in the various preparatory conferences that preceded the WJC's first plenary assembly in 1936. Indeed, the WZO stood fully behind the concept of a world Jewish congress, with its Executive declaring in 1935 that "the Zionist movement has from the very beginning affirmed the idea of a world Jewish congress." That same year, the Nineteenth Zionist Congress adopted a resolution stating that it considered "the creation of an authorized representative body [of the Jewish people] on a democratic basis as an urgent necessity, and that it "looks upon the World Jewish Congress as a suitable form of such a representative body."[29] Following Motzkin's death in November 1933, Goldmann became head of the Comité des Délégations Juives, and in 1935 he was appointed the Jewish Agency's representative to the League of Nations.

Two more preparatory conferences followed. Both took place in Geneva after Hitler and his National Socialist Party had come to power. At the second conference, in September of 1933, Wise called for an organized Jewish boycott of German goods and stressed that the situation of the Jews in Germany had become "the overshadowing Jewish problem, overshadowing all else, and marking this year in Jewish history with a new and unprecedented sorrow, filling the hearts of the Jewish people with a sense of grief if not despair such as we have not known for many centuries." The question, he declared, was no longer whether but when a World Jewish Congress would take place.[30]

At the third World Jewish Conference, August 20–23, 1934, the delegates reiterated their determination to establish a world Jewish congress and set forth the mission of the new organization in the following resolution that was unanimously adopted:

> It is a question of the creation of a permanent body representing Jews
> all over the world, whose task it will be, in the name of the whole of
> Jewry to defend the common interests, and to protect the rights of
> Jewish communities wherever they may be threatened. It follows from
> this declaration of aims and objects . . . that the World Congress and the
> organs elected by it will in no way have the task, or the competence, to
> occupy themselves with questions of the internal policies of the Jewish
> communities in the various countries nor with questions of internal

Jewish life in those countries. Furthermore, all questions of a religious character are outside the competence of the World Jewish Congress and its organs.[31]

To the extent that this resolution was meant to ease the concerns of Wise's critics and adversaries in the Jewish political arena, it had no such effect. The American Jewish Committee in particular kept up its opposition to the creation of a world Jewish congress, arguing vociferously against American Jews associating with Jews from other countries to create an international body that would presume to speak for American Jews.[32] In June 1936, with the World Jewish Congress scheduled to take place two months later, the American Jewish Committee announced that other American Jewish organizations, including the Jewish Labor Committee, B'nai Brith, the National Council of Jewish Women, and the Union of Orthodox Rabbis of the United States would also refuse to participate.[33] Wise's response was succinct: "We have to fight Hitler with one hand and the American Jewish Committee with the other."[34]

On August 8, 1936, 250 delegates from thirty-two countries (including Mussolini's Italy, but not Germany or the Soviet Union) gathered in Geneva for the first plenary assembly of the WJC, setting in motion what would become in very short order the most outspoken and arguably most effective Jewish organization advocating for Jewish rights worldwide. A detailed discussion of the proceedings of this plenary assembly can be found in *Unity in Dispersion* and therefore need not be repeated here.[35] For purposes of this introduction to the present volume, it is sufficient to cite the words spoken by one of the organization's founders and longtime leaders Maurice L. Perlzweig, a Polish-born, British-educated liberal rabbi, on that occasion:

> What is it that we, who venture to speak in the name and with the voice of the Jewish people, seek to achieve?
>
> First, we affirm the unity and integrity of the whole House of Israel in the hearing of the nations of the world. We demand for all Jews the full prerogative of citizenship as of right and not on sufferance, and whatever be the price of citizenship in sacrifices and loyalty we shall pay as we have paid without flinching even in all the step-fatherlands of the

Jewish diaspora; but in one thing we shall not yield. Emancipation is no emancipation if it denies us full place and partnership in faith and fellowship of Israel. Jewish loyalty is integral in the highest Jewish citizenship. We who are assembled in this Congress seek to bring a great gift to the world: we bring our Jewish heritage to the service of our citizenship.

Secondly, we shall seek to mobilize all the resources of the Jewish people in the struggle against those who have declared war on us. The truth of science no less than the inexhaustible capacity for courage and self-sacrifice of our people shall be our weapons in a struggle we shall wage for all humanity. First the Jew, then the Liberal, then the Christian, the sequence is governed by a logic, inexorable and ineluctable. Liberty is indivisible. If the Jew goes down in the struggle, then woe to the freedom of the world.[36]

Following the 1936 plenary assembly, the WJC continued seamlessly the activities of the Comité des Délégations Juives and interceded on behalf of beleaguered Jewish communities before the League of Nations and with various Eastern European governments. Goldmann and Perlzweig undertook most of these initiatives in what remained of the interwar years, with Goldmann, who had been elected chairman of the WJC's Administrative Committee, becoming the organization's de facto foreign minister.

One of the most notable early public WJC appearances was at the now infamous July 1938 conference on refugees convened at President Roosevelt's behest at the French spa of Évian-les-Bains. As it turned out, the conference accomplished precisely nothing, with Australian Minister for Trade and Customs T. W. White epitomizing the collective attitude of the participating governments when he declared that, "as we have no real racial problem, we are not desirous of importing one by encouraging any scheme of large-scale foreign migration."[37]

The WJC submitted a memorandum over Wise's signature in which it argued forcefully, among other points, that the refugee crisis that must be addressed should not be limited to Jews fleeing Germany and Austria:

It is desirable that the Evian Conference should not confine itself to consider the case of German Jews, which, although the most painful, is but one of the aspects of the refugee problem. Following the nefarious example set by Germany, several European states have, for some time, been enacting legal and administrative measures designed to evict Jewish population from employment and professions, to deprive Jews of their nationality and to force them to emigrate. In doing so, these states are violating their constitutions which guarantee to Jews equality of rights, and disregard the rights pledged to Jewish minorities by the peace treaties. We venture to think that one of the most urgent tasks incumbent upon the Evian Conference is to reaffirm the principle of equality of rights of the Jews in all countries, and to remind the states of eastern [sic] Europe that they have no right to create new masses of refugees through driving out of their boundaries their Jewish citizens.[38]

Numerous Jewish organizations attended the Évian Conference and were far from unified. Historian Yehuda Bauer observed:

It must be stressed that only the World Jewish Congress, represented by Dr. Nahum Goldmann, disregarded the appeals for moderation. It sharply attacked German practices, demanded that the Jewish problem be viewed as a whole, said that Jews fleeing from Eastern Europe should also be helped, and insisted that uncultivated areas be set aside for Jewish settlement. Also, WJC thought that government financing was indispensable because private agencies would not be able to support the emigration by themselves.[39]

Other Jewish groups espoused radically different positions. Rabbi Jonah B. Wise (no relation to Stephen Wise), chairman of the JDC, told *The New York Times* upon his return from Évian that the JDC and other American relief agencies were "Americans first of all," and that there would be no relaxation of US immigration regulations in favor of German or Austrian Jews. "After all," he said, "the people working for this movement are Americans, and their first interest here is for America and for Americans." He then added that "if our concern for groups in foreign countries who need assistance in escaping oppression would interfere with helping Americans, then we couldn't do it."[40]

After the Évian Conference had concluded, Goldmann conveyed his impressions in a letter to Rabbi Stephen Wise:

The Jewish organizations did not make up a very brilliant show in Evian. More than 20 of them appeared in Evian and created a deplorable impression. The British Council for German Jews is responsible for this ridiculous performance. We asked the British Council several times to invoke, together with the Executive of the Jewish Agency in London a conference of the Jewish organizations before the meeting in Evian in order to choose a united representation as it was done before the Lausanne Conference five years ago; I am sure that a united Jewish delegation composed of four or five people would have been received and heard by the whole Conference, and Weizmann would inevitably have become the speaker of this delegation. Unfortunately the British Council refused to call such a conference mostly because of Samuel's[41] fear for so-called "International Jewry," which should not appear united in Evian. Brodetzski[42] [*sic*] was not courageous enough to call such a conference on behalf of the Jewish Agency without the British Council, and so nothing happened. All the Jewish organizations came to Evian, swarmed around like bees and made a very bad impression on the Conference and the press. If ever a lesson for the necessity of Jewish unity representation was given, it was done in Evian. But I am afraid that Jewish notables have learnt nothing from this lesson.[43]

It is against this overall background that we hope that *The World Jewish Congress, 1936–2016* is read. The WJC has changed and evolved since 1936, as have the Jewish people in the aftermath of the Holocaust and the establishment of the State of Israel, and both will most certainly continue to change and evolve. However, as the different chapters in this book make clear, the WJC has consistently remained, and remains, true to its mission, which is to advocate for and defend Jewish communities and the Jewish people wherever and whenever necessary.

The Jewish Right to Equality

Judge Julian W. Mack

United States Circuit Judge Julian W. Mack (1866–1943), chairman of the Comité des Délégations Juives (Committee of Jewish Delegations) at the 1919 Versailles Peace Conference, was elected honorary president of the World Jewish Congress at the WJC's first plenary assembly in Geneva in August of 1936. The following are excerpts from an address by Judge Mack at a dinner of the Merchandising Council of the American Jewish Congress on May 10, 1937, in New York City:

I am proud to have been privileged in the course of the years to do what little I have done in aid of the struggle of my people. The guiding principle in endeavoring to secure the recognition of the human rights of the Jew and of the Jewish people, the guiding principle that animated us nearly twenty years ago when we were gathered together from all lands in Paris with the aims of securing the recognition of Palestine as the Jewish National Homeland and of securing for the Jews in the countries of oppression those fundamental rights that are accorded to all men in this glorious land of ours, that we ask for the Jew as an individual and for the Jewish people as a people no more, but on the other hand, no less than is accorded in any and each of these countries to the other individuals, be they of a minority or majority group.

We ask no more for the Jew than we do for anybody else and if it was the Jewish gatherings that were most insistent upon the recognition in Paris during the Peace Conference of minority rights, it was simply because the Jewish people felt the need of this international recognition more than did the other people, who even there were asking only that our Sabbath be recognized for us as the day of rest in most countries in Eastern and Central Europe. Not a line was asked to be written into those treaties with reference to the Jew or the Jewish people that was not asked for all peoples and for all individuals. And my friends, we shall always succeed, in the measure that it may be possible to succeed, if we recognize that fundamental principle—ask nothing exceptional for ourselves but demand that whatever be given to others be given in equal measure to us.

To put it another way, my friends, and it is the only way in which we can succeed, it is the way that every Jew at least ought to recognize—we must both in the interest of the world as Americans and in the interest of the Jewish people as Jews, be and remain thoroughly democratic. We can tolerate no Fascist movement; we must be no part of it. The totalitarian state, dictatorship of every kind, is absolutely foreign to the Jewish, as it is to the American, spirit. This is not mere theory. The American Jewish Congress and the World Jewish Congress, in contrast with some other organizations, are founded upon the principle of democracy. We American Jews, when we go to a World Jewish Congress, when we want a World Jewish Congress established, go there not in the spirit of superiority because we happen to be the richest in some respects or highly intelligent part of the Jewish people, there to lay down the law to the representatives of the Jews of other lands, there to attempt to tell them that in our judgment we, coming from a free land because of the opportunities that we have enjoyed through the centuries, know better than they do what is best for them—*no!* In a World Jewish Congress, the representatives of the American Jewish Congress enter into complete fellowship with their brethren of other lands. We go there not to dictate, not to control but to counsel together with them, to ascertain from their experience what they feel they need. Of course we present to them our point of view and urge upon them from time to time—and we did this twenty years ago in Paris, as we did last year in Geneva—we urge upon them what we believe to be best for them. But in truly democratic fashion we take counsel with them and having heard what they say, listening open mindedly, we are persuaded or they are persuaded, or neither is fully persuaded. Then it goes to a vote, and we unhesitatingly accept the decision of the majority and continue in fullest measure cooperating with them. That, my friends, is the true democracy of the American and World Jewish Congress.

The question that each one of you must feel at this time is this: Is this the wise, the sane, the safe method of procedure in our attempt to obtain freedom and equality for the Jew and the Jewish people throughout the world? And if it be that, is it or is it not up to you, in your own interest, in the interest of your children, in the interest of the Jewish people and of posterity—is it not in the interest of the Jewish people, that long suffering but eternal people, to contribute all your time, all your thought and all your money in support of an undertaking such as this?

The World Jewish Congress during World War II

Gregory J. Wallance

Just a few years after its founding in 1936, the World Jewish Congress was confronted with the greatest existential crisis in modern Jewish history: the Nazi scheme to exterminate European Jewry. The WJC discovered and reported the existence of the extermination plan; mobilized public opinion for action, especially in the United States and Great Britain; pressured Allied governments to issue war crimes warnings; persuaded neutral countries and the International Red Cross to rescue Jews; lobbied for a war crimes tribunal; and even secretly negotiated with one of the highest Nazi officials to free thousands of Jews from a concentration camp. These efforts were often undermined by callous, often anti-Semitic, career diplomats in the US State Department.

Many leaders of the World Jewish Congress were involved in these efforts, but two in particular, Gerhart M. Riegner in Switzerland and Rabbi Stephen S. Wise in the United States, played crucial roles in disclosing the Nazi extermination plan to the world and in rescuing Jews in Europe.

Gregory J. Wallance is a lawyer in New York City and the author of *America's Soul in the Balance: The Holocaust, FDR's State Department and the Moral Disgrace of an American Aristocracy*.

The Riegner Telegram

The World Jewish Congress was at the forefront of efforts to publicize German massacres of Jews. In late June 1942, based on reports from the Polish government-in-exile in London, the WJC accused Germany of murdering more than one million Jews since the start of the war as part of an extermination policy. But these reports apparently gained little traction in either the press or government circles in the United States.[1] Then, less than six weeks later, the World Jewish Congress received a report from a high-placed source within Germany that transcended even the horrific account from the Polish government-in-exile—and which ultimately revealed the full scope of Germany's unprecedented systematic biological extermination plan.

On August 1, 1942, Riegner, a thirty-year-old German-born lawyer and a representative of the World Jewish Congress in neutral Switzerland, met with a Jewish journalist on the terrace of the Hôtel du Château in Lausanne. The journalist told Riegner that he had been given a terrifying message from a prominent German industrialist, who had connections at the highest levels of the Nazi party, the German government, and the German military. The journalist regarded the industrialist, who loathed the Nazis, as highly reliable. The message was that the Nazis were considering a plan to exterminate European Jewry.

Riegner was no stranger to the Nazis. After Hitler took power in Germany in 1933, Riegner was dismissed from his position as assistant to a Berlin judge; his father, also an attorney, was disbarred; his older sister lost her job as a secondary school teacher in Frankfurt; and his younger sister was expelled from elementary school. One evening, Brownshirts (storm troopers) gathered outside the Riegner home, chanting *Juden raus!* ("Jews out!"). Riegner left Germany and, in the summer of 1936, joined the Geneva office of the newly formed WJC.

But now—in August 1942—the virulent, demonic Nazi hatred of the Jews had taken on a new dimension for Riegner, especially in light of reports that he had just received about massive roundups of tens of thousands of Jews from across occupied Europe. Even so, Riegner needed time to come to terms with the industrialist's message. "In spite of all the information in my possession," he wrote later, "in spite of what I had already experienced myself, I still needed another two days to convince myself that these events were possible and, finally, to believe in them."

Riegner drafted a cautiously worded telegram to Rabbi Stephen S. Wise, Chairman of the Executive Committee (and de facto president) of the WJC in the United States:

> RECEIVED ALARMING REPORT THAT IN FUHRERS HEADQUARTERS
> PLAN DISCUSSED AND UNDER CONSIDERATION ALL JEWS IN
> COUNTRIES OCCUPIED OR CONTROLLED GERMANY NUMBER 3-1/2
> TO 4 MILLION SHOULD AFTER DEPORTATION AND CONCENTRATION
> IN EAST AT ONE BLOW EXTERMINATED TO RESOLVE ONCE FOR ALL
> JEWISH QUESTION IN EUROPE STOP

Sending the telegram to Rabbi Wise through a Swiss telegraph service was out of the question. German intelligence intercepted every telegram or letter sent to Allied countries from neutral Switzerland. In any event, the Swiss, who employed strict military censorship to avoid antagonizing Germany, would simply have refused to transmit it. On August 8, 1942, Riegner went to the American consulate in Geneva. He handed over the telegram to an American diplomat and requested that it be sent to the State Department for delivery to Rabbi Wise in New York City and that the State Department investigate the industrialist's report.

Two weeks later, Riegner was contacted by the American diplomat, who explained that the career bureaucrats in the Division of European Affairs in the State Department in Washington, without conducting any investigation, had refused to pass Riegner's message on to Rabbi Wise because of "the fantastic nature of the allegation and the impossibility of our being of any assistance if such action were taken."[2]

The Riegner Telegram Reaches Rabbi Wise

But Riegner had prepared another, nearly identical telegram. He took this one to the British consulate in Geneva and requested that the consulate transmit the information to the British Foreign Office for delivery to Samuel Sidney Silverman, a Jewish member of the British Parliament and chairman of the WJC's British Section. The Foreign Office received the report on August 10, hesitated for a week, and then concluded it could not withhold the report from a member of parliament (MP). The Foreign Office gave the report to Silverman, but with the disclaimer that "we have no information bearing on or confirming this story."[3]

On August 28, Silverman cabled the report to the United States, where it reached Rabbi Wise, perhaps the most politically powerful rabbi in American history. Then sixty-eight years old, with a square face, slicked-back hair parted in the middle, and a jutting jaw that resembled the prow of an icebreaker, Rabbi Wise was the descendant of a line of distinguished Hungarian rabbis. He had been born in Budapest, immigrated as a child with his family to the United States, and became a rabbi with a passion for progressive causes and electoral politics. Rabbi Wise was a close political ally of President Franklin D. Roosevelt.

Wise contacted Undersecretary of State Sumner Welles, the second-highest ranking official in the State Department, whom Wise considered sympathetic to the plight of European Jewry. Wise reported the contents of the second Riegner telegram. Welles, unaware that career diplomats in the State Department had blocked the first telegram from Riegner, agreed to investigate Riegner's report, but asked Wise "not to release the information until an attempt had been made to confirm it."

Wise complied with Welles's request. By virtue of his promise to Welles, Wise did not disclose to his coreligionists that the greatest crisis in modern Jewish history was unfolding in Nazi-occupied Europe. No less a figure than Elie Wiesel has said, "How could he pledge secrecy when millions of lives were involved? How was he not driven mad by this secret?" On the other hand, no less a figure than Riegner rejected the charge that Wise had sacrificed Jewish interests for the sake of his relationship with President Roosevelt. "This is not true," Riegner wrote in his memoir. "Wise worked his entire life in the political world. He was certainly not naïve. And, in fact, he changed his attitude towards Roosevelt several times."[4]

In fact, Wise felt he was close to madness, whether from guilt at his self-imposed silence or from the knowledge of the terrible contents of the Riegner telegram, or both. At one point, Wise wrote to a prominent clergyman, "I am almost demented over my people's grief."[5] But Wise recognized that he first needed evidence that would silence the skeptics, especially in the Division of European Affairs at the State Department. He also knew that Roosevelt would only refer the matter to the State Department anyway.

The investigation by American diplomats in Switzerland took several months. In Geneva, Riegner had been profoundly shocked by the failure of the Allies to react to his information. "This pushed me to redouble my efforts to obtain additional testimony confirming the plan for total annihilation." The testimony obtained by Riegner included a statement from a Swiss law professor about his conversation with a senior official of the International Committee of the Red Cross with contacts in Berlin. The Red Cross official had described communications from German officials revealing a Nazi plan to make Germany and the occupied territories "free of Jews." The Red Cross official further told the Swiss law professor that, since there was no country to receive the Jews, there could be no doubt about the significance of the term.

In October, Riegner and a colleague provided the American diplomats in Switzerland with a report that left no doubt that something monstrous, in fact, had *already* begun behind the shroud with which the Nazis had covered the occupied countries of Europe.

> Expulsions, deportations, and mass executions are continuing thus decimating Polish Jewry to the point of complete annihilation. . . . [O]ne-third of the 180,000 Jews of the Netherlands have already been deported; the whole of Dutch Jewry is to be deported [by] June 1943 . . . the Romanian government itself admitted that since October 1941, about 185,000 Jews have been deported to Transnistria where there are by now only 112,000 left; the remainder have probably perished. . . . Thus, the deliberate policy of extermination of European Jewry is systematically carried out quite in accordance with the announcements made in the last speeches of the Head of the German Government.[6]

The American diplomats then transmitted the report and their own confirmatory findings to Sumner Welles. In November, Welles urgently requested that Rabbi Wise come to the State Department.

The patrician diplomatic scion of the Eastern establishment and the rough-and-tumble Budapest-born rabbi both understood the historic nature of their meeting. Arrayed on Welles's desk were documents from the Bern legation adorned with bright red seals. Wise could not avert his eyes from the seals. They were his people's blood, "pouring forth in rivers." Sumner Welles was suitably dignified and solemn. He held up the documents. He spoke quietly and movingly, as Wise later wrote: "every word etching itself into my heart." "I hold in my hands documents which have come to me from our legation in Bern," said Welles. "I regret to tell you that these confirm and justify your deepest fears."

Mobilizing Public Opinion

In Washington that evening, Wise held a press conference. He told reporters that the State Department had confirmed reports of a Nazi "extermination plan" to annihilate the entire Jewish population of Europe. The next day, Wise was back in New York, where he convened a meeting of Jewish leaders to plan a campaign to send telegrams to five hundred newspapers requesting editorials on the Nazi scheme; invite hundreds of prominent non-Jews to issue statements of condemnation; hold a national day of mourning; and seek a meeting with President Roosevelt. That afternoon, Wise held another press conference. He explained that his purpose in disclosing the reports from Europe was "to win the support of a Christian world so that its leaders may intervene and protest the horrible treatment of Jews in Hitler's Europe." However, officials in the State Department's Division of European Affairs insisted to reporters that Wise's report was unconfirmed.[7]

One week later, on December 2, a national day of mourning and prayer was held in the United States and twenty-nine foreign countries. In New York City, half a million Jewish union members, accompanied by non-Jews in their workplaces, stopped work for ten minutes. Religious and memorial services and moments of silence were held in other cities. A reporter for the *Dallas Morning News* was especially moved by the sobbing at the ceremony in Dallas.[8]

On December 8, 1942, Rabbi Wise and other leading Jewish leaders met with the President; they brought with them a report on the Nazi extermination of European Jewry. Roosevelt acknowledged that the American government had received "confirmation from many sources" of the Nazi extermination plan and promised to issue a war crimes declaration against the Nazis. Released on December 17, a joint US-British declaration, "German Policy of Extermination of the Jewish Race," confirmed the Nazi exterminations and vowed war crimes prosecutions against the responsible German officials.[9]

Second Telegram—"6,000 Jews Killed Daily at a Single Location"

In early 1943, Gerhart Riegner provided another, even more horrific, report to the American diplomats in Switzerland, also in the form of a telegram. The telegram was dated January 19, 1943. As he had with the first telegram the preceding August, Riegner asked the American diplomats in Bern to transmit his report to the State Department for delivery to Rabbi Wise. The telegram was precise in describing the acceleration of the Nazi plan: "6,000 [Jews] killed daily [at a single location in Poland] . . . required, before execution, to strip themselves of all their clothing, which is then sent to Germany." The telegram also emphasized the ongoing horror in Transnistria, a part of what was now Nazi-occupied Ukraine: "130,000 [Romanian] Jews were deported to Transnistria . . . approximately 60,000 [had already died] . . . 70,000 are starving . . . living conditions indescribable."[10]

The diplomats transmitted the telegram to the State Department in a cable sent on January 21. On February 9, the Division of European Affairs, apparently unwilling to run the risk of suppressing the report now that the US government had confirmed the existence of the extermination plan, reluctantly delivered a copy of the telegram to Rabbi Wise. The release of yet another Riegner report coincided with the plans by the World Jewish Congress and other Jewish groups to hold mass protest rallies, which would mount pressure on the State Department for rescue, the last thing the Division of European Affairs wanted to do. On February 10, the Division sent a cable to the American diplomats in Switzerland. The cable, specifically referencing Riegner's nightmarish cable of January 21, instructed the diplomats to stop transmitting any more reports from Riegner of the mass murders: "In the future we would suggest that you do not accept reports submitted to you to be transmitted to private persons in the United States."[11]

Attempt to Rescue Transnistrian Jews

That same month, an opportunity arose to rescue Romanian Jews trapped in Transnistria. On February 2, 1943, in a devastating defeat for Germany, the German Sixth Army had surrendered at Stalingrad. The Romanian government, no longer confident that its ally Germany would win the war and seeking to ease otherwise harsh peace terms, approached Jewish organizations about relocating the 70,000 Jews still alive in Transnistria. They could be relocated to an area of the Allies' choosing, although the Romanian government suggested Palestine and even offered to provide Romanian ships to transport the Jews. In return, the Romanian government wanted its expenses paid, allegedly about 20,000 Romanian lei ($50) per refugee.[12]

In Switzerland, Riegner put together a plan to meet the Romanian government's terms and managed to get a message to Rabbi Wise in New York City that he had urgent news. On March 31, Wise wrote to Welles that Riegner had "some further information of considerable importance" and asked Welles to instruct the American diplomats in Switzerland to obtain it. On April 5, Welles, still apparently unaware that the Division of European Affairs had been blocking reports from Europe, requested that the American diplomats contact Riegner."[13] They did so, and, based on Riegner's information, sent a lengthy cable to Welles that reviewed the possibility of getting aid to, or even rescuing, Jews in several locations in the occupied countries, including the Jews in Transnistria and Jewish children in France.[14]

To implement the rescue plan for the Jews in Transnistria, Riegner needed a license from the Treasury Department to transfer funds to accounts in Switzerland and then dispense them to Romanian officials. In a meeting with President Roosevelt on July 22, 1943, Rabbi Wise presented the plan to Roosevelt, who responded, "Stephen, why don't you go ahead and do it?" Roosevelt then called Secretary of the Treasury Henry Morgenthau, Jr. "Henry, this is a very fair proposal which Stephen makes about ransoming Jews." The Treasury Department issued a license for

Riegner to execute the rescue plan. However, the State Department—specifically, the officials in the Division of European Affairs—refused to even transmit the license to the American diplomats in Switzerland, effectively blocking the rescue plan.[15]

The Bermuda Conference

The State Department may have felt emboldened by its earlier success in orchestrating the "Bermuda Conference to Consider the Refugee Problem." In April 1943, at the Horizons Hotel in Bermuda, an American delegation conferred for twelve days with a British delegation on the plight of refugees. The requests of the WJC and other Jewish groups to attend the conference as observers were rejected. Assistant Secretary of State Breckinridge Long noted in his diary that "one Jewish faction under the leadership of Rabbi Stephen Wise" had been especially aggressive "in pushing their particular cause—in letters and telegrams to the President, the Secretary and Welles." Indeed, under the guidelines issued by Long, the delegates were not permitted to place special emphasis on the plight of the Jews or propose any measure that would solely benefit Jews.[16]

Throughout most of the conference, the American delegation maintained a unified position. But unity broke down, albeit briefly, over a suggestion by the one Jewish-American delegate to approach Germany through a neutral country to negotiate the release of Jews. The ensuing debate revealed the underlying fear of both delegations that such an initiative might be all too successful. A British delegate, Richard Law, a Conservative politician then serving as Parliamentary Undersecretary of State for Foreign Affairs, had stressed in a public statement that "every human life that can be saved is something to the good." In the confines of the conference, while debating the proposal, he and his delegation spoke differently. Law warned that

> [i]f Hitler accepted a proposal to release perhaps millions of unwanted persons, we might find ourselves in a very difficult position. For one thing, Hitler might send a large number of picked agents which we would be forced to take into our own countries. On the other hand, he

might say, "All right, take a million or two million." Then, because of the shipping problem, we should be made to look exceedingly foolish.

Another British delegate joined in the general condemnation of the proposal. "It would be relieving Hitler of an obligation to take care of these useless people."

No meaningful rescue proposals emerged from the Bermuda Conference. Today, no serious historian disputes that the Bermuda Conference was a public relations vehicle for relieving the pressure on the American and British governments to help Jews escape the Nazis. Indeed, many years later, Richard Law admitted that the conference was "a facade for inaction." The Bermuda Conference was deeply demoralizing to the WJC and other Jewish groups. And, within a few months, Sumner Welles, the one high-level State Department official sympathetic to the plight of Jews in Europe, became caught in a scandal and resigned.[17]

The War Refugee Board

Wise and Riegner did not know then that their efforts to rescue the Romanian Jews in Transnistria had triggered a furious behind-the-scenes battle between the Treasury Department and the State Department. In the late summer and fall of 1943, idealistic young lawyers in the Treasury Department, all Christians, had been repeatedly but futilely asking the State Department to transmit the license for the Romanian rescue to Riegner in Switzerland. Increasingly suspicious of the State Department's motives, the lawyers began an informal investigation that unearthed evidence of the State Department's appalling behavior, including the February 10 cable that directed the American diplomats in Switzerland to stop transmitting Riegner's reports on the extermination of European Jewry.

The Treasury lawyers, deeply angry at the State Department, wrote a damning indictment of the Department in a report to Treasury Secretary Morgenthau, who was Jewish. The report was titled, "The Acquiescence of This Government in the Murder of the Jews." Using the evidence uncovered by the lawyers, Morgenthau persuaded Roosevelt to take Jewish rescue and refugee affairs away from the State Department. On January 22,

1944, the White House announced the creation of the War Refugee Board. Between then and the end of the war, the War Refugee Board directly or indirectly rescued 200,000 Jews in Europe, including the surviving Jews in Transnistria.

The War Refugee Board, which was run by two of the Treasury lawyers who had battled the State Department, incorporated many of the earlier proposals of the World Jewish Congress for rescuing Jews into its own action plans. The WJC and the War Refugee Board collaborated closely on a number of these rescue efforts.[18]

The WJC War Emergency Conference

In November 1944, the WJC convened the War Emergency Conference of the World Jewish Congress. The five-day conference was the first international Jewish gathering since the start of the war. It was held in Atlantic City and was attended by three hundred delegates, including those from England, Canada, and ten Latin American countries. There were no delegates from the Soviet Union, which Rabbi Wise publicly regretted. He also explained to the delegates in his opening address that there were no representatives from the "millions of unarmed brothers and sisters, from infancy to old age, [who] have died because they are Jews."

The War Emergency Conference was not convened as a relief conference, although that subject was taken up. Rather, the Emergency Conference, as Rabbi Wise explained, was convened to assure Jewish freedom and security. The "Resolution on Palestine" urged the British government to open up Palestine to "unrestricted Jewish immigration and resettlement." The "Resolution on Rescue" called for the governments of liberated countries to demand that their Jewish citizens held in Germany as slave laborers "be accorded the same treatment as their non-Jewish citizens" also sent to forced labor in the Reich. The resolution on "Restoration of Jewish Legal Rights" demanded that governments in liberated territories abrogate all anti-Jewish legislation and fully restore the civil and political rights of Jews. The "Statement and Resolution on the Punishment of War Criminals" sought the prosecution for war crimes of the German officials who "devised and waged biological warfare and have exterminated whole groups and classes." The resolution noted that the "most monstrous of these crimes has had as its purpose the destruction of an entire people—the Jews of Europe."

The "Resolution on Indemnification" called for the payment of restitution and reparations to the Jewish people. The demand was supported by a study that quantified the Nazi destruction and looting of Jewish assets at $8 billion (not including the occupied regions of the Soviet Union) and by specific proposals on how the compensation could be obtained and distributed. But at the heart of the conference was the demand for a "Jewish Commonwealth" in Palestine. As Dr. Nahum Goldmann, chair of the WJC's administrative committee, told the delegates, "No program of Jewish demands has meaning or historic significance if it does not culminate in a demand for a Jewish Commonwealth in Palestine."

At the end of the conference, a memorial service was held for the fallen Jews of Europe.[19]

The WJC's Swedish Section, Raoul Wallenberg, and Heinrich Himmler

The WJC's Swedish Section had been founded by Hillel Storch, a successful Latvian businessman who happened to be in Sweden in July 1940 when the Soviet Union invaded Latvia. Even though he was a stateless refugee, Storch managed to get his wife and young daughter out of Latvia and bring them to Sweden the following year; however, he was not able to save other family members. Storch founded the Swedish Section of the WJC to undertake large-scale rescues. Neutral Sweden had maintained diplomatic relations with Nazi Germany throughout the war.

One of the best-known of all rescue efforts in World War II involved Raoul Wallenberg, a Swedish businessman. In 1944, Storch and some of his colleagues in Stockholm devised a plan for Wallenberg to undertake a rescue mission in Hungary. The US War Refugee Board supported the plan. The Swedish Government agreed to provide Wallenberg with diplomatic immunity, and Storch and his friends undertook to support the mission financially. In June, Wallenberg was appointed a Secretary of the Swedish Legation in Budapest. Upon arriving in July, Wallenberg distributed "certificates of protection" issued by the Swedish legation to Jews in Budapest. During his six-month stay in Budapest, Wallenberg was responsible for saving nearly 100,000 Hungarian Jews. In January 1945, the Soviet army liberated Budapest and took Wallenberg into custody. He disappeared into the Soviet gulag system and was never heard from again.[20]

In March 1945, Storch secretly arranged for a representative of the Swedish Section to meet with Reichsführer SS Heinrich Himmler to negotiate the freedom of Jews in concentration camps. Storch's intermediary for the meeting was Himmler's Finnish masseur, Felix Kersten. At that point, Himmler believed that notwithstanding the Allied policy of unconditional surrender and Germany's hopeless military situation, he could negotiate an agreement with the United States and Britain that would leave him in charge of Germany. Apparently, Himmler thought that he would improve his ability to achieve that delusional goal by freeing Jews.

The meeting was supported by the War Refugee Board. A Swedish Section representative, Norbert Masur, and Kersten flew into a bombed-out Berlin on April 20 and were driven to an estate seventy kilometers outside the city. Himmler was delayed by his attendance that evening at Hitler's birthday party in the Berlin bunker and did not arrive at the estate until 2:30 a.m. on the twenty-first. The encounter between the architect of Hitler's Final Solution and a WJC leader had a surreal quality. Himmler, wearing his SS uniform laden with medals and insignias, began with an extended defense of the Nazi extermination of the Jews. "We could not tolerate such an enemy at our backs. . . . The treatment in the camps was severe but just."

Masur, as he later wrote in a report of the meeting, was angry at Himmler's characterization of the concentration camps. "It was to my satisfaction, in the name of the suffering Jewish people, to tell him a thing or two about the atrocities in the concentration camps." Masur felt that "at that moment, I had the upper hand as the advocate of the bent over, but not destroyed rights of man. And I believe that Himmler felt the weakness of his position." Masur steered the conversation back to the release of Jews. Ultimately, Himmler agreed to free one thousand women inmates of the Ravensbrück concentration camp. Masur left Berlin, which Russian artillery had begun to shell, at the beginning of the Battle of Berlin. Within weeks, Himmler had committed suicide, and Germany surrendered. As a result both of this meeting and of the assistance of Count Folke Bernadotte of the Swedish Red Cross, the WJC ultimately was able to obtain the release of about seven thousand women from Ravensbrück. Approximately half of these women, who had been deported from over forty nations, were Jewish.[21]

The WJC had other successes, including its campaign for war crimes trials of Nazi leaders, which resulted in the Nuremberg trials and other clandestine rescue operations in Europe. Illustrative of these operations was the rescue of Jewish children in Portugal, a neutral country. Many of these children had been smuggled out of France to Portugal and Spain, where they had no legal status and therefore were at risk of being sent back. To mount the Portuguese rescue, Gerhart Riegner chose Isaac Weissman, a businessman who had escaped from Berlin in 1941 and now resided in Lisbon. Weissman, who came from a family of Russian origin, had good cover for a clandestine role because he had business interests in Istanbul (where he had been born), Cairo, Vienna, and Berlin, and was fluent in several languages. While Portugal did not have a common border with France, and therefore the refugees had to be transferred through Spain, Portugal appeared to WJC leaders to be relatively receptive to a clandestine operation on its territory.

Weissman, who operated clandestinely from 1941 until the end of the war, reached an agreement with the Portuguese government to accept three hundred children at a time. Under the agreement, after one group left Portugal, the next group could enter, and so on. The WJC offices in Lisbon and Geneva supervised the forging of thousands of documents, including identification cards and birth certificates. The WJC New York office raised funds from WJC members in the United States as well as from non-Jewish organizations, such as the American Quakers and the Unitarian Church.

To care for the children, a home, managed by Weissman's wife, Lily, was established outside Lisbon. The children went to classes at the home, where they were taught a variety of subjects. Particular emphasis was given to Hebrew because Weissman and the WJC leadership had chosen Palestine as the preferred destination for the children, in part because it ensured that they would be adopted by Jewish families. Between 1944 and

1945, Weissman sent hundreds of children to Palestine; dozens who had American relatives were sent to the United States.[22]

But, despite these successes, the WJC (as well as the War Refugee Board) had one great failure. The WJC failed to persuade the Roosevelt Administration to bomb the Auschwitz concentration camp and the railroads in that area. Assistant Secretary of War John J. McCloy wrote the WJC that such an operation would divert resources from the war effort and be of "doubtful efficacy." McCloy even made the bizarre argument that "even if practicable," such an operation "might provoke even more vindictive action by the Germans."[23]

Rabbi Stephen Wise died on April 19, 1949, at the age of seventy-five. His memorial service at Carnegie Hall was attended by three thousand people, while outside fifteen thousand more listened on loudspeakers. Three days after the memorial service, Albert Einstein wrote a letter to Wise's children: "In times of great adversity, he helped the Jewish people to maintain dignity and win their independence, and to every individual he was an understanding friend."

Gerhart Riegner worked for the World Jewish Congress for almost all of his adult life. He died in 2001 at the age of ninety, after devoting his life to the cause of human rights. In his autobiography, he wrote: "I belong to the tragic generation that saw the catastrophe coming and tried to contain its effects, but who, given the lack of foresight, the moral indifference, and the political opportunism of the world that surrounded us, lacked the means to do so."[24]

The Re-enfranchisement of the Jew

Rabbi Stephen S. Wise

As World War II was nearing its end, 269 delegates, representing Jewish communities and WJC representative committees from forty countries, gathered in Atlantic City, New Jersey, on November 26–30, 1944, for the WJC's War Emergency Conference. Rabbi Stephen S. Wise (1874–1949), who had served as chairman of the WJC's Executive Committee since 1936, was elected as the organization's president. The following are excerpts from Rabbi Wise's welcoming address at the War Emergency Conference on November 26, 1944:

This day, for the first time since the fateful day of September 1, 1939, Jews of many lands are met together. If it were not for my knowledge that immediately after my welcoming words we are to have a fitting service in memory of our beloved and martyred brothers and sisters, I would begin my salutation by proposing that we rise together in sorrowful tribute to our martyred and immortal dead. Their remembrance is our deepest sorrow and our most compelling challenge. Nor shall we rest as Jews and as members of humanity until we have done all that in us lies, not chiefly to express our tribute to the dead, but over and above all, in order to reach high and united resolve with regard to the future of our great people. Were we at this time to utter our grief, our truly immedicable woe, wailing and lamentation would be the form that remembrance would take. We feel, however, that we can best do honor to our martyred dead not by protest against injustice, but by plea translating itself into unwithstandable demand that never again shall the Jewish people be sacrificed upon the altar of those forces in the world which are resolved to crush free men and freedom everywhere.

We do not represent the entire Jewish world. For the largest number of Jews—of central Eastern Europe (this side of the Soviet Union)—we may not speak, for these are dead. Millions of unarmed brothers and sisters, from infancy to old age, have died because they were Jews, because a group of debased and degenerate madmen had resolved to overrule the free peoples and nations of the earth, and because the free nations of the earth resisted not the madmen until it was too late!

Proudly and rejoicing we welcome the delegates from many lands. We welcome our brother Jews from England and all English-speaking lands, for these have been a part of the great army of unafraid resisters to the devouring and, for a time it seemed, irresistible monster. We welcome our brother Jews from all American lands, including the Dominion of Canada, and all the Latin-American countries—ten or more—which are to have part as the delegates to the War Emergency Conference. Eagerly we welcome delegates from the liberated countries, above all, from immortal France and its North African lands, from Egypt, and above all, from Palestine, soon under God to be transformed into a free and democratic Jewish Commonwealth. Regretfully we note the absence of delegates from the second largest Jewish community of earth, that of the Soviet Union. But messages of sympathy from Jews in the Soviet Union have come to us, those who constitute one of the most effective anti-fascist and Nazi-resisting forces in the mighty Soviet Union. For the saving of mankind, Russia not only held Hitler and Nazism at bay for three years, but now is on the point of crushing to earth the military which was to win for him rule over mankind.

It has been declared by unfriendly observers that many of the delegates have not been chosen by the democratic process. . . . We have only this to answer: that, in the circumstances of war, it has not been possible for Hitler-conquered countries, such as Poland and Czechoslovakia, to choose their own representatives to this War Emergency Conference. But surely it is of deepest significance that the two Jewish members of the National Councils of the Polish Republic and of Czechoslovakia have journeyed from London, the seat of their war governments, in order to counsel with us, in order to have part in our deliberations. And this great assembly bids thrice welcome to the Jewish representative of the Polish National Council, Dr. Schwarzbart, and to the Jewish member of the Czechoslovakian National Council, Ernest Frischer.

Two things I would at once make clear. This is not a relief conference. This is not a charity conference. This conference is not called for consultation on the subjects of philanthropy. We are met as fellow-Jews and as brothers in order that we may take counsel together, not over our sorrow, our losses, our limitless tragedy, but over our common hopes and our common determination to share our common fate as Jews. If the Jews of other lands were our brothers before the overwhelming disaster which began not on September 1st, 1939, but on January 30, 1933—if, I repeat, these were our brothers before the moral chaos that has come to pass, they are doubly and trebly our brothers now. Not because they need us, not because we need them, but because in equal measure we need one another, and in the unity of our common faith and fate we are all indefectibly resolved to go forward together to do what may be done in order to repair the impaired fortunes and broken lives and, above all, to plan as one among the peoples of the earth for a happier, securer, and above all, freer future for all Jews. The motto of the world may be: *Ubi bene, ibi patria;* the motto of the Jew is: *Ubi male, ibi patria,* "my fatherland is wherever my brothers suffer wrong."

I thank God that victory is about to crown the glorious and incomparable strength of the United Nations. I thank God that free peoples are on the march and that they cannot be halted. We, who nearly thirty-five hundred years ago were the first of peoples to pilgrim for freedom, are at the side of all the free peoples, great and small, sharing the common lot and facing a common future not without high pride and loftiest hope!

Recently a volume has appeared, entitled "Justice for My People." In other days we thought of justice for my people as that which could only be achieved through the favor or bounty of other peoples. Too long we imagined that justice was something to be gained from without rather than wrought in large part from within. This War Emergency Conference of the World Jewish Congress is an affirmation of the deepening conviction of the Jewish people that there will be no justice to the Jewish people in the shaping and forging of which the Jewish people will not have its full and rightful part. As a people, we take counsel with the peoples of the earth, and even as we desire that the fullest justice be done to every people of the earth, we shall be satisfied with nothing less than the fullest measure of justice to the people of Israel.

Since the founding of the Congress, and even before its founding, I have felt, as its founder, by the side of Leo Motzkin and Dr. Nahum

Goldmann, my co-founders, that we are not to limit ourselves in relation to our brother Jews to the business of supplying them with food and clothing and shelter. We are to feel with them and think with them and plan together with them for that morrow on which once again they will become free and re-enfranchised members of the human race, with their enslavement forever behind them. The re-enfranchisement of the Jew! But such liberation of the Jew can only come if the democracies succeed in beating back the invading hordes of Nazism. Any other outcome of the war would mean blackest night for civilization, for religion, for freedom, and, therefore, for us Jews.

Whatever be the seeming exactions of neutrality, we Jews do not profess to be neutral as between democracy and dictatorship, as between freedom and enslavement, as between religion—which is the worship of God the Father and the doing of justice to one's brother man—and that idolatry, which is the worship of man and the unjust enslavement of one's fellow man. We were not morally neutral as between England and Germany, and any Jew who professes to be neutral between the democracies and the dictatorships is not loyal to democracy, nor faithful to Israel. Avoiding every act that violates the law of neutrality, our hearts, our hopes, our prayers, are with the democracies. Their fate is our fate; our future is bound up within their future. The unimaginable triumph of the dictatorships would mean the temporary eclipse of those values by which and for which the Jew has lived, which the Jew has done most to bring to the enrichment and ennoblement of the human race.

A word has come into use in the language of the world as a result of the most tragic circumstances, a word which it is our business to banish from the vocabulary of civilized nations. That word is "refugees." That term "refugee" is in itself a reproach to civilization. That reproach can and must be blotted out. It can only be blotted by the will of the peoples of earth, including the Jewish people. Protest may not avail amidst the turmoil and strain of war, but the day of peace will demand of us that we present to them that are to shape the destiny of the human race after the war, in such wise and temperate fashion as to make incontrovertibly clear, that Jews cannot be permitted to become a great body of refugees, that they have human rights and equal rights, and that a world at peace can deny those rights to Jews in every land in which they live only if they are indifferent to the causes of other and still more terrible wars. A world which permits Jews to be warred upon by any nation will find itself at war everywhere.

Dr. Beer-Hoffmann made the penetrating observation, "All peoples have a history; Jews have a destiny." Would it not be truer to put it that we Jews have a fate and that such fate is bound up with the fate of nations? When that fate is evil and bitter, it is not we Jews who communicate that evil fate to the nations, but the evil of nations results in an unhappy fate for us. Thus it is never Jews who are war-mongers, but the nations. And when we are charged with war-mongering, it is only because we are the first or earliest victims of war, even war waged within a nation of which we are a part as well as of war between nations. When Jews are permitted to live their lives as free men who know justice, then the peoples and nations are blessed. For the absence of strife against and war upon Jews is in itself the token of the highest status of the nations among whom and with whom the Jew lives. Peoples have their history; we have a destiny. Our destiny after centuries and millennia of injustice and hurt and wrong, to be pioneers in suffering the worst and in helping to achieve the best for all mankind. . . .

Zionism means the reconstituting of the Jewish people as a people in the Jewish homeland. I have only to add that it will come to pass as one of the moral triumphs of the global war. The English-speaking peoples, I am confident, desire it; the Soviet Union cannot fail to give it concurrence. The failure to establish the Jewish Palestine would mark the tragic failure of the global war. I venture to prophecy that the free and democratic Jewish Commonwealth will become one of the abiding achievements of the global war. The Jew owes it to himself to insist upon a free and democratic Jewish national home. The Christian world owes to the Jew reparation for all the centuries of wrong and hurt and humiliation—reparation for the awful and tragic Hitler years. That return will be afforded by the Jew. The Jew has taken his full part in the waging and in the winning of the war. The Jew has been the earliest and the greatest sufferer under the Hitler regime. A free and democratic Jewish Commonwealth means nothing more than justice to the Jew, freedom for the Jew, Jewish equality with all the free peoples of the earth.

Difficult it is to think of anything more regrettable, indeed, lamentable, than the recent assassination of Lord Moyne, the former Colonial Secretary of the British Government, and at the time of his death diplomatic agent of his Government in Cairo. There are some among us who availed themselves of the occasion in order to explain why some crazed young people in Palestine should be moved to rest their faith in the efficacy of violence, even to the point of assassination. The truth is that what must now be done is to put an end, at any and every cost, to that terrorism which prevails in Palestine. If such terrorism had the approval of the population of Palestine, it might be difficult to banish it; but it is a wicked aspersion upon the honor and integrity of the Jewish people even to insinuate that the terrorism has more than a handful of advocates and defenders among the Jewish people of Palestine. The Jews of Palestine best know and have given us reason to believe that they fully understand that Jewish terrorism, the policy and the work of a handful of misguided youth, must be uprooted at once. This is no time for pilpulistic augmentation about the cause of violence. The *havlaga*, or high self-restraint to which the Jewish population of Palestine rose in the midst of the unprovoked Arab disorders, must once again become the rule and the discipline of the Yishuv. The question is not whether terrorism can ultimately prevail. The fact is, if Jews are to be worthy of their traditions, if Jews are to be equal to themselves at their highest, if the moral law is to mean something for the Jewish people, terrorism must go and a handful of confused defenders of terrorism must not be suffered to stand in the way of the extirpation of that which can bring no advantage in itself, and, apart from every political consequence, is certain to bring infinite woe to the soul of the Jewish people.

Only yesterday, upon the eve of the convening of this assembly, I received a letter from a Jewish chaplain in the American Army, who writes:

> It is for the War Emergency Conference of the World Jewish Congress so to speak and act that the lot of Hitler's victims may be ameliorated and their faith in humanity maintained by providing for them equalities and opportunities for life, liberty and the pursuit of happiness in whatever country they may choose to live, especially in Eretz Israel.

The letter ends with the prayer: "May God grant you of the World Jewish Congress the necessary strength and endow you with a divinely inspired vision to perform these historic tasks." Whatever this War Emergency Conference of the World Jewish Congress does will be done on behalf of an eternal people by those sons and daughters who are resolved not to be unequal to the task or unworthy of their sacred and immortal heritage.

Nuremberg and Beyond: Jacob Robinson, a Champion for Justice

Jonathan A. Bush

Jacob Robinson (1889–1977) was arguably the most important and pro-lific legal scholar-activist in the Jewish world in the middle decades of the twentieth century. Working closely with his younger brother Nehemiah (1898–1964), the problems he addressed were enormous, from the rise of anti-Semitism in Eastern Europe and the destruction of minority rights in the 1920s to Nazi expansionism and domestic atrocities in the 1930s and, then, the Shoah. After the war he worked to bring war criminals to justice, arrange restitution and reparations for survivors, revive Jewish communal life, and gather Holocaust documentation. He participated in the early struggles of the State of Israel at the United Nations and fought for human rights for Diaspora communities in Eastern and Western Europe and North Africa. Working through the Institute of Jewish Affairs (IJA) of the World Jewish Congress, which he and then Nehemiah led for twenty-five years, and later with other groups and the Foreign Ministry of Israel, Jacob Robinson, "the first truly Jewish international jurist of front rank of mod-ern times,"[1] was at the center of the legal action.

Jonathan A. Bush is a lawyer and legal historian in Washington, DC.

Yet by 1970, Robinson was—outside of the circle of his aging colleagues—largely forgotten. In later decades when his work came to be remembered, he was the subject of a dozen published essays after his death[2]—all but two since the turn of the current century—as well as of a conference with published proceedings devoted to his life.[3] Although he is discussed in dozens of other essays and monographs, it is almost always for the same two activities: (1) as an advisor to American prosecutors at the first four-power Nuremberg trial (1945–1946) and (2) for his work with Israeli prosecutors at the Eichmann trial (1961), the integrity of which he vigorously defended. His contributions to both trials were important, but the emphasis says more about the recent revival of international criminal law than it does about Robinson's extraordinary and diverse career of scholarly Jewish advocacy.

Robinson was born in Seirijai, a small town in southern Lithuania, on November 26, 1889, one of seven sons born to David and Bluma Robinson. It was an observant family, but as Robinson's biographer Omry Kaplan-Feuereisen concludes, it was also progressive; Jacob's father was an early Zionist, and an uncle was one of the first Jewish researchers in Russia.[4] Conscripted into the Russian army in 1914 after earning the equivalent of a doctorate in law at the University of Warsaw, Jacob was captured and spent three years as a German prisoner of war. Upon his release, he settled in the Lithuanian city of Virbalis where he founded and ran a Hebrew *gymnasium*. He was admitted to the bar; moved to Kaunas (Kovno); began a legal practice, in which he was joined by Nehemiah in 1927; co-edited a Yiddish newspaper; and in 1923 was elected to the second Lithuanian parliament as one of seven Jewish members. He was the leader of both the Jewish faction and the minorities caucus for the parliament, posts he held until its dissolution in a December 1926 coup.

The dissolution of the Lithuanian parliament marked the start of the next phase of Robinson's communal activism. On the international Jewish stage he was active with the Committee for Jewish Delegations, established in 1919 to represent Jewish interests at the Paris Peace Conference, and participated in the early efforts to organize the World Jewish Congress (1927–1936). He is even credited with the idea for the Bernheim Petition (1933), a novel legal proceeding in which an exiled German Jew won a

League of Nations ruling against Germany.[5] At home he organized an informal group to promote Jewish rights, served as legal advisor to the Lithuanian Foreign Ministry (1931–1933), was his country's representative on the German-Lithuanian Permanent Conciliation Committee (1931), and helped present the country's successful claim at the Permanent Court of International Justice in the important Memel case (1932).[6]

The German invasion of Poland did not immediately bring Lithuania into the war,[7] but Robinson knew that his country was unlikely to be safe for long.[8] In May 1940, he, his wife, and their two daughters were granted visas to the United States but because they gave their tickets to two young students, their arrival was delayed until December. Within a few months, the World Jewish Congress and the American Jewish Congress announced through Rabbi Stephen S. Wise the establishment of the IJA to conduct basic research, based in New York and led by Jacob Robinson. The IJA was the first Jewish think tank addressing Nazism and war.[9] It faced a huge agenda with a tiny staff of refugee intellectuals. Jacob's brother Nehemiah started working at the WJC/IJA in 1941. From this modest beginning, the IJA began a program of research and the creation of substantial publications that would continue throughout the war.

The IJA's best-known book from the war years is probably *Hitler's Ten-Year War on the Jews* (1943), a useful book akin to Franz Neumann's *Behemoth* or Raphael Lemkin's *Axis Rule in Occupied Europe*, albeit with more solid research and less theoretical flash. An even more significant book may be the IJA's first work, *Jews in Nazi Europe, February 1933 to November 1941*, prepared for the Inter-American Jewish Conference in Baltimore in November 1941. At that gathering the principal speakers were Wise and US Undersecretary of State Sumner Welles. Circulated in mimeo for speedier dissemination, the book compiled Jewish human and material losses on a country-by-country basis and seems to have been the first study to show the scale of the Holocaust as it was about to enter its most murderous phase. Although it was mistaken about some details, cautiously offering figures that erred on the low side and relied in its methodology on published scraps of information, official estimates and leaks, and escapee accounts, the book was a clarion call not only for outrage among the delegates, but for further research.

Robinson wrote a book on the legal issues of the British Mandate, opposing the closure of immigration to Palestine. In another one of his books, *Were the Minority Treaties a Failure?* (1943), he drew on his positions in the Memel case to argue for the efficacy of better-designed minorities treaties. His brother Nehemiah, who had studied law at Berlin and Jena and practiced law with Jacob in Kaunas in the 1920s, joined the IJA and wrote one of the earliest and finest books—*Indemnification and Reparations: Jewish Aspects* (1944)—which deals with the legal issues relating to Jewish losses. Together with their half-dozen colleagues and outside allies, the Robinsons also wrote on refugees and migration, restitution, cultural revival, Zionism, federalism, an organization of united nations, assimilation, human rights, treaty protections, German demilitarization and rehabilitation, and Soviet Jewry. They shared data with and lobbied labor unions, Christian groups, and university experts, and worked with the WJC's Political Section and British Section despite differences of emphasis.[10] Jacob published frequently in *Congress Weekly* and other Jewish publications, gave courses on nationalism and minority protections to students and officer candidates at Columbia University, and played a prominent role at the WJC's War Emergency Conference in Atlantic City, New Jersey, in November 1944, which adopted an eleven-point program for war crimes accountability and another on reparations.[11]

Looking at Jacob's prominent writings and speeches from the period, one scholar has identified a shift in Robinson's wartime views from advocating reconstruction of Jewish life with treaty protections in a postwar Europe to robust Zionism. Another argues that the Institute shifted from policy advocacy to Holocaust documentation as the extent of the Final Solution became known.[12] But a different case can also be made from the writings by the Robinson brothers and their colleagues at the IJA. They were part of an entire generation of émigré lawyers and intellectuals who were searching for answers to the problem of "Germany and What Next?" Only a handful of these dozens of individuals—René Cassin, Franz Neumann, Hersch Lauterpacht, Hans Morgenthau, Hans Kelsen, and Raphael Lemkin—are familiar to most of us today. Some started with policy preferences, as Jacob did with minority rights treaties, and some became entrepreneurs for particular theories or approaches, most famously Lemkin with his notion of genocide, but those of a pragmatic bent, including the Robinsons, soon promoted more than one policy prescription. With authors such as the Robinsons, who wrote so much and so often with each other and other co-authors, it is particularly difficult to see a trend in their policy commitments. Still, it is not unlikely that with each new set of death estimates making the idea of renewed Jewish life in Eastern Europe less plausible, their commitment to Zionism, but also to life in North America and to legal accountability for the Holocaust, grew.

In May 1945, Supreme Court Justice Robert Jackson was announced as head of US planning for war crimes policy. Later when a trial plan for prominent Nazi war criminals was agreed upon with the major Allies, Jackson became the chief US prosecutor at the International Military Tribunal (IMT) at Nuremberg that followed (November 1945–October 1946). Jacob Robinson was an advisor to Jackson; and for the rest of his life, he was proud to identify himself as such. In many ways he was an ideal choice for Nuremberg: his work at the IJA meant he had sources about the Holocaust that complemented what the governments knew, and his writings on, and practice in, prewar international tribunals were unrivaled by the US staff. A trail of memos illustrates Robinson's role. In June 1945, newly returned from San Francisco where he was a WJC observer at the conference that founded the United Nations, Robinson met with Jackson and soon after was introduced to Charles Irving Dwork and Abraham Duker. Dwork and Duker were the two Jewish staff members who worked at the "Jewish Desk" for the Office of Special Services (OSS), the wartime intelligence agency whose chief, General William O. Donovan, was now the US deputy chief prosecutor and was sharing his agency's resources with the Nuremberg effort.[13]

Most likely it was Robinson and his IJA colleagues who prepared the comprehensive plan that Dwork proposed for viewing the Holocaust as a criminal conspiracy. In June, Robinson also took on the task for Jackson of assembling reliable estimates for presentation at trial about the Holocaust. He urged Jackson to consider including a Jewish chief prosecutor or official representative, giving the court an official Jewish submission amicus curiae, and above all, seeing the atrocities against Jews as crimes against a collectivity, a people, rather than a vast number of individual atrocities—all three points agreed upon at the Atlantic City conference.[14] Upon hearing rumors of the names of possible defendants, Robinson wrote Jackson in late July to urge that Adolf Eichmann be included alongside the Grand Mufti of Jerusalem, who was already under consideration. Stressing that "it has to date not been made public what has happened to Eichmann," he summarized Eichmann's enormous role in the Holocaust.[15] Throughout the summer, Robinson, Cambridge international law professor Hersch Lauterpacht, and a few others continued maneuvering to have a co-equal chief prosecutor of the Jewish people or an official witness who would testify, perhaps Chaim Weizmann, or both. In October 1945 Robinson lectured members of the US team still in London and in mid- to late-November, he went to Nuremberg and worked with the small team under Major William Walsh to prepare the American presentation of what was euphemistically called "the Persecution of the Jews." He went home and reported to the WJC on his time at, and impressions of, Nuremberg in December 1945, and later returned briefly to Nuremberg in the summer of 1946.[16]

Unfortunately, Robinson, like many other participants, left little evidence of his significance at Nuremberg.[17] Because of this, some have extrapolated about Robinson's role at Nuremberg with more speculation than evidence. Others have concluded that Robinson and other Jewish advocates made little imprint. But, they continue, this stemmed from Nuremberg's blindness to the centrality of what would become known as the Holocaust, to the absence of a Jewish voice and evidence at Nuremberg, a characterization that became conventional wisdom by the time of the Eichmann trial almost fifteen years later and is still widely accepted.[18] In this view, the charge against Nuremberg is twofold: that there were few Jewish participants and not enough focus on the Holocaust.

The truth about Jewish voices and influence at Nuremberg lies somewhere in between. Robinson and Jewish groups were right to feel that the Holocaust was not the focus of the trial. The largely American notion of deeming the war itself the supreme crime and encompassing everything related to it, including the Holocaust, into a criminal conspiracy model had been developed in autumn 1944, adopted by two successive presidents and Jackson, imposed on skeptical or surprised allies at the UN meeting in San Francisco, and adopted at the London planning meetings.[19] Even where theories were adopted that Jewish groups had pushed, such as the demand since 1942 of the British Section of the WJC that postwar accountability include wrongs done (1) prior to the war, (2) to enemy nationals (German and Austrian Jews), and (3) with the aim of exterminating whole peoples—in short, even where Jewish groups anticipated "crimes against humanity" and "genocide"—it was a case of *post hoc, ergo propter hoc*: Nuremberg planners arrived at the same place independently and without evidence that they heeded Jewish proposals.[20]

Despite this familiar story, Robinson's gloomy view that Jewish perspectives and voices were being ignored—a view broadly accepted today—was also wrong in many ways. From the start, Allied prosecutors did seek out émigrés—mainly German Jewish lawyers, political scientists, and historians—who could verify facts rather than legal theory, which is why Robinson himself was prized for his ability to document the hard figures of Holocaust deaths. The British staff does not appear to have consulted anybody aside from Lauterpacht, but the far larger American legal team sought help from the start from refugee scholars and others.[21] The most important refugee to whom they turned was not an academic or someone connected to Jewish think tanks but Robert M. W. Kempner, who had been ousted from the Prussian civil service and became a ranking prosecutor in both the IMT and the later Nuremberg trials, and who later showed his worth by discovering papers connecting field marshals on the Eastern Front to the *Einsatzgruppen* and what is still the only extant copy of the Wannsee Protocol.[22] Aside from Kempner, prosecutors seemed to feel, as litigators temperamentally do, that they didn't need outside help, either from new co-equal prosecutors or official witnesses as Robinson had hoped,[23] or from staff advisors. Robinson, Lauterpacht, Lemkin, and other eminences were consulted a few times, met chief or deputy prosecutors, and left—and were heartily thanked—with the theories that had preceded them largely unchanged.

None of which is to say that Jewish voices or concerns were not heeded. There were dozens of American Jewish staff prosecutors, investigators, and researchers on the large US team.[24] Their backgrounds ranged from assimilated but professional New Deal lawyers to more strongly observant Jews who were deeply committed to the specifically Jewish dimension of the case. Jewish and other survivors were not needed to testify in open court in a trial of German leaders, many of whom had never been to a ghetto or extermination camp. What was needed was testimony from knowledgeable senior Germans who could incriminate their colleagues, and this was gradually found in witnesses such as SS officers Erich von dem Bach-Zelewski and Otto Ohlendorf and diplomat Hans Gisevius.[25] Documentary proof was needed even more and was found by scores of investigators. A sequence of American prosecutors assembled hard documentary evidence about the Holocaust.[26] Other delegations, especially the Soviets, did so as well. In the end, the Holocaust featured prominently at Nuremberg. It was inescapable in the trial record. The extent to which an explicit Jewish voice was not featured or a story not told was due to the trial's legal premises about aggression and lawyers' self-confidence, and to a larger setback handed to Robinson and allies by the judges. Erring on the side of caution, the judges ruled that with a few exceptions they lacked jurisdiction over conspiracy to commit war crimes or crimes against humanity and over prewar atrocities.[27] Both were bitter blows to the prosecution and even more so to Robinson, for whom a conspiracy or central plan against Jews was the heart of the case. But even the Tribunal could not and did not want to minimize the Holocaust.

But this is skipping ahead somewhat. Back in the early months of the trial, when Robinson had only just returned from Nuremberg, he briefed his WJC and IJA colleagues about the trial and offered his critical view that while in principle the trial was important, and even historic, there was insufficient attention given to the Holocaust, and there was a second-rate quality to the American prosecutors presenting that case. In his confidential report, Robinson told colleagues that Jackson was "tremendous" and an ally, but that the trial premises he espoused derived from the UN War Crimes Commission; that the US team was estranged from the others; that the resignation of deputy US Chief Donovan had significance; that the French team might be the most supportive of the Holocaust case because of the Jewish background of alternate judge Robert Falco; that the broad expertise of the British prosecutors meant they would also be effective allies; that the Americans would be of little help because many of the staff were junior and second-rate and because no Jew had been assigned a speaking role in the case in chief; and that the composition of the prosecution demonstrates that overall "[w]e are witnessing the ebb of Jewish influence in the world."[28] As it happens, he was almost completely wrong in these conclusions. Nevertheless, he, and the WJC, followed the trials closely and kept this view for the next few years. In the winter of 1945 and spring of 1946, Robinson could not have known that Nuremberg would address the Holocaust with condemnation and stiff sentences, albeit with complicated and mixed legal rulings, nor could he have known that a number of the prosecutors and consultants on the Holocaust portion of the case would make important contributions to later trials or to the first wave of Holocaust scholarship.[29]

Robinson also could not have known that early in the second round of Nuremberg trials (1946–1949), Chief Prosecutor Taylor would send a memo to his deputies in February 1947 praising them for the current cases but urging them to view the Holocaust as the defining feature of the Nazi regime and to prepare prosecutions that would reflect this centrality. One result was the *Einsatzgruppen* case; another was the focus in the Weizsaecker case on crimes against humanity. But if Robinson could not have known those things, he and WJC President Stephen S. Wise should have shown better judgment than to send a November 19, 1947 letter over Wise's signature to Taylor, with copies leaked elsewhere, complaining about the paucity of cases and citing six uncharged SS leaders. One problem was that they were complaining about one of their best allies, for Taylor had sought to charge many more Nazis but had been reined in; another problem was that the list was factually wrong and most of the men either had been charged or were confirmed dead.[30]

While they stumbled by criticizing their allies in 1947, Robinson and the WJC were right about the larger fact that the Americans, at Nuremberg and elsewhere, and even more so the British, the French, and the liberated nations, were bringing few new cases and cutting back on resources, manpower, and enthusiasm for war crimes trials and punishment. In part this was due to war fatigue and Nazi fatigue, in part to unscrupulous Cold War politics. Whatever the balance, the WJC was accurate at its second plenary assembly in Montreux in July 1948 in identifying and denouncing the trend toward clemency and amnesty for Nazi war criminals. From then on, the

WJC was on the same side as the (former) prosecutors. Both Robinsons corresponded with Taylor to help lobby for publication of the Nuremberg record (the English language record of the first trial was published, but the record of the later twelve trials was severely cut and published in only limited print runs, while the German-language text was never released). They wrote Taylor to campaign for new trials and to oppose the pell-mell rush that began around 1951 to grant clemency to convicted major Nazi defendants. Nehemiah and his colleagues at the IJA published articles similarly urging trials and opposing clemencies.[31]

Back in late 1945 when he first returned from Nuremberg, Robinson rejoined his Institute. It continued to produce scholarly and policy studies, some two dozen in one series alone over the next few years, with a slight but noticeable turn to domestic issues such as civil rights in employment and schooling and veterans rights. Jacob wrote two of them, on Jews in the Soviet Union and the unfinished business of victory,[32] but he soon returned to international law. In May 1945, the WJC, American Jewish Conference, and the Board of Deputies of British Jews had submitted a memo to negotiators in San Francisco planning the United Nations—surely the first instance of an NGO petitioning the new organization and surely a document drafted by Robinson, perhaps with the support of his fellow delegate Alex Easterman—to urge a stronger basis for the UN protection of minorities; it had been rejected. Now, in May 1946, Robinson returned to the point with his prescient IJA study "Human Rights and Fundamental Freedoms in the Charter of the United Nations," with a focus on national and international jurisdictions and humanitarian intervention. Near the end of 1946, the UN Secretariat hired him as a consultant to plan the first meeting of the UN Human Rights Commission, held in early 1947.

There was little surprise that in April 1947 Robinson resigned from the IJA, which was safely in Nehemiah's hands, to become legal advisor to the Jewish Agency at the United Nations and, after Israel's independence, first legal advisor to Israel's UN mission. Within a few months of assuming his new role, he marked his presence at the United Nations with another book, *Palestine and the United Nations* (1947), documenting the legalities of the worsening situation in Mandatory Palestine and urging an even-handed constructive role for the United Nations. Abba Eban, Israel's first ambassador to the United Nations, later said that "Robinson did more than anyone else to educate us all to the potentialities and limitations of multilateral diplomacy."[33]

For the next ten years, the Robinson brothers were a Jewish-issues counterpart to West Point's famed football backfield of the mid-1940s that featured "Mr. Inside" and "Mr. Outside." Jacob was the insider at Israel's UN mission, working in the corridors of power, and Nehemiah was the outsider at the scholarly IJA, urging new programs, warning of new dangers, and advising the public. The brothers lived and worked together and were surely coordinating their tactics and strengths. Thus, on Holocaust compensation, Nehemiah continued to publish and update books and articles on West German and Austrian legislation for the IJA and work with Easterman and other experts from the WJC political and British sections. Jacob worked as the insider with Nahum Goldmann and others in the difficult Wassenaar negotiations and is credited with being one of the principal drafters of the Luxembourg Agreements (1952), which provided for historic reparations by West Germany to both Israel and individual Holocaust survivors. His hand-edited typescript of the agreement may be the closest thing to an ur-text for that landmark document.[34]

The brothers did the same with the emerging crime of genocide. Today, some say that genocide is the supreme crime and that the 1948 Convention on the Prevention and Punishment of the Crime of Genocide was an obvious outgrowth of the Holocaust. If so, it was not obvious at the time. Few nations initially ratified the Convention, and many had concerns about the definition of the crime and the incursions the Convention might permit on state sovereignty. Nehemiah's 1949 commentary is the first and, arguably, still the most important, gloss on the Convention, and he and other scholars at the IJA continued to track developments on genocide law in their publications. For his part, Jacob was almost certainly the strategist for the Israeli mission as it successfully petitioned the United Nations, along with the British and French, to permit them to ask the International Court of Justice (ICJ) for an advisory opinion on the question of reservations to the Genocide Convention. The question may sound academic, but for Israel, the issue was that Arab bloc nations ratified the Convention with variants of a reservation that the treaty did not bind them to renounce genocide against Israelis. Using Robinson's arguments, Shabtai Rosenne, then-legal advisor at the mission, and his two European counterparts persuaded the ICJ that reservations that undercut the heart of a treaty were deemed void (1951).[35]

After this victory, Jacob continued to make learned presentations for Israel to the UN Sixth Committee and other organs on the Genocide Convention, aggression, crimes against humanity, an international criminal court, slavery, and the Nuremberg principles. Other matters on which he was active were the Convention on the Declaration of Death of Missing Persons (1950) and the Convention Relating to the Status of Refugees (1951). Both were intended as temporary, retrospective agreements and both might seem technical, but they were of deep concern to a nation such as Israel, with hundreds of thousands of refugees and missing kinsmen. Joining Robinson at the negotiations was Gerhart Riegner, an old hand from the WJC and author of the crucial 1942 Riegner telegram that first alerted the world about the Holocaust. And, reliable as clockwork, the UN conventions on Refugees and on Declarations of Death of Missing Persons on which Jacob worked were then discussed in scholarly commentaries by Nehemiah at the IJA (1952).[36]

Jacob Robinson's most important moment at the United Nations came in the tense weeks before, during, and after the Suez incursion (October–November 1956). Meeting constantly with Ambassador Eban and occasionally with Foreign Minister Golda Meir, Robinson was the legal advisor as Israel sought to fend off diplomatic pressure while it negotiated withdrawal from Sinai. Soon after, in summer 1957, praised and respected by other delegations but disillusioned, he left the United Nations and returned to his life of research.[37] With Nehemiah still leading the IJA and publishing furiously about Jewish issues around the world—*European Jewry Ten Years after the War* (1956), and surveys of Jewish life in dozens of countries from Latin America to Iran—Jacob gathered bibliographic material on the Holocaust and on international law. In 1959 he was honored by scholars and communal leaders around the world on his seventieth birthday, and he continued to write.

His quiet routines as a scholar and institutional leader were interrupted by the arrival in Israel of Adolf Eichmann, abducted from Argentina on May 11, 1960. Israeli Attorney General Gideon Hausner, who would lead the prosecution, had only just taken office and had not previously been involved in legal planning. With the trial imminent, Hausner recruited Robinson, who had pressed the Allies to charge Eichmann as long ago as Nuremberg, as his international law specialist. Naturally, Nehemiah at the IJA was also involved, writing an essay in December 1960 about the sale of Eichmann's memoir to *Life Magazine* by Eichmann's wife, and another essay as the trial began about the same legal issues on which his brother was the chief advisor.[38] Unlike others on the small prosecution team, Jacob did not argue in court or examine witnesses, but he was indispensable and can be seen in trial photos sitting next to Hausner. He had declined an invitation to testify as the lead, expert witness—a role for which famed historian Salo Baron was picked, to mixed reviews—but he helped investigators sort through hundreds of survivor accounts to find witnesses, defended the planned trial in scholarly and other publications, and is credited with preparing the international law arguments used in court.[39] After a four-month trial, Eichmann was convicted, the conviction affirmed, and the defendant hanged at the end of May 1962.

Today the trial is widely seen as fair and the process praised for having been the first trial of a high-level war criminal since the Nuremberg era. It was the first case to feature the legal theories of universal jurisdiction and genocide, and the first to rely so centrally on survivor testimony. Yet it is often forgotten that at the time, the legal questions—seizure, jurisdiction, the Israeli statute, retroactivity, fair trial, venue, and execution—behind these, the political and moral issues, were enormously controversial. Without question, the most critical commentary on the trial was by the noted German Jewish émigré philosopher Hannah Arendt in her 1963 book, *Eichmann in Jerusalem: A Report on the Banality of Evil*, which was based on a series of articles she had written for *The New Yorker*. Arendt presented the defendant as guilty but ordinary, honest, free of anti-Semitism, mechanistic, and interesting rather than evil. She portrayed the prosecution as rigid and error-prone, the survivor witnesses as overly emotional, the Israeli government as producing a show trial, the charges as based on sectarian rather than universalistic grounds, and the Holocaust as so huge that it relied out of necessity on the complicity of Jewish communal leaders.

Robinson took on the task of rebutting Arendt's points, in places line by line, in his book *And the Crooked Shall Be Made Straight*, published in 1965. It is accurate on almost all points, and new research continues to endorse its findings, but it is poorly written and organized, more a dense list than the polished appraisal that would be needed against a polemicist as skilled as Arendt. The unfortunate fate of Robinson's best-known but least-successful book was that despite the favorable consensus of specialists about it, most readers still regard Arendt's book as brilliant if flawed, and Robinson's, when remembered at all, as an angry, nit-picking, even if accurate, book.[40]

Robinson continued to wear multiple hats in the world of communal Jewry.[41] From 1957, he had been legal advisor to the Claims Conference and helped establish the research branch of Yad Vashem, but he typically introduced himself as "research coordinator of the four Holocaust institutes," from which he encouraged joint scholarly projects to be undertaken and tried to assemble proposed lists of survivors who could be witnesses in war crimes trials. He worked with his brother's IJA, the national affiliates of the World Jewish Congress, and other groups. He corresponded with officials, rabbis, survivors, and old allies in Eastern Europe, Latin America, and of course Israel, Germany, and throughout the United States, and was seen as an indispensable counselor. He steered funds to a steady stream of survivors who came in penury to him and his brother, and to scholars and memorial projects, but he lived modestly, residing as he had since 1941 on Riverside Drive with his wife and two daughters, his brother, and a sister-in-law, all of whom helped in his work.

But his immediate world grew darker. His intimate co-author Nehemiah died young in January 1964, as another beloved co-author, his daughter Vita, had of leukemia in 1955. The appearance of other, more specialized research and advocacy groups meant that the IJA was less central, and perhaps because it no longer had Nehemiah's energy anchoring it in New York, it relocated to London in 1965. Jacob was left with more time for his research, which continued unabated. Continuing the bibliographic series of unpublished Holocaust evidence that he had begun with the late Philip Friedman in 1960,[42] he published new volumes together with scholars at Hebrew University starting in 1965. His bibliography of international law and legal sources (1967) is sadly forgotten today, but it itemizes and assesses over two thousand sources in dozens of languages, including older manuals and periodicals by Slavic and Asian authors that cannot be found in any major American library. His last major bibliographic work was, fittingly, a digest of the Nuremberg evidence, co-edited with Henry Sachs (1976). At a time when the Nuremberg trials are breezily cited everywhere but the body of evidence is too vast and unwieldy for all but a few specialists to access, Robinson's calendar is the gold standard for serious researchers. In 1977, soon after the digest was completed, Robinson died.

The author wishes to thank Carole Fink, Omry Kaplan-Feuereisen, Moris Kori, Michael R. Marrus, Henry Mayer, Myra Katz Sibrava, and Karin Sibrava-Cherches for their generous help, as well as Menachem Rosensaft and Isabella Nespoli of the World Jewish Congress and Lydia Deutsch for research assistance.

The State of World Jewry, 1948

Nahum Goldmann

*The following are excerpts from the keynote address delivered by Dr.
Nahum Goldmann (1895–1982), chairman of the Executive Committee
of the World Jewish Congress, at the opening session of the second WJC
plenary assembly in Montreux, Switzerland, on June 27, 1948. One of
the founders of the WJC, Goldmann became acting president of the WJC
in 1949 upon the death of Rabbi Stephen S. Wise and served as the
organization's president from 1953 until 1977.*

It is almost sixteen years since—at the first preparatory Conference for
the World Jewish Congress, held in the summer of 1932 in Geneva—it
fell to me to make one of a series of speeches dealing with the general
situation of the Jewish people in the world. . . . These few short years
have witnessed the greatest tragedy in Jewish history—the annihilation
of more than one-third of our people by the Nazi barbarians and their
allies. It has also seen the realization of the most cherished dream of many
generations of Jews: the proclamation and establishment of a Jewish state
in Palestine—the State of Israel.

These are two revolutionary events: the one marking the climax of our
galuth [exile] tragedy, and the other the beginning of the realization of the
most sacred ideal of our people. They are naturally the two governing facts
in determining the position of the Jews in the world today. Both events
are of such far-reaching importance and significance that it must take
years, perhaps generations, to evaluate their full meaning and take stock
of the tremendous consequences which they involve for our people, both
as regards our internal structure and in our external relations. We who
are still close to these events can only begin to realize their implications:

we can try to find out their historical meaning for our own and future generations of Jews, to estimate their effect, and to make a beginning with the readjustment of Jewish life and Jewish policies to these two governing factors. There is no problem of Jewish life today which will not be influenced, directly or indirectly, by them in the most radical and far-reaching way. There is hardly a problem that is not already feeling their influence. . . .

I think no one here needs to be reminded that these two events—on the one hand the annihilation of six million Jews and on the other, the establishment of the State of Israel—provide the fullest confirmation of the analysis of the Jewish situation developed by the founders of modern Zionism—an analysis, which is today accepted not only by Zionist thinkers and speakers, but by the overwhelming majority of the Jewish people. This analysis is based on the assumption that the Jewish situation in the world must remain abnormal and tragic: so long as it is determined solely by the fact of Jewish dispersion, so long as there is no real center for our national existence, so long as we have no place in the world to call our own—where we can live our own lives fully, after our own fashion, "like unto the nations," so long, in fact, as we are not recognized as an independent, sovereign state on a footing of equality with other sovereign states.

The terrible tragedy of the Hitler decade threw a ghastly but searching light on this abnormality of Jewish life: not even the most pessimistic analyst of the galuth situation could have seen so clearly in the years before Hitler as we all do today. Had the Jewish people had the courage and imagination ever to envisage—as the remotest of possibilities—the massacre of six million Jews, it might have taken some precautions in time; it might have heeded the warning the more clear-sighted of its leaders were already giving; it might have organized its fight against Hitlerism before it was too late and while the hydra head was still weak enough to be crushed without the catastrophe of a world war. Yet perhaps one had to be something of a Nazi oneself to envisage the possibility of gas chambers and concentration camps before they happened. Perhaps it was not only a lack of courage and imagination but also innate decency and a deep faith in human nature— what a German philosopher has called "the cursed optimism of the Jewish people"—which prevented the Jewish masses, and many Jewish leaders, from admitting even to themselves that such catastrophes might happen.

This is not the place for recriminations; nor have I any wish to make them. It is easy to say now that we should have reacted more vigorously in the early stages of Hitlerism. The Secretary-General's report will tell you much about these "sins of omission"—some of them dating from a time when the process of annihilation was well under way, but when, with a little more civic courage and daring in our policies, very large numbers of Jews might still have been saved.

To a greater or lesser degree, we are all responsible for these things: it was the tragic shortsightedness of a people which had got used to its abnormal situation, and which, confronted with a danger of unprecedented character and dimensions, could react only by the usual routine methods. More important than any admission of our past failures, is to apply to our future the tremendous results of the greatest tragedy in Jewish history....

If there is one ray of consolation in all this ghastly story of the decade of Hitler, it is the magnificent evidence it offers of Jewish vitality, and of our determination to survive all attempts to destroy us. If Jews in the United States and many other countries are today much more fully conscious of their Jewish identity and their Jewish responsibilities than they used to be, it is to a large degree due to the lessons forced upon them by the horrible tragedy enacted before their very eyes, and which they were powerless to prevent. Another striking proof of our will to live is provided to anyone who visits the DP camps. Hitler annihilated millions of individual Jews; he did not succeed in annihilating the Jewish people. He neither broke our will to live, nor delivered any mortal blow to the soul or spirit of Jewry. From the larger, historical viewpoint, he failed. *Am Yisra'el ḥai*....

Dangers in an Unstable World

The Hitler decade, with its annihilation of six million of our small people, is a grave threat to our existence, a threat to our ability to maintain our identity as a people. In the Diaspora, the permanent danger to Jewish life has always been the fact of our dispersion and disintegration. The more dispersed and disintegrated we are, the more difficult it becomes for us to maintain our solidarity as Jews, our unity as a collective entity. Five small communities can do far less than one large one. So the destruction of powerful and distinguished Jewish communities like the Polish, Hungarian, Rumanian, Lithuanian, and German, intensified this threat to our existence. Fortunately, Jewish history has provided us with one great new Jewish community—that built up in the last few generations in America. Seen as a whole, however, the safeguarding of our national identity is a much more difficult task today than it was before the Hitler decade.

There is another element in the present world situation which further increases this danger. We live in revolutionary times; new ideas are everywhere fighting to find concrete expression. Without expressing any opinion here on the merits of the various contending theories and systems, it must be clear to every thoughtful observer that we are headed towards a period of widespread ideological and political conflict and upheaval, even though—as we hope and pray—everything possible will be done to prevent it from degenerating into a shooting war. Whatever our opinions as to the various ideologies, it must be clear to everyone that we are not living, and for some time cannot hope to live, in a stable world. Perhaps the two great world wars were only the expression of revolutionary changes in the world. The next period will be one of instability, dissensions, new ideas of all kinds—political, economic, social, cultural, religious—which will make it impossible to maintain the status quo and to prevent great developments and changes.

As human beings and citizens of the world, we may welcome such developments or fear them; but however we feel about them, we have to realize the dangers inherent in them for the Jews as a people. If I here point out three such inherent dangers, it is not in order to advise the Jews to hold aloof from the current of world affairs; as heirs of an ancient civilization—grandsons of the prophets—we have to play our part and make our contribution with the other peoples of the world. I point them out in order that we may be fully aware of them, and may take what precautions we can to reduce their gravity and if possible counteract their effect upon our future as a people.

One danger flows from the fact that, whenever the world is in a state of instability and flux, of dissension, conflict and chaos, minorities are bound to be the first to suffer—and none is so vulnerable as the Jews. In the fight against new ideas, reactionaries—defenders of the past—must always seek a scapegoat and who more likely than the Jewish people—the classic scapegoat and object of attack from time immemorial for every reactionary movement in the world? In a world so unstable as ours is today . . . anti-Semitism is almost bound to become a permanent feature. You will hear during the present Session reports of anti-Semitic movements, of the revival of anti-Semitism in many countries, among them lands where anti-Semitism was formerly almost an unknown phenomenon—for instance Great Britain. In the United States, anti-Semitism is stronger today than maybe at any other period of its history; and though it is certainly not an immediate danger to the great and strong Jewish community there, it is still strong enough to constitute a serious problem and to do away with any facile notion that the democratic constitution and traditions of the American people are in themselves a permanent guarantee for Jewish life and equality of citizenship in that country. You will hear, too, about anti-Semitism in Latin-American countries, where new Jewish communities are beginning to make a notable contribution to Jewish life as a whole. I do not have to speak in detail about the grave situation of the Jews in Moslem countries, in some of which they have long lived under discriminatory regimes, and where the Palestine issue is now creating new dangers to their existence. You will also hear about the undiminished persistence of Nazi anti-Semitism in Germany and Austria, which may overnight grow into a serious danger—especially in view of certain tendencies to permit the reemergence of a strong Germany.

I hope the Jewish people has learned from the last fifteen years not to deal lightly with anti-Semitism, not to regard it as an isolated local phenomenon, for which antiquated and piecemeal methods are still adequate. Anti-Semitism always was, and today is more than ever, a general political phenomenon. It is one of the most popular disguises of reactionaries, Nazis and Fascists everywhere, one of the most formidable weapons for all aggressive movements. It has therefore to be dealt with by political methods: first by united action, by coordination of all efforts to fight it, and secondly by seeking the help of all progressive elements in the struggle. Anti-Semitism can never be dealt with adequately if it is regarded as a purely Jewish problem. It is much more a problem of world politics than a specifically Jewish one, and it is only with the help of all democratic, liberal, and progressive forces in the world that there is any chance of striking at it effectively, and preventing in the future catastrophes such as the one through which we have passed in the last decade or so.

Another consequence of the general world situation and its impact on our people is that revolutionary tendencies, and great political and moral movements in the world, are always apt to attract Jewish youth and Jewish intelligence: they draw the devotion and sympathy of large numbers of our people. We are not ashamed of it; on the contrary, as a people we have always been proud of our contribution to the life and thought of the civilized world. If there is something unique, something singular, about the life of the Jewish people, if there is a Jewish problem not comparable to the problem of any other people in the world, it is partly just because of the role we have played in all kinds of historical movements and causes—a role much greater than our numbers or political strength would suggest. The Jewish people has no intention of retreating to a self-imposed ghetto in the countries of the Diaspora, or of renouncing its ability or eagerness to play its part in the great movements which strive today to build a better world, a safer world, a happier world, based on a greater degree of social and political equality than the past centuries have shown. But the fact that those tendencies have so great an attraction for many of the best elements of our people should not distract our attention from the difficulty which this creates in the maintenance of our identity as people.

Most of our contributions to such world developments—except the contribution yet to be made in our own State of Israel (and one important *raison d'être* for a Jewish state is precisely this unique opportunity it would provide for us)—are made not simply as Jews, but as members of general or group movements. The stronger the attraction, the greater the strength and élan of such ideas, the firmer their hold on the devotion and imagination of sections of our people, the easier does it become for these sections to become submerged in the larger stream, losing their connection with the Jewish people and even their identity as Jews. How to strengthen this identity without abandoning our justifiable desire to participate in all forces engaged in the building of a better world, is one of the great problems of Jewish life in the galuth; and as long as the greater part of our people still live in the Diaspora (and this means certainly for us and our children), this problem will remain one of the great spiritual and moral problems of our life. There is no easy solution, and certainly no wholesale formula for solving it; but it has to be constantly borne in mind so that we recognize the dangers inherent in it and the difficulties it must create for us. . . .

The Jewish State Normalizes Jewish Existence

Now I come to the other great fact of the last period—no less important in its positive aspect than the Hitler decade in its negative aspect—a fact hoped for and dreamed of from time immemorial, but realized with dramatic speed. It is still so close to us that it is not easy to speak of it without emotion, still less to try and estimate the force of its impact, its meaning, and its consequences for Jewish life. The establishment of the State of Israel means the beginning of the normalization of our existence as a people; it does not mean the immediate end of the Jewish problem. There are no miracles in history; there is no historical process which does not require its proper time. The proclamation of our State does not mean the end of the Diaspora, and I could wish that in a time like ours, when we face great developments and great changes, we might be able to reduce the ideological debates and discussions of which we are masters. To overdo such discussions is one of the characteristics of the galuth.

Living for centuries the life of the ghetto, unable to establish their own realities for themselves, the Jews have been the objects of history rather than its subjects. They have depended for their lives, for the form of their existence, on the good or ill-will of their neighbors and protectors, of the nations among whom they lived. So far as our own life was concerned, we have been reduced to the world of thought and dialectic, of poetry and dreams, and have therefore over-developed the art of ideological discussion and purely logical, abstract argumentation. How often do we split on purely theoretical definitions? How often do we discover that, once we leave the field of such abstract ideology, and approach a problem from its practical angle, we are able to unite, despite all theoretical differences? I am not of those who have no respect for ideological differences. I know that ideologies are among the main instruments given us to shape realities.

But what we are here for is to do actual work in shaping realities for the Jewish people. Therefore I plead for a minimum of ideological discussions and a maximum of realistic and practical approaches to the problems we have to face.

I say this as the first of my observations on the problems involved in the establishment of the State of Israel, in order to warn this Session not to indulge in unnecessary discussions between Zionists and non-Zionists; between those who have a positive relation to the *golah* [Diaspora] and those who reject it. . . . The fact is that for a long time to come, the majority of our people will live in the *golah*. The fact is also that those Jews living outside the State of Israel will continue to owe their allegiance to the states whose loyal citizens they are, and I think it is both in the interests of our people, and of the State of Israel, to make as clear as possible what has always been said in unmistakable terms before the State was established: that this state will be composed of citizens like every other normal state, and that Jews outside of the State, not being its citizens, will owe no political allegiance to it.

The bogey of dual loyalty, which some reactionary non-Zionists— learning nothing and forgetting nothing—are trying to raise in some countries, should thus be disposed of from the very first moment. There are many similar and parallel cases to this of the Jews abroad in their reaction to the State of Israel: there are millions of Irishmen in America, millions of Poles, millions of Italians. For them there is no problem of dual loyalty; and there is none for us. But at the same time, it is natural—and every decent non-Jew will understand—that Jews all over the world will have a special sentimental and spiritual relationship to the State of Israel; will help it financially and morally; will do everything to further its development; will help to train such Jews as desire to go to Palestine, and to prepare them for their life there. The Jewish people everywhere will also, quite naturally, regard Israel as a spiritual and cultural center for Jewish life, and be largely influenced by its spiritual achievements. . . .

The main significance of the creation of the State of Israel is not that it will solve the Jewish problem overnight; so long as Jewish minorities remain in many countries of the world, the problems of anti-Semitism, of discrimination, of securing their position, will remain as actual [*sic*] as ever before. There is no contradiction between the Jewish state on the one hand, and the safeguarding of Jewish rights and positions, and the strengthening of Jewish life in the Diaspora on the other. The theory of anti-Zionists that Zionism aims at the annihilation of the Diaspora was always sheer nonsense—a silly or malicious misconception.

Israel Needs a Strong Jewish Diaspora

The State of Israel requires a strong Jewish Diaspora, just as the Jewish *golah* requires the State of Israel. The greatest reserve line in support of this Jewish state, which will have in its early years tremendous difficulties to overcome, will for years to come be a strong and united Jewish people in the Diaspora, ready to support it morally, spiritually, and practically. The existence of the State of Israel, on the other hand, will immediately relieve us of many galuth problems, and in the long run provide a solution of such problems as Jewish migration, persecution, and so on. Above all, it will give the Jewish people a voice among the nations of the world, and put an end to the anonymity of Jewish existence. But it would be naïve to believe that the creation of the state will resolve all the detailed problems of Jewish life overnight. It is quite enough if it does what it is doing for the solution of the essential Jewish problem.

This problem was the lack of a normal center for our existence as a people; the lack of a home where a Jew could go if he wished or was obliged; the lack of the possibility of appearing as a nation recognized by other nations of the world; the anonymity of our existence—what Pinsker called "the ghost-like existence of our people."[1] All these fundamental aspects of what was the Jewish problem are being removed by the creation of the state. It normalizes our existence. It makes us fundamentally a people like any other. The world now sees for the first time (to mention only one expression of this fact) Jews fighting as Jews, and I venture to say—and in this I am sure I do not speak only as a Zionist in the narrow sense of the word—that nothing has so increased Jewish prestige and respect for our people for the last two thousand years as the phenomenon of a Jewish fighting army defending Jewish soil and Jewish honor, identified under their own flag as Jews. . . .

We hope that at the next Assembly, the State of Israel will be admitted to the United Nations, so that when in the future Jewish problems requiring United Nations action arise, there will be at least one official representative of the State of Israel at the Council table, ready to speak out and take care of them. But again, we should not regard the State of Israel, eo ipso, as the formal representative and spokesman of Jewish communities in the Diaspora, which it cannot be—in its own interests as well as in those of the communities themselves. Just as Jews in the Diaspora, without any political tie-up with the state, will be entitled and able to look to the state for moral support, in the same way the state will have the right to give the moral support of its authority and presence in the United Nations to the justified complaints and claims of Jewish communities in the Diaspora, or to general Jewish demands of the Jewish people; but directly the Jews of the Diaspora are admitted—as they must be—to have no political ties with Israel, it becomes clearly impossible for the State of Israel to act in their behalf.

From this it follows that there can be no contradiction between the State of Israel (and our natural obligations to support it) and the need for an organization of world Jewry to act for Jewish communities whenever necessary, and for the Jewish people when desired. The future of the Jewish people in the Diaspora, and the future of the State of Israel alike require close relations of trust, of mutual help, of interest, of cooperation, in many cases; but at the same time they will be distinct and different entities: the state representing its citizens and speaking for them, the World Jewish Congress representing the Jewish people and speaking for them—so far as authorized to do so.

Jewish Unity in the World Jewish Congress

All this leads me to the conclusion of my remarks. Both the analysis of the tragedy of Jewish life in the last fifteen years, and this preliminary evaluation of the greatest creative achievement in Jewish life—the establishment of the state—lead to the same conclusion: the necessity of maintaining and strengthening an organism which will express the unity of the Jewish people and which can speak and act on its behalf. I wish that this problem, too, may be dealt with in a practical way. Certain critics in American Jewry have developed a new bogey: galuth nationalism. They are ready to acquiesce in, or even welcome, the existence of the Jewish state, but maintain their stubborn opposition to an organization like ours, basing themselves on the dislike of what they call "galuth nationalism." It is yet another of those bogeys which confuse Jewish life, and I regret that distinguished leaders of American Jewry like the President of the American Jewish Committee, who have taken up the right attitude with regards to the Jewish state, still seem to remain imbued with this confusing and nonsensical idea of "galuth nationalism."

The World Jewish Congress does not intend to represent, still less to create, a Jewish political nation in the Diaspora. So far as the Jews are a nation, in the legal and political meaning of this term, the Jewish nation is represented by the Jewish citizens of the State of Israel. As I said before, the definition of what constitutes a Jew is unimportant for the problem of the World Jewish Congress. Whatever we are by theoretical definition (I personally believe, and have long believed, that there is no non-Hebrew term defining properly the collective entity called the Jewish people), what is essential is to recognize that this entity has the right and duty to organize itself for common activity and to do it in an open, public, and organized manner.

Where is it laid down that only "nations" have international organizations? Are there no international organizations representing churches, social groups, trade unions, writers, and all kinds of collective conglomerations of individuals, based on professional, social, and other common interests? If we recognize that there are problems common to Jews all over the world, which are best dealt with by common approach, by cooperation, and coordination, the existence of the World Jewish Congress is fully justified, and is indeed essential. . . .

A Voluntary Association for Political Action

This does not mean galuth nationalism; it does not mean the existence of a political Jewish nation in the Diaspora; it does not mean, either, any abolition of the full autonomy of individual Jewish communities. The World

Jewish Congress has never tried to interfere with such autonomy. It is an organization of voluntary affiliation, of autonomous Jewish communities and organizations, freely joined in one world organization to deal with common problems. It is obvious that no internal Jewish problem, or political problem of a Jewish community in any country of the world, is within the jurisdiction of the World Jewish Congress. There is not one case in all the twelve years of its existence where Congress has made the slightest attempt to interfere with the internal problems of any of its constituent Jewish communities—not to speak of trying to interfere in the political problems of Jewish communities—their allegiance to various political parties, and so on.

The World Jewish Congress does not even act internationally, or with regard to various governments, on behalf of any community unless asked by that community to do so. The Congress is an organ of the Jewish people and its parts; it acts when asked by those parts to do so. At the same time, respect for the autonomy and identity of individual Jewish communities and their organizations cannot go so far as to deny and destroy the principle of common action. If certain Jewish bodies refuse to join the Congress because they would lose their identity, and desire to insist on a form of cooperation in which every action has first to be discussed by all the cooperating bodies, every document submitted has to be signed by all these bodies, then the principle of common action becomes ludicrous and impossible, because such procedure presumes that what is valid for one Jewish community must be valid for them all. . . . The only way to efficient action is for us all to join in one organization, maintaining the identity of the national Jewish organizations within the jurisdiction of their national activities, but at the same time regarding them as parts of the larger body for whatever action may need to be taken on an international scale. . . .

Two Major Problems Facing the World Jewish Congress

I do not want in this opening address to enter into any discussion of the concrete program and detailed tasks which await the World Jewish Congress. I am sure that this Session will discuss these matters fully, and that differences of opinion will develop—especially with regard to questions of relief and the concrete work of reconstruction. But I am sure that anyone will agree that the World Jewish Congress must concentrate on two major problems: political work to safeguard Jewish positions and secure the status of Jewish communities all over the world, especially in view of the grave dangers which menace us; and secondly, cultural work. More than ever, today it is necessary to initiate and coordinate a program of constructive activities, to rebuild Jewish cultural institutions, to bring up Jewish boys and girls in knowledge of and respect for the Jewish past, and for the great treasures of Jewish history and cultural achievements. . . .

In this world of great ideological conflicts, with the strong appeals made by many new movements to our young people, it is more than ever essential to strengthen their Jewish consciousness—not only politically and sentimentally, but also culturally and spiritually. We can do this by giving them a chance to know what the Jewish people has created and achieved in its long history—by giving new meaning to their Jewish consciousness. It has always been our pride that to be a Jew meant much more than just having some vague sentiment about it; that it meant to know, to learn, to study. Without Jewish learning—in all its forms—the Jewish people would have disintegrated long since, and perished from the earth. And although facilities for Jewish learning are today very different from what they were some centuries ago, we still have to do everything we can to inspire our people—and especially our young people—not only with emotions of pride and devotion, but also with knowledge, without which those sentiments cannot be firmly rooted. . . .

A People's Fight for Survival

Our fight for survival is a political fight. It is the fight of a people. It has to be directed, coordinated, and organized by political methods; and the fear that some Jewish groups show of all political work really needs to be overcome once and for all. It is perfectly legitimate for the Jewish people as such to take common action in defense of its main interests; no decent Gentile and fair-minded government will misunderstand or resent it— nor have they misunderstood or resented it in all the history of the twelve years' work of the World Jewish Congress, or the history of the Committee of Jewish Delegations before that. We have no need to be ashamed of organizing ourselves politically, as long as there is a danger to our position, and as long as anti-Semitism and other kinds of discrimination prevail in all parts of the world.

And just as the world has learned to admire and honor the Jews in Palestine who have established their state and are fighting to maintain it, the world at large will respect a Jewish people, which is ready to fight for its position wherever they live and have a right to live. Nothing has done more harm to our prestige, to our position in the world, than the weak reaction of the Jewish people to the massive assault of Nazism. If not for the revival of Jewish consciousness and the heroic achievements of modern Zionism which have led to the establishment of the State of Israel, Jewish prestige after the Hitler decade would have sunk to its lowest ebb. Something of the spirit which has brought about the establishment of the state must now imbue the Jews of the Diaspora in their fight for survival. So long as a people is prepared to fight for its future, no enemy can destroy it. The murder of a people is not recorded in history. Whenever a people was destroyed, it was through its own fault—because it had lost faith and courage, had given up the struggle in face of superior forces; in fact, had committed suicide.

More important than all our organizational arrangements, more important than all financial means, more important than all political action as such, is the revival of the fighting spirit of our people. We have gone through the greatest tragedy in our history; we have come out weakened, but not broken. We have mobilized our resources and our will to live, and have realized the ideal of our ancestors in the establishment of the State of Israel. It is on similar lines that we have to proceed, spiritually, with regard to the large majority of our people who for the time being remain in the Diaspora. We are one people, with one spirit and one policy. If we are resolved to secure and strengthen Jewish positions where they are, not to yield one of them, if we are ready to fight together for our survival, with all progressive and decent elements in the world, then we shall succeed in normalizing our own existence. That means having the State of Israel at the center and a strong and creative Jewish Diaspora at the periphery. In doing this, our generation, which has witnessed the greatest tragedy in Jewish life, without being able to prevent it, will also witness the laying of solid foundations for a new and better future for the Jewish people in a world which, if full of dangers, is also full of opportunities.

In the long run the fate of a people is determined by itself. That is why peoples and nations exist. In the end it will depend on our own determination—both in Palestine and in the Diaspora—whether we are weakened and destroyed by the great changes now in process or impending, or whether we are able to use the opportunities they offer to become one of the recognized and respected peoples of the world—a people with a secure home, a life, a future—making its own distinctive contribution to the progress and future of humanity.

Gerhart M. Riegner:
Pioneer for Jewish–Catholic
Relations in the Contemporary World

Monsignor Pier Francesco Fumagalli

In the second half of the twentieth century, Gerhart M. Riegner (1911–2001) played a guiding role in the promotion of the relationship between Jews and Christians, in particular between the Jewish people and the Catholic Church. This followed the positively revolutionary change in the Church's attitude toward Jews contained in Section 4 of the declaration *Nostra Aetate* (In Our Time) promulgated on October 28, 1965 by the Second Vatican Council. Riegner was inspired by a desire to protect Jewish rights and dignity and did so in the context of the universal human rights and fundamental freedoms as recognized by the United Nations.

I first encountered Riegner in Milan on September 6, 1982 at the tenth meeting of the International Catholic-Jewish Liaison Committee (ILC). Human rights and religious concern were at the heart of this meeting, the theme of which was "The Sanctity and Meaning of Human Life in Relation to the Present Situation of Violence." Delegates raised many issues. One of them—a gentleman speaking in a warm, calm voice with passionate undertones, revealing moral integrity—stressed that for a Jew, to be religious implies a strong commitment to promoting justice, peace, and

Monsignor Pier Francesco Fumagalli is Vice Prefect of the Biblioteca Ambrosiana in Milan.

cultural values; a concern for pacifism; opposing violence, anti-Semitism, and terrorism in the world; and promoting religious freedom and relations with Israel and the Holy See. When I heard this honest man for the first time in my youth, I felt I was meeting a person of unambiguous courage, a true *mensch*: this was Gerhart M. Riegner. But I had no way of knowing that day, as I showed the delegates the ancient illuminated Hebrew manuscripts in the Ambrosiana Library, that our paths were to cross again so closely in the following two decades.

Serving as Secretary of the Holy See's Commission for Religious Relations with Jews over several years (1987–1993), working in Rome or traveling, particularly to Eastern Europe, it was quite customary for me to receive visits or to cooperate closely with Dr. Riegner. All the major issues in Catholic-Jewish relations were always on his agenda, but what is more relevant in my opinion was his universal—that is, "ecumenical"—regard for every concrete situation of human suffering and violation of human rights. Without forgetting the tragic memories of history, he looked with great hope toward the future, calling for pooling resources and efforts with the Church, within and without the boundaries of faith and culture. Jerusalem, Auschwitz, and Geneva are among the places where we met frequently in an effort to promote the new brotherly relations between the Church and Judaism, as was the dream of the giants of the Second Vatican Council when they wrote *Nostra Aetate*. Our cooperation was specifically devoted to continuing the joint work in meetings of the ILC, which, according to Cardinal Johannes Willebrands, was the only official body linking the Holy See and the Jewish community.

Forced to flee his native Berlin in May 1933 after the Nazis had come to power, Riegner settled in Geneva, where he joined the World Jewish Congress soon after its establishment in 1936. He devoted himself to that organization for the remainder of his life, serving for many years as director of its Geneva office, then as secretary-general, and finally as honorary vice president. In 1942, in his famous Riegner telegram, he provided the first news of the Nazi holocaust against the Jews to the free governments.

After the defeat of Nazism and the end of the Shoah, Riegner was one of the leading Jewish personalities who wanted to forge a constructive relationship between the Jewish people and the Church, but not at any cost. He insisted that the condemnation of both the crime of genocide and anti-Semitism had to be among the preconditions for Jewish-Christian dialogue and cooperation. It was his hope that this dialogue would lead to, in addition to the creation of a common front against racism and anti-Semitism, the recognition of the State of Israel by the Holy See. This indeed occurred in 1993, concurrent with the start of direct negotiations between Israel and Palestinians.

Among the first Jews to seek an audience with Pope Pius XII after the end of World War II was WJC Secretary-General A. Leon Kubowitzki who was received by the Catholic pontiff on September 21, 1945. Kubowitzki thanked the Pope on behalf of the WJC for his actions during the war, and asked for the Catholic Church's help and cooperation on two important issues.

The first of these was practical and specific, the second theoretical and general. The urgent practical item concerned the WJC's request for the Church's intervention in the search for many Jewish children, saved during the years of the Holocaust and hidden in Catholic religious institutions, where many, if not most, had been baptized. Kubowitzki asked that the Church return these children to their families, or, if there were no surviving relatives, to the Jewish people.

The more general issue concerned the possibility of the Church promulgating an encyclical, which, recognizing the spiritual link between Jews and Christians, would put an end to the ancient accusation of deicide aimed at the entire Jewish people, and the source of so much anti-Jewish hostility and anti-Semitism over the centuries. Neither of the two requests was acted upon, as Riegner later recalled in his autobiography.

In November 1945, Riegner was in Rome to attend a gathering of displaced persons who had survived the Shoah. On that occasion, at Kubowitzki's request, he met with Mgr. Giovanni Battista Montini, the future Pope Paul VI, who at that time was one of the Pope's two deputies. Riegner was accompanied to this meeting by Raffaele Cantoni, the president of the Union of Jewish Communities in Italy. Riegner explained to Mgr. Montini, again without success, the magnitude of the tragedy that had struck the Jewish people. Riegner recalled:

> I said to the deputy, "We, the Jewish people, have lost a million and a half children. We cannot allow ourselves to lose one more. We are very

grateful to the institutions and to the Catholic faithful for what they have done to save Jewish children and to help them survive. But we now judge that the danger is past, and they should be restored to us. Since we do not know where they are, we are asking you to help us find them."[1]

To Riegner's surprise and profound disappointment, Mgr. Montini at first did not believe the extent of the Jewish losses. After a conversation that lasted twenty minutes, Mgr. Montini said, "Point out to me where these children are and I will assist you in recovering them." Riegner replied that if he knew where the children were, he wouldn't need the Church's assistance.[2]

Similar initiatives, undertaken after May 1948 by the leaders of the State of Israel in the hope of creating a climate of trust that would lead to diplomatic relations between the Holy See and the nascent Jewish state, were equally unsuccessful. It seemed that the Jewish-Catholic relationship was destined to remain unchanged since this issue was not a priority for the Church.

The possibility of a Catholic-Jewish rapprochement was given a vigorous boost on June 13, 1960, when the French-Jewish historian Jules Isaac had a private audience with Pope John XXIII. The Pope was receptive to Isaac's idea of the Church condemning its traditional "teaching of contempt" for Jews and Judaism and placed this item on the agenda of the Second Vatican Council.

Riegner, who was closely following the efforts to "update" the Catholic Church, saw that the time had come for decisive action to build a new relationship between Jews and Christians. A natural mediator and forger of daring and creative briefs, he was convinced that in both the Jewish and Christian communities, as well as in wider civil society, there was no longer a daunting separation between secular and religious life, and this allowed him to act incisively as the representative of world Jewry in the workings of the Vatican Council.

One result of this work was an important memorandum dated February 17, 1962, which WJC President Nahum Goldmann and Label Katz, president of B'nai Brith International, sent to Cardinal Augustin Béa, to whom Pope John XXIII had entrusted the sensitive beginning of a Jewish-Catholic dialogue.[3] This memorandum summarized the Jewish point of view on the issues the Council was proposing to address. This document emphasized, with biblical foundation, the universal values that would be discussed by the Council and included in its documents, concluding with the prophetic statement:

> Have we not all one Father? Hath not one God created us? The challenge of the Prophet lays upon all of us the most solemn obligations. The differences which separate us are real and important; it were [sic] foolish to overlook and underrate them. But they cannot nullify the commandment to love our neighbour.

Elsewhere, the memorandum declared that:

> As Jews we consider the fight against anti-Semitism as an integral element of these aspirations for a better world. What constitutes for us— as it does no doubt for the Church—a source of deep distress is that the anti-Semitic agitation and incidents are occurring, with rare exceptions, in European countries or overseas countries with European populations, which are, or have been, ingrained by the influence of Christianity. We venture to express the conviction that in the contemporary world wherever anti-Semitism poses a danger to the Jewish community, it constitutes at the same time a threat to the Church.[4]

Among those who had approved the wording of the memorandum were two individuals who seemed antithetical, but were in fact complementary, representing as they did the different strands of Judaism: on the one hand, Nahum Goldmann, the president of the WJC and a principal exponent of secular and liberal Judaism, and on the other, Rabbi Joseph Dov Soloveitchik of Boston, a renowned professor at Yeshiva University who was then considered the highest authority in Jewish modern Orthodoxy. It was Goldmann who had consulted Rabbi Soloveitchik regarding establishing a dialogue with the Church, and it was Soloveitchik who insisted that any overture in this regard be initiated by secular as opposed to religious Jewish groups, so as to make clear that any such dialogue would be secular rather than theological.

Upon rereading the memorandum and some of the statements made by the Council, one easily notes substantial similarities and convergences:

One is the community of all peoples, one their origin, for God made the whole human race to live over the face of the earth.[5] . . . We cannot truly call on God, the Father of all, if we refuse to treat in a brotherly way any man, created as he is in the image of God. Man's relation to God the Father and his relation to men his brothers are so linked together that Scripture says: "He who does not love does not know God." (1 John 4:8)[6]

It is in this context that *Nostra Aetate* contained the then-revolutionary declaration that the Church "decries hatred, persecutions, displays of anti-Semitism, directed against Jews at any time and by anyone."[7] Published on October 28, 1965, *Nostra Aetate* immediately became the fundamental Church text that revolutionized the Jewish-Christian—or, more accurately, the Jewish-Catholic—relationship.

Between 1965 and 1970, thanks to the work of Cardinal Béa and his successor, Cardinal Willebrands, the Council's rejection of the charge of deicide against the Jews and its repudiation of anti-Semitism were disseminated around the world and backed up by solid theological studies. At the same time, the promulgation of *Nostra Aetate* aroused intense emotion in the Jewish community throughout the world and led to new forms of cooperation between Catholics and Jews.

Riegner, for his part, devoted his energies to creating a Catholic-Jewish institutional dialogue at the highest level, placing great emphasis on exploring the content and motivations underlying the ideals and cultures on both sides. On January 6, 1969, he accompanied Goldmann and Rabbi Joachim Prinz, chairman of the WJC's executive committee, to an audience with Pope Paul VI. It was during that audience that the Pope referred for the first time to the Jewish, or Hebrew, people—in Italian, *populo ebraico*—followed by an almost epiphanic incident that Riegner described in his memoirs:

> In pronouncing the words "Jewish people" the Pope [*sic*] suddenly broke off to add with some emotion, "You know, we have known each other for such a long time, but we are really only starting to reflect on our relationship." The phrase had visibly affected him. He realized all of a sudden that he had never before spoken of the "Hebrew people," that previously he had considered Jews solely as adherents of a religion. This

was an extremely moving moment, and we all saw the sincerity of the pope's reaction.[8]

However, to establish and promote effective and stable relations between Jews and Christians, both within individual countries and internationally, it was necessary to interpret in a dynamic and creative manner the opportunities and existing tensions between orthodoxy and secularism, religion and civil and political society.

Accordingly in 1970, the World Jewish Congress, at Riegner's initiative, joined with other Jewish organizations—the American Jewish Committee, B'nai B'rith International, the Jewish Council for Interreligious Consultations in Israel, and the Synagogue Council of America—to set up an international Jewish committee for interaction with the Catholic Church and other religious organizations, which was to be called the International Jewish Committee on Interreligious Consultations (IJCIC), with offices in Geneva and New York. Responding to this Jewish initiative, in December 1970 Pope Paul VI appointed five Catholic delegates to form, together with IJCIC delegates, the ILC, which is in existence to this day, on the basis of an *Intesa* or memorandum of understanding.

The decisive inaugural meeting of the ILC, which would have an extraordinary and lasting impact, took place in the Palazzo della Congregazione Orientale, then the seat of the Secretariat for Promoting Christian Unity, to which the Vatican Office for Jewish Relations was attached. Cardinal Willebrands, the president of the Secretariat, attended this meeting on behalf of the Holy See together with officials from the Secretariat of State and from the Congregations for the Doctrine of the Faith, for Catholic Education, and for the Oriental Churches, as well as from the Pontifical Commission for Justice and Peace. Riegner participated in the meeting for the WJC together with other representatives of IJCIC. The memorandum of understanding that was agreed upon at the conclusion of the session on December 23, 1970 reflected, in accordance with Riegner's ideals, the convergence between the Jewish and Catholic perspectives on matters of common interest, without compromising the legitimate diversity of faiths of the two religious communities or the secular point of view on the subject of human rights.

This document focused on two "main areas of concern," namely, questions concerning the Jewish-Catholic relationship, including confronting and working toward the elimination of all manifestations of anti-Semitism and promoting mutual understanding, and questions of common concern such as "the promotion of justice and peace in the world, as well as of human freedom and dignity; the fight against poverty and racism and all forms of discrimination; and the protection of human rights, both of individuals or groups."[9]

The ILC's authority was strengthened in 1974 when Pope Paul VI set up the Holy See's Commission for Religious Relations with the Jews (CRRC), which, under the leadership of Cardinal Willebrands (and later of Cardinals Edward Idris Cassidy, Walter Kasper, and Kurt Koch), has been the IJCIC's direct partner for over forty years.

Riegner was the principal protagonist in the activities of the ILC and IJCIC for many years. Other WJC leaders and personalities who played important roles in the many meetings and activities held under ILC auspices over the years have included Fritz Becker, the long-time head of the WJC's Rome office; Jean Halpérin of Geneva; Rabbi Joachim Prinz; Rabbi Arthur Hertzberg; WJC President Edgar M. Bronfman; Rabbi Israel Singer; and Betty Ehrenberg.

To measure the extent of the progress made in almost half a century of joint activities, it must be borne in mind that in addition to the plenary sessions of the ILC, there was a smaller executive committee, led by Riegner for many years, which was very active. It called two special meetings of the ILC in 1987 and in 1990, and in February 1991 successfully organized an international mission to Poland, Hungary, and Czechoslovakia, nations that had just shaken off the Soviet yoke.

These positive results were due to the wide horizon outlined in the founding memorandum. Between 1970 and 1985, the ILC focused on two main areas related to Jewish-Catholic relations and common action. The first dealt with issues such as anti-Semitism, mutual understanding, education, and, in particular, religious relationships between the people, the nation, and the country. The second area concerned matters relating to justice and peace, religious freedom and human rights, poverty and racism, interreligious dialogue, and relations with Islam.

At the end of the twelfth plenary session in Rome in 1985, the joint action plan was unanimously extended to six goals, including the dissemination of the results achieved, the overcoming of remaining prejudice, cooperation in opposing religious fanaticism, theological reflection, the commitment to justice and peace, and the beginning of "a joint study on the historical events and the theological implications of the extermination of European Jews."

To offer a particularly meaningful example of the atmosphere in which the ILC meetings took place, I share a personal memory of the preparatory talks that preceded the extraordinary session of the ILC, scheduled to take place in Rome at the end of August and the beginning of September of 1987. At that time Vatican officials were preparing the apostolic trip to the United States that the Pope would begin shortly. A further source of concern was (and it was certainly not a novelty) the tension that was disturbing the Vatican's relations with international Jewish organizations such as the WJC. The main worries during the summer had been caused by the papal audience granted to Austrian President Kurt Waldheim, whose Nazi past had been exposed by the WJC and, more generally, by a certain impression that there was a deliberate strategy to "Christianize" the Shoah or to turn it into something more banal. Among the catalysts of that particular debate were the controversies surrounding the Carmelite convent in the "Old Theatre" at Auschwitz and the beatification of Edith Stein in Cologne, a few months earlier on March 1, 1987. The latter had been harshly criticized because of the Jewish origins of the Carmelite nun, who had been deported and murdered at Auschwitz along with millions of other Jews, and who was now being put forward as a model of martyrdom for the Catholic faith.

For these reasons, Rabbi Mordechai Waxman, President of the Synagogue Council of America and then-chair of IJCIC, and Cardinal Willebrands agreed to call an extraordinary session of about twenty delegates and experts. This session took the form of a special meeting of the International Catholic-Jewish Liaison Committee. On the afternoon of Sunday, August 30, 1987, Riegner, together with Rabbi Waxman and Fr. Pierre Duprey, vice president of the Vatican commission, met with Willebrands in the Cardinal's home in Rome to prepare the details of the sessions. I was also present in my capacity as secretary of the ILC.

I vividly remember Riegner's remarks during the discussion. After emphasizing the importance of taking a new step on the road of dialogue, he came to his main point in a tone that was calm, but at the same time vibrant and full of the memory of suffering. To overcome the suspicions and the lack of trust on the part of the Jewish communities as to the sincerity of the Jewish-Catholic dialogue, and to reaffirm the authoritative orientation that the Pope gives through his teaching (as he had recently done in Warsaw), the time was ready for a Church document (maybe even an encyclical letter) that confronted in a comprehensive manner the difficult themes of the Shoah and of anti-Semitism in its historical and religious roots—aspects that in some way are connected with the history and the future of Jewish-Christian relations. At the same time, however, he concluded:

> This is not a project that we, as Jews, can suggest or ask you to consider; you alone can autonomously begin such an initiative, which, however, would certainly have an extraordinarily positive effect on world Jewry. In particular, if announced now, on the eve of the Pope's trip to the United States, the decision would deeply and positively impress the large and lively Jewish communities of America, which are now agitated by doubts and suspicions as to what the Church really thinks of the Shoah [author's recollection of Riegner's words].

Riegner stopped—there was a brief silence, full of intensity, a pregnant expectation, redolent with the weight of memories, as happens when two people recognize each other after a long separation. But it was little more than a moment. The words of Willebrands's decisive assent sounded short but appeared to reflect a long, earlier reflection, as if they had been pronounced to fulfil an ancient expectation, answering a gesture of fraternal trust and truth, a gesture as strong as a cry. From this encounter would come the process of repentance, of *teshuvah*, and reconciliation that is still in progress now, within which we ought to include the important document "We Remember: A Reflection on the Shoah," that was eventually signed by Cardinal Cassidy in 1998.

Another serious issue affecting Jewish-Catholic relations at that time should be mentioned here. Beginning in 1984, when a controversy erupted in Poland following the establishment of a convent of Carmelite nuns on the grounds of the concentration and extermination camp of Auschwitz-Birkenau, Riegner devoted all his energies to explaining to numerous interlocutors and Catholic friends that it was essential to be able to contemplate in silence the memory of all victims of the Shoah and Nazi brutality. It took him a decade of patient persuasion until finally—in 1993—Pope John Paul II addressed a letter to the "Dear Sisters" of Carmel that brought this long-running affair to a close with the relocation of the convent to a more appropriate location, and with the creation of a center for education and dialogue in Oswiecim.

No less important were the joint documents of the ILC, which with the cooperation of many Jewish thinkers, such as Emmanuel Lévinas and Jean Halpérin, and Catholics, such as Bernard Dupuy and Cardinal Roger Etchegaray, deepened and promoted Jewish-Christian initiatives in defense of human rights and religious freedom around the world, as a contribution to *tikkun olam* [repairing the world] in the spirit of the prophets of Israel.

One of the many fruits of Riegner's tireless work is recognizable in the brief but significant statement condemning anti-Semitism disguised as anti-Zionism published in 1988 and signed by the president of the Pontifical Commission for Justice and Peace, Cardinal Roger Etchegaray, and the vice president, Cardinal Jorge Mejía, then-president of the Bilateral Commission between the Holy See's Commission for Religious Relations with the Jews and the Chief Rabbinate of Israel. It states:

> Among the manifestations of systematic racial distrust, specific mention must once again be made of anti-Semitism. If anti-Semitism has been the most tragic form that racist ideology has assumed in our century, with the horrors of the Jewish "holocaust," it has unfortunately not yet entirely disappeared. As if some had nothing to learn from the crimes of the past, certain organizations, with branches in many countries, keep alive the anti-Semite racist myth, with the support of networks of publications. Terrorist acts which have Jewish persons or symbols as their target have multiplied in recent years and show the radicalism of such groups. Anti-Zionism—which is not of the same order, since it questions the State of Israel and its policies—serves at times as a screen for anti-Semitism, feeding on it and leading to it. Furthermore, some countries impose undue harassments and restrictions on the free emigration of Jews.[10]

Subsequently, another significant milestone for the ILC was marked by the establishment of diplomatic relations between Israel and the Holy See on December 30, 1993. Once again, this milestone in Jewish-Catholic relations owes a great deal to Riegner's behind-the-scenes diplomatic efforts over the course of many years.

Riegner was particularly tenacious in Jerusalem in May of 1991 at the ninth plenary assembly of the WJC, where his actions were decisive in overcoming the impasse that blocked the first official relations between the Holy See and representatives of the State of Israel. He was always ready to seize any opportunity to discretely promote meetings that could contribute to an increase in mutual trust and understanding, and he knew how to create networks that served to improve relations between peoples and nations. In large part due to Riegner's efforts and personal intervention, there were many opportunities at the 1991 WJC plenary assembly for high-level informal meetings between Israeli officials and representatives of the Vatican, including with Monsignor (today, Cardinal) Andrea Cordero Lanza di Montezemolo, the Apostolic Nuncio to Israel and Palestine. The constructive atmosphere of those informal meetings laid the groundwork for a subsequent institutional meeting between the Holy See and the State of Israel.

It is not surprising, therefore, that on the occasion of Riegner's ninetieth birthday, Rabbi David Rosen, the American Jewish Committee's Director of Interfaith Relations and Liaison to the Vatican, called Riegner "the Jewish doyen of relations with the Christian world," adding that he "deserves no small amount of credit for the remarkable achievements of the last half-century, and in particular with the Catholic Church over the last thirty-six years since the promulgation of the Church's ground-breaking document *Nostra Aetate*."[11]

Following Riegner's death on December 3, 2001, Cardinal Walter Kasper, president of the Pontifical Council for Promoting Christian Unity, said, "I think Gerhart Riegner was one of the witnesses of our time and played an outstanding role in the relations between Christians and Jews. With his experiences in World War II, he worked for mutual understanding and improving the Church's relationship with Jews. We have lost one of the most important and competent partners in Jewish-Christian dialogue."[12]

May his memory be a blessing and an inspiration to all of us.

The World Jewish Congress and the State of Israel: A Personal Reminiscence

Natan Lerner

The Jews are a group, unified mainly, but not exclusively, by religion or faith, that developed a system of ethical values derived from their beliefs. They lost their independent state more than two millennia ago and since then have been dispersed all over the world. There may be different views about the nature of the Jewish people—a religious, ethnic, or cultural group, or a civilization—but beyond a doubt, Jews are a rather coherent, easily identifiable group or community. The judiciary of several countries state that it is not so important to define precisely the nature of a human group; important are the historical ties, the self-perception, and the perception by others of the group—or community—as a group.[1]

Since their dispersion, Jews have maintained diverse forms of relative communal autonomy, with loose ties among themselves.[2] In the twentieth century in the period between the two world wars, some European Jewish communities enjoyed, under the League of Nations, a special system of autonomy protected by international law.[3] During the Holocaust, many of

---

Natan Lerner is Professor of Law Emeritus at IDC Herzliya and was director of the WJC's Israel Branch from 1966 until 1984.

those communities were annihilated by the Nazis and their accomplices. A few years after the end of the war, in 1948, an independent Jewish state, Israel, was established, with the support of the United Nations, more or less on the same territory on which the ancient biblical Jewish state—or, more accurately, two states—had existed.

Even though the State of Israel has enjoyed wide international recognition for almost seven decades, it remains involved in a struggle for its existence. At the time of this writing, about half of the Jews of the world live in the sovereign state—where they constitute about 80 percent of the population—and the other half continue to be dispersed on all but one of the continents, keeping their cohesion through more or less organized communities, under different legal regimes, according to the constitutional framework of the host state.

The Jews living in the Diaspora as well as those who are inhabitants of Israel are conscious, in general, of the fact that they belong to the same unit of humanity—that they are described as the Jewish nation, the Jewish people, or world Jewry, although there are different understandings of what constitute the cohesive factors or the nature and extent of the reciprocal obligations or duties, as well as rights, involved. The legal and sociological dimensions of that relationship are beyond the scope of this article. What seems beyond a doubt is that the relationship exists and demands attention.

An Uneven Bilateral Relationship

It is against this theoretical backdrop that the relationship between the World Jewish Congress and the State of Israel should be considered. It is an uneven relationship between two unequal partners that need each other: an independent, sovereign, modern, relatively powerful state on the one hand, and a loose federation of minority communities based on voluntary affiliation on the other. The WJC, founded in 1936, is the most well-articulated effort to create a political framework or federation involving all the Jews of the world, namely, those who live in the independent State of Israel as well as those living abroad, in the Diaspora.

Already in its founding assembly, the WJC affirmed "that the Jewish people of the whole world, without distinction of groups or party affiliation, are united in their support of the heroic battle of the *Yishuv* for the maintenance of its right to life and labor, and pledges its full support in the task of safeguarding the right of the Jewish people to the widest opportunities for immigration and construction work in Palestine."[4] In all its subsequent major assemblies, the WJC reiterated that support emphatically. The third plenary assembly, in 1953, in Geneva, for instance, stressed that the rebirth of the Jewish nation within Israel has given the Jewish people "a new inspiration, a revived dignity and confidence, as well as a new pride, which have transformed them from a diversity of minorities . . . to a people prideful of a restored nation worthy of the respect of the world."[5]

At the same time, it seemed evident from the moment the State of Israel came into being in 1948, if not before, that the interests and concerns of the State might not always be identical to those of Jewish communities in the Diaspora. Nahum Goldmann made precisely this point in his keynote address at the second WJC plenary assembly in Montreux, Switzerland, in June of 1948.[6] The distinction was not lost on Israeli leaders either.

Addressing the fourth WJC plenary assembly in Stockholm in August 1959, the former Israeli prime minister as well as foreign minister Moshe Sharett spoke at length about the respective and distinct priorities of Israel and world Jewry. "Israel's primary concern," he said, "must, of course, be its own survival," and in that context Israel expected the Jews of the Diaspora "unquestioningly to accept its authority in determining its interests and policies." At the same time, he said:

> There is a wide margin of points at issue regarding which the Diaspora as a whole, or certain sections of it in particular cases, are in their turn entitled to expect consideration on Israel's part for their own interests, viewpoints, and susceptibilities.[7]

Moreover, Sharett continued:

> There are functions of Jewish life and items in the program of Jewish public activity which lie outside the plane of Israeli affairs, such as most of the tasks assumed by the World Jewish Congress in defending Jewish rights in the Diaspora and tendering advice and assistance to communities in need thereof. Inasmuch as there are points of contact

between the respective spheres of activity of the Israel Government and the World Jewish Congress, co-ordination is perfectly feasible. What is eminently desirable in this regard is the prevention of unnecessary overlapping. Yet, in any case, the World Jewish Congress remains an independent body, bearing complete and sole responsibility for its work and program.[8]

The Representative Character of the WJC

The WJC is a non-governmental political entity that aspires to represent the totality of world Jewry, including Israeli Jewry. In fact, it never managed to become fully representative of all Jewish communities. There are a number of reasons for this. Certain communities are not organized in a single political—or quasi-political—structure, and as a result, no one entity represents all the Jews of that community. Historically, the organizations that represented a number of Jewish communities did not want to join an international Jewish umbrella organization, perhaps out of a desire not to give up independence by delegating to an international agency any freedom of action. On occasion, the reluctance had ideological components; at other times, the reasons were less clearly defined and had to do with personal motives or just isolationist trends. Thus, it took many years for the Board of Deputies of British Jews and the Conseil Représentatif des Juifs de France, better known as CRIF, to formally affiliate with the WJC. The most pronounced absence today, that of an all-embracing voice representing US Jewry, must be seen in light of the lack of a central Jewish organization in the United States that deals with the total spectrum of issues on the communal agenda, such as the one existing in Canada. Jews in the United States have created representative Jewish bodies, but primarily for specific purposes, such as affiliation with a specific stream of Judaism (Orthodox, Conservative, Reform, or Reconstructionist), fighting anti-Semitism, advocating on behalf of Soviet or Ethiopian Jewry, or political support for Israel. This absence of a single US representative body is obviously reflected within the WJC. Nonetheless, the WJC's American Section, made up of many diverse American Jewish organizations, successfully represents a substantial cross-section of the US Jewish community.

Who Should Speak for Diaspora
Jewish Communities?

The State of Israel does not claim, formally at least, to represent or to speak in the name of Jewish communities abroad. David Ben-Gurion, its first prime minister, stated in the early years after independence that Israel would not interfere in Diaspora affairs, and the State for the most part does not pretend to represent Jews who are not citizens of Israel.[9] In its short existence, full of dramatic developments, the State formally kept to this position, but in more than one case acted in a different way, frequently because of a feeling of solidarity and responsibility for the welfare of Jews everywhere across the globe. In practice, therefore, occasional friction and misunderstanding occurred in the relations between the WJC and Israeli officials that implied a departure from the principle.

Personal Experience

I served on the staff of the WJC from 1963 to 1984, when I resigned because of my disagreement with organizational decisions affecting my position and work. From 1959 I represented Argentine Jewry on the World Executive of the WJC and was a delegate to the 1959 WJC plenary assembly in Stockholm. From 1963 to 1966, I was employed by the WJC in its New York office, working with one of the heads of its International Affairs Department, Rabbi Maurice Perlzweig, and dealing mainly with United Nations and Latin American affairs. Perlzweig, under whose leadership I represented the WJC at the UN, was a British Reform rabbi, an eloquent speaker with great expertise in international relations. He was strongly committed to the WJC and played a central role in the drafting of most of the important documents elaborated in the name of the Congress.

In addition to my responsibilities concerning the UN, my work in New York included close cooperation with the Latin American Jewish Congress. The director of the Buenos Aires office, Mark Turkow, was a colorful international civil servant and leader of Latin American Jewry. He was a member of the Turkow family, well known in the performing arts and in Jewish cultural life in Poland. Turkow integrated into Jewish life in Latin America and was a senior advisor to most, if not all, Jewish communities on the continent. He was efficiently assisted by Dr. Paul Warszawski and by Manuel Tenenbaum, a Uruguayan Jewish scholar and leader who became Turkow's successor as the director of the Buenos Aires office.

In 1966, I settled in Israel and was appointed director of the WJC's Israel Branch and office, working with three chairmen: Professor Arieh Tartakower and Members of Knesset Yitzhak Korn and Zalman Abramov. I was, therefore, in a position to follow the ups and downs of the interaction and cooperation, or occasional lack thereof, between the WJC and the Israeli authorities, primarily at the Ministry of Foreign Affairs and the World Zionist Organization. Those ups and downs were, in some cases, the result of differences of approach to problems affecting Jewish life. In others, they were the consequence of organizational rivalry, the desire by one side to impose views and political attitudes on the other.

It must be pointed out that the WJC presence in Israel has a double character: on the one hand, it is the instrument of contact, consultation, and cooperation between the Israeli Branch, as one of the regional branches of the WJC (similar to the other regional branches, such as those in Europe or in Latin America) with WJC headquarters. On the other hand, it is the instrument through which the central office of the WJC, located in the Diaspora, communicates and consults with Israeli authorities and institutions. The WJC's Israel branch is also expected to represent Israeli Jewry within the WJC. I discuss the structure of the Israel Branch below.

WJC Support for the State of Israel

Without reservation, since its creation in 1936, the WJC extended full support to the aspirations and program of the Zionist movement although during the horror of the Holocaust and its aftermath, its work was dictated by the needs of rescue and reparation of Jewish life in Europe.[10] After the establishment of the State of Israel in 1948, the WJC gave its total support to the Israeli struggle for international recognition, security, and development, as reflected in the declarations and resolutions of its governing bodies. In some areas there was full cooperation. In others, there were occasional differences and disagreements. The WJC played a major role in the advancement of global Jewish interests.

WJC plenary assemblies and executive meetings produced statements and documents voicing full and unreserved support for the State of Israel and its policies. It should be kept in mind that the WJC embraces almost all the political trends and factions in Jewish life, including dissenting groups such as, at certain times, Communist groups or supporters of the Soviet Union and what was left of the Bund, as well as different trends within the Jewish religion. Despite these differences, the WJC always expressed complete solidarity with the Jewish state as such, irrespective of changes in the composition of the Jerusalem government.

The Israel Branch

The Israel Branch, or Section (the nomenclature changed over the years), of the WJC is based on the Israeli political parties that describe themselves as Jewish or mainly Jewish. The composition of the Israeli Executive follows the pattern of distribution of mandates of Jewish or partly Jewish parties in the Knesset, with all the consequent political implications. While I was director of the Branch, the Israeli political parties did not overestimate the importance of the WJC and did not attach too much weight to the role of their representatives on its Israeli Executive. This fact alone had an impact on the overall relationship between the WJC and the State. A stronger and more influential Israel Branch might have produced a more efficient and effective framework for cooperation, but political parties have their priorities. In the same vein, Professor Arieh Tartakower, Chairman of the WJC's Israel Executive, wrote in 1961:

> The organizational strength of the Congress in Israel unfortunately does not reflect the Congress position as regards public opinion in Israel generally. Large sectors of Israel's population, especially the younger generation, have little knowledge of or interest in Diaspora affairs. They are also preoccupied with grave security problems, relations with their neighbours, the ingathering [of] the Exiles, so that little attention is paid to other matters. Under such circumstances those responsible for Congress work in Israel were faced with the arduous task of influencing public opinion towards a concept of unity of the whole Jewish people, not only in the organizational sphere, but morally and spiritually as well.

A satisfactory solution could not be achieved by mere propaganda or by long debates.[11]

Tartakover was aware of the problem. He was much more of a serious scholar than a politician. He was absolutely loyal to the idea of the WJC and to Nahum Goldmann's leadership. He was also a member of the then-ruling party in Israel, Mapai, and had to find a balance between both loyalties.

Nahum Goldmann's Leadership

Anyone familiar with Jewish history since the 1930s, and with the development of the young State of Israel and its policies concerning Jewish issues of global significance, cannot ignore the central role played for much of that period by Dr. Nahum Goldmann, who was for years simultaneously the president of the WJC and the first co-chair of the Jewish Agency and then the president of the World Zionist Organization (WZO).

It is beyond the scope of this article to analyze Goldmann's personality, views and actions, his influence on Jewish life, or his differences with the policies of successive Israeli governments.[12] Still, when one deals with the relationship between the WJC—that is, world Jewry—and the State of Israel, one cannot ignore the impact of Goldmann's ideas and policies on the entire spectrum of that relationship. His was a unique personality, with a brilliant intellect and an unwillingness to bend to anyone else's demands, especially when it came to issues of principle. He also exuded a cosmopolitan internationalism that was often at odds with the narrower, necessarily more introverted, views of Israeli government leaders and officials, from David Ben-Gurion down.

By presiding simultaneously over both the WJC and the WZO, Goldmann was able to prevent or sidestep many difficulties. At the same time, however, this double-leadership role proved to be a source of conflicting tensions. Needless to say, officials of the State and the Jewish Agency, on the one hand, and of the WJC, on the other, were frequently led to oppose or support the attitudes of the strong Diaspora leader, whose outspoken, often controversial, ideas could hardly be ignored. In addition, Goldmann's often personal relations with many major international governmental leaders were the source of conflict with, as well as not infrequently, jealousy on the part of, Israeli leaders—attitudes that often trickled down to the lower echelons of power.

The main points of disagreement with Goldmann were related to the areas of Middle East politics and the modalities and tone of the struggle with the Soviet Union. Broadly speaking, Goldmann was a dove when it came to the Israeli-Arab conflict, especially after the June 1967 Six-Day War, and a strong advocate of quiet diplomacy as opposed to public protest with respect to efforts on behalf of Soviet Jewry.[13]

Goldmann's unwillingness to support—or at least not appear publicly critical of—Israeli government actions and policies got him into trouble on numerous occasions. In 1968, shortly before he announced that he would not seek reelection as president of the WZO, he was denounced by members of the Israeli government for supposedly asking Senator J. William Fulbright, chairman of the US Senate Foreign Relations Committee, to help bring about a resolution to the Israeli-Arab conflict, a charge Goldmann vigorously denied.[14] Two years later, Prime Minister Golda Meir blocked a possible meeting between Goldmann and Egyptian President Gamal Abdel Nasser.[15]

Nothing brought Goldmann's independent and nonconformist views into focus as much as an article he wrote in the April 1970 issue of *Foreign Affairs*, in which he called for the "neutralization" of Israel, going so far as to suggest that such neutralization

> may even mean that a permanent symbolic international force may have to be stationed in the State of Israel so that any attack on it would imply an attack on all the states guaranteeing Israel's existence and neutrality and participation in this international force. (To avoid misunderstandings, I would add that this does not signify the demilitarization of Israel and the abolition of its army, as long as there are no proof and experience to show the effectiveness of the international guarantee.)[16]

Small wonder, then, that more than a few Israeli leaders saw Goldmann's activities as interference in affairs they considered to be exclusively under their jurisdiction. When Goldmann was reelected WJC president in 1975, he had to overcome bitter opposition from the Herut Party as well as from some Labor Party leaders such as Golda Meir. He was, however, supported by an overwhelming majority.

Other Issues

While my assigned topic for this book is the WJC's relationship with the State of Israel, I would be remiss were I not to reflect on other WJC activities and priorities during my time with the organization, and to recall at least a few of the individuals with whom I had the privilege of working.

SOVIET JEWRY

Israeli authorities frequently complained that in the struggle for Soviet Jewry, mainly their right to immigrate to Israel, the WJC under Nahum Goldmann followed a softer line than the State of Israel and most Jewish communities of the world. The WJC consistently maintained that world Jewry had to detach itself from involvement in Cold War policies. This caused frequent disagreements concerning some particular steps, but the development of the relationship with the Soviet Union and the changes in its policies finally determined the course of events.[17]

NORTH AFRICA

In the first years after the creation of the State of Israel, it was necessary to follow a very cautious policy concerning Jewish life in the Muslim countries of North Africa, particularly with regard to emigration to Israel. It was a very delicate situation, and the Congress displayed a ramified action that could not be expected to be undertaken by the State. The Paris office, directed by Armand Kaplan, and the London office of the WJC's Department of International Affairs, headed by Alex Easterman, were especially active in this area.[18]

GERMANY AND REPARATIONS

There is no doubt that the WJC, its president, and members of its staff were of central importance to the process that finally led to the agreements between the Federal Republic of Germany, on the one hand, and the State of Israel and a representation of world Jewry under the leadership of Nahum Goldmann, on the other. The agreement with Jewish organizations constituted an important development in the recognition of the international personality of world Jewry and its legal status. The historical significance of the building of a new relationship with Germany and the material importance of the reparations for the wellbeing of Israel and of the hundreds of thousands surviving victims of the Holocaust also is beyond the scope of this article. Nonetheless, it should be noted that the WJC's approach, approved by the Israeli mainstream and the Israeli government, was met with strong opposition in some quarters, sometimes of a violent nature.[19]

Interfaith Relations

In the area of interfaith relations, the WJC also played a role that the State of Israel could not perform. Led by WJC Secretary-General Gerhart M. Riegner, the organization worked for the improvement of interfaith activities and the establishment of a positive relationship between the Jewish people and the Holy See. The new climate and the new Catholic attitude achieved progress, culminating in the agreement on diplomatic ties between the Vatican State and Israel and a positive relationship with the Jewish people.[20] The Congress was also instrumental in the advancement of relations with Protestant denominations and the World Council of Churches.

Riegner was probably the most important personality who dealt with interfaith relations on the Jewish side. He played significant roles in the process that led to Vatican II and in the promotion of a creative relationship between the Jewish people, the Vatican, and the other Christian churches. A jurist and a scholar, he symbolized the best creative trends of German Jewry. He spoke several languages fluently and for many years was seen as the personification of the WJC.

United Nations

The WJC is one of several Jewish non-governmental organizations (NGOs) that enjoy consultative status with the United Nations. There was close cooperation between the Congress and the State, in which WJC functionaries played a constructive and creative role widely appreciated in international affairs, from the perspective of political action as well as research. The role of the WJC Institute of Jewish Affairs (IJA) should be mentioned especially with regard to the important support it gave the State of Israel. The research and publications of Nehemiah Robinson and other members of the WJC staff are well known, in and outside Jewish circles. Robinson was an outstanding jurist who devoted most of his work to the problems related to the Holocaust, reparations, human rights, and all other major issues that occupied the WJC. I had the privilege of working with him in the same office for about a year before his untimely death. I was also the translator into Spanish for his classic commentary on the Genocide Convention (1960). Nehemiah Robinson provided the Congress with authoritative legal commentaries, appreciated in all international circles. After the IJA was moved to London, it continued to produce a wide variety of research work under the efficient direction of Stephen J. Roth.

Who Speaks for the Jewish Communities?

Frequently, the question has been raised of whether the State of Israel should be at the forefront of the protection of Diaspora interests in international forums, mainly at the UN, or whether it is preferable to leave these interests in the jurisdiction of Jewish NGOs. It is a delicate topic involving issues of principle as well as practical matters. Having been involved in this matter while working for the WJC as well as afterward, I think that non-state entities can serve global Jewish interests in international organizations more efficiently than powers involved in interstate, frequently conflictive, matters can. One condition for that would be to ensure reasonable coordination between Jewish NGOs. The WJC should take a leading role in this respect. Of course, the right and duty of the State of Israel to act in favor of Jewish communities in distress is undeniable. It is fair to mention that the WJC's work at the UN, as well as in other international bodies, was frequently made more difficult as the result of anti-Israeli bias.

Conclusions

At the present time, the debate surrounding the WJC's relationship with the State of Israel seems to have become far less contentious and dramatic than in the past. There are several reasons for this, including the fact that the State has changed. There have been many sociopolitical changes in the Diaspora; and certain political trends both within the State and within the

Jewish communities have resulted in broadening rather than narrowing the gaps between the two. Conflicting views on the signification of the term "Jewish State," as well as on the meaning of being Jewish in the Diaspora, have resulted in a further emotional and psychological distancing, if not estrangement, between Israel and the Diaspora, with the entire issue of the interaction between the State of Israel and the Jewish religion playing a major role. All of this has organizational implications, but this discussion, too, is beyond the scope of this article, in which I attempted to summarize my own experience.

The author thanks Menachem Rosensaft for his guidance and help in the preparation of this article and acknowledges the documentation provided by WJC archivist Isabella Nespoli.

The World Jewish Congress, the League of Nations, and the United Nations

Zohar Segev

The Establishment of the World Jewish Congress

The inaugural convention of the World Jewish Congress, which was attended by 280 delegates from thirty-two countries, took place in Geneva in August 1936. Although the organization itself was new, its ideological roots lay in the transformations experienced by the Jewish communities in the United States and Europe in the wake of World War I and in the Balfour Declaration. The purpose of the WJC was twofold: to continue in the tradition of the American Jewish Congress (founded in 1918) and the Committee of Jewish Delegations (founded in 1919) by operating as a voluntary organization, representing Jewish communities and organizations worldwide vis-à-vis governmental authorities and international bodies, and to foster the development of social and cultural life in Jewish communities around the world.

For the founders of the WJC—most notably Rabbi Stephen S. Wise and Dr. Nahum Goldmann—the new organization was a direct extension

---

Zohar Segev is Professor of Jewish History and Head of the Wolfson Chair in Jewish Religious Thought and Heritage at the University of Haifa.

of the Committee of Jewish Delegations, which had been established to represent Jewish interests at the Paris Peace Conference that followed the end of World War I. They considered the Committee to have been a turning point in modern Jewish history in that it had advocated not only for individual Jewish rights, such as civil and political equality and freedom of worship, but also for collective rights that called for recognition of the right of Jews to internal autonomy within their countries of residence with regard to their culture and national existence.[1]

The concept of the Jews as a people whose national life should be conducted throughout the world and not in a separate territory is expounded extensively in the works of Simon Dubnow, a writer and historian as well as a founding member of the autonomist movement.[2] Like Dubnow, the founders of the WJC regarded Jewish existence in the Diaspora as a legitimate part of Jewish existence. Unlike Dubnow, however, they did not seek to establish Jewish autonomy, but were actively engaged in integrating Jews within their countries of residence while underscoring their cultural characteristics and the need for an organizational structure that would ensure the rights of Jews in particular and of all minorities.

The League of Nations: First Steps

The worldview of the WJC leadership found expression in a memorandum submitted by the directorate of the WJC to the institutions of the League of Nations in 1936.[3] The memorandum reviewed the traditional Jewish support for peace and international cooperation and underscored the organization's contribution to the struggle for these ideals. It was intended to secure the League of Nations' support for the rights of minorities in general and of the Jews in Europe in particular, and to position the Congress as the exclusive representative of the Jewish people in the Diaspora. For this reason, the members of the Executive Committee of the WJC, who authored the document, stressed that the organization represented the Jews of the Diaspora and was fighting for minority rights, but likewise supported the Jewish community in Palestine and was working to stabilize the mandated government there.[4] Thus, they clarified their worldview:

advocating a complex Jewish reality that combined a Jewish national existence in the Diaspora with the founding of a national home in Palestine.

The WJC was the ultimate manifestation of the dual reality they presented, and through its very existence and modus operandi could address the complex nationalism encompassing both the Jewish Diaspora and the Land of Israel. Rabbi Stephen S. Wise, the de facto president of the WJC, developed the argument that the organization was fulfilling an essential purpose. According to Wise, the establishment of a democratic Jewish organization prepared to take robust action on behalf of world Jewry was a vital matter because of the situation of European Jewry. He maintained that the founding of the WJC constituted a historic turning point, the full significance of which lay in the establishment of a democratic Jewish organization precisely at a time of deep crisis.[5] Wise went on to describe the voting process whereby each Jewish home in the United States would receive a voter card for the price of ten cents. The election was to be supervised by a national election committee that would determine the number of delegates each community would elect to the Congress's institutions. Toward the end of the letter, Wise underscored in large print that the appropriate response to the attack on millions of Jews around the world by anti-democratic forces was the mass participation in this democratic process by American Jews, which would signify their commitment both to the struggle for democracy and the Jews of the world.[6]

The memorandum submitted in 1936 was actually the tip of the iceberg of intensive activity of the WJC leadership in general, and Nahum Goldmann in particular, at the League of Nations. The WJC leadership emphasized the League's obligation to protect the rights of minorities in general and those of European Jews in particular. They maintained that since the issue of minority rights was high on the League's agenda, it was obligated to promote the rights of Jews not only among its members, but also in non-member countries. This position enabled Congress leaders to demand that the League protect the rights of Germany's Jews, even though Germany had left the League.[7]

Despite the League of Nation's significant inherent structural problems, which came to the fore in the latter half of the 1930s, WJC leaders went out of their way to operate in this arena. The grave state of Europe's

Jews left them no choice in the matter; they sought every available channel through which to ameliorate their situation. They thus made energetic efforts at the League's September 1938 assembly in Geneva. They held meetings with the British deputy foreign minister, senior members of the Romanian regime, and League of Nations functionaries responsible for addressing the refugee issue, among others.[8]

The WJC and the United Nations

As World War II came to an end, the cooperation and interaction between the WJC and the United Nations was considered a WJC priority. As Natan Lerner, then the director of the WJC's Israel Branch, explained in 1978:

> As soon as the war was over and the UN came into existence, Congress [i.e., the WJC- Z.S.], as the Jewish people's political organ in the international arena, did its best to help establish an international order based on law, justice, tolerance and freedom. Next to its support for the existence and security of the State of Israel [and] the rights and status of Jewish communities in distress, the struggle for human rights became its direct concern.[9]

The WJC sent a delegation to the San Francisco Conference, held from April to June 1945, at which the UN Charter was drawn up. The WJC delegation was headed by Rabbi Maurice L. Perlzweig and the legal scholar Jacob Robinson, founder and director of the WJC's Institute of Jewish Affairs (IJA).[10] One of the WJC's priorities at the San Francisco Conference was to place Jewish rights in, and claims to, Palestine at the forefront of the international agenda. Together with the American Jewish Conference and the Board of Deputies of British Jews, the WJC submitted a memorandum to the Conference stating, among other things that:

> the reconstitution of Palestine as a Jewish Commonwealth is of prime importance for the future of the Jewish people as a whole, and an affirmative solution of this question is the condition sine qua non for Jewish rehabilitation, especially after the horrors and tribulations of the last decade.[11]

However, as Lerner noted, the adoption of "an effective system of human rights" was of equal concern in San Francisco.[12] Indeed, at the November 1944 WJC War Emergency Conference in Atlantic City, New Jersey, assembled delegates passed a resolution that called for:

> [t]he promulgation of an international Bill of rights securing full protection of life and liberty for the inhabitants of all countries without distinction of origin, nationality, race, faith or language, and the enforcement of such a Bill of rights by an adequate international machinery.[13]

Accordingly, at the San Francisco Conference, the WJC, again together with the American Jewish Conference and the Board of Deputies of British Jews, also submitted a proposal to strengthen the wording of the UN Charter with respect to human rights and freedoms. Specifically, according to Jacob Robinson, the proposal "demanded that the words 'promote respect for human rights' be replaced by 'protect (or safeguard)' those rights and freedoms; and that Chapter I be enlarged by the explicit inclusion of international protection of these rights and freedoms."[14]

In 1947, the WJC became the first Jewish organization to receive consultative status with the UN Economic and Social Council, thereby gaining judicial, public, and international authorization of its singular status as the representative body for world Jewry. According to Natan Lerner:

> As soon as the drafting committee of the Human Rights Commission was established in 1947, the WJC urged it to take measures providing for the recognition of the right of petition for individuals and nongovernmental organizations, and for the establishment of appropriate machinery to implement the substantive principles.[15]

As early as 1948, Dr. Gerhart M. Riegner, then the WJC's de facto secretary-general (he would formally assume the title in 1965), actively participated in the conference of non-governmental organizations (NGOs) with consultative status, serving on the permanent committee of the conference for many years. In 1951, Riegner was elected deputy secretary-general of the conference committee in Geneva. In 1953, he was unanimously elected president of the conference and assumed the position that same year; he subsequently served as the conference's treasurer.[16] In Geneva,

Riegner was also an observer at the UN Commission on Human Rights beginning in 1946. "This advisory capacity," he wrote, "gave us the right to attend meetings, to submit written briefs, and to address the Commission orally. On the Commission there were generally two WJC representatives, at times even three of us."[17] Among other accomplishments, the WJC significantly influenced the drafting of a number of articles of the Universal Declaration of Human Rights. For example, Riegner recalled in his autobiography, the original draft of Article 29 of the Declaration:

> envisioned that the exercise of human rights could be limited by law. We made the case that this was exactly what Hitler had done. . . . We then suggested that every national law that restricted human rights should not be considered valid from the perspective of international law unless it conformed to the principles and objectives of the United Nations. We had complete success.[18]

The WJC leaders wished to keep their independent status at the United Nations even after the State of Israel had been granted membership in 1949. One key example of the WJC's independent activity in the international arena is its insistence on retaining official status at, and being extremely involved with, the United Nations. Various committees of the WJC submitted papers, distributed memoranda, and presented data to the United Nations, addressing not only matters of specific concern to the Jewish people or to Jewish communities, but also broader issues. Nehemiah Robinson, who succeeded his brother Jacob as the director of the IJA, noted in 1955:

> The World Jewish Congress was the first Jewish non-governmental organization to be granted consultative status with the United Nations Economic and Social Council. It also has the distinction of being the only Jewish and one of the very few non-governmental organizations at large which has intervened with the competent organs of the United Nations and the delegations thereto in practically all matters relating to the drafting of new international law rules, protection of minorities, prevention of discrimination, protection of human rights, and protection of Jewish communities, and similar subjects, regardless of whether

these topics were discussed in the Economic and Social Council, its subsidiary bodies (Commission on Human Rights, Sub-commission on Freedom of Information), in the General Assembly, in Conferences of Plenipotentiaries, Ad Hoc Committees, the International Law Commission, the Committee on International Criminal Jurisdiction, etc. As a result, the activities of the World Jewish Congress connected with the United Nations reflect, in a measure, the activities of the United Nations itself. [19]

Perlzweig, who had been one of the founders of the WJC together with Wise and Goldmann, was the WJC's principal representative at the United Nations in the late 1940s and early 1950s and drafted many of the documents submitted by the WJC to the UN Commission on Human Rights. In a 1953 report on WJC activities at the United Nations, he wrote, "To support the United Nations and its principles and purposes as embodied in the Charter has been, since the San Francisco conference, one of the principal tasks of the World Jewish Congress." Perlzweig went on to provide the rationale and context for the WJC's in-depth involvement in UN activities:

> It is one of the primary purposes of the World Jewish Congress to seek to safeguard the rights and freedoms of Jews and Jewish communities wherever they may happen to be. But these rights and freedoms are not conceived of as existing or being able to survive in isolation. They are fundamentally an expression of general human rights and of the reign of law in international and domestic relations; and in this view we are sustained alike by Jewish tradition and the unique experience of the Jewish people. Accordingly, the World Jewish Congress has devoted an important part of its resources and energies to the struggle for human rights in the broadest sense, and to the development of international law through the United Nations. [20]

The WJC's desire to gain recognition of Jewish displaced persons' extraordinary condition and its attempt to influence policy toward them is also apparent in its endeavor to become involved in shaping the policy of the UN Relief and Rehabilitation Administration (UNRRA). This organization was founded in 1943 and became a part of the United Nations after 1945. It operated as an international agency until 1947, initiating, administering, and implementing welfare programs in Europe. The WJC involved itself in UNRRA's activity from its inception by submitting memoranda to the body's various branches and seeking to place Jews, especially Congress representatives, on its staff in Europe.[21] In September 1944, Wise and Goldmann submitted a signed memorandum to UNRRA. In it they applauded the body's policy of conducting welfare activity directed at Europe's entire population, irrespective of origin, religion, or race, without differentiating between those in need of assistance who were nationals of enemy states and citizens of countries liberated from Nazi occupation. They added, however, that "those discriminated against by the Nazi oppressors must be given the same opportunities of recovery as the others. Thus, the Jews should be given equitable priorities in the distribution of food, medical aid and shelter, as well as in the return, repatriation, and resettlement of displaced persons."[22]

These attempts to influence the activities of the administration and UNRRA were accompanied by a supreme fundraising effort among WJC member nations to provide the money required to finance welfare and rehabilitation of European Jews. The WJC raised ten million dollars during 1944. At the same time, it criticized other Jewish organizations, particularly the American Jewish Joint Distribution Committee, for raising considerable sums of money but continuing to conduct only philanthropic activity rather than engaging in broad, politically significant rehabilitation efforts. An opinion piece in the December 1944 *Congress Weekly* addressed the issue:

> On this need for a centralized Jewish authority is based the decision adopted by the War Emergency Conference of the World Jewish Congress to raise a fund of $100,000,000 for rehabilitation and reconstruction. Unlike other organizations which attempt to separate Jewish relief work from political activities, the World Jewish Congress, primarily a political organization, realized from its inception that the two are inseparable parts of a single task.[23]

In preparation for the reconstruction of the communities, the WJC established a training facility on the outskirts of Paris to teach personnel, primarily women, how to operate within European bureaucratic systems.

In March 1946, thirty young women were selected to commence the study program.[24] They received training in a variety of areas, including education, community organization and action, Jewish festivals, selected issues pertaining to Jewish tradition, Zionism, and the Palestine problem. While all of this was going on, the WJC was also investing considerable effort in cultural rehabilitation within the communities. Hundreds of thousands of books were dispatched to Europe: basic textbooks on Jewish issues, Yiddish and Hebrew literature, prayer books, and Bibles. Particular emphasis was placed on the dispatch of more than sixty Torah Scrolls, most of them donated by communities in New York and Chicago, with the express intention of reviving the religious life of European Jewry.[25]

In subsequent years, the WJC continued to regard itself as being responsible for the overall cultural life in the communities. Its institutions sought to encourage Jewish youth in Europe to choose a career in Jewish education, and it actively promoted the establishment of teacher-training institutes. In the papers of the Congress's European bodies, there is documentation of programs for the preparation of textbooks on Jewish history between 1848 and 1938; for the founding of scientific journals addressing Jewish culture; and for adult education activities using the modern technology of the day, such as radio, gramophone, and movable displays.[26]

Both Wise and Goldmann rejected the view that Zionism should be the sole constituting force of Jewish life following the Holocaust. Addressing the second WJC plenary assembly in Montreux, Switzerland, on June 27, 1948, Goldmann stressed that the WJC, rather than the government of Israel, should be the official voice of Diaspora Jewry. He expressed the hope that Israel would be admitted to the United Nations

> so that when in the future Jewish problems requiring United Nations action arise, there will be at least one official representative of the State of Israel at the Council table, ready to speak out and take care of them. But again, we should not regard the State of Israel, eo ipso, as the formal representative and spokesman of Jewish communities in the Diaspora, which it cannot be—in its own interests as in those of the communities themselves. . . . The future of the Jewish people in the Diaspora, and the future of the State of Israel alike, require close relations of trust, of

mutual help, of interest, of cooperation, in many cases; but at the same time they will be distinct and different entities: the State representing its citizens and speaking for them, the World Jewish Congress representing the Jewish people and speaking for them—so far as authorized to do so.[27]

In this vein, within the United Nations, the WJC emphasized not only the role played by the organization in presenting the perspective of the Jewish Diaspora to international bodies and agencies, but also its status as the only organization dedicated to protecting the rights of Jews around the world. This outlook was clearly expressed in a report submitted in 1948 by Dr. Robert Marcus, chairman of the WJC's political committee, to the UN Commission on Genocide. Marcus maintained that the organization's proposals to the commission should be given serious consideration, as the WJC represented all of world Jewry. He added that the experience of the world's Jews as a minority group that had resisted the attempts to annihilate it during the Holocaust and was now struggling for its rights lent added weight to the WJC outlook on the issues of genocide and minority rights. On the strength of his Jewish experience, Marcus proposed that several measures be taken, including the passage of international legislation designating the infringement of minority rights as a crime; the creation of an international system of intervention in the case of infringement of minority rights; and the formation of a reparations mechanism to facilitate the rehabilitation of victims.[28]

While WJC leaders attributed great importance to the international recognition they received through the United Nations, their involvement in its activity stemmed from their overall support of the organization. WJC papers indicate that the organization's leaders called upon its members and on the general American Jewish public to actively support the United Nations. They maintained that as an intellectual collective upholding a progressive worldview, the Jews were obliged to support the UN, and emphasized that international peace and cooperation as manifested by the UN were particularly vital to Jews, given the suffering and catastrophe they had experienced during World War II. Nevertheless, Jewish support for the United Nations did not stem from narrow self-interest but emanated from a sense of mission that recognized the importance of the organization to the entire world. Jews should commit themselves both to supporting the founding of the UN and to reinforcing it, so as to ensure that the ideals underlying its establishment would not remain only within the realm of utopia.

The WJC leadership in New York also endorsed the Bretton Woods Agreement, concluded during the course of an international economic summit held in July 1944 in the town of Bretton Woods in New Hampshire, which comprised a series of trade agreements determining the exchange rates of currencies among the developed countries. The forty-four countries attending the conference established the International Monetary Fund and the World Bank. WJC representatives participated in public activity in the United States to promote the agreements. The organization's American members were called upon to lobby their representatives in Congress to support the agreement, and its institutions distributed information pertaining to the agreements to their members and conveyed their support of the agreements and the financial arrangements concluded in their wake.[29] The activities of the WJC in and for the United Nations can be properly understood only in connection with the relevant steps taken by the respective organs of the UN and the bodies connected with it. We must understand these activities not in isolation, but within the framework of the action taken in the respective field by the organs of the UN and the result achieved.

The issues of human rights and fundamental freedoms were ones to which the WJC had devoted the largest part of its work at the United Nations. From the very beginning the WJC considered it critical that the new world organization, established in the immediate aftermath of the Holocaust and World War II, deal with the rights of the individual to a greater extent than had been the case at the League of Nations. This consideration stemmed from the experience of the Nazi and Fascist regimes, which had demonstrated the degree to which the most elementary human rights could be violated and the depth of inhumanity that resulted from that violation. Mindful of the failure of constitutional guarantees for the protection of the individual against abuse, particularly since 1933, the WJC has regarded the international protection of human rights as the only solution to the problem, and the establishment of international machinery for the protection of the rights so proclaimed as the only effective safeguard against their violation.[30]

The main agency of the United Nations dealing with human rights was the UN Commission on Human Rights (UNCHR). It was a functional commission within the overall framework of the UN from 1946 until it was replaced by the UN Human Rights Council in 2006. It was a subsidiary body of the UN Economic and Social Council (ECOSOC), and was also assisted in its work by the Office of the UN High Commissioner for Human Rights (UNHCHR). It was the UN's principal mechanism for, and international forum concerned with, the promotion and protection of human rights. Practically no single session of the Commission on Human Rights passed without the WJC having submitted memoranda on the task before it and its representative appearing before the Commission to present the views of the WJC on the points under discussion.

An expression of the specific interest of the WJC and the United Nations in non-discrimination and the protection of minorities was the establishment of the Sub-Commission on Prevention of Discrimination and Protection of Minorities. The function of the Sub-Commission consists mainly of undertaking studies and submitting recommendations to the Human Rights Commission. The Sub-Commission was viewed by the WJC as the "conscience of the United Nations" in the field of discrimination. The WJC therefore supported the work of this Sub-Commission, and when the ECOSOC decided in 1951 to discontinue its activities for a certain period of time, the WJC made strenuous efforts to have this decision reversed by the General Assembly, in official statements and intervention with UN member states and their representatives. In written submissions as well as in oral statements (before the fourth session of the Sub-Commission), the WJC contended that the Sub-Commission had made an important and distinguished contribution to the problems with which it dealt, and deeply deplored the decision of the Economic and Social Council to discontinue its work.

The General Assembly accepted the WJC point of view and disagreed with the ECOSOC. It decided on February 4, 1952 that since prevention of discrimination and protection of minorities is one of the most important tasks undertaken by the United Nations, it must be enabled to continue its work to fulfill its mission.[31]

John P. Humphrey, director of the UN Human Rights Division, said in his address at the opening of the third WJC plenary assembly in Geneva on August 4, 1953:

> One of the most interesting and significant developments in international organizations since the Second World War has been the increasing participation of non-governmental organizations like the WJC in the work of the United Nations and of its specialized agencies. Among the non-governmental organizations having consultative status with the Economic and Social Council, none have contributed more than the WJC. I am informed that the WJC alone has had some 44 written statements circulated to various United Nations bodies and this impressive figure does not include the many oral interventions of your representatives. Even more important, however, in my opinion, are the more subtle influences that you are able to bring to bear on governments and delegations, a diplomatic function, which none could be more delicate or require. Not only have you taken full advantage of the procedures provided by the United Nations for consultations but you also played a brilliant role in the working out and development of these procedures.

Professor Humphrey's address pointed out the tremendous role and contributions of the WJC to the United Nations.[32]

Summary

As an Israeli scholar engaged in the study of American Jewry, I take particular interest in the WJC's role in shaping the Jewish Diaspora in Europe and rehabilitating the Jewish communities there following World War II. Most studies undertaken during the initial decades after the founding of the State of Israel addressed the various contexts of this dramatic event. The discussion among American Jewry became a part of this trend, and their political and economic contribution to the establishment of the state was used as a kind of counterbalance to the criticism leveled at the limited success of their contribution to the rescue of Jews during the Holocaust.

As the defining impact of the founding of the State of Israel gradually receded into the past, historical discourse began to address broader issues relating to the essence of Jewish existence following World War II as well as to the establishment of Israel. In this paper I have tried to examine the attempt by WJC leaders to operate within the United Nations as a representative Jewish organization. Rather than conducting this effort from an anti-Zionist worldview, they emphasized that the recovery effort would function alongside their public, economic, and political support for the young state.[33]

The efforts of the WJC at rehabilitating the Jewish communities of Europe and its activities within the United Nations reinforce the conclusion that the founding of the State of Israel was but part of the process of shaping the postwar Jewish world, and that the WJC's role in this process is of critical importance. It behooves us as scholars to broaden the scope of the study and discussion of this issue within academia, and to contribute to the evolution of the discourse on this topic within the State of Israel, in the United States, and throughout the Jewish world.

From Pariah to Partner:
The Jews of Postwar Germany
and the World Jewish Congress

MICHAEL BRENNER

In May 1990, when the World Jewish Congress had organized a three-day conference in Berlin to mark the forty-fifth anniversary of the end of World War II in Europe, a substantial number of invitees refused to attend, many arguing that it was still too early for a major international Jewish organization to meet in Germany.[1] In September 2014, the WJC Governing Board met in Berlin, Germany. According to WJC President Ronald S. Lauder, there were still serious discussions on whether the 2014 meeting—which took place in close proximity to the Wannsee Villa, where the mass murder of European Jews was conceived—would indeed be the right choice almost seven decades after the end of the war. In the end, Lauder concluded: "This was the best decision."[2] The 2014 meeting gave the final stamp of approval not only for decades of German-Jewish reconciliation but also for the legitimation of Jewish life on German soil.

Sixty-six years earlier, at the first postwar plenary assembly of the WJC in Montreux, Switzerland, no one could have foreseen the possibility

Michael Brenner is Professor of Jewish History and Culture at Ludwig Maximilian University Munich and Seymour and Lillian Abensohn Chair in Israel Studies at American University, Washington DC.

that there would ever again be a meeting of worldwide Jewish leaders in Germany. In 1948, the political commission of the WJC made clear what its representatives thought regarding any future for Jews in Germany when it passed a resolution stressing "the determination of the Jewish people never again to settle on the bloodstained soil of Germany."[3] There was broad consensus that no Jews should live in Germany, and certainly that no international Jewish meetings should be held on this "bloodstained" soil. This article tells the story of the gradual change in recognition and acceptance of Jewish life in postwar Germany by the WJC and the slow process of German-Jewish reconciliation to which the WJC, and especially its president, Nahum Goldmann, contributed considerably.

It is one of the ironies of history that Germany became a center for Jewish life in post-Holocaust Europe. The officially registered number of Jewish displaced persons or DPs (concentration camp survivors, Jews who had survived in hiding or on forged papers or who had fought in partisan units, and Jews who had fled to the Soviet Union during the war) in the American Zone of Germany alone increased from 39,902 in January 1946 to 145,735 in December of the same year.[4] Until the late 1940s, about a quarter million Jewish DPs from Eastern Europe lived at least temporarily in Germany, the vast majority of them in the American Zone, even though the single largest DP camp, Bergen-Belsen, was located in the British Zone.

Most had barely escaped the Nazi death machines and were in dire need of assistance. The American Jewish Joint Distribution Committee (JDC) and other American and British Jewish organizations were able to help them on the ground, as it were, to start a new life. The WJC, too, gave priority to questions concerning the national and political rights and demands of the survivors, as well as their wellbeing, their material indemnification, and their resettlement in Israel, the United States, or elsewhere.[5] As Zohar Segev wrote in his account of the WJC, "What set the WJC apart from other Jewish organizations was that its leaders sought not merely to institutionalize the relationship between Israel and American Jewry, but involved themselves in the Jewish world as a whole, particularly in Europe where they worked vigorously to rehabilitate the Jewish Diaspora and to assist those survivors wishing to reestablish their lives there."[6]

Josef Rosensaft, the chairman of the Central Committee of Liberated Jews in the British Zone of Germany and of the Jewish Committee that in essence ran the Bergen-Belsen DP camp, observed: "The World Jewish Congress engaged itself in political aid, which was given us not in the spirit of pity on poor Jews in reduced circumstances, but in true brotherly fashion, in full cooperation with us and through continuous consultations as between equals. This is what made the assistance of the World Jewish Congress so different from that of other Jewish organizations."[7] The WJC was involved in influencing the policies of the United Nations Relief and Rehabilitation Administration (UNRRA) toward the DPs and tried to shape policies for the future. In this respect, its leaders disagreed with the JDC's philanthropic approach, which they considered shortsighted. In contrast, the WJC was interested in long-term political strategies that would result in a lasting solution for the Jewish survivors in Germany and the rest of Europe.[8] The WJC did, however, also undertake steps to facilitate immediate relief for the survivors, such as training American Jewish social workers who could help survivors and providing assistance to children, many of whom were orphans. The WJC encouraged the adoption of Jewish orphans by Jewish families in the United States and Palestine, and initiated long-term strategies for Jewish life in Europe.[9] As the 1948 Montreux resolution demonstrated, however, long-term planning for Jewish life in Germany was not on the WJC's agenda.

In the meantime, however, it became clear that Jewish life in Germany had not come to a complete end. While most Jewish survivors had left Germany after the State of Israel was established in 1948 and the United States lifted its strict quotas for Jewish immigration in 1949, approximately 10 percent of the 250,000 Jewish DPs, who were temporarily living in Germany, remained there. They were joined by a small group of German Jews who had survived the Nazi terror within Germany itself. Approximately 15,000 German Jews were liberated in 1945, some of whom had been in concentration and death camps, others in hiding. Most of them had had only very loose contacts with the Jewish communities before 1933, and a high percentage of them had survived only because they had been protected to a certain degree by a non-Jewish spouse or parent.

A considerable number of Jewish communities were officially reestablished as early as 1945. By 1948, more than 100 Jewish communities had been founded, and a total of some 20,000 members were registered in the reestablished communities in 1948. This reality was acknowledged in the same resolution adopted by the WJC plenary assembly in Montreux, which demanded that "[t]he legal status of Jews and their communities [in Germany] be guaranteed internationally."[10] It is a psychologist's task and not that of a historian to analyze the reasons why Jews stayed or settled in postwar Germany. It may suffice to state here that there was more than one reason. Some were just not able to move again to a foreign place and to learn a new language after all they had been through; others had found German non-Jewish partners; still others had established themselves economically; and, finally, there were those German Jews who returned immediately after the war to help build a new and democratic Germany. Those political idealists could be found more frequently in the East, where the more prominent Jews lived in the first postwar years. The writer Arnold Zweig returned from Palestine, Anna Seghers from Mexico, and quite a few leading Communist politicians were of Jewish descent. In absolute numbers, however, the Jewish presence in East Germany was almost negligible, especially after many Jews had left in the tumultuous weeks of anti-Semitic propaganda in the final Stalinist years of 1952 and 1953. This wave of emigration left only about fifteen hundred, mainly elderly, Jews in the Jewish communities of East Germany, a number that was further reduced to 350 by the late 1980s.[11]

The WJC's 1948 de facto ban on Jews residing permanently in Germany is often mentioned in connection with an analogous reciprocal ban allegedly issued by Jewish authorities after the 1492 expulsion from Spain. Apart from the fact that no credible evidence exists of such an official rabbinical ban or ḥerem, the situation was indeed quite different from that in post-1945 Germany. After all, it was the Spanish monarchy that expelled the Jews and did not allow them to resettle in their realm for a few centuries. Even if some rabbis had declared a ban on Jewish life in Spain in the sixteenth or seventeenth century, it would not have made any difference. They could not have settled there anyway.

In Germany, the situation after 1945 was quite the opposite. As two German states arose a few years after the war had ended, the presence of Jews served as a litmus test for the new states. John J. McCloy, the US military governor (and later high commissioner) for Germany, stated at a conference on the future of the Jews in Germany, convened in Heidelberg in 1949: "What this community will be, how it forms itself, how it becomes a part and how it merges with the new Germany, will, I believe be watched very closely and very carefully by the entire world. It will, in my judgement, be one of the real touchstones and the test of Germany's progress towards the light."[12]

As the Declaration of Montreux indicated, most of the Jewish world thought differently. Chaim Yachil (Hoffmann), the first Israeli consul in Munich (who was accredited with the US authorities), declared categorically: "All Jews must leave Germany." Those who stayed were, for him, "a source of danger for the entire Jewish people. . . . Those who are tempted by the fleshpots of Germany must not expect that Israel or the Jewish people should provide them with services for their convenience." This, of course, was a thinly veiled threat signifying that the world Jewish community, and Israel in particular, were about to isolate the few remaining Jews in Germany. The American-Jewish writer Ludwig Lewisohn shared this opinion and predicted that the remaining Jews not only of Germany but of Europe as a whole would become "outcasts, paupers, untouchables, in separate quarters of Europe" who would live a "life without dignity, creativity, and hope."[13]

Perhaps the clearest expression of rejection concerning the Jewish community of Germany was a letter from the second Israeli consul in Munich, Eliahu Livneh, to his foreign ministry, in which he wrote, "The Jewish world considers this Jewish community to be a result of chance selection and will under no circumstances grant it the right of its own political will." The response from the foreign ministry was telling, however. After acknowledging that it would be ideal but unrealistic to believe that the Jewish community would dissolve itself, the foreign ministry official suggested that "you continue with your policy of resistance [to official relations with the Jewish community], which you had practiced so far, with the inside knowledge, however, that in the long run this position is untenable. Thus, it is not worth that you put too much energy into the matter."[14]

It goes without saying that the WJC did not always speak with a single voice on this, as on other matters. There were different offices—the most important ones at the time were in New York, London, and Geneva—all with their particular perspectives, and even within the various offices the position on this question was not always uniform. One may divide the different views inside the WJC into three general categories:

- Those who were categorically opposed to a permanent or lasting Jewish presence in Germany
- Those who had no ideological objections to Jews living in Germany but did not believe in a future Jewish life there
- Those who in principle were against rebuilding a Jewish future in Germany but who argued pragmatically that as long as Jews were living there, they would have to receive support from international Jewish organizations

The first of these positions was taken by a broad variety of Jewish officials, but most prominently by those in Israel, a state that, after all, forbade its citizens to travel to Germany. The Israeli passport contained the well-known stamp: "Valid for all countries except Germany." If Israel did not want its citizens even to *visit* Germany, how could they be agreeable to the idea that other Jews would make their *living* there? Thus, in 1950, the Israeli office of the WJC broke all ties with the Jews remaining in Germany. This was a minority position within the WJC.[15]

The second position may have been best expressed by an official report of the WJC-sponsored Institute of Jewish Affairs, in 1949: "Despite the intensive social and cultural activities of the Jewish Communities in Germany, the conclusion appears inescapable that German Jewry will cease to exist. . . . Those who are able to leave will leave the country. The others will die off."[16] Jewish leaders made similar statements over the years. One example was British Rabbi Isaac Chait who toured Germany in 1962 and, according to the *Jewish Chronicle*, reported that there was no future for Jews in Germany. "When the old people die and the younger ones leave for Israel," he wrote, "there will be nothing left save the beautiful synagogues."[17]

The third position was adopted by Nahum Goldmann and became the WJC's dominant position. During a meeting with the London members of the WJC Executive in October 1948, Goldmann argued that "the slogan that no Jew should live in Germany after the Hitler catastrophe was unrealistic."[18] Thus, the WJC took a rather pragmatic position. In 1949, the WJC decided to establish its own office in Frankfurt to assist Jewish organizations and communities in Germany; to maintain a liaison between them and the WJC; to maintain contact with the Allied authorities; and to collect material on the revival of anti-Semitism.[19]

A crucial moment came in 1949, when West Germany was about to become a sovereign state. At that time, much of the discussion among the European members of the WJC Executive was dedicated to the future of Germany in general, and Jews in Germany in particular. Guest speakers at this session included delegates representing the DPs still living in Germany and raising critical voices about a future in Germany.

Thus, Chaim Eife of the Central Committee of the Liberated Jews in the US Zone expressed his hope concerning the remaining DPs that "steps be taken to ensure they remain under the jurisdiction of the occupying authorities." His colleagues from the British Zone, Josef (Yossel) Rosensaft and Norbert Wollheim, both of whom were planning to leave Germany, also stressed the problematic side of staying there in the face of continuing anti-Semitism. On the other hand, Hendrik George van Dam, the main spokesman of the Central Council of Jews in Germany, expressed a more confident position when he "favored the establishment of an overall representative body of Jews in Germany" and stressed that the WJC "should restrict its action on Germany to two matters: the legal protection of the Jews in Germany, and the protest against the reinstatement of Nazis." Similarly, Heinz Galinski, chairman of the Berlin Jewish community, expressed his belief in the construction of a new democratic German state in which Jews would find a place, too.

These discussions were embedded within more general positions toward postwar Germany, with some delegates advocating the boycott of German goods. Not surprisingly, those in favor of a strict boycott envisioned a Germany without Jews. As one delegate, Dr. S. Levenberg stressed, "The Congress should advocate the evacuation of the Jews from Germany." Maurice L. Perlzweig, the WJC's Director of International Affairs in New York, echoed this sentiment when he demanded that "we should take all Jews out of Germany, so that they should not remain there as hostages." Rabbi R. Kapel went so far as to state that "Germany constituted danger no. 1 for the Jews in the world."[20]

In 1950, on the eve of the establishment of the Central Council of Jews in Germany as the umbrella organization of those communities that were there to stay, the WJC majority opinion was expressed in the following statement by Alex L. Easterman, Director of International Affairs in the WJC's London office: "While it was the opinion and policy of the World Jewish Congress that Jews should leave Germany, those who chose to stay in Germany would be gladly given advice, if they should call on the World Jewish Congress."[21] It was in fact the Central Council that initially did not want to be associated with the WJC, as it had taken up contact with other Jewish organizations, such as the American Jewish Committee. Only in 1954, four years after its establishment, did the Central Council officially approach the WJC concerning terms of affiliation. There was some controversy among the London WJC European Executive members, ranging from strong advocacy of the affiliation to the opinion that it "would be a mistake, since it would encourage Jews to remain in Germany." In general, there was agreement that while it was not a good thing for Jews to remain, those who did should be affiliated with the WJC.[22]

Once the Central Council was established, conflicts arose again and again about the question of who should represent Jewish issues before German authorities and politicians—the German-Jewish representatives or the WJC. Thus, a 1951 meeting of the London members of the WJC Executive criticized the Central Council for writing a letter to West German President Theodor Heuss. The Council had asked to establish formal relations with the government, without prior consultation with the WJC.[23]

The WJC representative in Germany, Saul Sokal, reported to the London office in May 1952 his concerns about a new self-confidence on the part of Jews living in West Germany:

> Some German Jews are beginning to develop a new "ideology" according to which German Jewry is called by history to assume the role of a mediator between Germany and world Jewry. . . . The very small group of people who speak for the Jews would like to establish a standing for the Jewish community in Germany. The attitude of the postwar forties, even of 1950, has been reversed. They do not consider the existence of Jews here as transitory, nor do they pretend their stay is transitory. Just

the opposite is now the prevalent philosophy. "The history of the Jews in Germany is not finished." This is the slogan. . . . Although they do not know what is the mission of the Jews in Germany, or what they would like it to be, they want it very emphatically.[24]

This new attitude among German Jews is confirmed by other sources. Thus, in 1951, the Association of Jewish Communities in northwestern Germany passed a resolution "rejecting all attempts to denounce the Jews who remained in Germany. . . . The Jews in Germany consider themselves an integral part of world Jewry."[25]

When the next WJC plenary assembly was held in 1953 in Geneva, Jews were still living in Germany. Among them was a group called the "hard core," referring to those DPs who for a variety of reasons still had not moved out of Germany. The most visible of this group were the two thousand Jews living in the Föhrenwald DP camp. In this connection, it is fascinating to examine the minutes of the early postwar WJC plenary assemblies, where different languages, including Spanish, Yiddish, Hebrew, and French, were spoken. While quite a few delegates—namely exiled German Jews—spoke in German, a delegate from Germany, Maurice Weinberger, chose to speak at the 1953 WJC plenary assembly not in German but rather in his native Yiddish, which can be taken as symptomatic of the new situation. He stressed more than anything else that the remaining Jews in Germany were old and sick, and that 90 percent of them wanted nothing more desperately than to leave Germany. It was, he said, the WJC's duty to help them get out. Weinberger, himself a DP in Munich, did not distinguish between German and East European Jews and represented the position of the communities in the south of Germany, to which few pre-war German Jews had returned.[26] Several other observers referred to the postwar German-Jewish community as a "broken people who were earning a precarious living."[27]

These different views were still reflected during a special session of the 1966 WJC plenary assembly in Brussels. By that time, after the restitution accords of the early 1950s, the first major German trials against Nazi perpetrators in the early 1960s, and especially after the establishment of diplomatic relations between Bonn and Israel in 1965, West Germany had become more accepted in the Jewish world. Against much resistance from both the right-wing (Herut) and left-wing (Mapam and Ahdut Ha'avoda–Poalei Zion) delegates from Israel, Nahum Goldmann insisted on a session that would be dedicated to the question of "Germans and Jews." In an emotional statement, made in Hebrew and in Yiddish, the Herut delegate Isaac Remba explained why he could not be present for this discussion, as Jews should not help Germans to rehabilitate themselves among the family of nations.[28] He was not only supported by the left-wing Mapam and Ahdut Ha'avoda-Poalei Zion delegations,[29] but also by the delegation of *mizraḥi* Jews—that is, Jews originally from Arab countries—from Israel, who stressed that while they had not suffered directly from the Nazi atrocities, they remained steadfast in their opposition to a German-Jewish reconciliation at this early point in history.[30] And Hungarian-born, Orthodox, New York Rabbi Bernard Bergman sent a letter to the WJC leadership in which he declared: "We call upon every Jew to limit the relations with Germany to the minimum. The blood of our brethren is crying out and demanding from us not to have any treaty with Germany."[31]

It was again Nahum Goldmann who called for a pragmatic approach toward Germany. "This symposium has caused some doubts and many misunderstandings," he declared in a statement released to the press prior to the opening of the plenary assembly. He continued:

> The leadership of the World Jewish Congress regards the open and frank discussion of this difficult and delicate problem as necessary, just because the problem is far from being solved, despite the indemnification payments and the normalization of relations between Israel and the German Federal Republic.
>
> After what happened in the Hitler period, it is obvious that it will take quite some time until German-Jewish relations will be psychologically and spiritually normalized, and recent symptoms of a new anti-Semitically colored nationalism in Germany have given cause to worries and fears. On the other hand, to ignore this problem and not to take note of Germany's growing importance is a most unrealistic attitude, based on pure emotionalism.[32]

In his introductory remarks at the beginning of the session, "to avoid distortions and misunderstandings," Goldmann elaborated further: "the problem of German-Jewish relations exists; it is unresolved. . . . It is both historically and realistically one of the most complex and important problems of our Jewish generation of today." That was precisely why the WJC leadership had put the topic on the agenda despite opposition.

> We shall not find a solution tonight—I am not so naïve as to believe that we will—but I think it is much better that the problem be discussed by people from both sides—by Germans whose record is perfect and who opposed Hitler, and by Jewish historians and scholars who can give us the historical background of the problem. . . . The purpose of what is on the agenda here tonight is to find a way of coexistence between Jews and Germans in a world in which the Germans exist and are growing in importance, and in which—thank God—the Jewish people exists despite the Nazi attempt to annihilate it; to find a way of coexistence between two peoples who, in light of the realities and in spite of whatever happened, must find means of dealing with one another. All the sentiments behind it are a matter for the individual. It is not for the World Jewish Congress or the State of Israel or the Knesset of Israel to determine these emotional and sentimental aspects. We have to deal collectively with the hard realities.[33]

Goldmann assured the delegates that this special session was not to be an "orgy of reconciliation," and that "our people will never forget what happened in the Hitler period. . . . I would be ashamed to be a Jew if Jews could forget it."[34] At the same time, he also opposed "being *broiges*"—that is, being angry—as a policy, and rejected "the advice to ignore Germany" as being "unrealistic and not practical." A people that wants to be the master of its own fate, Goldmann proclaimed in essence, cannot conduct politics by "being *broiges*."[35]

Speakers at the meeting included Jewish scholars Gershom Scholem and Salo Baron, as well as Rabbi Joachim Prinz, Chairman of the Conference of Presidents of Major American Jewish Organizations, who would be elected chairman of the WJC Governing Council at the end of the 1966 Brussels plenary assembly. The speakers on the German side were historian Golo Mann—a son of Thomas Mann and on his mother's side the descendant of a family of Jewish background—and the speaker of the German *Bundestag*, Eugen Gerstenmaier, known for his anti-Nazi past. While

Scholem emphasized the complex history of Jews in Germany, Gerstenmaier spoke about the German efforts toward reconciliation. Among the Jewish speakers, only Baron, the respected professor of history at Columbia University who had also presided over the Jewish Cultural Reconstruction after the end of the war, expressed his conviction that Jews would remain in Germany, and would even increase in numbers.[36]

The most notable fact about the remarks delivered by Hendrik George van Dam, Secretary-General of the Central Council of Jews in Germany, was not what he said, but that he was invited to speak at all. He was not on the original list of speakers and it was only after much pressure from the Central Council, even involving threats that it might leave the WJC altogether, that a German-Jewish representative was added to the panel.[37] In his speech, van Dam took a clear position against any collective punishments or bans, such as in the case of Spanish Jewry half a millennium earlier. "History has shown that the Jews are not interested in the isolation of peoples," he concluded.[38]

The words spoken by Rabbi Prinz, who had been a courageously outspoken anti-Nazi figure in the early Hitler years before being expelled from Germany by direct order of Adolf Eichmann,[39] were especially poignant. "It is very difficult," he said, "to talk about an encounter of Jews and Germans if there are no Jews in Germany. It is fair to say that for all practical purposes there are no Jews in Germany today, because their number is so small and their spiritual influence so limited that the average German rarely meets a Jew. There are hundreds of German communities in which no single Jew exists. Therefore the image of a Jew, both physically and spiritually, has disappeared for Germany and it will remain so for a long time, certainly as long as our generation lives and probably much longer."[40]

As it turned out, Rabbi Prinz was mistaken. By the mid-1960s, the Jews in Germany felt a growing acceptance among the worldwide Jewish community. An official report of the Central Council in 1964 made this clear: "The Central Council has been insisting since its establishment that the Jewish community of Germany has a right to exist. . . . We fought for this right against much resistance, especially against world opinion. Now we see success in that we are represented in many world Jewish organizations."[41]

By the end of the 1960s, it was clear that Jews would remain in Germany. A second generation had grown up, and while many of them had left for Israel or other countries, quite a few stayed. They were joined by new immigrants from Poland, Czechoslovakia, Israel, and Iran. New synagogues were built, new schools opened. Even in East Germany, the tiny Jewish community was briefly in the spotlight in 1988, when WJC president Edgar M. Bronfman led controversial talks with the last Communist party leader, Erich Honecker, which involved the restoration of the ruined Oranienburger Strasse synagogue.[42]

The brief encounter between the WJC and East Germany proved inconsequential, while the fall of the wall in 1989 brought 150,000–200,000 Jews from the former Soviet Union to a now unified Germany, thus increasing the total German-Jewish community six to seven fold. A new chapter of German-Jewish life had begun. To the surprise of the rest of the world, Germany was now the country with the fastest-growing Jewish community in the world. This was the new reality at the time of the 2014 WJC meeting in Berlin, which seemed a world apart from the 1948 plenary assembly in Montreux and even the 1966 symposium in Brussels.

Part of this article was previously published as the Ina Levine Annual Lecture 2008 by the Jack, Joseph and Morton Mandel Center for Advanced Holocaust Studies at the United States Holocaust Memorial Museum.

Diplomatic Interventions: The World Jewish Congress and North African Jewry

Isabella Nespoli
Menachem Z. Rosensaft

During World War II, the principal focus of the World Jewish Congress understandably was on the annihilation of European Jewry, and, where feasible, rescue efforts however minimal in nature. The immediate post-war years saw the focus shift to providing political and other assistance to Holocaust survivors in the displaced persons (DP) camps of Germany, Austria, and Italy; the creation of the United Nations as successor to the League of Nations; and intensive efforts to establish a Jewish state in what was then Palestine. Very shortly thereafter, the future of North African Jewry received a prominent place on the WJC's agenda.

Gerhart M. Riegner, then head of the WJC's Geneva office and later the organization's secretary-general, recalled that

> [a]fter the loss of six million Jews, we began to rediscover some of the surviving communities, especially those throughout the Maghreb; these constituted a population of more than a half-million persons. This redis-covery led the WJC to undertake a series of political actions designed to

Isabella Nespoli is the archivist of the World Jewish Congress.
Menachem Z. Rosensaft is general counsel of the World Jewish Congress.

protect the large Jewish communities in Morocco, Tunisia, and Algeria. In the face of the profound political transformation that was under way, but which all parties were far from anticipating, the WJC was resolved to follow political developments closely and assist those communities to meet the difficulties they would face. With this objective in mind, in 1949 we created the WJC North African bureau in Algiers under the competent direction of Jacques Lazarus.[1]

Pre-1948

Although the best known efforts of the WJC in North Africa occurred after the establishment of the State of Israel, the organization in fact had a connection to the region since its inception. Delegates from Algeria, Egypt, Libya, Morocco, and Tunisia took part in the WJC's founding plenary assembly in Geneva in August of 1936.[2] During the war, the WJC intervened several times on behalf of the North African Jewish communities. In August 1943, for example, after British troops had liberated parts of Italian-occupied Libya, the WJC held talks with the British military officials to rescind the racial laws that had been imposed by the Italian dictator Benito Mussolini.[3]

The WJC also worked to reinstate the Crémieux Decree of 1870, which had granted French citizenship to Jews in Algeria, and which had been abolished in 1940 by the collaborationist Vichy Government. Following the November 1942 Allied landing in Algeria, General Henri Giraud, the high commissioner of North Africa, confirmed the abrogation of the Crémieux Decree, arguing in a speech of March 14, 1943, that it was discriminatory in that it differentiated between Jews and Moslems in Algeria. Outraged, the WJC joined a delegation of the French Jewish Representative Committee in presenting a memorandum on the issue to US Undersecretary of State Sumner Welles on May 20, 1943, in which the abrogation of the Crémieux Decree was denounced as "the most unjust racial discrimination ever inflicted upon the French citizens of Jewish faith who are natives of Algeria," and "a violation of the sacred rights of the human personality, and the legal principles respected by all civilized nations, as well as the organic Laws of the French Republic."[4]

In September 1943, Rabbi Stephen S. Wise, the chairman of the WJC

Executive Committee, received a personal letter from General Charles de Gaulle, assuring Wise that "in the war for human rights . . . we shall continue . . . to make it possible for all men to participate in the benefits of that victory." De Gaulle and the WJC had had a positive relationship ever since Rabbi Maurice Perlzweig, the chairman of the British Section of the WJC, had recognized the general as the leader of the Free French in 1940.[5] It is unclear whether de Gaulle in fact interceded with Giraud, but on October 21, 1943, the WJC's British Section was advised by the Free French that the Crémieux Decree had been reinstated, restoring to the Jews of North Africa "their status as French citizens."[6] Two days later, the French Jewish Representative Committee adopted a resolution stating that "the guidance, authority, solidarity, and devotion of the WJC Executive Committee were instrumental in the success achieved."[7]

In November 1944, delegates from Algeria, Tunisia, and Morocco took part in the WJC War Emergency Conference held in Atlantic City, New Jersey.[8] Over the next twenty years, the WJC would expend much effort on behalf of Jews in the three countries. WJC President Nahum Goldmann wrote:

> [O]ur most important—and less known—activities were undoubtedly our contacts with the liberation and independence movements of the new North African states, especially with Algeria and Morocco. In the days of French dominion there were more than a hundred thousand Jews in Algeria and more than two hundred thousand in Morocco, most of them very Gallicized. . . . The WJC had the foresight to realize in time that the process toward independence was irresistible. That being so, it was not hard to imagine some sort of retaliation against the Jews, with persecution perhaps going so far as pogroms. We therefore had to get in touch with the leaders of the independence movements, which required all the more discretion and secrecy because official French Jewry would have made violent protests. We took the precaution of confidentially informing the French government about the step we had taken, and I must say that we found them very sympathetic.[9]

In June of 1952, the WJC convened its first North African Jewish Congress. This was at a time when decolonization was an ever increasingly popular political ideology and the nationalist movements in Morocco, Tunisia, and Algeria were on the rise. The principal question the WJC wanted to highlight was how the overall political situation there would affect the Jewish communities. "Our task," wrote Riegner, "was . . . to make the Jewish communities, beginning with their leaders, familiar with the idea of not considering the status quo as fixed and immutable."[10] The WJC's policy was clear. In Riegner's words, "either the Jewish populations should leave, or they should negotiate with the revolutionary movements in sufficient time that they could reach an understanding in order to preclude attacks."[11]

In 1954, Goldmann met with French Prime Minister Pierre Mendès-France, who assured the WJC president that his government would take the situation and rights of Jews, as well as other minorities into account in its negotiations regarding the future of North Africa. On the other hand, as Goldmann acknowledged, he personally "had very little to do" with the WJC's contacts with the North African nationalist leaders.[12] These were undertaken by Alexander Easterman, the WJC's director of international affairs in London, and Joseph (Joe) Golan, described by Goldmann as "an Israeli WJC official" and in effect a key advisor to Goldmann on North African issues.[13]

For purposes of this chapter, it is clearer to describe the WJC's activities on a country-by-country rather than a chronological basis.

Morocco

Initially, the French authorities in Morocco were opposed to allowing Jews—especially young Jewish men of military age—from traveling to Israel. Postwar aliyah (immigration to Israel) from Morocco, therefore, mostly took place within an illegal smuggling framework. Even those lucky enough to obtain legitimate documents often had to acquire them through illegitimate means, such as bribing medical professionals to lie to French authorities.[14] In contrast, aliyah from Spanish Morocco was "often tolerated by the authorities," according to a 1951 report by Dr. I. Schwarzbart, head of the WJC's Organizational Department in New York.[15] The first destination for those engaged in illegal aliyah was Algeria, where they would then depart for France and then to Israel, since the French authorities in Algeria generally allowed Jews to leave.[16]

The situation in Morocco began to change in December 1948, when, according to historian Michael M. Laskier, "the French were beginning to sense a decline in Muslim opposition to *aliya*," likely due to the evident victory of Israeli forces in the war there; with the Jewish state being an established fact, opposition to emigration (i.e., the Jews leaving) among the local Muslim population fell.[17] At the same time, the French authorities were forced to acknowledge that they could not put a stop to the illegal aliyah. They were ready, and perhaps even eager for some sort of compromise. That same month, Marc Jarblum, a member of the WJC Executive based in Paris, travelled to Morocco "to discuss with French authorities the prohibition on Jews leaving Morocco, and to investigate the situation of Moroccan Jewry." While in Morocco, Jarblum met with Alphonse Juin, French Resident-General in Morocco. Although Juin remained generally opposed to Jewish emigration, citing the usual reason of local opposition to Jews leaving the country to fight Muslims in Palestine, he conceded that the authorities might eventually have to allow a legal pathway for the many Jews seeking to leave. Juin's comments indicated that the Residency was open to compromise, but this meeting with Jarblum did not produce it.[18]

However, it was becoming clear that the prohibition was unviable; even Francis Lacoste, a Residency official with whom Jarblum had met during his trip, and who had been implacably opposed to aliyah only a year or so earlier, was now open to allowing some emigration. In a letter to French Foreign Minister Robert Schuman, dated June 1949, Lacoste said: "It would not be just to prevent young and healthy Moroccan Jews from emigrating and to confine them to profound social and economic misery. . . . The only future they would have for improving their lot would be in Israel, which we are going to recognize as having the right to become a member of the family of nations."[19] In mid-1949, the French authorities began to regularly issue exit visas to Moroccan Jews (albeit, with quotas and restrictions) and allowed for the creation of Cadima, a group founded by Jacques Gershuni that would assist Jews in making aliyah.[20] In 1949, the WJC established a section in Morocco, with its central committee based in Casablanca. This section answered to Jacques Lazarus, who ran the WJC's North Africa office in Algiers.

While the WJC was supportive of aliyah, it was unwilling to allow the situation for Jews remaining in Morocco to deteriorate. Indeed, given the young State of Israel's difficulty in absorbing the deluge of refugees from Europe and the Arab world, creating a safe environment for Jews in the Diaspora remained a high priority for the organization. Despite some episodes of violence (including riots) between 1949 and 1953—in 1953 the WJC's Moroccan Section, in Laskier's words, "thought it prudent to encourage *aliya* by quality rather than in quantity"[21]—Jews lived relatively peacefully in Morocco.

Independence was already on the minds of Moroccans, as it was in many of the countries still governed by European powers in the post-war period. Recognizing that French rule would not last, Easterman and Golan established contacts with Moroccan nationalists, including with the progressive wing of the Istiqlal party led by Mehdi Ben Barka, who, according to Laskier, held the WJC in high regard.[22] Indeed, in a 1952 meeting, Goldmann successfully convinced several Moroccan Zionist activists to support the independence movement in Morocco.[23] As independence approached, and violence against Jews increased, the WJC continued to tread carefully on the issue of aliyah. It now recognized that while a number of Jews might prefer to stay in Morocco, options were needed for those who wished to emigrate. In 1955, following the advice of Easterman, who had a more pessimistic outlook than Goldmann, the WJC in Morocco, in tandem with the local Zionist organization, "called for an *aliya* of at least 5,000 persons per month"—more than double what the Jewish Agency had allotted for the country. Despite the efforts of Goldmann and Meir Toledano, a Moroccan Jewish leader affiliated with the WJC, to bolster Jewish support for independence, Moroccan Jews remained skeptical and did not hide their pro-French sympathies.[24]

The ascendant pro-aliyah camp did meet some internal resistance, particularly from Toledano, who continued to publicly express support for Jewish assimilation in Morocco and sought to influence French policy in the direction of granting independence.[25] The WJC tried to balance support for aliyah on the one hand, and securing the rights of Jews in Morocco on the other. Jacques Lazarus, the director of the WJC's North African office based in Algiers, spoke out in favor of aliyah but stressed at the same time that aliyah was not the preference of Moroccan Jews of wealth, even modest wealth, and status.[26]

Easterman, arguably the strongest supporter of aliyah within the WJC, was a moderate in comparison to some, including a few Jewish Agency officials, who insisted that Moroccan Jews were facing an immediate existential crisis. Easterman believed that the interests of aliyah were best served by a slow approach that showed deference to post-independence Moroccan leaders.[27] At the same time, the WJC made efforts to cooperate with the emerging political leadership in Morocco. This reasoning was influenced by meetings the WJC leadership had with Moroccan nationalists between 1954 and 1955, prior to independence. These meetings in turn had been facilitated by the personal relationships that Golan had developed with these Moroccan leaders.

One of the relationships cultivated by the WJC was with Mbarek Bekkay, who would become Morocco's first prime minister following independence. In February 1955, he met with Easterman, Riegner, and Perlzweig, then the WJC's director of International Affairs in New York, and Armand Kaplan, the secretary-general of the WJC's French Section. In addition to Bekkay, the leaders of the Istiqlal party and the Democratic Independence Party (PDI) also attended. It was here that the Moroccan nationalists pledged not to harm Jews and even went as far as committing to naming a Jewish cabinet member in the new government.[28] Riegner later held a follow-up meeting with the PDI's leader, Mohammed Hassan Ouazzani, in Geneva.[29]

Lazarus was more skeptical of the nationalist leaders, whom he feared would buckle under Arab League pressure after independence, and emphasized that the French still had a role to play when it came to the protection of Jews. In October 1955, Easterman, Lazarus, Golan, and Riegner visited Morocco again and attempted to persuade local Jewish officials to adopt a more positive attitude toward the independence movement. However, unlike Goldmann's meeting with the Moroccan Zionists in 1952, this effort did not prove successful.[30] But the situation for Jews did not dramatically change for the worse as a result. In fact, Sultan Muhammad V—who had helped save Jews during Vichy rule—told the WJC delegation that,

"I have always seen my Jewish subjects as completely free citizens, and as Moroccans who are completely equal to my Muslim subjects."[31]

Lazarus's caution proved prescient. Mindful of its relations with the Arab world, particularly Egypt, the new Moroccan government was opposed to aliyah on the grounds, among others, that emigrants would join the Israeli armed forces,[32] and that mass emigration could be damaging to the young state.[33] In May 1956, several Cadima (the aliyah-oriented group) leaders were told by government officials to slow down the aliyah process. As the hostility toward emigration increased, thousands of Jews found themselves stranded in Cadima's transit camp. At this point, the relationships that the WJC had developed over the years proved to be productive. In 1956, Israel's Prime Minister, David Ben-Gurion, enlisted Goldmann and the WJC to try to negotiate with the king and government officials on resolving the crisis.[34]

In May 1956, Easterman began a five-month-long trip to Morocco, and met with Leon Benzaquen, the Jewish minister in charge of the postal service. Easterman expressed his disappointment that the nationalists had misled him on their willingness to permit aliyah. When Benzaquen presented the economic and political concerns of the government, Easterman replied that middle class Moroccan Jews were not the ones considering emigration, at least not at this point, and restricting their rights to emigrate would damage Morocco internationally. A split in the Moroccan government led to the next hurdle. While most of its members opposed aliyah, Prime Minister Bekkay was inclined to allow those in the transit camp to leave for Israel. When Easterman was unable to obtain a meeting with Bekkay, Golan was brought into the process. Golan met with Mohammed Laghzaoui, one of Morocco's top security officials, whom he had helped obtain connections at the United Nations during the independence struggle. Laghzaoui strongly opposed Jewish emigration and considered Cadima's activities as nothing less than subversive, although he readily acknowledged this was a reversal of previous commitments.

Easterman, perhaps fearing talks would permanently break down, contacted the Moroccan Interior Minister in hopes he could break the logjam. After listening to Laghzaoui's long list of allegations against Cadima, the Interior Minister put forward the following compromise: for three months, Cadima would be allowed to function and process visas pursuant to the previous rules, after which Cadima would close and large-scale aliyah would end. Golan and Laghzaoui then continued to meet to work out the details, and reached several understandings. First, camp residents with legal visas would be allowed to leave for Israel "in an orderly fashion." Second, those emigrating would have to leave at night so as not to draw attention to themselves. Finally, the camp's closure would also mean the end of the recognition of so-called French "collective exit visas."[35] The next day, the government reneged and asked that the Cadima camp be shut down and the exit visas cancelled.[36] Goldmann responded forcefully to the government's reversal. "The Jewish people," he said, "will never renounce its right to emigrate to Israel or elsewhere and will insist in Morocco as in other countries, on full respect for this fundamental human right."[37]

Easterman and Golan once again were tasked with trying to resolve the crisis. It turned out that Laghzaoui was the main obstacle. In the end, the Moroccan cabinet voted to approve a plan allowing "the evacuation in small groups of two hundred to three hundred people at a time."[38] Laghzaoui then added one final condition: the repayment of debts of the emigrants had to be guaranteed. The WJC agreed to cover such debts and the plan proceeded.[39] WJC involvement in Morocco continued over the next few years at a modest pace. As Riegner would later recall:

> On balance, our Moroccan policy was quite satisfactory. The evidence of mass emigration without profound upheaval, without any apparent friction . . . and without victims constituted an unquestionable success. The understanding, even friendly, attitude and flexibility of the sultan and Moroccan authorities toward the Jews, often displayed with regard to Israel, were important milestones in our political activity. The small remaining Moroccan Jewish community has for many years taken part in the deliberations of the WJC.[40]

TUNISIA

The WJC, along with several other organizations, had been assisting the Jewish community in Tunisia since the end of World War II.[41] According to Riegner, the WJC had extremely positive relations with Tunisia in large part as a result of a meeting Easterman had in August 1954 with the Tunisian nationalist leader and future head of state Habib Bourguiba in the Ferté-Montargis fortress, where Bourguiba was interned. In the course of this meeting, Bourguiba reportedly assured Easterman that Tunisian Jews would enjoy "equality of all civic and political rights including the right to emigrate to Israel" in a future independent Tunisian state.[42]

At the same time, many Tunisian Jews were concerned by the rise of the nationalists and the corresponding likelihood that French sovereignty was likely to come to an end. This subject was debated by the delegates to the first North African WJC conference in Algiers, June 7–10, 1952. According to Laskier, Maître Charles Haddad, the president of the Jewish community of Tunis, said that while he considered the French presence to be essential, he, together with most Tunisian Jews, were reluctant to publicize this view. In contrast, Mathieo Ganem, another Tunisian delegate at the conference, considered Jewish emigration from Tunisia, encouraged by the WJC, to be inevitable.[43]

On the other hand, the WJC looked at the appointment of Tunisian Jewish lawyer Albert Bessis, whom Riegner knew well, to Tunisia's negotiating team with France as an opportunity to protect the rights of Tunisian Jews. Riegner provided Bessis with numerous documents on the protection of human rights. The WJC also submitted to the French minister for Tunisian and Moroccan affairs a memorandum containing suggestions for insertions into the Franco-Tunisian convention that would be advantageous to the Tunisian Jewish community. The result was a success, with the drafters of the convention adopting the WJC's recommendation, including a clause that guaranteed all residents of Tunisia "the rights and guarantees of the individual as set out in the Universal Declaration of Human Rights."[44]

In July 1958 after a four-day visit to Tunisia, Perlzweig told *The New York Times* that the Jews of that country, numbering between 60,000 and 70,000, were "in no way being discriminated against and the Government is sincere in its efforts to give the Jews an even break."[45] In the same vein, Riegner observed that, "All the promises of President Bourguiba and the texts of the convention were scrupulously respected. The friendly relations between President Bourguiba and the World Jewish Congress continued for years in mutual confidence and amity."[46]

ALGERIA

Algeria of the 1950s was perhaps the toughest case for the WJC. As was the case in Morocco and Tunisia, the local Jewish communities had a long-standing relationship with France and favored continued French rule. In Algeria, however, the stark differences between the Jewish community and the majority Arab population were amplified. According to Riegner, "The Arabs did not hide their resentment in the face of a situation they judged to be unjust and a status they envied."[47] Once again, the WJC wanted to prepare for the triumph of nationalist forces over European powers. However, this time the prospects for success in convincing nationalist forces—mainly the National Liberation Front (FLN)—to be inclusive of Jews post-independence were less than certain. Although the FLN often did explicitly instruct Algerians not to target Jews, this did not always translate into policy on the ground, with Jews in the city of Constantine being driven out by violence.[48] Therefore, emigration was an option likely to be seriously considered by Jews in Algeria in the event of French rule ending. When it came to aliyah to Israel, the WJC and others trying to warn Jews of coming events in Algeria were also sensitive to the concerns of a French government still committed to Algeria.

In July 1958, the Algerian Jewish Symposium was held at the WJC offices in Algiers. It was a critical moment for Algeria. Although the Franco-Algerian War was already underway, the organizers dedicated several sessions to youth and cultural issues as well as topics such as community activities, Zionism, and social order. The main issue facing the Algerian Jewish community was the lack of positive social change at a time when the war had deprived many young people of hope, particularly in the remote areas of the country.

Lazarus, the director of the WJC office in Algiers, was tasked with organizing the symposium in recognition of the important role that the WJC played in Algeria. The gathering was the first and the last of its kind; four years later, the doors of the WJC Algiers office were shuttered. By the time of the 1958 meeting it was evident that there was a growing schism between the Jewish community and the wider Algerian society, and it was increasingly clear that a Jewish community that had once been an integral part of Arab society would soon be all but extinct. The Jewish community was perceived as strange and foreign. A year earlier, Lazarus had written to Nehemiah Robinson, the director of the WJC's Institute of Jewish Affairs, that, "in addition to ethnic and religious [prejudices] can be added a nationalist prejudice based in race, meaning that increasingly Arabs buy from Arabs and go to Arab doctors and lawyers, even if, in certain cases, the services offered by Jews proves [*sic*] more advantageous."[49]

However, the closure of the Algiers office certainly did not mean the WJC had abandoned the Algerian Jewish community. In 1961, Golan met with the FLN's Karim Belkacem in Tunisia, who told Golan in no uncertain terms that he could not protect the rights and safety of Algeria's Jews, and even suggested they leave the country. Golan did not disagree, believing emigration to be inevitable. However, he also believed that Algerian Jewry should be warned about the dangers of remaining in Algeria. Golan's meeting with Belkacem put him on a collision course with Israeli Foreign Minister Golda Meir who was furious with Golan for meeting with the enemy of a close ally in an Arab country. Afraid of angering France, Meir insisted that Golan refrain from communicating Belkacem's advice to the Jews in Algeria. Meir believed that French protection would ultimately be sufficient for Jews in the country. Golan disagreed strongly and defied Meir's request and soon found that he could not renew his Israeli passport. Golan, however, was not contrite. Writing in his journal, he observed: "Had I obeyed Golda's instructions, hundreds of Algerian Jews, maybe even thousands, would have been murdered."[50]

That same year, Goldmann, Easterman, and Kaplan also met with FLN officials and tried to enlist the help of Tunisia's Habib Bourguiba, Jr.[51] Although it is unclear whether these meetings resulted in significant changes, the meetings are further evidence of the WJC's independent policy. It sought a different path than the Government of Israel and was in direct communications with the Algerian nationalist movement. While the WJC's limited contact with the FLN did not result in preserving the Jewish community in Algeria, its relationship with the nationalists did allow it to see the situation more clearly and determine early on that the Jewish community would not remain safe following a French departure. As Goldmann concluded:

> The WJC was the one organization that took a grip on the problem, because all the rest were openly pro-French. Not that we ourselves were anti-French, but we were certain that the independence movements would win the battle in the long run. . . . Our approaches probably saved tens of thousands of Jews: there were no pogroms, and in fact I believe that not a single Jew was killed after independence.[52]

Conclusion

The WJC's activities in North Africa were not the only WJC initiatives with respect to the persecution and oppression suffered by Jews in Arab countries. WJC leaders regularly met with political leaders in Arab countries in an effort to safeguard the interests of the surviving Jewish communities there. The WJC also took on the task of reminding the international community of its responsibilities toward these communities, highlighting at the United Nations and elsewhere the discrimination and worse to which they were being subjected, As early as January 19, 1948—four months before the establishment of the State of Israel—the WJC submitted a memorandum to the UN Economic and Social Council (ECOSOC) calling for "immediate and urgent" consideration of the discrimination and persecution to which Jews and Jewish communities were being subjected in Arab and Muslim countries.[53] In February 1950, to cite just one other example, Dr. Robert S. Marcus, the WJC's political director, advised ECOSOC that there had been "further deterioration in the position of Iraqi Jewry" since ECOSOC had adopted a resolution calling for the protection of minorities the previous year.[54] And in 1951, the WJC's Institute of Jewish Affairs provided a comprehensive overview of the conditions of Jews in the Middle East with the publication of an authoritative study, *The Arab Countries of the Near East and Their Jewish Communities* by Nehemiah Robinson.[55]

The WJC never stopped campaigning to ensure the rights of Jews who had fled or been expelled from Arab countries. In September 2012, at an event held at UN headquarters in New York co-sponsored by the WJC, the Israeli Mission to the UN, and the Conference of Presidents of Major American Jewish Organizations, WJC President Ronald S. Lauder declared:

> Now is the time to set the historical, diplomatic, and legal record straight. Lasting peace can only be built on historical facts—both the issues of the Jewish refugees and the Palestinian refugees must be addressed. Only addressing the historical facts can help bring about peace.[56]

The suffering endured by the Jewish communities and by individual Jews in Arab and Muslim countries lies at the heart of the WJC's mission. In this context, the critical political assistance provided by the WJC to the Jews of North Africa constitutes a page of honor in the organization's history. As Riegner wrote, "The WJC was the only Jewish organization that foresaw the unfolding of potentially destructive political events in this region. We had no choice but to draw the appropriate dire conclusions."[57]

The authors gratefully acknowledge the assistance provided by Abraham Silberstein, an intern at the WJC in the summer of 2016, in the preparation of this article.

Bourguiba's Jewish Friend

S. J. Goldsmith

Speaking at a press conference in Tel Aviv and dealing with the contribution of the World Jewish Congress to contemporary Jewish life and Jewish politics, Dr. Nahum Goldmann made a pointed reference to the personal friendship of two vastly different types of men—Habib Bourguiba, president of Tunisia, and Alex L. Easterman, the international affairs director of the World Jewish Congress. And so the silence was broken.

In the prevailing circumstances, the story of this connection is as remarkable as it is unique. On the personal level, the friendship between Bourguiba and Easterman remained intact through all the vicissitudes of the last decade. It is even more remarkable if we consider the totally opposite temperaments and backgrounds of the two men. One is the leader of a North African people in a successful struggle for independence against a great power—mercurial, tempestuous, given to explosions of temper, single-minded, impatient but realistic, and on the ball all the time; the idol of the masses and the redeemer. The other, a son of a Lithuanian Jew, born in Scotland, with the analytical mind of the Litvak and the reflective habits of a son of the Scottish soil, a cautious, perhaps over-cautious, foreign

---

S. J. Goldsmith was European Editor of the Jewish Telegraphic Agency (JTA) from 1958 until 1975.

correspondent and editor turned politician, a man given to puff twice at his pipe before committing himself once on any subject, sometimes brooding but always clearheaded. How could these two extremes get along even without a clash of interests? But they took to each other when they first met. What they do have in common is a sense of humor.

The story must be traced back to the forties and early fifties, when Tunisia was clamoring for independence, and there was no apparent prospect of her attaining it in the foreseeable future. Easterman and a few of his intimate friends had the imagination and perception to assume that, however bleak it might look for the Tunisians, their independence could not be long delayed, that France would be bound to give way without a colonial war, and that Bourguiba, the virulent leader of the Neo Destour, would be the ruler of the free nation and a free country within a short time.

The foresight proved to be correct. Having made this assumption, Easterman and his friends acted accordingly, whenever the opportunity arose, and sought contacts with the dramatic personae in the North African drama. The Tunisians, and other North Africans for that matter, were quick to notice it. People fighting for their freedom against odds never despise allies.

Easterman went to see Bourguiba for the first time in 1954. They met in very dramatic circumstances. Bourguiba was under detention in the French countryside. But France being a civilized country, certain people did get permission to visit him, and Alex Easterman was one of those. The place of Bourguiba's detention was under strong military guard; but once inside, the two men were free to talk and talk. They discussed many things, including the Jewish position and Israel and the Jews of Tunisia and their fate in the event of Tunisia's independence. It was a frank and uninhibited exchange of views. This was less than two years before Suez, when the Israel-Arab conflict was at its height.

As to Tunisian Jews, Bourguiba said at the time that they would be treated as equal citizens of the country. He has rigidly and meticulously kept this pledge. Tunisian Jews enjoy full citizenship rights, and the authorities do not interfere with their religious life or their communal institutions. Any Jew who wants to leave the country can do so, on the same terms as other citizens.

During the dramatic meeting between Bourguiba and Easterman,

Bourguiba expressed substantially the same views on Israel which he propounded this spring in his now famous speeches, radio and television appearances, and press interviews. He was not in favor of a Jewish State and would in principle have opposed it. But it was there and had come to stay, so there was no alternative but to accept its existence. Here was the realist talking.

Bourguiba's clash with Nasser is not only based on their different attitudes to Israel. Bourguiba never accepted Nasser as leader of all Moslems, from Dakar to Karachi. He also refuses to accept the notion that North African Moslems and the Arabs of Egypt, Arabia, and the Levant are the same nation, divided only by geography.

Bourguiba's constant efforts to assert the independence of North Africa from Nasser received a new impetus after the last elections in Tunisia, in November 1964. Bourguiba was given a vote of confidence by 96.43 percent of the electorate, to be exact. He is now the unchallenged leader of his people. As soon as he quarreled with Nasser over Israel, the students came out in his support. No one is glad to see buildings burned down anywhere, but the demonstrations were spontaneous and the support for Bourguiba whole-hearted.

Bourguiba, with his education, experience, political knowhow, and flare for leadership and dramatic action, has a big part still to play in the shaping of his vast region.

This article must not be taken as a plea to consider Bourguiba's proposals regarding Israel. What Bourguiba suggests is utterly unacceptable to any Jew. But Habib Bourguiba has broken the front of implacable Arab hostility to Israel, and has accepted the fact that Israel is there for good. The Arab world is now astir. It will never be the same again after Bourguiba has spoken.

Distributed by JTA and published in *The Canadian Jewish Chronicle*, May 28, 1965. Republished by permission of Professor Tessa Rajak.

Soviet Jewry: Debates and Controversies

Suzanne D. Rutland

Nahum Goldmann's Strategy

One of the major issues facing world Jewry from 1948 until 1988 was the plight of the Jews in the former Soviet Union (USSR). In May 1967, a resolution of the World Conference of Jewish Organizations (COJO), a worldwide body created by Dr. Nahum Goldmann in 1958, stressed that "the survival of the Jewish people in the USSR has become the greatest and most critical problem of world Jewry in the Diaspora and calls for the utmost efforts being made for their salvation as Jews."[1] During this period, there was strong conflict over the best tactics to follow in the campaign. Goldmann, the president of the World Jewish Congress, believed in a policy of accommodation, but other Jewish leaders, especially from the student movement, opposed this approach and advocated a policy of protest. By 1968, the actions of Soviet Jewish activists themselves had made it clear that they considered the better approach to be worldwide protest to focus attention on the plight of the Jews under Communist rule.

Following the death of Joseph Stalin in March 1953, Goldmann campaigned to improve the position of Soviet Jewry. At the third plenary

Suzanne D. Rutland is Professor Emerita at the University of Sydney.

assembly of the World Jewish Congress, held in August 1953 in Geneva, Goldmann stressed that while the Jews of the Soviet Union did not face physical death, they were facing spiritual annihilation.[2] Throughout the 1950s, he continued to raise concerns about the position of Soviet Jews and highlight the difficulties faced by the Jews of Poland and Romania.

The position Goldmann took was a policy of accommodation. He was consistent in his assertions that there was no official policy of anti-Semitism in the Soviet Union and that Jews enjoyed full civil rights.[3] He also stressed that the campaign to improve the position of Soviet Jews had to be kept completely separate from the Cold War. He believed that efforts should be made to create a representative body through the federation of syna-gogues in the USSR and that Yiddish publications and cultural life should be resumed. He was keen to ensure that a delegation of Soviet Jews would again be present at meetings of the WJC, and at the Geneva WJC Assembly of August 1953, he expressed regret that the Jews of Eastern Europe were "sealed off from the rest of the Jewish people" despite the efforts of the WJC. He believed that "[t]his division must be regarded as a great mis-fortune. The unity of the Jewish people is the basic condition for Jewish survival."[4] Goldmann consistently worked to create links between the WJC and Soviet Jews.

Goldmann was concerned that a policy of protest would have negative repercussions for Soviet Jewry. He believed that the correct approach was quiet diplomacy and he feared that public criticism of the Soviet Union would undermine any chance of success. He remained firm in this position from 1953 until 1968 when he was overtaken by events.

In 1952–1953, in response to growing evidence of Soviet anti-Semitism, the Israeli Ministry for Foreign Affairs created an unofficial, secret com-mittee to assist Soviet Jews. Initially known as the "Office with No Name" it became known as Lishkat Hakesher (Liaison Bureau). Its aims were to sup-port Soviet Jews against Stalin's heightened anti-Semitism and to encour-age emigration to Israel. Spearheaded by Shaul Avigur and Dr. Binyamin Eliav, it recruited a small group to create awareness of the situation in the West. This group included, for the French branch of the operation, Meir Rosenne (Rosenhaupt), who was originally from Romania and had com-pleted his doctorate in law in Paris in 1957; the well-known author Emanuel

Litvinoff in London; and Moshe Decter, who established an office called Jewish Minorities Research in New York.[5] In 1958, Avigur also involved Isi Leibler, a young Australian Jewish leader from Melbourne.

It was decided that Israel's direct involvement should be kept secret because of the strong pro-Soviet feelings of many left-wing Jews in Israel and the Diaspora, as well as the sense that Israel was experiencing enough problems in the United Nations because of the Arab-Israeli conflict and should not further alienate the USSR leadership. Goldmann was approached and agreed to become a member of this secret committee and also allowed Rosenne to work out of the WJC offices in Paris.

Goldmann's approach was to try to work through prominent left-wing personalities, such as former French Prime Minister Pierre Mendès-France and Soviet ambassadors, to gain entry to the corridors of power in the USSR. In 1956, he also tried to organize a meeting with Yugoslav leader General Tito to discuss Arab-Israeli relations and Soviet Jewry, but this did not eventuate.[6]

With the Suez crisis of 1956–1957, the position of Soviet Jews deteriorated. At the WJC Executive meeting held in London in May 1957, Goldmann advocated a change of policy. He noted that since 1953, there had been a few minor improvements, such as the publication of the first Hebrew prayer book since 1917, the establishment of a "so-called yeshiva," the arrival of a few rabbinical delegations, and the holding of a few Yiddish concerts. However, unlike in other Communist countries such as Poland and Romania, emigration from the Soviet Union had not been permitted. Goldmann presented the Communist explanations for the lack of Jewish life: the fact that Jews were not concentrated geographically and that most Russian Jews were assimilated and not interested in maintaining Judaism. However, he rejected these arguments and stressed that the younger generation had become more Jewish than their parents in response to Stalinist anti-Semitism. In his opening address he stated:

> We have become aware of this problem more and more in the last few
> years. We did not deal with it so much publicly as we hoped that it will
> be possible with the leaders of the Soviet Union to bring about some
> solution to the problem. . . . I think that the time has come when Jewish

organizations and certainly the World Jewish Congress, speaking for the many communities, should not hesitate any more to put the problem of Eastern European and especially Soviet Jewry before the world as maybe the major Jewish problem of today.[7]

Goldmann felt very concerned that after the loss of six million Jews during the Holocaust, a further three million Jews in the Soviet Union might be lost due to inaction on the part of world Jewry. In a press release issued after this meeting, the WJC pledged to "secure the survival of East European Jewry as a distinctive group . . . we shall neither rest nor relax until the Jewish communities of Eastern Europe have been brought back into the mainstream of Jewish life, and Israel has been made secure with the help of all Jews, including Soviet Jews."[8]

Despite Goldmann's cooperation with the Israelis, key WJC figures continued to advocate silent diplomacy and to oppose open protest by Jewish groups. He also continued to persist in trying to invite a delegation from the Soviet Union to WJC plenary meetings. In January 1959, Goldmann, together with US-based WJC Executive member Rabbi Maurice Perlzweig, visited the Soviet Embassy in Washington to see if representatives of Soviet Jewry could attend the WJC plenary assembly planned for August 1959 in Stockholm. In July 1959, the rabbis of both Moscow and Odessa sent negative replies to the WJC invitation, explaining that they could not participate in political activities and, since the WJC supported Israel, it was "Zionist-orientated." At the end of his letter, Rabbi Dimant of Odessa stated, "We regret that you attempt to draw us into the sphere of activities of your organization."[9]

In 1959 a series of arrests of Romanian Jews was carried out and an internal debate ensued as to how the WJC should react to this situation. In November 1959, Alex Easterman, Director of the WJC Department of International Affairs in London, arranged for a letter to be published in *The Times*, signed by leading non-Jewish personalities and criticizing the sentences handed down to the Romanian Jews.[10] Goldmann supported this move and wrote to Easterman that the letter was "an excellent piece of work" and that he was sure "it [would] make some impression on the Rumanians."[11]

In Paris, Rosenne was experiencing problems with Armand Kaplan, the secretary-general of the WJC's French Section, and at the end of 1959, he decided to move to the offices of the Jewish Telegraphic Agency (JTA). Tensions between Rosenne and the WJC personnel increased in early 1960. In March 1960, Khrushchev planned to visit Paris, and Rosenne decided to prepare a brochure and booklet on the situation of Soviet Jewry, to be published in the name of the French WJC branch just before Khrushchev was to arrive. Rosenne consulted closely with Goldmann about these two publications, but when they came out, Kaplan claimed that they had been published without WJC authorization.[12]

During the early 1960s, the situation of Soviet Jewry continued to deteriorate as a result of official, state-sponsored anti-Semitism. In 1960, matzah baking was prohibited in Kiev, Odessa, Kishinev, and Riga, and the supply of matzah continued to be a problem in subsequent years.[13] Synagogues continued to be closed and by 1960, there was not a single Jewish school still open. Anti-Semitism became more widespread, with anti-Semitic articles being published throughout the Soviet press.

In 1960, in the face of this growing persecution, Meir Rosenne, working closely with his friend and colleague Saul Friedlander, decided that an international conference should be convened in Paris with leading intellectuals, writers, artists, scientists, and above all "men of spiritual standing . . . to appeal to the Soviet leadership about the ominous situation of Jews in the Soviet Union."[14] Goldmann agreed that this conference could be held under his aegis, together with Daniel Mayer, President of the French League of Human Rights and former Socialist Labour Minister of France.

In early September, just before the conference was to start, Rosenne received a telegram from Nehemiah Levanon of the Israeli Ministry of Foreign Affairs. Levanon had replaced Binyamin Eliav in the Lishkat Hakesher, and he instructed Rosenne to stop all preparations for the conference. This was due to a telegram Goldmann had received from the USSR informing him that if the conference was held, Romania would stop all Jewish emigration to Israel. Rosenne believed that it would be an enormous mistake to cancel the conference at the last minute, and he flew to Geneva, where Goldmann was staying at the time, to try to persuade him to change his mind. After failing to ascertain the exact source of the information from the USSR, Rosenne sent a telegram stating that there was no proof of the Soviet request and that it would do more damage to cancel the conference. The following day, *Yedioth Ahronoth* announced that Ben-Gurion had insisted that the conference take place. The headline of the article was "Under pressure from Ben-Gurion, Goldmann decides to go on with the conference." This article was picked up throughout the Israeli and European media.[15]

On September 15, 1960 the conference took place with fifteen countries represented, spanning four continents including Africa. The array of participants was most impressive, and included key figures in the world of letters, art, science, and politics. Afterward, a statement was issued stressing the dispassionate nature and the lack of partisanship of the gathering. It further stated that after the destruction of six million European Jews—one third of the Jewish people—by the Nazis, the Soviet Jews, numbering some three million, were "the largest surviving Jewish community in the continent of Europe. Their wellbeing is surely therefore the joint responsibility of our civilization."[16] The statement pointed out that all aspects of Jewish cultural life had been repressed in the USSR and requested that the Soviet Jews be allowed the same rights as other minority groups in the Soviet Union.

Subsequently, Goldmann produced two "interim reports" for those who attended the Paris Conference, one in July 1961 and another in September 1963. These stressed the increasing problems facing Soviet Jews, especially in light of the death sentence introduced for economic crimes. In his 1961 report, he emphasized that:

> [t]he situation of Soviet Jewry has, for many years, been a "forbidden" subject. Breaking the wall of silence, beginning open discussions and exchanges of opinion can contribute a great deal towards fostering a rethinking, eventual improvement and positive solutions, of the situation.[17]

Goldmann also continued to work with Decter to enlist prominent figures to support the campaign for Soviet Jewry, such as Martin Luther King, Jr.[18] At the same time, Goldmann continued his efforts for quiet diplomacy and, as key historian of this period Yaakov Ro'i has written, he "never gave up hope that he would be invited to the USSR to discuss the lot of Soviet Jewry with the leadership of that country as the plenipotentiary of Western Jewry."[19] In 1964, Goldmann opposed the decision of the American Jewish Conference on Soviet Jewry (AJCSJ), which rejected the quiet diplomacy approach, to meet with President Lyndon Johnson and Secretary of State Dean Rusk. He wrote, "Demagogic speeches and exaggerated resolutions may do a lot of harm."[20]

In the meantime, the AJCSJ moved ahead in 1965 with its campaign of protest, holding two major events in early June 1965: a rally at Madison Square Garden on June 3, 1965 followed by a vigil in Washington on June 4. On June 10, in keeping with his opposition to open protest, Goldmann responded with a strong and controversial press statement featured on the front page of *The New York Times*. He criticized those who accused the Soviet regime of being anti-Semitic or of denying Jews their civil rights, and claimed that "accusations are being made against Russia which are not justified, and which can only delay the solution of the problem, and even harm Soviet Jewry."[21]

Some papers defended Goldmann. In a major editorial published in *The Times of London*, the following was written:

> Recently there have been loud protests in the west about the condition of Soviet Jews. . . . But if, as seems likely, Moscow's gesture is a response to foreign opinion it is more likely the product of some quiet talks that the World Jewish Congress has been having with the Russians. . . . If Soviet Jews want a position in Soviet society similar to that of the Orthodox Church, it does not help to constantly show them as the "ward" of American and other western organizations. A quiet, diplomatic approach to the Russians is more likely to be effective. Using this method, the World Jewish Congress has been trying to bring about the creation of a central body to represent Jews of the Soviet Union. . . . It has been said that religion is like a nail and the harder you hit it, the deeper it penetrates. The same may apply to Soviet antisemitism, which should certainly be hit—but the blows have to be carefully aimed.[22]

In October 1965, Rabbi Maurice Perlzweig, the WJC Director of International Affairs in New York, expressed his concerns about the negative effects of public demonstrations. At this time, a resolution was introduced at the United Nations condemning ideologies such as racism and fascism. An effort was made to include anti-Semitism, which led the Soviet Union to also add Zionism to the list. In the end, both anti-Semitism and Zionism were excluded, but Perlzweig expressed the fear to Goldmann that "this marks the opening gun in a Soviet campaign to reply to the use of the UN as a platform from which to attack the Soviets on the Jewish question."[23]

In 1966, the publication of Elie Wiesel's *The Jews of Silence* further highlighted the problems facing Soviet Jewry. Wiesel later told a Toronto audience, "I went to Russia drawn by the silence of its Jews and I brought back their cry. What torments me most is not the 'Jews of Silence' I met in Russia, but the silence of the Jews I live among today."[24] In response, Goldmann criticized public campaigns on the basis that the existence of three million Russian Jews could be endangered. Elie Wiesel replied: "How can we be sure that our complaints and protests will not have harmful results for them? . . . Only the Russian Jews themselves can answer that question and they do: 'Keep calling! Awaken public opinion.'"[25]

In February 1967, Alexei Kosygin visited London, and the community met to discuss the correct tactics. Key members of British Jewry were in favor of holding a public meeting of protest, a proposal that Easterman strongly opposed, and managed to prevent from happening by insisting on postponing discussion of the idea until it was too late. However, Jewish students organized a protest rally with around one thousand students marching to the Soviet embassy. The third secretary met a small delegation and invited them in. They presented him with a memorandum on Soviet Jewry. Easterman congratulated the students afterward on their success,[26] but when they asked if that meant "a 'new wind' [was blowing] regarding Soviet Jewry" in the WJC,[27] he insisted that in his opinion, they still needed to work "through political and diplomatic channels."[28]

Diaspora Opposition to Goldmann

One of the strongest critics of Goldmann's policy in the Diaspora was the young Australian Jewish leader Isi Leibler. In November 1962, Australia was the first country to raise the issue of Soviet Jewry and human rights at the

United Nations, as a result of the lobbying of Melbourne Jewish leaders Maurice Ashkanasy and Isi Leibler. Following his success in having the issue raised by Australia at the United Nations, Leibler worked assiduously at establishing contacts with members of the Communist Party of Australia (CPA), maintaining consistent contact through telephone conversations and meetings with key figures. He was able to persuade Rex Mortimer, Communist leader and editor of *Arena*, a Melbourne-based Communist newspaper, of the problems facing Soviet Jewry.

Given this Melbourne record of consistent campaigning and protest on behalf of Soviet Jewry, a clash with Goldmann over the issue of tactics was inevitable. Already in April 1965, Leibler wrote an extremely critical letter to Litvinoff about Goldmann, referring to "his public statements minimizing Soviet antisemitism." At the WJC Executive meeting held in early June 1965 in Geneva, a clash between Leibler and Dr. Goldmann was reported as follows:

> Leibler, whose published survey has attracted worldwide attention, thrustfully advocated a harder line in Jewish approaches to the Soviet Union in order to enlist support of non-conforming leftist circles. Dr. Goldmann, in turn, with a formidable display of forensic fireworks, insisted that his quiet diplomacy was the better course. In general, the consensus was that Dr. Goldmann had won on points but Mr Leibler's pugnacity and tenacity was admirably commented upon. The encouraging thing about the lively exchange was its implication that new voices are beginning to be heard and new ideas to emerge.[29]

Leibler then decided to attack Goldmann at the Strassbourg meeting held on July 13 and 14, 1965, when he claimed that "*shtadlonus* [intercession] and private diplomacy used since 1956 have been abysmal failures as actual conditions deteriorated," and that the only approach was "a militant campaign designed to mobilize public opinion."[30] Leibler concluded his address with the following words: "And let's not hear any talk about restraint. Principled, factual, well-documented approach, *yes*! But based on militant public campaigns, not on *shtadlonus* or silent diplomacy."[31] Goldmann's response was highly critical, and he accused his own critics of "extreme naivety and even stupidity," stressing his right to make decisions about tactics.[32] He also accused the activists of undermining any chance he had of coming to an understanding with Soviet authorities.

At the World Jewish Congress plenary session held in Brussels in August 1966, the debate over tactics in relation to Soviet Jewry continued, with Leibler again being highly critical of Goldmann's approach.[33] *The Jewish Chronicle* described the debate as follows:

> While delegates accepted Dr. Goldmann's warning to keep the issue of Soviet Jewry out of the cold war and avoid exaggerated accusations which cannot be substantiated, his cautious approach was challenged by some delegates.
>
> Dr. Goldmann said that while others liked to beat the drum, he himself preferred to play the flute.
>
> One of his most persistent critics on the Soviet issue, the Australian Mr I. Leibler, complained that the Congress President's role was not to play one instrument but to conduct the whole orchestra. To which Dr. Goldmann retorted: How can I be the conductor when I have no assurance that my baton would be followed?[34]

Following the Six-Day War and the defeat of the Arab armies, the Soviets intensified their attacks on Israel and Zionism. In response to these policies, Goldmann increased his level of criticism of government policy toward Soviet Jews. In October 1967, at the time of the fiftieth anniversay of the Bolshevik Revolution, he sent a message complimenting the Soviet Union on its achievements, but stressed that the promises made to the Jewish community in 1917 had not been fulfilled. Then, in January 1968, the WJC Governing Council again criticized the anti-Israel and anti-Zionist statements emanating from the Soviets, and appealed to the Soviet leaders to grant full equality to Jewry, on the basis of rights afforded to other religious and ethnic minorities. Similar statements were made at a conference of the Institute of Jewish Affairs in December 1969, with Goldmann reinforcing these concerns in a statement in March 1970:

> The current violent anti-Israel and anti-Zionist campaign organized by the Soviet authorities is the most convincing confirmation of the desire of a large number of the three million Jews in the Soviet Union. This

campaign has culminated in the use of Soviet Jews to deny the plight of their community and to denounce Israel.[35]

He appealed to the Soviets to allow freedom of movement for Soviet Jews, in accordance with the Universal Declaration of Human Rights. Later in 1970, the Institute of Jewish Affairs published a collection of essays by key scholars of the area, edited by Lionel Kochan,[36] and expanded its biannual journal dealing with Soviet and East European affairs to a higher quality one renamed *Soviet Jewish Affairs*.

The Leningrad Hijacking and Revision of Approach

On June 15, 1970, eighteen Russians, nine of whom were Jewish, were arrested at Leningrad's Smolny airport and accused of planning to hijack a small plane, which was scheduled for a domestic flight, and take it out of the country. At the same time, another eight Jews were arrested in Leningrad, Moscow, Riga, and Kharkov. Further arrests were made in July and August in the Kishinev and Riga areas. All the Jews arrested had applied to emigrate to Israel. The KGB seized letters from Israel, Hebrew textbooks, articles on Jewish history, tape recordings of Hebrew songs, and even a copy of Leon Uris's *Exodus*, as "evidence." These events led to heightened activity of Jews throughout the world.

The Leningrad trial, which lasted a week, began on December 16 and took place in camera. No member of the Western media was allowed in. The accused were prosecuted under "Article 64 of the Russian Federation's Criminal Code, which defines 'flight abroad or refusal to return to the USSR from abroad' as one of the treasonable offences which may be punishable by death."[37] When the trial began, Goldmann issued a very strong statement condemning the Soviet actions:

> The current trial of Soviet Jews in Leningrad must be regarded as the most disturbing development in the difficult situation of Jews in the USSR. Available information indicates the silencing of their ever more openly expressed affirmation of their Jewish identity and desire to emigrate to Israel.[38]

He again asked that Soviet Jews be permitted to emigrate freely to Israel if they so desired, and if they chose to remain, that they be offered "full opportunities for the enjoyment of Jewish cultural, religious, and communal life."[39]

All of the defendants were given prison sentences ranging from four to fifteen years, with two of them—Mark Dymshits and Edward Kuznetkov—receiving the death sentence. The Soviets claimed that they had all pleaded guilty. These harsh sentences were thought to be a warning to would-be hijackers, as well as an effort to prevent Jews from applying for the right to emigrate.

The severity of the sentences led to a worldwide outcry, with protests being made by key international leaders, Nobel prize winners, and US Members of Congress. The press also highlighted the injustice of the death sentences. Goldmann immediately sent a strongly worded cable to the chairman of the Soviet Presidium Nikolai Podgorny, Foreign Minister Andrei Gromyko, and the Soviet ambassadors in Washington and Paris, Anatoly Dobrynin and Valerian Zorin, respectively. He stressed that the sentences were "incredibly harsh and repugnant" and requested intervention to commute the death sentences and release all of the accused. He also cabled other international leaders, including Presidents Tito and Ceaucescu, Prime Mininster Indira Ghandi, and Federal Chancellor Brandt, as well as the Swedish Foreign Minister.

In response to international pressure, the Soviets reduced the death sentences for Dymshits and Kuznetkov to life imprisonment, which Goldmann welcomed. However, Goldmann initially opposed a proposal to hold an international conference of world Jewry to discuss the situation in the Soviet Union, which led to the first Brussels Presidium convened in February 1971. Goldmann believed that the Soviets would never permit significant emigration and that world Jewry should focus on campaigning for religious and cultural rights, rather than family reunion. Others, including the Jewish Agency, "advocated an all-out struggle for emigration."[40]

However, by the early 1970s, it was clear that the demands for emigration were meeting with a successful response and that the only way forward was to continue the policy of protest. In response to the new developments, including the Leningrad hijack trial, the WJC Governing

Council agreed to become a sponsor for the Brussels Presidium at its meeting in January 1971. Its delegation included Secretary-General Gerhart Riegner, Armand Kaplan, and other officers of the Governing Council, but Goldmann himself did not attend.

In March 1971 Goldmann cabled Leonid Brezhnev before the 24th Congress of the Communist Party of the Soviet Union (CPSU) requesting the party to adopt resolutions favorable to the Jewish community. The Governing Council continued to issue critical statements about Soviet policies, including a public cable sent to Brezhnev before his visit to Paris in October 1971. On the twentieth anniversary of the execution of twenty-four Jewish Soviet writers on August 12, 1952, Goldmann also issued a strong statement reiterating demands for freedom of emigration, the end of harassment of Jews who had applied to emigrate, and freedom of religious and cultural practices within the Soviet Union. At the same time, the WJC expressed its strong opposition to the radicalism and violent actions of the Jewish Defense League led by Rabbi Meir Kahane.

In November 1971, the idea of insisting on people who had tertiary education being taxed before their departure was raised by the Soviets, but it was not until August 3, 1972 that this concept was approved by the Supreme Soviet and implemented on August 14. Officially, the head tax was not discriminatory, since it applied to both Jews and non-Jews. In September 1972, specific restrictions for Soviet citizens wishing to emigrate to "fascist" countries such as Israel, South Africa, Spain, and Portugal were added. In reality, however, it only affected Jews, since non-Jews could leave the country on a tourist visa, and then apply for residency once outside the Soviet Union. Those applying to travel to one of the "fascist" countries, however, had to renounce their Soviet citizenship and pay 500 rubles for an exit visa and an additional 400 rubles for renouncing their citizenship.[41] This Soviet initiative to contain Soviet Jewish emigration again led to a world outcry. Goldmann issued a strong statement condemning the imposition of the "diploma tax" (also known as a "ransom tax"), describing it as "an unworthy blot on the [Soviets'] record [for] free education."[42] The WJC and its affiliates were also active protesting the tax at the UN Sub-Committee on the Prevention of Discrimination and Protection of Minorities.

The WJC Governing Council expressed further objections during the WJC British Section's Emergency Conference of Jewish Communities in September 1972, and again in November 1972 at its Paris meeting. In December 1972, Goldmann issued a plea for the Soviet Union to grant amnesty to the "Prisoners of Zion" who had been incarcerated simply because of their application to emigrate to Israel. In June 1973, the WJC World Executive expressed its satisfaction at the increasing numbers of Soviet Jews being granted permission to emigrate, and this was also noted in January 1974. However, when the Soviets reduced emigration in mid-1974, the leadership expressed its distress at its meeting that summer in Lausanne, Swizerland.

In addition, Goldmann continued to appeal for the restoration of full, equal rights to Soviet Jews. This policy led to great controversy. At the mid-year meeting of the WJC Executive in 1973, Dr. Ben-Zion Keshet, a Likud Member of Knesset, strongly criticized Goldmann's policy, stating that his actions were "contrary to the majority of the members of the WJC." Keshet also said that a request for more Jewish culture might lead to greater promotion of publications such as *Sovietish Heimland*, and other anti-Zionist and anti-Israel propaganda. Other Israeli speakers also referred to the intense Soviet hostility to Zionism and Israel, with Dr. Moshe Levran claiming that it would be "extremely naïve to hope for the revival of Jewish cultural life in the USSR."[43]

Thus, although Goldmann had recognized the need for public protest, he still continued to believe that the Soviets could be persuaded to change their domestic policies toward Soviet Jewry through private diplomacy and requests to the leadership. In its October 1974 report on Soviet Jewry for the period 1966–1974, the WJC expressed its hope that this internal change would occur. It also stated, "The World Jewish Congress will continue its efforts to obtain a breakthrough with regard to this important issue as well. It does not abandon hope that one day it will be able to welcome Soviet Jewry within the ranks and councils of world Jewry."[44] This hope was finally fulfilled in February 1989, with the opening of the Samuel Mikhoels Center in Moscow, the first official institution to promote Jewish culture in the Soviet Union, supported by the WJC and spearheaded by Isi Leibler, then a WJC vice president.[45]

Conclusion

In hindsight, it is easy to claim that the policy of quiet diplomacy was not going to succeed, as the Soviet Union did respond to open, public protest. However, Goldmann remained firm in his convictions and was not prepared to change his position. Indeed, as late as 1979, after he had resigned as WJC president, he was still writing that "public protest was 'dangerous and immoral' because it might put Russian Jews at risk rather than help them."[46]

Advancing the Best
in Jewish Culture

Philip M. Klutznick

Philip M. Klutznick (1907–1999) served as president of the WJC from 1977 to 1979 when he took a leave of absence after being appointed US Secretary of Commerce by President Jimmy Carter. The following are excerpts from his keynote address at the Diamond Jubilee Congress of the South African Jewish Board of Deputies in Johannesburg on May 27, 1978:

There is a rarely remembered exchange of correspondence between Dr. Albert Einstein and Dr. Sigmund Freud, which took place before Hitler's election victory and World War II. It provides the kernel of thought which I would like to apply against these crucial days. On July 30, 1932, Dr. Einstein asked Dr. Freud: "Is there any way of delivering mankind from the menace of war? Is it possible to control man's evolution so as to make him proof against the psychoses of hate and destructiveness?" While he posed these questions, he proposed "the setting up, by international consent, of a legislative judicial body to settle every conflict arising between nations."

Freud's response was delayed a few weeks and was several times the length of Einstein's letter. It was not an optimistic one. He did not accept the contention that

> in some happy corners of the earth, where nature brings forth abundantly whatever man desires, there flourishes races whose lives go gently by, unknowing of aggression or constraint. . . . The Bolsheviks, too, aspire to do away with human aggressiveness by ensuring the satisfaction of material needs and enforcing equality between man and man. To me, this

hope seems vain. Meanwhile, they perfect their armaments and their hatred of outsiders, [which] is not the least factor of cohesion amongst themselves.

How well do we know the verity of this conclusion; sixty years after the revolution, the Jew remains an outsider under anti-Semitic attack. Freud then commented on ideal utopian conditions which he believed then unattainable. He agreed with Einstein's view of a central establishment which could have the last word in any conflict of interest. But he foresaw the recent weaknesses of the United Nations when he added, "obviously such notions as these can only be significant when they are the expressions of a deeply rooted sense of unity shared by all." Then he added the following:

> The cultural development of mankind (some, I know, prefer to call it civilization) has been in progress since immemorial antiquity. To this process we owe all that is best in our composition, but also much that makes for human suffering. Its origins and causes are obscure, its issue is uncertain, but some of its characteristics are easy to perceive. . . . On the psychological side two of the most important phenomena of culture are, firstly, a strengthening of the intellect which tends to master our distinctive life, and, secondly, an introversion of the aggressive impulse, with all its consequent benefits and perils. Now war runs most emphatically counter to the psychic disposition imposed on us by the growth of culture; we are therefore bound to resent war, to find it utterly intolerable. With pacifists like us it is not merely an intellectual and affective repulsion, but a constitutional intolerance, an idiosyncrasy in its most drastic form.
>
> How long have we to wait before the rest of men turn pacifist? Impossible to say, and yet perhaps our hope that these two factors—man's cultural disposition and well-founded dread of the form that future wars will take—may serve to put an end to war in the near future, is not chimerical. But by what ways or by-ways this will come about, we cannot guess.

The cultural development of mankind still remains the single best answer to our search. Culture, as Freud meant it, was not just intelligence or intellectualism but something much more—the making of the whole man. As he states it so well, "not merely an intellectual and affective repulsion but a constitutional intolerance." This is a large order and none can guess any more than did Dr. Freud as to when that day can be reached. Nor can each of us or many of us, organized as you are or as the World Jewish Congress is, expect to tackle the encompassing challenges that surround this generation of man. But, as it is said, even if it be not our lot to complete the goal, it is our duty not to desist from the work.

The breath-taking pace of the last seventy-five years which brought both opportunity and peril leaves us not much removed from the content of the Einstein-Freud correspondence of over forty years ago. In recent weeks, Gore Vidal published his latest book *Kalki*. It is a fantasy in which an ordinary soldier from New Orleans assumes the role of the Hindu god reincarnated to bring about the end of the world. By use of his own discovery for biological warfare, he does destroy the world leaving five to rebuild it. But only he and one other can produce offspring and they fail. The loneliness of the few left and the thought that it would take two centuries to repopulate the world with but one million people are indeed fantasies. But the walls that grow up between only a few who roam the earth suggest that destruction and rebuilding is no less hazardous an enterprise than undertaking patiently to solve the problems we face now. Each of us, in our own way, can make contributions to problem-solving if we would first permit ourselves the time to try to understand the problem. A culture must be based on knowledge and understanding, not ignorance and passionate reaction.

On the fortieth anniversary of the Holocaust, all of us and certainly we Jews, should understand the ultimate price of abysmal ignorance and passionate prejudice. Over the life history of our own people, many generations in one way or another have paid an enormous price for the indignity and oppression visited upon our ancestors and on some of our co-religionists in certain parts of the world until this day. Forty years ago, the world by a miracle moved back from the abyss of universal doom as millions stood by and permitted the inhuman deprivations of a false god and a servile people. But millions of humans were destroyed in a fiery conflagration that would be considered a Sunday school picnic compared with the awesome instruments of warfare available these days.

I know that in many places even after the establishment of the United Nations and the adoption of the Universal Declaration of Human Rights and the Helsinki Accord, there is a tendency to soft pedal the issues involved as if we can long isolate those who suffer indignity from the rest of the world. But, the pains of human misfortune cannot be quarantined forever without the rest of the world ultimately paying the price of blindness to such pains. We came of a people who believe in one God and that men, all men, are fashioned in His image. We believe, too, that to destroy one man is as if you destroyed the world. This is basic to our culture and our hopes. So for us to contribute our best to universal demands, we must drink deeply of our history and culture and act in accord with its precepts. Whether in the Jewish Board of Deputies or the World Jewish Congress, advancing the best in Jewish culture is our solemn duty.

I want to be clearly understood. There are many types and methods of problems affecting human dignity throughout the world as there are many types and methods of solution. I am not here as an American or as the president of a world organization, to tell you or your government what the formulae might be for the solution of your problems no more than I expect you can tell others how to solve theirs. My purpose is simply this—forty years ago, when it was easier to hide, the whole world paid a tragic price when it failed to recognize that there are no borders when hate and prejudice start their foreboding march. Today, modern communication, transportation, and capacity to destroy have virtually reduced the universe to a compact abode for us all. One nation's serious potential conflict unsolved cannot leave the rest of the world untouched for long.

But there is another area to which I have alluded that is weighted with great urgency. The continued potential for warfare, whether in the Middle East or Southern Africa, which international experts continue to identify as current hot spots, does not limit concern to these areas. Maybe, the convergence of culture and a realization of the awesome implications of war are nearer than we think.

The Struggle for Historical Integrity at Auschwitz-Birkenau

Laurence Weinbaum

On January 17, 2015, the seventieth anniversary of the liberation of Auschwitz, Ronald S. Lauder, president of the World Jewish Congress, addressed a solemn audience gathered at the gates of Birkenau—perhaps the most iconic material remnant of the Shoah. Inside a vast tent in which thousands of dignitaries from around the world were present, together with many of the camp's last survivors, he declared:

> I am not a survivor, although I am grateful for the survivors who are here today. I am not a liberator, although I salute the courage of the veterans who are among us today. I am here, simply, as a Jew. And, like all Jews everywhere, this place, this terrible place called Auschwitz, touches our souls. . . . What was the reason that over one million Jews were murdered right here? The reason was they were Jewish. Nazi Germany believed Jews had no right to live.[1]

At that ceremony, beamed around the world in real time and circulated through innumerable newspapers and social media outlets, it was unequiv-

---

Dr. Laurence Weinbaum is Director of the Israel Council on Foreign Relations (ICFR) and founding Chief Editor of *The Israel Journal of Foreign Affairs*.

ocally clear to all, that 90 percent of the victims of Auschwitz-Birkenau had been dispatched to the camp and murdered there for no other reason than the fact that they were Jews. The event, held under the auspices of the Polish government, the WJC, the State Museum at Auschwitz-Birkenau, and the USC Shoah Foundation, was the symbolic culmination of an intense struggle for memory and truth. It was a struggle in which the WJC had played an important role, sometimes publicly and sometimes behind the scenes, and one to which Lauder personally, many years before he was elected president of the organization in 2007, had dedicated himself wholeheartedly.[2]

That victory overcame a relentless, often shameless attempt to denude the Jewish victims of their ethnic, national, and religious identity and to appropriate their suffering and death. That process of usurpation of history began almost immediately after the camp was liberated in January 1945, when the wider world learned of the horrific tragedy that played out in Auschwitz-Birkenau in the otherwise unspectacular Polish city of Oświęcim. The very fact that in 1947 Polish law recognized Auschwitz-Birkenau as a "Monument to the Martyrdom of the Polish Nation and Others" was telling, preliminary evidence that the Jews who made up most of the victims were to be excluded from the pantheon of suffering and martyrdom, or simply subsumed into the "Polish Nation" or "Others." It was, as sociologist Iwona Zarecka called it, "Auschwitz without Jews."[3]

In 1967, Alex L. Easterman, the Scottish-born director of the WJC's International Affairs Department in London, attended the Polish state ceremony at which the "International Monument to the Victims of Fascism" at Birkenau was unveiled between the ruins of crematoria II and III. Upon his return to London, he bitterly described the way in which the Jewish victims had been internationalized and "polonized," consonant with the political agenda of "People's Poland."

> The hour-long address of the Polish Premier, Mr. [Józef] Cyrankiewicz, inaugurated the ceremony of remembrance and homage. His speech was an amalgam of eloquence in poignant tribute to the four million martyrs of Auschwitz; of powerfully phrased, indignant denunciation of the infamies of Hitler and his Nazi Third Reich, of violently sharp criticism of the West German Federal Republic. Although the Prime

Minister described in deeply emotional terms the sufferings, the degra-
dation and the final ghastly massacre of the four million [*sic*] annihilated
in Auschwitz, a thorough examination of the official text of his speech
yielded, alas, not one single mention of the word "Jew'" or "Jewish"
throughout the whole great length of the dramatic speech.[4]

The focal point of the monument unveiled on that occasion was a row
of bronze plaques with an inscription in some twenty languages (including Hebrew and Yiddish) that read "Four million people suffered and died
here at the hands of the Nazi murderers between the years 1940 and 1945."
The tablets were topped by a marble checkerboard, one of the national
symbols of Poland, with a triangle (symbol of the non-Jewish prisoners)
superimposed on it. There was no reference at all to the Jews who had
perished there. The Magen David that most Jewish deportees wore when
they arrived at Auschwitz, and which some wore as inmates, was altogether
absent.[5]

"Although no arrangements had been made beforehand," wrote Easterman, "the Jewish delegations assembled at the commemorative ceremony
went to the monument and improvised a religious service there under
the direction of the Chief Rabbi of Rome, Professor Elio Toaff. Grouped
in front of the monument, the Jewish participants in the proceedings,
many of them in tears, solemnly recited the *Kaddish* and intoned *El Ma·le
Raḥamim*. This—unofficial, improvised—was the only Jewish aspect of
the commemoration of the devastation and annihilation of more than two
million Jews."[6]

For successive generations, Auschwitz has been a metonym for the
Holocaust—the premediated, industrial destruction of European Jewry—
and was widely seen in Jewish circles and beyond as the epicenter of that
unprecedented tragedy. That was so, in part, because of its cosmopolitan
nature—the victims of Auschwitz were brought to the killing grounds
from across the length and breadth of Europe and the fact that many thousands of Jews, having been used as slave laborers, survived. It was also
because the Germans had failed to destroy most of the material evidence
of their crimes and when the camp was overrun, it was discovered almost
completely intact.[7]

The WJC was born in 1936—in the shadow of the burgeoning threat of Nazism, though at that time the murderous potential of the sinister Nazi ideology was unimaginable. In the authorized first history of the organization, upliftingly titled *Unity in Dispersion*, it was noted:

> As World War II was progressing, the people of the world were confronted with the inescapable reality that the Jews had been singled out by Germany for complete annihilation, and that while the plight of most inhabitants of the occupied countries was deplorable, and, in the case of some, terrible, it could not be compared with the fate of the Jews, whose only destination in the scheme of the Third Reich was cruel death. Yet, for many years, the Allied and neutral governments clung obstinately to the concept that legally, the Jews as such did not exist as specific subjects of law, and consequently as subjects of their official policy, diplomacy or strategy. There existed only citizens of recognized nations: Poles, Czechs, Rumanians, etc.[8]

This situation was especially evident in the countries of East Central Europe that had once been the heartland of world Jewry and were now shackled behind the Iron Curtain. The tragedy that engulfed the Jewish communities of those countries, now Communist "peoples' democracies," was to be downplayed or utterly erased from public consciousness. Certainly, the fact that Jews had often perished with the encouragement of elements of the autochthonous population and/or of collaborationist regimes was never to be a part of the national narrative. There were Jews who also sought relief in that internationalist view of suffering: in the sincere belief that a less parochial view of what had happened would engender greater sympathy and solidarity.[9]

In Communist Poland, the fate of Jews during the wartime German occupation was generally seen within the context of the suffering of Polish society—and certainly not as a distinct tragedy of an entirely different magnitude. Posthumously, the victims of the German Final Solution were appropriated as Poles, prompting the journalist Paul Lendvai to observe in his book *Antisemitism without Jews* that "dead Jews make good Poles."[10] Seeking to explain what lay behind this phenomenon, Polish scholar Piotr Osęka explained that "[i]n the early years, the authorities focused, to a much greater extent, on patriotic rather than revolutionary self-creation and initially strove to achieve control over historical representation in accordance with the motto 'That which we don't commemorate, did not happen.'"[11]

Nowhere was this tendency toward the manipulation and even falsification of history more pronounced and disturbing than at the museum at Auschwitz. And it was manifested in the way the story of the camp was presented to the Polish and foreign public that visited the site, in the guide and history books, and in the media. Over the course of the forty-five years that elapsed between the liberation of the camp and the eventual collapse of Communism in Poland, Jews were routinely presented—in the most generous case—as merely another one of the nationalities that had suffered and died there, but not the primary victims. That was done without ever explicitly denying that the vast majority of victims were Jews.

At the end of the 1950s the International Auschwitz Committee announced its initiative to establish national pavilions in some of the barracks of Auschwitz I, the former *Stammlager*. It was intended that these barracks display information on the Nazi occupation of these countries and the fate of their citizens deported to Auschwitz. The first to open were those of Czechoslovakia and Hungary in 1960, followed in 1961 by the Soviet Union. That same year, in a particularly cynical move, the pavilion of the German Democratic Republic was dedicated to "Germany and the Anti-Fascist Resistance Movement 1933–1945."[12] For the most part, to the extent that the sufferings of Jews were depicted at all, they were subsumed into the nationalities of the countries from which they arrived, and were thus treated as Hungarians, Greeks, Dutch, or French.[13]

Initially, some senior Polish officials supported the idea of creating an Israeli pavilion, but this suggestion was overruled. The opponents of that idea argued that Jews were citizens of the countries in which they lived and should therefore be represented in the pavilions of Poland and other nations. Clearly, no Israeli citizens had perished there, as Israel had not yet come into existence. It was also argued that the State of Israel did not represent the Jewish people as a whole.[14] Of course the WJC could and did claim to represent the Jewish people in the Diaspora and actively sought to prevail upon the Polish authorities to allow for a Jewish pavilion.

In April 1963, Easterman visited Auschwitz and in a meeting with Deputy Foreign Minister Józef Winiewicz, Easterman told him

> [t]hat the Polish government should consider the sense of deepest indignation which will inevitably arise throughout world Jewry if the Government persisted in excluding a distinctive Jewish memorial building from its plans, because not only were Jews the overwhelming majority of the millions destroyed in Auschwitz, but the very name Auschwitz, had become the symbol of the whole tragic martyrdom of the six million European Jews annihilated by the Nazis. . . . The essential issue was that Jewish martyrdom was *sui generis* in the whole sordid story of Nazi savagery and must not be obscured.[15]

In his extensive monopgraph on Polish-Israeli relations, Marcos Silber writes that Easterman later reported to Israeli Foreign Minister Golda Meir that Winiewicz "without replying . . . picked up the telephone and spoke for several minutes to someone in Polish. When he had finished he said to me 'You will have the Jewish Pavilion; the plans will be worked out in this ministry and under the direction of the man with whom I have just been speaking.'"

On August 3, 1964, the Jewish Telegraphic Agency (JTA) reported on a meeting of the World Conference of Jewish Organizations (COJO) that had taken place in Geneva at which WJC President Nahum Goldmann announced that he had concluded negotiations with the Polish government for inclusion of a Jewish pavilion: "one of a complex of pavilions memorializing victims of various nationalities murdered in Auschwitz." Goldmann said that he had conveyed "appreciation" to the Polish government for its efforts to keep alive the memory of the martyrs of the Nazi era. The participants at the COJO meeting had voted to endorse the memorial and urged Jewish groups to "participate actively" in plans to make the Jewish pavilion "a fitting monument to Jewish martyrdom." According to Goldmann, the WJC would also assist Poland in underwriting the cost of the exhibition and said that the organization had given "a considerable amount of money—many governments gave less."[16]

By the time that the pavilion, dedicated to "The Struggle and Martyrdom of the Jews" was finally opened in Block 27 in April 1968—and with almost no input on the part of those who had urged it be created—Poland had severed diplomatic relations with Israel and embarked on a bitter domestic purge that led to the expulsion of more than 20,000 Polish citizens of Jewish origin, many of whom had only tenuous ties, if any, to Jewish life and regarded themselves as Poles. Therefore, no representatives of international Jewish organizations agreed to take part in the opening ceremony that incidentally was held on the last day of Passover. In Jewish circles, the event was rightly seen as a flagrant attempt to divert attention from the terrible events taking place in Poland, and perceived as the tragic finale to the thousand-year history of Polish Jewry. Significantly, the exhibition highlighted Polish aid to Jews as well as the notion that Poles and Jews had shared a common fate. Attention was drawn to the western Allies' failure to come to the rescue of European Jewry and the WJC was also singled out for its purported shortcomings.[17]

By the mid-1970s, beset by economic crisis, and seeking western credits, Poland's government adopted a more pragmatic, less ideological stance. At Goldmann's urging, the Poles agreed to revamp the exhibition in the Jewish pavilion. This more palatable display was opened in April 1978, with Goldmann and a WJC delegation present for the ceremony. On that occasion, the former WJC president delivered an emotional speech in Yiddish. In 1979, the WJC, together with the Polish government, successfully petitioned to have Auschwitz-Birkenau added to the list of UNESCO world heritage sites.[18]

However, in the autumn of 1984, a challenge emerged from another quarter. With the financial support of a group of Belgian Catholics, a Carmelite convent was established at the edge of the *Stammlager* in Auschwitz I, in the derelict theater building that had been used for the storage of Zyklon-B gas cannisters. The idea of a convent at Auschwitz enjoyed the full support of Cardinal Franciszek Marcharski, the archbishop of Kraków, who claimed that the nuns would "live in seclusion offering prayers of expiation for the crimes committed at Auschwitz-Birkenau." After establishing themselves in the building, the nuns proceeded to erect a twenty foot-high cross. This move largely escaped public notice, but a bombastic appeal in 1985 by the European "Aid to the Church in Distress," with funds collected in Luxembourg, Belgium, and the Netherlands, suddenly placed it in the limelight.[19] Jews were especially upset by the triumphalist militant language of the appeal in which the convent was described as "a spiritual fortress and a guarantee of the conversion of strayed brothers from our countries as well as proof of our desire to erase outrages so often done to the Vicar of Christ."

The WJC had been a pioneer in the development of relations with the Roman Catholic Church and was uniquely placed to spearhead the struggle to persuade the Church that the presence of the nuns at Auschwitz was unacceptable and an affront to Jewish sensitivities. In December 1985, WJC President Edgar Bronfman arrived in Warsaw to discuss the issue with Poland's Minister of Religious Affairs Adam Łopatka who told the WJC president that he would take up the issue with the Polish Church in an attempt to convince the nuns to relocate. As Bronfman explained: "it is not only a matter of the Auschwitz convent, but the broader implications of historical revisionism in which the uniqueness of the Holocaust and the murder of the Jewish people is being suppressed."[20] Bronfman—and many other Jews—believed that the nuns were "praying to convert the souls of the dead Jews to Catholicism."[21] To be sure, at the root of this tension was also the theological clash between how Jews and Catholics viewed suffering and death.

Meanwhile, former WJC Secretary-General Gerhart M. Riegner, who had been actively involved in interfaith relations for many years, led the WJC's efforts vis-à-vis the Catholic hierarchy.[22] As it later transpired, there was a disconnect between the Church in Western Europe and in Poland, and the WJC was successful in appealing to the more liberal representatives of the episcopate. Looking back at that time, Riegner wrote:

> No other problem in Jewish-Catholic relations entailed so much work for me nor so many urgent negotiations and discussions. . . . After several years of observation and reflection, I became convinced that this problem could not be resolved without the Pope [John Paul II] taking a

clear stand. He had avoided personal intervention to keep himself free of the divergences and tensions that divided the Polish episcopate. We understood that in these circumstances it was a delicate matter for a Polish pope to intervene officially in such a quarrel.[23]

After long negotiations, an agreement was reached in Geneva at the end of February 1987 to relocate the Carmelite convent from Auschwitz to a nearby site within two years. This second site was to serve as a Catholic center of information about both the Holocaust and the martyrdom of Poles and other peoples. Cardinal Macharski was charged with overseeing the implementation of this project, while the bishops of other countries agreed to raise the funds to underwrite the cost of the project realization within two years of the signing. This deadline came and passed without any sign of the relocation of the convent.

Although there was nothing remotely resembling a consensus among Jewish organizations, and although the State of Israel (then in the process of attempting to restore relations with Poland and gain a foothold in East Central Europe) did not want to get involved in a controversy over Auschwitz, the WJC saw this as an especially distressing phenomenon that could not go unanswered. Recalling the atmosphere at that time (and the WJC's insistence that world Jewry not back down), Rabbi David Rosen, who was deeply engaged in dialogue with the Roman Catholic Church on behalf of the Anti-Defamation League, observed:

> The ADL didn't want to make a thing of it. Their attitude was, it is not as if there are Jews there at the time who are involved in it and it's not as if it's actually on the property itself. By making a big thing, you're basically trying to go to war with the Catholic Church. . . . To some extent the WJC determined the tune. Their style created the atmosphere in which no public Jewish organization could not get involved. Had the WJC not got involved, those issues might not have developed in the way they did.[24]

By the summer of 1989, the situation had reached an impasse and even a boiling point. It was then that Rabbi Avi Weiss from New York and a group of six young Jewish activists arrived in Poland in the hope that he could draw international attention to the situation. They climbed over the fence surrounding the convent and brought their protests to the nuns' front doors. Rabbi Weiss and the protestors were roughed up by Polish workers renovating the building and ejected by force. Neither the nuns nor the local police intervened.[25] The reaction in the press was immediate.[26]

Although Rabbi Weiss was seemingly acting on his own as a "lone wolf," it turned out that the WJC had quietly but discreetly encouraged his activities and even underwritten them. Recalling the genesis of his plans to protest at the convent in Auschwitz and how the WJC facilitated them, he told me in a telephone interview:

> The idea came from the activists. We met in the courtyard of the Jewish Theological Seminary in New York but then moved on to the WJC office. I'm not convinced that we could have done it without the WJC. I knew Israel Singer and Elan Steinberg and worked closely with them going after Waldheim. The WJC worked on the inside and we were the foot soldiers. The 1989 protest at the Convent was planned in Sruly's [Israel Singer] office. This was a classic example of how activists can work with mainstream organizations and can do wonderful things together. Edgar [Bronfman] and the WJC funded the whole operation.[27]

This, of course, was a far cry from Goldmann's quiet diplomatic engagement that some derided as mere *shtadlanut*. In his memoirs, Goldmann made clear his own modus operandi: "With us, the watchword is confidentiality."[28] After the changing of the guard in the late 1970s, the WJC, under the leadership of Bronfman and Israel Singer adopted a very different, "in your face" approach to the way in which it advanced its agenda. Bronfman insisted "You don't go as a supplicant. You say 'Look fellow, this is good for me and you.' If you don't understand how it's going to be good for them, you are not going to get through to them."[29] Not surprisingly, the reaction in both Polish and many Jewish circles was highly critical of Rabbi Weiss's actions, which were seen as inflaming tensions and as a setback to the unfolding process of Polish-Jewish reconciliation.[30] There was no denying, however, that it hurled the convent crisis onto the front page of newspapers worldwide and introduced a new sense of urgency.

Eventually, the WJC succeeded in mobilizing moderate elements in the Roman Catholic Church to prevail upon their Polish coreligionists to relocate the convent. But as it turned out, even their leverage was limited. In September 1989, the Holy See announced that it would help pay for the construction of a new interfaith prayer center farther from the camp and that the Carmelite nuns would be relocated to the center. This did not happen swiftly and it was only in April 1993, in a last-minute letter apparently intended to calm Jewish sensitivities on the fiftieth anniversary of the Warsaw Ghetto uprising, that Pope John Paul II told the Catholic nuns to relocate. The Pope instructed the fourteen Carmelite nuns to move to another convent within the diocese or return to their old homes. So ended one of the most contentious chapters in the postwar history of Auschwitz-Birkenau.

Over the years, the WJC has maintained its engagement at Auschwitz. In 1995, a Polish commercial firm sought to erect a shopping center within the camp's protected zone—directly across from the visitor parking lot. The WJC and other Jewish groups protested, and eventually the Polish government intervened to put a halt to the plans. The WJC also protested when hundreds of crosses were planted in the ground around the gravel pit at Auschwitz I by a hard core nationalist group led by Kazmierz Świtoń; these were ultimately removed by the Polish authorities in 1999.[31] Beginning in the 1990s, the French Section of the WJC, and later the European Jewish Congress, both under the professional direction of Serge Cwajgenbaum, were especially active in raising consciousness about the camp and its significance. They brought a steady stream of high school students and teachers, journalists, and other influential members of civil society to visit the site. In 1995, it dispatched a "memory train" from Birkenau with a travelling exhibition devoted to the history of the camp that stopped in Budapest, Prague, Berlin, and Strasbourg. During this period, the WJC issued a number of publications explaining the history of Auschwitz and the sensitivities of both Jews and Poles in relating to the site.[32]

Although Auschwitz will continue to be remembered and understood in many different ways, its association with the suffering and death of European Jewry can never again be concealed or subsumed. The pathology of deliberate obfuscation, which long bedeviled the site, is finally gone.

Auschwitz-Birkenau is no longer the "Museum of the Martyrology of the Polish Nation and *Other* [italics mine] Nations." Nothing better symbolizes this transformation than the speech of WJC President Ronald Lauder on the seventieth anniversary of the liberation of the camp as well as the prominence of his role on that occasion. Speaking in the name of world Jewry, the successors to the victims, he poignantly affirmed the centrality of the horrifying Jewish experience at Auschwitz.

The author expresses his heartfelt gratitude to Isabella Nespoli, Alex Feder, and Yvette Shumacher for their assistance in the preparation of this text.

New Directions and Priorities, 1985

Edgar M. Bronfman

Edgar M. Bronfman (1929–2013) served as acting president of the WJC from 1979 to 1981 and as WJC president from 1981 to 2007. Under Bronfman's leadership, the WJC moved from primarily behind-the-scenes diplomacy to a more aggressive, often confrontational stance. The following is his address at the meeting of the WJC Governing Board in Vienna on January 26, 1985:

Mr. Chancellor, before I begin my prepared remarks, I would address a few comments on a matter of major immediacy. You are no doubt aware that it was not with unanimity that the Governing Board of the World Jewish Congress, a human rights organization from its very beginnings, chose to meet in Vienna. On the very eve of our meeting, a man convicted for crimes against humanity was not only repatriated to Austria, but received what was tantamount to a hero's welcome!

To say that we are devastated is to put it mildly. Shocked, furious, and deeply angered is our mood. [Walter] Reder represents all that was unspeakably evil about Nazism and Austrian participation therein.[1] Your government has promised to teach its young about the horrors of a past era. I cannot think of a worse example. We ask how Nazism can be dead anywhere such a disgusting display can take place? I hope, Mr. Chancellor, I have adequately conveyed to you the depth of our feelings.

Convening this World Jewish Congress Governing Board session here in Vienna reflects a historic milestone. We cannot—we must not—ever forget what happened in the past, but the central meaning of our presence here lies in what we hope will be the reality of tomorrow. It is in the future that the importance of this gathering of Jews from so many nations will be found.

Two months ago, this city was host to a remarkable series of multimedia exhibitions celebrating and mourning the "Vanished World" of pre-Holocaust Europe. Its impact must not be underestimated. It came at a time when many Austrians are confronting their country's anti-Semitic past and when Jews are undertaking the task of building a viable community for the future. The Austrian Jewish community, though but a fraction of its past size, is a proud, dynamic, and thriving component of the World Jewish Congress. Through its president Ivan Hacker, we thank the community for serving as gracious and generous host for this meeting.

Vienna is influenced not only by history but by geography as well. Austria stands between East and West, on the geo-political boundary line that has divided Europe since the end of World War II. The Jewish people, too—in both East and West—have been challenged by the political realities of this divided world. Our passionate determination to maintain the unity and vitality of our people is manifested in the presence here of Jews from both Eastern and Western countries, and indeed from every continent on this globe.

In the last year we have witnessed significant changes impacting on the Jewish world. Developments affecting Israel remain central in the concerns and the hearts of Jews everywhere. We will be discussing the situation in the Middle East at length during the sessions of this Governing Board. But let me state here that the emergency airlift of Ethiopian Jews to Israel represented all that is best in the Jewish moral tradition. It is the manifest refutation of that base slander against the Jewish people that Zionism is racism. We salute the State of Israel and former Prime Minister Begin for undertaking this noble endeavor and pledge that the entire Jewish world will not rest until all Ethiopian Jews are rescued.

The course of events in Latin America—specifically the move toward democracy—has been welcomed not only by Jews in the region but by Jewish communities everywhere. I have met this past year with President Alfonsín of Argentina, President Lusinchi of Venezuela, and President Monge of Costa Rica and sensed the anticipation and excitement with which these three great exponents of democracy have imbued their nations. As the plenary assembly of the Latin American Jewish Congress declared in São Paulo, we express full support for this commitment to human rights.

I am pleased to report also that during the last year we have met with some success in efforts to quash the pernicious lie that Zionism is a form of racism. Through the good offices of various world leaders with whom we intervened, the meeting of the Inter-Parliamentary Union this year did not adopt that heinous anti-Zionist resolution.

In discussions with President Reagan, we received assurances that the United States would vigorously oppose any insertion of an anti-Zionist text at the upcoming Nairobi conference on the UN Decade for Women. In fact, he told a small group under WJC auspices that should such resolutions be adopted, the US delegation would be under his instructions to walk out. Perhaps most significantly, even the enabling resolution for the forthcoming UN Decade to Combat Racism no longer refers to the Zionism-racism canard. These are moves in the right direction. They indicate the growing worldwide recognition that the true struggle against racism cannot afford to be diverted by extraneous political matters.

We must continue to guard against political extremists of all shades. The World Jewish Congress has made clear that it condemns the anti-democratic philosophy that Meir Kahane expounds, and accordingly, through its Institute of Jewish Affairs in London, has—at the request of Israel's Attorney General—sent documentation to the Israel Minister of Justice to assist in preparing anti-racism legislation to be brought before the Knesset.

In Europe, economic and social problems have engendered a disturbing increase in neo-fascist trends and personalities. These extremists still represent a small minority to be sure, but they merit increased vigilance. History demonstrates that radicalism of both right and left are always a threat to the stability of democracy in general and to the well-being of Jews in particular.

There are still, sad to say, Jewish communities which as a whole find themselves in precarious conditions. They and the world must know that they are not forgotten. No matter how small or isolated they may be, the Jewish people everywhere are committed to safeguarding their interest.

We are moved by the Talmudic injunction: "He who saves but one life, it is as if he saved the entire world." It has been—and remains—the credo of the World Jewish Congress that our efforts to strengthen the security and unity of the Jewish people pose no threat to the political or social system of any country. We will continue to follow this principle in expressing our concern for the dignity of our brothers and sisters wherever they need our help. We have done this with particular energy with respect to Jews in the Soviet Union. I have done so directly in dealings with Soviet officials. I will continue on this course unrelentingly. At the same time, the World Jewish Congress has made clear that our concern is not motivated by any anti-Soviet disposition. We reject enlistment as Cold Warriors, and it serves no purpose for the World Jewish Congress to be involved in East-West struggles.

World Jewry and the Soviet Union share much common emotional ground and mutuality of past interest. The victory over the Nazis and fascism forty years ago was a historic moment for both the Jewish people and the Soviet people. One million Jews fought in the Red Army against Nazi barbarism. In remembering the Holocaust, we cannot forget that brave Soviet troops liberated most of the tattered remnant of European Jewry from the death camps. In my talks with Soviet officials, the possibility has been raised that the USSR join with world Jewry in the various events that will commemorate the fortieth anniversary of the defeat of the Nazis. Let us hope that cooperation in this endeavor will bring positive movement in other areas as well. There is no doubt that constructive development toward easing the plight of Soviet Jewry will help ease the tension between East and West, just as we believe that diminishing tensions between East and West will improve the condition of Soviet Jews. And in this not only Jews, but the entire world would benefit.

In concluding, I wish to express our gratitude to the government of Austria for serving as a national host for this gathering. We are a people with long memories. While we may speak often here of past deprivations and horrors, we would fail morally if we ignored what the Austrian government has done in recent years on behalf of the Jewish people. Austria's record in assisting the flow of refugees is shining testimony to a national spirit of humanity and good will. In that same spirit, and on behalf of the

World Jewish Congress, I look forward to a continuing dialogue with the Austrian Government and people in addressing matters of mutual concern and those present-day problems that demand a just resolution.

We all recognize that we must establish many more milestones especially in countries where Jewish life is threatened. As all of you know, the World Jewish Congress is committed to that course. It is not an easy road, but I am confident that if we find mutual understanding and respect along the way, it will lead us to security and peace.

Fighting Delegitimization: The United Nation's "Zionism Is Racism" Resolution, a Case Study

EVELYN SOMMER

On November 10, 1975, the UN General Assembly adopted G.A. Resolution 3379, which declared Zionism to be "a form of racism and racial discrimination." The resolution also cited the political declaration adopted at the Conference of Ministers of Foreign Affairs of Non-Aligned Countries held at Lima, Peru, on August 25–30, 1975, which had condemned Zionism "as a threat to world peace" and a "racist and imperialist ideology."[1]

This resolution—most commonly referred to as the "Zionism is racism" resolution—came onto the scene against the backdrop of the Cold War. At that time, the United Nations was a forum in which countries often vied for the approval of, and were aligned with, one of the two great powers. Beginning in the 1960s, following the June 1967 Six-Day War, the Soviet Union began promoting the concept of "Zionism-equals-racism" as a way to strengthen its relations with, and support for, the Arab countries in their ongoing conflict with the State of Israel. The very essence of Zionism as the Jewish movement of national liberation and self-determination, which created the only democratic society in the Middle East where Jews and Arabs could live alongside one another, was deliberately distorted into

Evelyn Sommer is Chair of the North American Section of the World Jewish Congress.

its own antithesis. According to Israel's enemies, which after 1967 included almost all of the Communist states and many of the so-called non-aligned countries, any manifestation of Jewish national rights was deemed hostile to Arab claims to the entirety of the territory between the Mediterranean and the Jordan River. Thus, anti-Zionism became a staple of foreign policy not just for Arab and Communist governments, but also for those countries that wanted to burnish their so-called "anti-imperialist" credentials. This process accelerated as Egypt, the Arab world's most populous country, began moving away from the Soviet sphere of influence in the Middle East. In 1973, the UN General Assembly passed an anti-apartheid resolution that condemned "the unholy alliance between Portuguese colonialism, South African racism, Zionism and Israeli imperialism."[2]

Such corrosive atmospherics had their effect. To give only one example: at a workshop on anti-Semitism and anti-Zionism at the sixth plenary assembly of the World Jewish Congress, held in Jerusalem in February of 1975, several delegates from Latin America reported that "anti-Zionist pressure, foremost by certain groups sympathizing with the Third World, was so strong that many Jews, especially at the universities, preferred to dissociate themselves from Zionism."[3] That same WJC plenary assembly adopted a resolution that drew "attention to the fact that anti-Semitism today frequently appears under the cloak of anti-Zionism" and urged "all people to oppose anti-Semitism, whether appearing openly or in the guise of anti-Zionism."[4]

In fact, Resolution 3379 can be said to have been born at the "World Conference of the International Women's Year," held in Mexico City on June 19–July 2, 1975. I represented WIZO, the Women's International Zionist Organization, at this conference. I was WIZO's representative at the United Nations at that time and recall how Marc Schreiber, the director of the UN Division of Human Rights, approached the Israeli delegation with the draft of the final declaration of Mexico, which included an insertion, in pencil, of Zionism among the "isms" deemed to constitute the ills of the world. We all dismissed this as inconsequential, but by the next morning, the term had been typed into an official UN document—the "Declaration of Mexico on the Equality of Women and Their Contribution to Development and Peace"—with Article 24 calling for "the elimination of colonialism and neo-colonialism, foreign occupation, zionism [*sic*], *apartheid*, and racial discrimination in all its forms."[5] From then on, Zionism was always listed among the great evils of the world.

Another seminal moment on this road came less than one month before the resolution was passed, at a meeting of the UN's Social Humanitarian and Cultural Committee, or Third Committee, which had convened to decide whether to advance a Zionism-equals-racism resolution to the General Assembly. While many of the Arab, Communist, and other supporters of the resolution purported to praise Judaism as a religion, they in effect rejected, and often slandered, the Jewish people's national aspirations. Saudi Arabia's ambassador Jamil Baroody declared that for Jews to claim to be "a single people . . . was a feeling of exclusivity very much akin to racism." The Palestinian Liberation Organization (PLO) representative was even more offensive when he likened Zionism to Nazism.[6]

Chaim Herzog, Israel's permanent representative to the United Nations, who would later go on to serve as the country's sixth president, was eloquent in his denunciation of the resolution, but that was to be expected. As American Jews, we were gratified and heartened by the strong support we received from our government. Leonard Garment, counselor to the US Mission at the United Nations, denounced the resolution as an "obscene act." He said that the language of the resolution:

> distorts and perverts. It changes words with precise meanings into purveyors of confusion. It destroys the moral force of the concept of racism, making it nothing more than an epithet to be flung arbitrarily at one's adversary. . . . Zionism is a movement which has as its contemporary thrust the preservation of the small remnant of the Jewish people that survived the horrors of a racial holocaust. By equating Zionism with racism, this resolution discredits the good faith of our joint efforts to fight actual racism. It discredits these efforts morally and it cripples them politically.[7]

The World Jewish Congress was one of the first Jewish groups to sound the alarm about this attempt to demonize Zionism. Following the Third Committee's initial approval of the resolution, WJC President Nahum Goldmann condemned it as "a travesty of historical facts and a defamation of the national liberation movement of a people that for two millennia was deprived of a national existence and the right of self-determination, and was subjected to most cruel persecution."[8] Dr. Gerhart M. Riegner recalled in his memoirs:

> We had to mobilize all the forces of goodwill against the draft resolution as we tried to prevent its adoption by the General Assembly itself. On October 23, as WJC secretary-general, I sent a circular letter to all our affiliates urging them to do everything in their power to convince their governments to oppose the draft resolution.

The WJC then mobilized the other Jewish organizations with consultative status at the United Nations to submit a joint protest to the president of the General Assembly.[9]

The vote breakdown on the resolution in the General Assembly reflected the frightening hostility to Israel at the United Nations. While the United States, Canada, Australia, Western and Northern European countries, and a handful of Latin American, African, and other countries opposed the resolution, the Soviet Union and virtually all Communist nations voted for it, as did the Arab and Islamic states, as well as many African countries. To our great disappointment, with the additional support of Brazil and Mexico, the resolution passed 72–35. Thirty-two countries chose to abstain, including several from Latin America, and three did not vote.[10]

Two speeches during the General Assembly debate captured the revulsion we all felt at the "Zionism is racism" resolution. "I do not come to this rostrum to defend the moral and historical values of the Jewish people," declared Herzog. He continued:

> They do not need to be defended. They speak for themselves. They have given to mankind much of what is great and eternal. . . . I come here to denounce the two great evils which menace society in general and a society of nations in particular. These two evils are hatred and ignorance. These two evils are the motivating force behind the proponents of this resolution and their supporters. These two evils characterize those who would drag this world organization, the ideals of which were first conceived by the prophets of Israel, to the depths to which it has been

dragged today. . . . To question the Jewish people's right to national existence and freedom is not only to deny to the Jewish people the right
accorded to every other people on this globe, but it is also to deny the
central precepts of the United Nations.[11]

Ambassador Daniel Patrick Moynihan, the US Permanent Representative
to the United Nations, was equally forceful. The United States, he said,

> rises to declare before the General Assembly of the United Nations,
> and before the world, that it does not acknowledge, it will not abide
> by, it will never acquiesce in, this infamous act. . . . A great evil has been
> loosed upon the world. The abomination of anti-Semitism . . . has been
> given the appearance of international sanction. The General Assembly
> today grants symbolic amnesty—and more—to the murderers of the
> six million European Jews. Evil enough in itself, but more ominous by far
> is the realization that now presses upon us—the realization that if there
> were no General Assembly, this could never have happened.[12]

I also want to pay tribute here to Father Benjamin Núñez Vargas, Costa
Rica's UN Ambassador, who was one of the most eloquent opponents of
Resolution 3397 and one of Israel's best friends.

After the resolution was passed by the General Assembly, Nahum
Goldmann issued another statement in which he expressed the sentiments
of virtually the entire Jewish world:

> The resolution of the UN General Assembly condemning Zionism is one
> of the worst and most immoral decisions that the UN has unfortunately
> indulged in the last few years. To define Zionism as "racist" is an absurd
> distortion of the basic facts and a denial of the right of the Jewish people
> to have its own homeland and its own state, which was established by
> overwhelming decision of the same United Nations. . . . It is the duty
> of the Jewish people to react in the most decisive manner against this
> resolution, by identifying itself with the Zionist ideal and giving its full
> solidarity to the State of Israel.[13]

Goldmann's call proved prescient as "Zionist" increasingly became a term
of abuse in some circles. Although a cursory glance at the vote tally shat-
tered any illusions of a quick turnaround and repeal, it was now clear

that the United Nations had become a critical front in the fight against anti-Semitism and delegitimization of the State of Israel.

In 1982, the WJC commissioned and published a study detailing the damage done in the years that followed Resolution 3379. The study found that the word "Zionist" had, in some parts of the world, become a catch-all word for nefarious behavior. "International Zionism," a self-contained contradiction and fiction, became a popular object of denunciation for regional Middle East leaders—often in the context of something with which Israel had nothing to do. For example, the study noted that during the Iran-Iraq war, Saddam Hussein accused Iran of being party to an international Zionist conspiracy. In turn, Iran accused Saddam of "being entirely in the hands of international Zionism."[14]

Although the WJC boycotted a UN anti-racism conference in 1978 because of its targeting of Israel and Zionism,[15] it did not disengage from the United Nations or decelerate its efforts to convince countries, particularly those that had abstained in the 1975 UN vote, to rescind the "Zionism/racism" resolution. The early 1980s saw various efforts to fight off new resolutions, build important relationships, and ultimately advocate the repeal of Resolution 3379. The rhetoric of Herzog and Moynihan gave way to the concrete efforts of hundreds of community leaders and activists around the world.

On June 25, 1982, WJC President Edgar M. Bronfman told the UN Special Session on Disarmament, "The charge that Zionism is racism is an abomination," and that "world peace cannot tolerate the denial of the legitimacy of Israel or any other nation-state."[16] In October of that year, Dr. Riegner and other senior WJC officials met with the president of the UN General Assembly Ambassador Imre Hollai of Hungary to discuss, among other things, the continued negative effects of the "Zionism is racism" resolution, as well as efforts to expel Israel from the world body.[17] In September 1984, Bronfman protested a resolution planned for a meeting of the Inter-Parliamentary Union that would have reiterated the Zionism-equals-racism claim. The resolution was eventually withdrawn.[18] And in December 1984, the WJC, together with the World Zionist Organization and B'nai B'rith International, organized a conference in Washington, DC, hosted by the State Department, entitled "Zionism is Racism: An Assault on Human Rights."[19]

A critical turning point in the US posture toward the United Nations and Zionism-equals-racism was reached in 1985. In July of that year, the US Senate unanimously adopted its own resolution in which it "soundly denounces and condemns any linkage between Zionism and racism," and called Resolution 3379 "a permanent smear on the reputation of the United Nations."[20] In July of that year, I was one of the delegates to the conference in Nairobi, Kenya, which marked the end of the UN Decade for Women. The US delegation was headed by Maureen Reagan, President Ronald Reagan's daughter, who declared publicly that if Zionism were again to be included among the ills of the world, the American delegation would walk out of the conference. I was chosen to address the conference on behalf of all the Jewish non-governmental organizations (NGOs) in attendance, including the WJC, WIZO, and the International Council of Jewish Women, but when the time came to do so, I was informed that the Algerian chair of that particular session would not call on a Zionist representative to speak. Later the same evening, however, the overall chair of the conference, Margaret Kenyatta of Kenya, did call on me during the closing plenary. In my statement, I told the assembled delegates that:

> Zionism, the national liberation movement of the Jewish people and probably the world's oldest liberation movement, is intrinsically an anti-racist movement of a people that, historically and continuously, has been the victim of many brutal forms of racism and racial discrim-ination. We note with great sorrow that the branding of Zionism as racist . . . contravened the most basic principles of the United Nations charter and fueled the dangerous flames of anti-Semitism in many parts of the world.

As it turned out, Nairobi proved to be the first substantive milestone on the road to the repeal of Resolution 3379. In contrast to Mexico City ten years earlier, the Zionism/racism equation did not appear in the Nairobi declaration.

A few months later, on November 10—the ten-year anniversary of the resolution—President Reagan sent a message to the Conference on Israel, Zionism and the United Nations (held at the United Nations despite a formal protest to the UN Secretary-General by Arab states) in which he pledged his "support for the removal of this blot from the United Nations record."[21] Throughout this period, the WJC, together with other major Jewish organizations, continued its fight against Resolution 3379. In August 1985, the WJC'S Latin American office held a meeting with the World Council of Churches, where the latter's opposition to the resolution was "reaffirmed."[22] Shortly before the tenth anniversary of the UN resolution, Bronfman, together with Bernice Tannenbaum, president of the World Zionist Organization-American Section, and Gerald Kraft, president of B'nai B'rith International, called on Jewish communities around the world to urge their governments to support the repeal of the resolution.[23]

US policy regarding Resolution 3379 remained consistent in the administration of George H. W. Bush. Addressing the AIPAC annual policy conference in May 1989, Secretary of State James Baker said that Arab countries should "take concrete steps toward accommodation with Israel, not in place of the peace process but as a catalyst for it; end the economic boycott; stop the challenges to Israel's standing in international organizations; repudiate the odious line that Zionism is racism."[24]

The WJC continued to press the case against the UN resolution in international forums and in meetings with diplomatic and government officials. In January 1990, Brazilian President-elect Fernando Collor de Mello told Bronfman that Brazil's 1975 vote in support of the resolution had been "a mistake," and that his country would not vote that way again.[25] The following month, I was part of a group of WJC leaders who met Dr. Luis Alberto Lacalle, the newly elected President of Uruguay. When I asked Dr. Lacalle whether Uruguay, which had opposed the resolution in 1975, would lobby other Latin American countries to support repeal, he promised to do so, saying that "in Uruguay, the efforts against this resolution were originated by me."[26]

In July 1991, Bronfman met with French Prime Minister Edith Cresson and urged France to support rescinding the resolution.[27] In the same year, the WJC achieved a crucial breakthrough. Mexico, which had voted in favor of the 1975 resolution, announced following a meeting with Bronfman that it no longer supported the principle that Zionism was akin to racism.[28] Also in 1991, Mexican President Carlos Salinas de Gortari told Bronfman at a meeting in Mexico City that his country had reversed its position and now opposed equating Zionism with racism.[29]

On September 24, 1991, President George H. W. Bush urged the repeal of Resolution 3379. "To equate Zionism with the intolerable sin of racism is to twist history and forget the terrible plight of Jews in World War II and, indeed, throughout history," he told the UN General Assembly. "To equate Zionism with racism is to reject Israel itself. . . . By repealing this resolution unconditionally the United Nations will enhance its credibility and serve the cause of peace."[30] That same day, Soviet Foreign Minister Boris Pankin followed suit, telling the General Assembly that the United Nations "should once and for all leave behind the legacy of the ice age, like the obnoxious resolution equating Zionism to racism."[31] And WJC Executive Director Elan Steinberg told the JTA that Ukrainian President Leonid Kravchuk also supported repeal of the resolution.[32] As a result, we were all hopeful that the injustice perpetrated in 1975 would at long last be undone. But there remained one last bit of drama. President Bush's Chief of Staff, John Sununu, was undermining efforts to rescind the resolution. On December 3, Bronfman asked the President directly why Thomas Pickering, the US Ambassador to the United Nations, had not received the necessary instructions to bring repeal to a vote. Bush replied that he had indeed authorized the vote, excused himself for a few minutes, and when he returned told Bronfman apologetically that "my now former chief-of-staff held things up."[33]

On December 16, UN General Assembly Resolution 46/86, which declared that the Assembly "decides to revoke the determination in its resolution 3379 of 10 November 1975," was overwhelmingly adopted by a vote of 111–25, with thirteen nations abstaining and seventeen, including Egypt, Kuwait, and China, not voting. Cuba, North Korea, and Vietnam were the only Communist countries that opposed repeal. India, Nigeria, Singapore, and the Philippines, which had voted for Resolution 3379 in 1975, now voted to repeal it.[34] It was a distinct privilege for me to represent the WJC on the floor of the General Assembly at the historic vote, together with WJC Secretary-General Israel Singer and Executive Director Elan Steinberg. That evening, Bronfman was kind enough to call me on his way to Idaho to say, "We did it!" Following the vote, Israeli Foreign Minister David Levy met privately with Bronfman to thank him both personally and on behalf of the government of Israel for what Levy called the "unparalleled efforts on the part of the WJC in helping realize this important diplomatic triumph."[35]

For the entire period from November 10, 1975, until December 16, 1991, the WJC representatives at the United Nations had to navigate tortuous roads to continue participating in positive UN programs that guaranteed human rights while at the same time fighting the delegitimization of the State of Israel and the condemnation of Zionism. I believe that the role played by the lay and professional leadership of the WJC brought great pride and honor to our organization.

Navigating the Communist Years:
A Jewish Perspective

Maram Stern

I was born in Berlin in 1955, ten years after the end of the Second World War, to parents who had fled Eastern Europe, having survived the Shoah, and who had decided to settle in Berlin. In 1961, we awoke to find a wall, built during the night by the German Democratic Republic (GDR) authorities, called the *Antifaschistischer Schutzwall*: the anti-fascist protective wall. It had supposedly been constructed to protect the Germans in the Eastern sector from a potential return of fascism; in reality, the wall was intended to prevent escapes from the GDR to the West.

Already as a child, I understood that this barrier would affect my life, as it would the lives of all Berliners. However, I could never have imagined that the Berlin Wall, which dissected *my* city, would become *the* symbol of division for almost three decades—cutting Europe in two, splitting the world into two ideological blocs, and separating European Jewish communities. We had to wait until 1989 to see this wall tumble down like a house of cards. At the time, I had just joined the World Jewish Congress, an organization that had always been dedicated to overcoming barriers.

Maram Stern is Deputy CEO for Diplomacy of the World Jewish Congress.

In this chapter I focus on the social and diplomatic engagements of the WJC, and how the organization experienced history, in the years following the Second World War and then during the Cold War years, with respect to Communist countries other than the Soviet Union (USSR). I do not touch here on the question of the WJC's role in the struggle for Soviet Jewry, which is a separate issue and is addressed in a separate chapter of this book.[1]

1936 to 1948

If we look back on history from the perspective of the WJC, the Communist years, just like the Nazi years before them, never prevented the organization from fighting for imperilled or persecuted Jewish communities. Isaac I. Schwarzbart, in charge of the Organization Department of the WJC, noted succinctly in 1957 that: "[t]he WJC struggled, with considerable success, to achieve constructive unity of the Jewish people."[2]

In 1936 in Geneva, during the inaugural plenary assembly of the WJC, representatives of virtually all European Jewish communities were in attendance to discuss the problems for which they all needed to take a common stand.[3] It is worth noting that two absent communities were those of Nazi Germany and the Soviet Union. On this occasion, the situation of Jewish communities in Eastern Europe was presented by sociologist Jacob Lestschinsky,[4] who was living in Warsaw at the time, where he had arrived in 1934 from Berlin. He gave a detailed report in Yiddish,[5] the common language of all the communities in Eastern Europe. For us today, his exposé on Jewish life represents much more than an account. It is a warning alarm from a world under threat and a detailed snapshot of the social condition of these communities before the Shoah swept them away. I think it is important for everyone to be aware of this broad and comprehensive panorama of the communities that Lestschinsky outlined in 1936 to understand the complete disarray in which the communities found themselves after the implementation and extension of genocide.

Following the Shoah, the communities of Central and Eastern Europe had to overcome additional ordeals. They had to fight for many years until the rights of the victims and the survivors were finally recognized and, to a greater or lesser extent, addressed. Geopolitical transformations, added to the years of migrations, the acts of expropriation, the redrawing of borders, and the forced displacement of millions of people after the geno-cide, imposed new political models. All of these changes caused fundamen-tal upheaval for the Jewish communities in Eastern and Central Europe. In 1946, many became victims of anti-Semitic pogroms, such as at Kielce in Poland, where the WJC sent a delegation to demand an explanation of the situation and to explore the possibility of Jewish emigration.[6] On this occasion, the WJC obtained the right for Polish Jews to emigrate, and many of them left for Sweden, where the Stockholm office of the WJC had arranged for work permits to be issued.[7]

Between 1947 and 1948, WJC delegations had the opportunity to travel to Central European countries. Community representatives in these coun-tries were able to participate unhindered in continental and global meet-ings of the WJC. In April 1947, a year before the Communist takeover of Czechoslovakia, a meeting of the WJC European Consultative Council was held in Prague.

The declaration of the State of Israel in May of 1948 was, of course, the watershed moment in Jewish post-Holocaust history. It also provided the hope that Jews would be allowed to leave Eastern Europe. At the sec-ond WJC plenary in Montreux, Switzerland, on June 27, 1948, in his last major speech as WJC President, Rabbi Wise proclaimed: "The State of Israel is established and it will stand. Politically it has been recognized by two mighty nations, the United States of America and the Soviet Union."[8] Still, while delegates from Bulgaria, Czechoslovakia, Hungary, Poland, Romania, and Yugoslavia participated in the Montreux plenary assembly, Nahum Goldmann, then chairman of the WJC Executive, said in his key-note address at that gathering:

> We deeply regret that one great Jewish community—that of Soviet Russia—is not represented here today. We have done our best to have them with us; and—optimists as we are—we do not give up hope that very soon they will be able to come into this framework of world Jewry which we call the World Jewish Congress, taking their rightful place and making their contribution as one of the essential parts of a united Jewish people.[9]

Unfortunately, this hope did not materialize. By 1951, all Jewish communities from Communist countries other than Yugoslavia had left the WJC.[10] Nevertheless, the WJC policy of trying to maintain equilibrium between East and West remained. Thus, at the third WJC plenary assembly in Geneva in August 1953, the delegates adopted the following resolution on the Status and Rights of Jewish Communities in Eastern Europe:

> The Third Plenary Assembly of the World Jewish Congress feels it its inescapable duty to draw attention to the unsatisfactory conditions which make it increasingly difficult for Jewish communities to maintain a distinctive Jewish tradition and life in the Soviet Union and the other States of Eastern Europe. . . . The Congress records its most earnest hope that the opportunity will be accorded to Soviet Jewry to organize itself, to revive and maintain the great traditions of Russian Jewry, and to establish appropriate institutions through which it could co-operate with the rest of the Jewish people. . . . The Plenary Assembly is encouraged to hope that developments and changes in the structure of international relations may result everywhere in such lessening of tensions as will permit and encourage the organization or strengthening of Jewish community life in all these countries, so that they may take or resume their appropriate place in the councils of world Jewry and within the framework of the World Jewish Congress.[11]

1949 to 1954

In Europe, Jews started to reclaim their lives in different ways depending on whether they were in the West or in the East: Western Europe embodied the spirit of reconstruction with the Marshall Plan. At the heart of NATO, military alliances were first established, followed by political alliances, as old enemies became allies. Eastern European countries and the new Communist regimes began to suffocate under the weight of propaganda: they were busy constructing a new mindset, in which the responsibility for the *fascist* past was put squarely on the shoulders of the West, and most if not all contact with the West was forbidden.

Despite all these political problems, whenever possible the WJC was at the side of Jewish communities, tirelessly active as the only Jewish forum in which communities could discuss, in complete freedom, both the problems that affected them and the challenges that lay on the horizon.

Construction of the Berlin Wall

The construction of the Berlin Wall demonstrated that Europe and the world were divided in two. To cross "the Wall" was the universal symbol of freedom and not only for Berliners.

The restrictions on Jewish life in the USSR and in most Communist countries reached extremely alarming levels, but the efforts by the WJC to allow "Jewish life in freedom"[12] were performed with tenacity, obstinacy, and sometimes through mediation. They were often the subject of strong criticism, notably because they required establishing and maintaining good working relations with Communist governments. One by-product of this approach was the re-establishment of formal contacts with the Jewish community of Romania. In 1966, Chief Rabbi Moses Rosen of Romania attended the fifth WJC plenary assembly in Brussels as an observer. The WJC leadership believed that through a combination of diplomacy and political wisdom it could bring about a reintegration of this community into world Jewry. That is why the WJC supported Chief Rabbi Rosen throughout his term as head of the Jewish community of Romania and as chief rabbi of the country. Rosen undeniably had a strong relationship with his government, which sent him frequently as its unofficial envoy to the United States in a successful effort to obtain and then retain Most Favoured Nation status for his country.

In general, neither the Berlin Wall nor the Iron Curtain made WJC leaders forget the communities in the Communist countries; they always thought that it must be possible to breach the barriers in one way or another and to reunite with the communities on the other side—they just needed to seize the right opportunity at the right time.

This opportunity came at the end of the 1960s.

In October 1966 Armand Kaplan, based in Paris and the deputy director of the International Affairs Department of the WJC, was invited to Sarajevo. The trip was organized by the Yugoslavian Federation of Jewish Communities, officially to celebrate the 400th anniversary of the arrival of the Jewish community in Sarajevo. In celebrating this event, Kaplan had various opportunities: an official visit to a socialist country; a visit to the local Jewish community; initial contact with representatives of other Jewish communities in Eastern Europe, who themselves could travel freely to Yugoslavia; and to lay the foundations for a potential visit by WJC President Nahum Goldmann to countries of the Soviet bloc. Kaplan's visit was so successful that in December of the same year, a delegation from the Czechoslovakian Jewish community was able to meet with Goldmann and other representatives of the WJC in Geneva.[13]

In January 1967, Kaplan was sent to visit Jewish communities in Central and Eastern Europe. The purpose of his trip was to finalize the first visit of a WJC president behind the Iron Curtain since the start of the Cold War. Kaplan visited the communities and organized with them a series of official meetings, which took place from March to April 1967. It was a historical visit, which took the WJC delegation, headed by Goldmann, to Belgrade, Budapest, Bucharest, and Prague. In addition to Kaplan, Goldmann was accompanied by Gerhart M. Riegner, who was secretary-general of the WJC at the time, Stephen J. Roth, executive director of the European branch of the WJC, and Yitzhak Korn of the Israeli Executive of the WJC. The trip was simultaneously a voyage of hope and sadness: the hope of improving relations with the Jewish communities and the governments of Yugoslavia, Hungary, Romania, and Czechoslovakia through negotiation, and sadness because, for the first time, global Jewry could, through the WJC, officially pay homage to the victims of Nazism in these countries. The WJC delegation met with the leaders of these communities, and visited the places of remembrance of the genocide and other atrocities: the former Pinkas synagogue in Prague, the site of the Nazi concentration camp at Theresienstadt (Terezin), the remains of the destroyed village of Lidice, the monument in Budapest to the victims of forced labor camps, and the monument to the victims of Nazism in Romania.

On his return on April 17, 1967, Goldmann held a press conference in Geneva where he declared: "The identification with the Jewish people and their collaboration with the World Jewish Congress, as the expression of the unity of the Jewish people, is understood and appreciated by their governments."[14] This declaration by Goldmann enabled the communities in Hungary and Czechoslovakia to resume contact with the WJC and for the WJC to visit them. Unfortunately, this improved atmosphere did not last long. The Arab-Israeli Six-Day War in June 1967 changed the game once again. With the exception of Romania, the other countries of the Soviet bloc decided to sever diplomatic relations with the State of Israel.

A new period of difficulty began for the Jewish communities. In Poland, in particular, anti-Semitic acts were carried out against the community under the guise of anti-Israeli propaganda. On several occasions, the WJC condemned the situation in Poland on the world stage, and firmly protested to the Polish authorities. In 1968, the invasion of Czechoslovakia by Soviet troops persuaded a portion of the remaining Czech Jewish community to emigrate[15] because the general situation of political repression in the country had become intolerable. At the end of the 1960s, the WJC led a worldwide campaign aimed at the leaders of East Germany (GDR) to extend the statute of limitations for the crimes committed by the Nazis. Besides these examples, we should not forget that, undeniably, throughout the 1960s the destiny of the Jewish communities in Central and Eastern Europe was linked to that of Soviet Jews, which had become much more sensationalized in the media, as a consequence of the confrontation between the United States and the Soviet Union.

The 1970s

As already indicated above, numerous organizations, personalities, and communities of the western Jewish world were engaged in campaigns to support the cause of Jews in Russia. The 1970s were the years of struggle for obtaining the right of Jews from the USSR to emigrate. The WJC was at the heart of this fight.

While the WJC, along with other Jewish organizations, was fighting for the recognition of the rights of Russian Jews, it did not neglect the communities of Central and Eastern Europe, and its relations fluctuated according to the course of political events. The Romanian and Yugoslav communities remained active within the WJC, thanks to the "flexibility" of their regimes, and other communities were allowed to send observers to the conferences and meetings of the WJC. In my view, the personal relationship that existed between Yugoslav President Josip Broz Tito and Nahum Goldmann played a critical role. At the time Tito wanted to be the leader of the so-called non-aligned movement, which pitted him against Indira Gandhi of India and Fidel Castro of Cuba. It was for that reason that he sought to open his own diplomatic channels with the West. Goldmann was a person of ambition and vision, both personally and for the WJC. He met Tito several times in the 1960s, and the two leaders discussed plans for a solution to the conflict in the Middle East, as well as the situation of Eastern European Jewish communities and Jewish communities in Muslim countries.[16]

In 1975, the countries of the Soviet bloc were among those countries that signed the Helsinki Accords. This enabled the WJC to demand at every opportunity that the principle of free movement should be granted not only to the Jews in the USSR, but to all Jews living in Communist countries. The Helsinki Accords helped to instill a desire for freedom in the Communist countries, and the political scene began to stir.

Toward the "Thaw"

The 1980s ushered in political change. In 1980, the Federation of Hungarian Communities requested to become a member of the WJC.[17] At the time, I had been elected to my first term as president of the European Union of Jewish Students, and it was in this capacity that I took part in the meetings of the WJC.

At the WJC, these were the years following the Goldmann presidency. In 1977 Goldmann was briefly succeeded by Philip M. Klutznick. The presidency of Edgar M. Bronfman, who took over from Klutznick in 1979, shifted the cultural and political center of gravity of the WJC from Europe to the United States. Bronfman, formally elected WJC President in 1981, made the plight of Soviet Jews a top priority. He paid several visits to Central and Eastern Europe during the first years of his presidency.

In 1983, the WJC decided to send a delegation led by WJC Secretary-General Gerhart M. Riegner to Poland on the occasion of the fortieth anniversary of the Warsaw Ghetto uprising.[18] From February 28 to March 8,

1985, Riegner also paid a visit to East Berlin. Although he was no longer secretary-general of the WJC at this time, he remained responsible for the WJC's Geneva office. Berlin was Riegner's hometown, and I remember that in 1985, he still travelled with a Nansen passport[19] because his German citizenship had been revoked by the Nazis in 1935. Riegner did not want to reclaim his German passport or obtain another nationality. For Riegner, the visit to Berlin was not a political visit; it was a personal return heavily loaded with individual sensations, values, and emotions.

Riegner had always been engaged in Jewish-Christian dialogue, which is why it was logical that he was invited by the Theological Department of the Von Humboldt University and the Evangelical Academy of East Berlin to conferences on interreligious dialogue. Of course, Riegner met the Lutheran bishops of Brandenburg and the secretary of state for religious affairs, as well as members of the Jewish communities of East Berlin, Dresden, and Leipzig. Riegner was invited to an event, which was both religious and academic, although not really political or institutional. Something had changed in the rigid GDR.

The Berlin Wall

In 1985, we found ourselves once again in front of the Berlin Wall, which had started to show cracks due to the fresh wind of *glasnost* and *perestroika* that was blowing in Russia. The world learned these two words with great enthusiasm; they meant transparency and restructuring. That same year in the Soviet Union, Mikhail Gorbachev had become Secretary-General of the Communist Party. He planned to change the USSR, and like a game of dominoes, his changes had repercussions around the whole world—in Europe and, of course, in Berlin. We hoped that the Jewish communities would also benefit from this wind, which was imbued with renewal.

In December 1986, Bronfman led a large WJC delegation on an official visit to Poland. This was an opportunity for the organization to officially open negotiations with the Polish government on the protection and restoration of Jewish cultural heritage in Poland.[20] This was a broad agenda for a country that still struggles to recognize the extent of this heritage and which, in its self-proclaimed role of first victim of Nazism, has enormous difficulty sharing the grief of other victims, and resisting the temptation to prioritize suffering.

In May 1987, a WJC Executive meeting was held in Budapest, the first of its kind since the European Executive meeting in Prague in 1947. The presence of the WJC leaders in Budapest was an opportunity for political meetings, but they also had the opportunity to participate in an event the likes of which had not been seen in that part of Europe for decades: the ordination of two rabbis from the Soviet Union at the Jewish Theological Seminary of Budapest. In July 1987, Bronfman paid yet another visit to Central Europe, leading an official WJC delegation to Hungary—the country with the largest Jewish community in East-Central Europe outside the USSR—and to Yugoslavia.[21]

At about the same time, just two years after Riegner's visit to East Berlin, the WJC considered it the right moment to make an official visit to East Germany. In 1987, I was still president of the European Union of Jewish Students when the WJC asked me to open negotiations with the leaders of the GDR. Bronfman did not only want to see the *Schutzwall*—he wanted to go to East Berlin, to the other side of the Wall, to get the leaders of the GDR to face up to their responsibilities.

I am a Berliner, and following a very pragmatic and logical idea, Bronfman asked me to get the process moving and obtain what he wanted. On paper, he found it simple and very natural. This visit would be a first as there had never been any official consultations of any international Jewish organization with the GDR, but above all, there had never been any recognition of responsibility for the Nazi crimes on the part of the East German regime. In the opinion of the Communist leaders, upon the division of the remnants of the German Reich into two Germanys, it was West Germany that had inherited all the debts of Nazism, including ethical debts of responsibility for the collective conscience of the German nation. According to their worldview, the Wall had created a clean and precise division, with the good and innocent on one side and the bad and guilty on the other. It was the perfect dichotomy: there was no place in East Berlin for mea culpas or admissions of responsibility.

The WJC, in contrast, wanted the leaders of the GDR to recognize and assume its fair share of responsibility for Nazi crimes. For the Jewish people, the Wall did not represent any division of responsibility. The WJC had asked me to do the groundwork for the negotiations on the recognition of this debt to the Jewish people so that we could also discuss the subject of reparations at Pankow, then the heart of East Berlin. In April 1988, after making numerous visits and taking part in endless discussions with the Ministry of Foreign Affairs of the GDR, I managed to organize a secret meeting between the Minister of Foreign Affairs of the GDR and Israel Singer, the WJC's secretary-general, and Elan Steinberg, the executive director of the WJC.

In the meantime, on another front, I was aware that private discussions had started between the GDR and the Conference on Jewish Material Claims Against Germany, more commonly known as the Claims Conference, over possible compensation payments for Holocaust victims by East Germany. The sometimes difficult and always discreet discussions continued for months, as did my trips to East Berlin. These trips also allowed me to establish contacts with the Jewish community in East Berlin, which was always a source of support during complicated negotiations that often gave me the feeling that it would be difficult to bring the process to a positive conclusion. It isn't easy to play the intermediary between two worlds: one in disarray and wanting to defend itself with a dying ideology, and the other a paragon of the struggle for fundamental rights. Two worlds at two different levels: fortunately the links had been established and deepened, which allowed me to continue the mandate that had been entrusted to me.

In June 1988, after more or less one year of claims, instructions, and controversy, the GDR government at long last announced "its willingness to provide humanitarian aid to the victims of the Shoah." Announcing such willingness in the socialist language of the time meant that the GDR government publicly recognized for the first time that it shared at least some responsibility for making reparations toward the Jewish people. It was the signal that the WJC had been waiting for and in October 1988, the first official delegation of the WJC, led by Bronfman, visited East Berlin. The official photograph captured the moment in the iconography of the Communist regimes: an oversized room, a large table with flowers, and the flashbulbs of the press from the whole world ensuring the publicity of the event.[22]

Just one year later, in October 1989, the Berlin Wall was demolished for good by the will of the people. I was present for this event, which would shake my native city and the rest of the world. To conclude the chapter on the GDR before the country was consigned to the dustbin of history, I continued my talks: effectively, we could not stop with a simple recognition of "willingness for humanitarian aid." In February 1990, GDR Prime Minister Hans Modrow, who had replaced Erich Honecker as the GDR's last Communist leader, sent a letter to Bronfman in which he assumed, on behalf of the East German government, the GDR's responsibility for German crimes committed against the Jewish people by the Nazi regime.

This was the statement that the WJC had been waiting for since 1945. The declaration said: "The German Democratic Republic stands unalterably by its duty to do everything against racism, Nazism, anti-Semitism, and hatred among peoples, so that, in the future, war and fascism will never again start from German soil, but only peace and understanding among people."[23] In July 1990, a few weeks before the GDR united with West Germany, I managed to obtain a letter, addressed to Bronfman from Modrow's democratically elected successor, Lothar De Maizière, in which there was mention of reparations.[24] On October 3, 1990, German unification took place, spelling the end of the GDR.

Other Communist regimes and even entire countries disappeared; and the geopolitical situation of the European continent was remodelled. Berlin is no longer divided into four zones, Germany is reunified, some states changed their names, others changed their borders, some separated peacefully, and others imploded following ethnic conflict.

The Jewish communities have followed the destiny of their respective states and have adapted to their new institutions not without difficulty and sadness, but always with a constructive spirit looking to the future. I conclude with a reflection on Berlin. Today, Berlin is once again the capital of a unified Germany, in which we struggle to find the remnants of Nazism and Communism and where the Wall seems to be just a distant memory. The city is still a gigantic construction site, and its Jewish community is one of the liveliest in Europe and growing demographically. Berlin is not a neutral city, nor is it indifferent. It is still a symbolic city, even if it is no longer the symbol of a Europe divided in two. Instead, Berlin has become symbolic of a Europe that fights anti-Semitism, as we witnessed during the mass demonstration at the time of the meeting of the WJC Governing Board in September 2014. On that occasion WJC President Ronald S. Lauder reminded his German audiences, standing alongside Chancellor Angela Merkel and President Joachim Gauck, "We are your neighbors and your friends. We all share the same values, we hold the same beliefs."[25]

As it always has done, the WJC monitors events and continues to be present in the countries of Central and Eastern Europe, perpetuating its mission, which is to remain alert to events, always persevering for the distinctiveness and survival of every Jewish community, without allowing the WJC to become a political instrument of any government or regime.

The Kurt Waldheim Affair

Eli M. Rosenbaum

As 1985 drew to a close, the international public profile of the World Jewish Congress was slowly but steadily growing, in large part as a result of the efforts of Executive Director Elan Steinberg.[1] Arriving at the organization in 1978 at the age of just twenty-six, he brought to the WJC a preternaturally sophisticated media savvy and a brash determination to restore the estimable international stature that the WJC had enjoyed during the early part of the Nahum Goldmann era, but had long since forfeited. Steinberg's audacious goal was to return the WJC to its former position as a major player on the world stage, defending and advancing the interests of the Jewish people, and especially protecting Israel and imperiled Jewish communities throughout the world. Crucially, Steinberg gained strong backing for his vision of "American-style assertiveness" from Edgar M. Bronfman, the prominent businessman and philanthropist who had been elected

Eli M. Rosenbaum is Director of Human Rights Enforcement Strategy and Policy of the US Justice Department's Human Rights and Special Prosecutions Section. During the events described in this chapter, he served as general counsel of the World Jewish Congress. Although he is employed at this writing by the US Department of Justice, the views expressed in this chapter do not necessarily represent those of the Department of Justice or any other component of the US government.

president of the organization in 1981, succeeding Philip Klutznick, as well as from WJC Secretary-General Israel Singer. Bronfman in particular was virtually fearless in matters involving fundamental justice and security for the Jewish people and Israel, and so the bold tactics for which the WJC soon became known won his early backing.

A son of Holocaust survivors, Steinberg was instinctively and passionately drawn to issues involving the escape from justice of Nazi criminals. The fact that the vast majority of the perpetrators had eluded justice offended him deeply. We first met in 1985 when I was practicing law at a Manhattan law firm after working for three years in Washington as a prosecutor in the US Justice Department's Office of Special Investigations (OSI). That unit was tasked with investigating and bringing legal actions to deport participants in Nazi-sponsored crimes of persecution who had come to the United States after World War II. I initially reached out to Steinberg in the spring of 1985 to seek his assistance in publicizing the determined efforts being mounted principally by activists and groups based in the Baltic- and Ukrainian-American communities, with the support of unorthodox political figures such as Patrick Buchanan and Lyndon LaRouche, to undermine OSI's work and even shut it down. Steinberg was immediately receptive to my appeal, and the WJC held a press conference and issued a short report on the activities of these persons and groups, highlighting documented instances of anti-Semitism in the campaign against the Justice Department's prosecutorial program. The WJC's revelations garnered extensive media coverage, including in *The New York Times*.[2]

I also introduced Steinberg to then-OSI Director Neal M. Sher, and the two soon became close allies on issues involving fugitive Nazi criminals. Their working relationship endured for the remainder of Sher's distinguished fifteen-year tenure at the Department of Justice, and their collaboration soon established the WJC as the leading non-governmental organization (NGO) supporting OSI. Steinberg frequently reminded interlocutors that the World Jewish Congress had been founded in 1936 to prevent further anti-Jewish depredations by the Hitler regime and that, despite the organization's valiant efforts (which included informing the Allies for the first time, in 1942, about the Nazis' diabolical "Final Solution" to exterminate European Jewry), the WJC had failed in that life-and-death mission, with ghastly consequences. He was determined that no stone be left unturned in the effort to ensure that surviving perpetrators were held accountable—an effort in which the WJC had already been engaged, in one capacity or another, since the time of the International Military Tribunal at Nuremberg in 1945–1946. For example, the WJC's Jacob Robinson was a key advisor to Justice Robert H. Jackson, the lead American prosecutor at Nuremberg, and later to Israeli prosecutors in the Adolf Eichmann case. The WJC had also long assisted prosecutors in West Germany and elsewhere in locating and contacting Holocaust survivors who might serve as trial witnesses.[3]

Several important lessons were learned by the WJC leadership from the organization's April 1985 experience exposing the efforts that were being directed against the US prosecutorial program. One such lesson was that despite the passage of more than four decades, public and media interest in the horrific crimes committed by the Nazis remained strong. The most important of these lessons was that the organization could make a powerful impact (despite its very small staff, especially compared with those of other well-known Jewish organizations) by identifying an issue or problem that was undiscovered, or at least under-advocated; seizing the initiative on that issue in key public forums; assiduously developing a constituency for the issue, especially through press outreach efforts that fed the media's constant thirst for new and significant (and preferably sensational) information; and, as a consequence, acquiring, in effect, global "ownership" of that issue.

In this regard, comparison with another World War II–related issue on which WJC leadership had labored that year is instructive. The WJC had been actively engaged, at roughly the same time in 1985, in the ultimately unsuccessful effort to dissuade US President Ronald Reagan from making a ceremonial visit with German Chancellor Helmut Kohl to the German military cemetery at Bitburg, where former Waffen-SS men were buried alongside former German soldiers.[4] However, the WJC's voice had been just one of many raised around the world in protest against the proposed visit; it had not been the first to denounce it, and the WJC's public activism broke no new ground factually. As a result, the organization's efforts did not distinguish the WJC in the court of public opinion from those of other Jewish groups that spoke out against the Bitburg visit. More importantly, the WJC was not in a position to significantly shape public discourse on the issue or, in the end, to influence the outcome.

An additional lesson learned from the WJC's successful public exposure of the efforts that were being made to thwart the US prosecutorial program in the Nazi cases was that because the WJC's professional and lay leadership cadres were so small, and because lay leadership approval for most activities was only needed, if at all, from Edgar Bronfman, the WJC had the ability to move swiftly, unhampered by a sizeable professional bureaucracy. (I had, in fact, brought the matter of the anti-OSI campaign first to another major Jewish organization, but because the approval process in that group dragged on for months, I decided to reach out to the much more nimble World Jewish Congress, which ultimately spoke out first on the issue, even though the other organization had a very substantial lead time on the WJC.) As it happened, all of these lessons would be put to use in just a few months' time when, in early 1986, the WJC almost singlehandedly exposed what arguably was the most sensational and shocking Nazi scandal in postwar history.[5]

I left private practice in late 1985, accepting an offer from the WJC to fill the newly created position of general counsel. At the time of my arrival, the organization's professional staff (which numbered less than twenty worldwide) was almost completely occupied with making preparations for the WJC's global plenary assembly, a conference held every four or five years, often in Israel, that brought together leaders of Jewish communities from nearly every country in which Jews lived. The next such gathering was scheduled to be held in January 1986.

At the plenary assembly, the Austrian Jewish community was represented by, among others, Leon Zelman, a Holocaust survivor and long-time head of Vienna's Jewish Welcome Service. Zelman was eager to speak with me about Kurt Waldheim, the Austrian diplomat who had served two terms as Secretary-General of the United Nations (1972 through 1981). Waldheim was now running for the largely ceremonial position of president of Austria, on the slate of the Österreichische Volkspartei (ÖVP) [the Austrian People's Party], which was the out-of-power conservative rival to the long-dominant, liberal Sozialistische Partei Österreichs (SPÖ), the Socialist party.[6] When I was introduced to Zelman, it was immediately apparent that he was agitated about something. He showed me a half-page article that had been published the previous Sunday in *Profil*, an influential, if comparatively small, Austrian weekly magazine. The article concerned an ongoing controversy in the city of Wiener Neustadt, where the Austrian military academy, with the support of Austria's defense minister, was refusing to remove a newly installed plaque that honored the late General Alexander Loehr—despite the fact that he had been hanged as a Nazi war criminal by the Yugoslav government in 1947. The final three lines of the article mentioned a "rumor" that "presidential candidate Kurt Waldheim" had once been Loehr's "personal adjutant in the Wehrmacht." However, this rumor was refuted, the article reported, by the head of Vienna's Institute for Military History, who explained that "Waldheim was only an *Ordonnanzoffizier*"(special missions staff officer) on the staff of Army Group E, "whose *Kommandant* Loehr was." (Waldheim's declaration of his candidacy for president had plainly inspired persons affiliated with the Socialist Party to look, however belatedly, into his wartime past. In fact, I soon learned that the small *Profil* item linking Waldheim to Loehr had been planted by the Socialists as a trial balloon. To their chagrin, it had attracted no "outside" follow-up interest either in Austria or abroad.)

During his decade as UN Secretary-General, rumors had occasionally circulated that Waldheim, who had always acknowledged serving as a soldier, but only briefly, in the German Wehrmacht after the *Anschluss* (literally "connection," the country's annexation by Nazi Germany in 1938), had done something sinister, or even criminal, during that service. Waldheim had always succeeded in quickly swatting down those rumors so that he could continue to present himself to a global public as "the chief human rights officer of the planet Earth."

In light of my experience investigating suspected Nazi criminals, Zelman pleaded with me to return to Vienna with him at the conclusion of the plenary assembly to see what I could find out about Waldheim's war record. I was skeptical. After all, Waldheim had been a prominent political figure for many years in New York City, which had long been called (especially by New Yorkers) the media capital of the world. If he had been concealing a Nazi past, wouldn't at least one of New York's famously aggressive investigative reporters have uncovered it years earlier? Also, when the rumors reached a fever pitch in 1981, they had been publicly refuted by no less impressive and persuasive a figure than Israel's UN representative Yehuda Blum, himself a Holocaust survivor. He assured an interviewer that while his government had "many differences" with the Secretary-General (particularly on the Israeli-Palestinian issue), "[w]e don't believe Waldheim ever supported the Nazis and we never said he did."[7] This arguably constituted the definitive exoneration. After all, Israel possessed a highly regarded foreign intelligence service, and if the government of the nation that arguably had the strongest interest in discrediting former Nazis (and in shaming Kurt Waldheim for what Israeli officials openly described as his hostility to Israel's interests) had cleared the UN chief, one might reasonably conclude that this should end the discussion. Also, the Soviets, who seemingly never tired of exposing the hidden Nazi pasts of senior political figures in Western Europe, especially West Germany, had been the strongest champions of Waldheim's selection as secretary-general. And our own CIA had vouched for Waldheim when a congressman inquired about him in 1981, assuring the legislator that Waldheim had been discharged from the German military early in the war after sustaining a combat injury and that there was no evidence he had participated in any crimes.

Zelman was unfailingly charming but also unremittingly insistent, and he persuaded Singer and Steinberg to dispatch me to Austria. A few days later, I was in Vienna, sitting in Zelman's office. Zelman quickly put me in touch with an individual who was working with a small group of people who were digging into the scattered records left behind by the defeated Nazi regime to try to learn more about Waldheim's war service. Soon, I made contact with Karl Schuller,[8] perhaps the most devoted of the former Secretary-General's behind-the-scenes pursuers. Schuller and I spent several hours discussing what he and his fellow researchers had found thus far. He showed me that Waldheim had publicly and repeatedly claimed that he had sustained a leg wound during the German invasion of the Soviet Union in 1941 and that after recuperating, he had returned to Vienna to resume his law studies. But documents that Schuller shared with me showed, among other things, that Waldheim had in fact *returned* to German military service, that he had been a senior intelligence aide to General Loehr, and, most ominously, that he had been present in Podgorica, Montenegro, on

May 22, 1943, precisely at the time that a large-scale massacre of civilians and captured partisan fighters, code-named "*Unternehmen Schwarz*" (the "Black Operation"), was underway there.

Schuller's newfound proof regarding Podgorica came in the form of a glossy, eight-by-ten, black-and-white photo of four uniformed officers, in an obviously posed shot, standing on a grassy airstrip. Two parked airplanes were visible in the distance. The officers stood next to another plane, the left wing of which extended most of the way across the top of the picture. In the background, a small group of soldiers marched in formation, with rifles raised. In the foreground were two automobiles from the late thirties or early forties. Three of the officers wore German uniforms of the Nazi period; the fourth wore a uniform unfamiliar to me. "The tall fellow," Schuller said, "the second from the left—that is our friend." The stiff, slim, hawk-nosed *Oberleutnant* in the black-and-white photo was glancing to one side. The profile did, indeed, appear to be a young version of Waldheim. "Turn it over," Schuller directed. I did as he asked. The reverse side bore what looked like an original black-and-red stamp of the photographic branch of the Prince Eugen Division of the Waffen-SS, along with identifying information, typed in German: the date (May 22, 1943) and location ("landing strip at Podgorica") of the picture, the photographer's name, the film roll and frame number, and, finally, the typed words, in German, "From i. to r.: Excellency Roncaglia Escola, Italian Commandant of Montenegro, *Oberleutnant* Waldheim, Adjutant of the Colonel, Col. Macholz, and *Gruppenfuehrer* Phleps." If the photo was authentic, it was a bombshell, placing Waldheim at the scene of an ongoing massacre, posing with some of its principal perpetrators, including *SS-Gruppenfuehrer* Artur Phleps, who was commander of the Prince Eugen Division, one of the most notorious of all of Hitler's Waffen-SS units.

I agreed to take the original photo and copies of the few documents that Schuller's people had found back to the United States, and, if I could verify their authenticity and import, try to persuade the WJC leadership to make them public. When I returned to the United States, I was able to confirm the bona fides of the photo (with the assistance of a retired CIA photo analyst) and to piece together an undeniable narrative that the self-described "anti-Nazi" Waldheim had been concealing key aspects of his

German war service for decades, along with prewar membership in several Nazi organizations. It was decided that I would present these materials and findings to *The New York Times*. Editors there assigned reporter John Tagliabue to the story and, after we met, he agreed that the discoveries merited further inquiry. I introduced him to some of my sources in Austria, and he obtained an interview with Waldheim, who had no idea that the *Times* was looking into his long-ago past. In his interview with Tagliabue, a plainly shocked Waldheim denied that he had concealed anything and insisted that he had been opposed to the Nazis and had certainly taken no part in any Nazi-sponsored crimes.

On March 4, 1986, *The New York Times* ran Tagliabue's exposé of Kurt Waldheim on its front page, under the headline "FILES SHOW KURT WALD-HEIM SERVED UNDER WAR CRIMINAL," giving prominent placement to the Podgorica airstrip photograph, attributing the photo and other evidence to the WJC. The story proved to be a worldwide phenomenon, garnering front-page newspaper coverage and lead-story status on news broadcasts throughout the free world. (The state-controlled Soviet media did not report the story.) WJC officials were eagerly sought out for media interviews by US and foreign journalists, and Edgar Bronfman became the first Jewish leader in decades to receive the honor of being featured by West Germany's *Der Spiegel* magazine in its weekly *Spiegel-Gespräch* newsmaker interview.

The WJC's US-based leadership, naïvely appraising the situation from an American perspective, unanimously assumed that in the wake of the international furor generated by the *Times* expose, Waldheim would end his presidential campaign. Our expectations in this regard were informed by the fact that American politicians had been forced from campaigns, and even from elective office, for far less serious cover-ups, such as concealing extramarital affairs. However, Waldheim never did abandon his run for Austria's presidency. It turned out that enough Austrian voters were unconcerned about the question of his Nazi-era past that he remained a viable candidate. The WJC leadership simply had not imagined such a possibility. We also underestimated Waldheim's determination to win the presidency. Most important, there were two key developments that we did not predict. The first was that Waldheim would be defended, very aggressively, by the famous Vienna-based Nazi-hunter Simon Wiesenthal. (A public feud soon erupted between the WJC and Wiesenthal and the mutual antagonism had scarcely diminished when, two decades later, in 2005, Wiesenthal died at the age of ninety-six.) The second was that the Austrian People's Party would respond to the revelations by running an openly anti-Semitic and xenophobic campaign on Waldheim's behalf—the first such campaign by a major European political party since the Nazi Party of Germany had shocked the world in the 1930s.

In the ensuing months, the WJC responded to this surprising outcome by conducting additional research in the US National Archives and in European archives. To my surprise, I found myself once again directing a worldwide investigation of a suspected Nazi criminal—but this time without the subpoena power and other impressive resources I had been accustomed to having at my disposal when I had investigated and prosecuted Nazi cases at the Justice Department years earlier. Despite the comparatively meager resources available to us, we plunged ahead in pursuing a labyrinthine evidentiary trail. Over a period of months, we managed to unearth, in archives in Europe and the United States, a large number of pertinent captured wartime documents, including many that named Waldheim or were initialed or signed by him, along with other evidence. Witnesses were found as well, including a former American medic who was the lone survivor of a British-American commando unit captured on the Aegean island of Kalymnos (Calino) and interrogated, according to one of the captured documents, "by Army Group E" on July 17, 1944.

The fruits of that investigative work linked Waldheim ever more closely to Nazi crimes, including crimes committed against Jews. And when I presented each new discovery to Steinberg, he promptly released it to the media, typically accompanied by a statement of outrage about Waldheim's ever-more incredible denials. Waldheim and his campaign team were increasingly on the defensive. To cite but one example, we found captured documents establishing that Waldheim had signed off on propaganda leaflets containing vicious anti-Semitic invective about "the accursed Jews" and "blood-sucking Jews," including one leaflet that exhorted Red Army soldiers to join the Nazi side. "Enough of the Jewish war," it proclaimed before reaching its moral nadir: "Come over. Kill the Jews." Those last three words, *Erschlagt die Juden*, were an explicit incitement to mass murder.

The investigation also yielded considerable evidence that the Soviet and Yugoslav governments had, for decades, known much of the truth about Waldheim's hidden past but had kept the facts secret for their own Cold War geopolitical and intelligence purposes, including during Waldheim's service as Austria's Foreign Minister and then as United Nations Secretary-General. At a press conference held on June 2, 1986, the WJC released a ninety-one-page preliminary report that I had prepared,[9] which largely attained its goal of helping journalists make sense of the torrent of revelations that we disseminated over the preceding months in unavoidably piecemeal fashion (as we discovered new facts).

One extraordinarily surprising discovery by the WJC arguably provided the single most dramatic moment in what quickly came to be known internationally as "the Waldheim affair." Postwar documentation we found at the US National Archives showed that Kurt Waldheim had been listed in February 1948 as wanted by—irony of ironies—the UN War Crimes Commission (UNWCC), for murders in which he was said to have participated during his service in Yugoslavia on General Loehr's staff. A Commission fact-finding committee composed of a Briton, a Norwegian, and two Americans had given Waldheim the UNWCC's "A" classification, a designation the committee reserved for suspected war criminals whose apprehension was considered to be of the highest priority. Only those persons against whom a prima facie case was assembled were branded with that modern-day scarlet letter.

A pitched and very public battle ensued to obtain the release of Waldheim's UNWCC charge file, which was held under lock and key, like all of the other UNWCC records, by the United Nations Archive in Manhattan. Eventually, I obtained a copy of the still-sealed file from a UN source and the WJC made its incriminating contents public. A successful WJC campaign followed to press the United Nations to open the UNWCC files to researchers; the UN opened the files in late 1987, and scholars have been utilizing them ever since.

Month after month, the WJC continued its campaign of disclosures, with hardly a week going by without a new investigative revelation. The story remained a major focus of international media attention into 1987, and almost always it was the WJC that was cited as taking the lead in pursuing the truth about Waldheim. Those efforts notwithstanding, on June 8, 1986, Waldheim won the presidential runoff, and a month later he was inaugurated as president of Austria. In what was almost universally reported as a diplomatic snub, the US Ambassador to Austria, Ronald S. Lauder, did not attend the inaugural ceremonies. Twenty years later, in 2007, Lauder succeeded Bronfman as WJC President.

Although Waldheim's election stunned the WJC leadership, the organization did not give up. It did, however, have to identify an attainable goal. Preventing Waldheim's ascension to Austria's presidency and fomenting a criminal investigation in Austria were, obviously, no longer achievable objectives. At Elan Steinberg's initiative, the WJC leadership decided to press for Waldheim to be barred from entering the United States, under a 1978 US immigration statute that rendered participants in Nazi-sponsored acts of persecution inadmissible to the United States. The WJC shared with Neal Sher at the US Justice Department all of the evidence it had amassed, and under his leadership the Office of Special Investigations investigated Waldheim's wartime whereabouts and actions.

On April 27, 1987, the US Department of Justice announced that the Departments of Justice and State had determined that US law required that Kurt Waldheim's name be added to the border control watch list on the basis that he was ineligible to enter the United States because "the evidence . . . establishes a prima facie case that Kurt Waldheim assisted or otherwise participated in the persecution of persons because of race, religion, national origin, or political opinion." Thus, Kurt Waldheim became the first sitting head of state in history to be formally barred from entering the United States. OSI's lengthy investigative report, detailing evidence found by that office in support of its recommendation that Waldheim be barred from entry, was later released publicly after a Freedom of Information Act lawsuit was brought to compel its release. Illustrative of the report's damning findings is the following:

> The available evidence demonstrates that under established legal principles, Lieutenant Waldheim "assisted or otherwise participated" in the

following persecutorial [*sic*] activities: the transfer of civilian prisoners to the SS for exploitation as slave labor; the mass deportation of civilians to concentration death camps; the deportation of Jews from the Greek islands and Banja Luka, Yugoslavia, to concentration and death camps; the utilization of anti-Semitic propaganda; the mistreatment and execution of Allied prisoners; and reprisal execution of hostages and other civilians.[10]

The 204-page report (available to this day on the Justice Department's website) noted that "a full opportunity was afforded to Waldheim and his attorney to provide information and to comment on issues" and that "Waldheim took full advantage of this opportunity. Between April and December 1986, Waldheim made seven submissions to the government in an effort to demonstrate that he did not engage in persecutory activities during World War II."

Unexpectedly, the exposure of Waldheim's Nazi-era past also precipitated a long-overdue reckoning, in Austria and beyond, with the truth about the country's own mid-century past. The Waldheim controversy led directly to a belated, and in many quarters anguished, confrontation with the myth, cherished in Austria for more than four decades, that the country had been "Hitler's first victim," when, in fact, it was actually his homeland and enthusiastic ally, a nation whose citizens had played a disproportionate role in perpetrating the Holocaust and other Nazi-era atrocities.

On the heels of the Reagan Administration watch list announcement that effectively vindicated the WJC's position on Waldheim's involvement in Nazi crimes, the WJC leadership soon commenced a similarly successful effort to persuade other countries to close their borders to Waldheim. In the end, during his six-year presidency, the Austrian Foreign Ministry's tenacious efforts to secure invitations from foreign governments for official visits by Austria's controversial president succeeded solely in a few Arab and Muslim capitals and in tiny Lichtenstein. *Der Spiegel* characterized President Waldheim as a man who "crosse[d] Austria back and forth," appearing at minor functions to deliver "empty discourses."[11] Not one major Western head of state visited Vienna during Waldheim's term of office, so fearful were they of having to decide whether to meet with—or snub—him.[12]

The WJC's high-profile, successful leadership in the effort to expose Kurt Waldheim's Nazi past and to win his banishment from Western countries empowered the organization to deal with other challenges as well, including some that it determined were best handled quietly, behind the scenes. There was, for example, the matter of widespread anti-Jewish threats that began appearing on posters and graffiti in the Paraguayan capital of Asunción in the summer of 1986. Paraguay's tiny Jewish community was terrified, and for good reason. Paraguay was a police state, run with an iron fist by General Alfredo Stroessner, a brutal dictator who reveled in his German ancestry and seemed little troubled by his country's reputation as a haven for fugitive Nazi war criminals. Indeed, Jewish leadership there had been warned repeatedly over the years that the Jews of Paraguay would pay a steep price—in lives—in the event that any attempt were made to apprehend Nazi criminals hiding in the country. If anti-Jewish outrages were being committed in public now, it could only be happening with the connivance, or at least the tacit approval, of Stroessner's dreaded secret police. The leaders of the Paraguayan Jewish community desperately, if quietly, reached out to the WJC for help.

We immediately drafted a strongly worded private letter from Bronfman to Stroessner and within just two weeks, the wave of venomous anti-Semitic agitation came to an end. Stroessner sent a warm, almost obsequious, reply letter to Bronfman, assuring him of his steadfast commitment to ensuring the security of Paraguay's Jews. A WJC official in Latin America telexed us shortly thereafter to relay the happy news that "Stroessner personally gave orders to put an end to the anti-Semitic wave," and that his contact in Asunción "is grateful for the WJC intervention, which he considers decisive." According to the contact in Asunción, "Stroessner enormously fears being accused of being an anti-Semite, because of the repercussions in the United States." Later, we learned from another of our Latin American representatives that what Stroessner had in mind was the possibility that, as our contact put it, "Bronfman would do to him what he has done to Waldheim."

The Waldheim Affair, and the highly effective manner in which the WJC led the successful effort both to expose Waldheim's Nazi past and to secure significant measures of historical and political justice (but not, alas, juridical justice—Austrian law enforcement authorities refused even to commence an investigation), rocketed the WJC back into the international forefront of Jewish NGOs and restored its worldwide stature, thus achieving the ambitious goal that Elan Steinberg had envisioned for the organization long before the question of Kurt Waldheim's Nazi-era past first appeared on the WJC's radar. The experience also greatly elevated expectations, both within and without the WJC, of what the organization could achieve. It correspondingly increased the confidence of WJC leadership in its ability to impact international events and decisions in which important Jewish interests were implicated. Those elevated expectations and that newfound confidence—and especially the credibility that the WJC had regained on the world stage—led directly to the organization's history-making and highly successful efforts in the 1990s to take on powerful Swiss banks for failing to disgorge the contents of bank accounts that had been opened by European Jews who subsequently fell victim to the Nazis.[13]

For more than twenty years, the WJC's landmark work in the Kurt Waldheim matter served not only as the hallmark of its belatedly restored capabilities and international leadership, but also as the best known— and perhaps most remarkable—of the many important achievements recorded by the World Jewish Congress during the Bronfman era.

This chapter is adapted in part from the author's 1993 book (co-authored with William Hoffer), *Betrayal: The Untold Story of the Kurt Waldheim Investigation and Cover-Up* (New York, 1993).

In Search of Justice:
The World Jewish Congress
and the Swiss Banks

Gregg J. Rickman

August 13, 1998

On August 13, 1998, the Swiss people awoke to find that a three-year "war" over Holocaust assets had ended. The day before, a group of Swiss banks had agreed to pay $1.25 billion to thousands of Holocaust survivors and their heirs, after more than fifty years of stonewalling over the fate of their assets.

Among those who had worked hard to achieve this settlement were US Senator Alfonse D'Amato from New York, the chairman of the Senate Banking, Housing and Urban Affairs Committee, who held multiple hearings on Swiss banks and the status of Holocaust survivors or heirs; US District Judge Edward R. Korman of the Eastern District of New York, who had presided and would continue presiding over a series of class actions brought against the Swiss banks by survivors; and Ambassador Stuart E. Eizenstat, who, first as US Undersecretary of Commerce and then as US

Gregg J. Rickman was on the staff of US Senator Alfonse M. D'Amato and, from 1995–1998, led the US Senate Banking Committee's examination of the Swiss banks and their treatment of Holocaust-era assets during and after World War II.

Undersecretary of State, had led negotiations between the various parties to the controversy. But no one deserved the credit for this enormous victory as much as the World Jewish Congress and its president, Edgar M. Bronfman, Sr.

December 7, 1995

At 12:20 p.m. on December 7, 1995, Bronfman arrived at the US Capitol building to meet with D'Amato, accompanied by WJC Secretary-General Israel Singer and Stephen Herbits, Executive Vice President of Corporate Policy and External Affairs at Seagrams Co. Ltd., and one of Bronfman's senior aides. Bronfman had come to Washington because he wanted to recruit D'Amato to join the WJC in pressuring Swiss banks into providing an accounting of the assets belonging to the Jewish people—assets dating back to the end of World War II. Once into the conversation, Bronfman and Singer began to detail for D'Amato the events of that year, and what the WJC had done to bring the banks to the table.

Over a bowl of soup, Singer told D'Amato how the Swiss bankers claimed to only have found 774 dormant accounts, opened between 1933 and 1945, and left unclaimed since that time. He said that the Swiss banks had agreed to provide information to the WJC but were not doing so. Singer meticulously detailed the steps of the negotiations and the preliminary findings the Swiss Bankers Association (SBA) had made to date. Yet, he said, the SBA was stalling, and the WJC leadership was getting nervous. "They're taking advantage of you," said D'Amato. "They think that they can wait you out. I wouldn't trust them." "That's why we're here," said Singer. "We want to ask you," Bronfman interrupted, "to help us. What can you do?" Without as much as a thought about its implications, D'Amato said quite simply, "We'll hold hearings. We'll research it, and we'll look into the problem." Simple as it might seem, with this Bronfman had found his man, but neither he nor D'Amato really grasped the significance of D'Amato's decision. Soon the Swiss bankers and the Swiss people would find out.

Bronfman and the senior professionals at the WJC, primarily Singer and WJC Executive Director Elan Steinberg, had been sharpening their knives for the Swiss bankers for some time. The three made a formidable team. In large part through his jet-setting trips to Eastern Europe and the Soviet Union, Bronfman had raised the public profile of the WJC considerably since becoming president in 1981. Singer, an ordained Orthodox rabbi, had tremendous energy, commitment, and charm; was outspoken and often provocative; and liked the idea of access to royalty and presidents. While Bronfman and Singer were the WJC's public face, Steinberg was the planning and strategic force in the organization's hierarchy and thrilled in the daily conduct of relations with the press. With the irrepressible D'Amato, who took pride in his reputation as a pit bull, on board, the fight was on.

It is rare in life that one is fortunate enough to be a participant in a great enterprise. Moreover, it is rarer still to see such an enterprise through to its conclusion. I feel honored to have been a part of just such an effort. From 1995 to 1998, I was a senior aide to Senator D'Amato, and Project Director for the US Senate Banking Committee's Swiss banks investigation. The campaign to squeeze out a measure of justice was long and tortured by our standards. Still, while money cannot solve all the ills of the world, we could only hope that by bringing the Swiss banks to justice, those victimized first by the Nazis and then by the Swiss could rest a bit easier.

Prologue: Setting the Stage

In the years after World War II, a number of Jewish organizations, including the WJC, tried unsuccessfully to establish that Swiss banks held money and other property of Jews who had perished in the Holocaust. At that time, however, the Jewish groups' position was weak, and the Allied governments had other things on their minds, such as rebuilding Europe and fighting the Cold War. Four and a half decades later, however, conditions had changed. By the mid-1990s, it was time for Swiss bankers to face up to the sordid truth that they were wrongfully in possession of hundreds of millions—if not billions—of dollars that belonged to Holocaust victims or their heirs.

In 1992, following the collapse of the Soviet Union and other Eastern and Central European Communist regimes, the WJC, together with other major international Jewish organizations, established the World Jewish

Restitution Organization (WJRO), with Bronfman as president and Singer as one of two co-chairs of the Executive Committee. The WJRO's mission, in Bronfman's words, was "to coordinate claims for the return of Jewish community property and the transfer to the Jewish people of heirless holdings. We also worked to secure for individual Jews no longer resident in the countries in question the same rights that would obtain for local Jews who remain."[1] In October of that year, Jacques Picard, a historian with the Institute for Social Research in Bern, received a request from Lawrence Lever, the financial editor of the *Mail on Sunday* and a BBC film producer to write a report "to examine from a professional standpoint . . . a preliminary study on the subject of the administration of assets in Switzerland of Jewish Holocaust victims, and the use to which they had been put."[2] The result was a thirty-page paper entitled "Switzerland and the Assets of the Missing Victims of the Nazis," which Picard subsequently expanded into a full-length book entitled *Switzerland and the Jews, 1933–1945.*

In July 1994, Itamar Levin, a journalist with *Globes*, an Israeli business newspaper, was sent to Davos, Switzerland to write an article on Orthodox Jews vacationing in the Alps. While there, he met with Professor Yehuda Blum, a former Israeli ambassador to the United Nations and a Holocaust survivor, who informed him that the "real story of the Jews in Switzerland is the bank accounts left by Holocaust victims."[3] In October 1994, Levin applied to S. G. Warburg Bank for information on an account of a relative from Poland and was denied any information.[4] Within a year, Levin would begin publishing articles on Holocaust victims' assets in Swiss banks.

On May 8, 1995, the fiftieth anniversary of the end of World War II in Europe, Swiss President Kaspar Villiger admitted "unforgivable" guilt in a televised message to the Swiss people, and apologized for the Swiss government's turning back of Jewish refugees at the Swiss border during World War II.[5] With Picard's and Levin's writings and Villiger's pronouncements as catalysts, the Swiss Federation of Jewish Communities (SFJC) approached the Swiss Bankers Association regarding assets that had belonged to survivors. Michael Kohn, the vice president of the European Jewish Congress, asked SFJC President Rolf Bloch to inform Bronfman and Singer of this development. In so doing, they set in motion the opportunity for the WJC to become involved.

September 14, 1995

On September 14, 1995, Bronfman, along with Singer, Avraham Burg—Chairman of the Jewish Agency for Israel and the other co-chair of the WJRO Executive Committee—and Bloch met with the SBA, and the two sides announced the establishment of a working dialogue as well as a central office with a Swiss banking ombudsman. Bronfman had come armed with a letter from Israeli Prime Minister Yitzhak Rabin, declaring that he, as president of the WJRO as well as of the WJC, represented "the Jewish people and the State of Israel" in negotiations with the Swiss banks. George Krayer, head of the SBA, told Bronfman and the others that the banks had found nearly $32,000,000 in dormant assets. It also appeared to Bronfman and Singer that the SBA was willing to do only the bare minimum to resolve the problem.

According to Maram Stern of the WJC Brussels office, the Swiss were under the misapprehension that Bronfman was in this simply for the money. The Swiss, Stern explained, asked Bronfman to "name a price" for a lump-sum payment. According to Singer, the Swiss suggested that $32 million was a workable number with which to start. Bronfman held out, as he would later tell D'Amato, for a full accounting of the assets in Swiss banks. But what angered Bronfman the most was the arrogance of the Swiss bankers. As Bronfman related many times, when he walked into the room with the Swiss, he was not even offered a chair. The bankers abruptly gave him an ultimatum: "Take it or leave it." However, the Swiss would live to regret their callous omission of such a common courtesy.

February 6, 1996

Between the September encounter with the Swiss and Bronfman's meeting three months later with D'Amato, the Swiss had been silent. Promised some word on the assets and the search for their owners, Bronfman and Singer became convinced, as D'Amato also warned, that the bankers were trying to stall. Yet, at a meeting between the WJRO and the SBA in Bern on December 12, the two sides agreed to a six-point plan calling for, among other things, secrecy in their dealings. It was the violation of this point by the SBA that would signal the descent of Swiss fortunes and the beginning of the search for the truth about the behavior of Swiss banks during World War II.

On February 6, 1996, the WJC was notified that the SBA was going to hold a press conference the following day to announce the final results from their examination of the banks. Considering this a "blatant disregard" of their agreement, the WJC condemned the upcoming announcement.[6] The next day, the WJC went even further in declaring the Swiss move to be unilateral and unacceptable.

The Senate Banking Committee Investigates

By the end of February 1996, the Senate Banking Committee under D'Amato's chairmanship had begun its inquiry and was seeking the assistance of any federal agency that might be able to provide relevant information. To help us locate and review documents, we enlisted Willi Korte, a German-born attorney-turned-researcher and a tracker of Nazi-looted artwork who had previously worked with the WJC on the Waldheim case, and Miriam Kleiman, a University of Michigan graduate who had worked for a number of Jewish organizations in Washington.

As Korte and Kleiman settled down in the Archives II building in suburban College Park, Maryland, it did not take very long for them to find pertinent records. Korte found 2,100 boxes of documents from the "Economic Intelligence Division" of the Treasury Department. Then, after only a few days of sifting through the dusty brown boxes of onion-skinned papers with the original rubber bands and paper clips, last seen decades before, Kleiman found records relating to "Operation Safehaven." Up until that time, no one really remembered much about this wartime operation, but soon the world would come to learn a great deal about the effort by the US government to track German external assets in Europe and elsewhere during and after the war. The Safehaven documents would open the door for us to the history of the Swiss banks.

Within a few weeks, documents began to pour in detailing Nazi gold shipments, stolen securities, looted artwork, stolen jewelry, and Swiss collaboration with the Nazis. All the horrors and misdeeds of the past were being brought back to life in the pages of the documents Kleiman and Korte were copying. Within a short time, it became readily apparent that this project was bigger than the two weary researchers could handle, and it was obvious that what was initially thought to be a few days' work would require weeks and perhaps months of effort.

Trial by Public Opinion

By March, we were preparing to go public. Throughout the 1940s and 1950s during long and fruitless negotiations with the Swiss, American diplomats and negotiators dealt with the Swiss bankers and diplomats on legal terms. At each session with their Swiss counterparts, they laid out their arguments in a legalistic and methodical manner, trying to convince them of the merits of their case. Each time the Swiss would listen and argue back as if they were in a court of law. The mistake our diplomats made then was that they let the Swiss determine the agenda.

By the sheer weight of the information we gathered in less than a month of research, it became clear that we could not, and most assuredly would not, re-fight the battles our diplomats had lost fifty years earlier. Our goal was simple. We would bring the Swiss bankers into a court, but not one like the ones they were used to. In the court of public opinion we controlled the agenda. The bankers would be on our turf and conveniently we would be judge, jury, and executioner. Like it or not, the Swiss bankers would have to play by our rules. As it turned out, they were not very good at it.

On April 23, 1996, the first Congressional hearing in fifty years on the World War II role of the Swiss banks was set. Senator D'Amato had assembled a prestigious group of witnesses for the hearing. Undersecretary of Commerce and Presidential Envoy for Property Restitution Stuart Eizenstat, WJC President Edgar Bronfman, claimant Greta Beer, and Chairman of Julius Baer Bank and a member of the Executive Board of the SBA Hans J. Baer would testify before the packed audience in the Banking Committee Hearing room in the Dirksen Senate Office Building. Bronfman's testimony set the tone for this fight. His message was simple:

> Fifty years after the Holocaust, as Germany and the collaborationist countries have sought to face their responsibilities and make restitution,

> there remains the glaring void in the behavior of the banks of Switzerland.
> . . . Mr. Chairman, many Jews in Central Europe, and many others in
> those countries, saw the Nazis coming and made the trip to Switzerland
> because they thought their assets could be held safely there. They put
> their faith and trust in Swiss neutrality and the integrity of that nation's
> banking system. It appears they were betrayed.[7]

Representing the six million "who cannot speak for themselves," Bronfman
was in search of, in a word, "justice."[8]

The Swiss, meanwhile, were being somewhat cautious. The Swiss Jewish
banker Hans J. Baer testified that the SBA was planning to form a joint
commission with the WJC to study the dormant accounts in a detailed way.
Independent accounting firms would be appointed "to review funds and
property held by Swiss banks that belonged to Holocaust victims," and the
commission would then "verify that the banks have properly implemented
the methodology."[9] He declared that it was the SBA's "determination that
at the end of the current process, any dormant assets in Swiss banks that
may have belonged to Holocaust victims will have been distributed to the
rightful heirs of the victims, or otherwise to worthy charitable causes."[10]

Unbeknownst to us, there was about to be another significant development. One day before the hearing, Bronfman had met with Hillary
Clinton in New York and told her about the Swiss banks. He also asked
her to arrange a meeting for him with the president the next day, which
she did. On the afternoon of April 23, Bronfman met with Bill Clinton in
the Oval Office and enlisted the president's support. The following day,
among the many clips reporting the events of the previous day, we found
one in *The New York Post* quoting President Clinton as having said that at
Bronfman's suggestion, he would even work with Senator D'Amato to solve
the problem. Owing to the events of the time—in particular the pending
Whitewater investigation—this was quite a statement.

Meager Results

From the beginning of the campaign against the Swiss banks, the WJC
had claimed that the banks were holding as much as $7 billion in Jewish

assets that had been placed with them before or during the Holocaust. They arrived at this figure by including looted artwork, jewelry, securities, bonds, and of course bank accounts. Many in Switzerland doubted the validity of this figure and attacked the WJC for estimating such a high number. The SBA insisted that the sum was $32 million and no more. After exhaustive searches, the SBA maintained that it could find no additional assets.

Following the creation of the Banking Ombudsman's Office to investigate claims against the banks, the ombudsman Hanspeter Haeni received thousands of claims from all over the world. On November 12, 1996, Haeni held a press conference in Zurich to deflect criticism that his office was doing little to help claimants. In announcing the findings, Haeni characterized the WJC estimate that Swiss banks held $7 billion in Jewish funds as "unrealistic to any unprejudiced eye." He claimed to have uncovered only $1.3 million in undisclosed assets belonging to only eleven claimants, with only $9,000 belonging to five Jewish account holders. The WJC dismissed Haeni's findings as "pathetic."[11] Others criticized Haeni's methods and correctly described the meager results as adding to the growing mistrust of the banks and Switzerland as a whole.

Unfortunately for the Swiss, among those who did not take Haeni's representations at face value was former Federal Reserve Chairman Paul Volcker. He had been appointed chairman of the joint SBA/WJC commission that Hans Baer had heralded in his testimony before the Senate Banking Committee, and that was formally announced nine days later. Formally titled the Independent Committee of Eminent Persons, the purpose of what became known as the Volcker Commission was to essentially audit the Swiss banks' dormant accounts. One of the Volcker Commission's members was the WJC's then-treasurer Ambassador Ronald S. Lauder, who is today the organization's president.

Volcker was so bothered by Haeni's results that he announced the next day that he would examine Haeni's methodology to determine why more money was not found. It did not take long for Volcker's concerns to be validated. By June of 1997, as the Volcker Commission was about to begin its audits, the Swiss banks acknowledged that there were far more so-called "dormant" accounts—including thousands that might have been opened by Swiss citizens for the benefit of persecuted Jews—than the paltry number they had been willing to concede to Bronfman two years earlier.[12]

The Eizenstat Report

On September 26, 1996, Bronfman wrote to President Clinton that "not one ounce" of the hundreds of metric tons of looted Nazi gold recovered by the Allies after World War II "had gone to Holocaust survivors or victims of Nazi persecution." On October 25, Clinton replied to Bronfman, "The subject of allied and neutral nations' actions during and after the war to handle Nazi assets and dormant accounts is both important and complex," and "I have asked Ambassador Eizenstat to look into the matter thoroughly and consider your views."[13]

On May 7, 1997, Eizenstat released a 210-page study entitled "U.S. and Allied Efforts to Recover and Restore Gold and Other Assets Stolen or Hidden by Germany During World War II—Preliminary Study," more commonly referred to as the "Eizenstat Report." Among other things, Eizenstat wrote in his introduction, "The neutrals continued to profit from their trading links with Germany and thus contributed to prolonging one of the bloodiest conflicts in history."[14] One week later, on May 15, Eizenstat testified before the Senate Banking Committee that:

> Swiss actions after the War are the least understandable. After the War, despite appeals from Allied negotiators to consider the moral imperative, the Swiss demonstrated an obdurate reluctance to cooperate with Allied efforts to retrieve and redistribute looted gold. Despite repeated Swiss protestations after the War that they had never received any looted Nazi gold, this report is incontrovertible: the Swiss National Bank and Swiss bankers had to know, as the War progressed, that the Reichsbank's own coffers had been depleted, and that the Swiss were handling vast sums of looted gold. In postwar negotiations, Switzerland used legalistic positions to defend their interest, regardless of the moral issues also at stake. . . . Until last year, the Swiss banks were notably uncooperative in helping identify dormant bank accounts."[15]

If there had been any doubt before, it was now clear that the Clinton administration, Senator D'Amato, and the WJC constituted a formidable front against the Swiss bankers, whose image was reeling in international public opinion.

"Nothing Less than Extortion and Blackmail"

While on a trip to Switzerland in November 1996, British parliamentarian and WJC vice president Greville Janner suggested the creation of an interim fund, with contributions from the major Swiss banks, from which elderly Holocaust survivors could receive pensions, however modest, to alleviate their suffering. Both Bronfman and D'Amato reacted positively to this proposal, but the Swiss insisted that it was too soon to start talking about money.[16] Calls for such a fund, however, were about to boil over into an international uproar caused by the unfortunate remarks of the Swiss president.

In a year-end interview with the *Tribune de Genève*, Jean-Pascal Delamuraz, the outgoing president of the Swiss Confederation, rejected out of hand the creation of a $250 million compensation fund. "This is nothing less than extortion and blackmail," he said, adding, "Such a fund would be considered an admission of guilt."[17] Delamuraz also accused his country's critics of attempting to undermine Switzerland as a world financial center. WJC Executive Director Elan Steinberg responded that Delamuraz "was not only insulting, but he couldn't even get his facts straight." According to Steinberg, "The Jewish side never attached a figure to the good-faith gesture that was proposed. The offer of $250 million came from the Swiss side."[18] The spokesman for the Swiss Jewish Community said that "the Jewish community feels deeply hurt and finds the remarks are an insult to the victims of the Holocaust."[19] State Department Spokesman Nicholas Burns commented, "Frankly to make a charge that somehow an agency of the United States government is attempting to destabilize the Swiss banking system, or is blackmailing the Swiss government, is ludicrous."[20] The Israeli Foreign Ministry formally expressed "regret" concerning Delamuraz's words.

Sensing an opening, WJRO Executive Committee co-chairs Israel Singer and Avraham Burg declared that normal discussions with the Swiss would be impossible as long as the Swiss government did not denounce Delamuraz's remarks and that Swiss businesses would face a worldwide boycott if the Swiss government failed to do so. Threats of a boycott had their intended effect within the Swiss political system. The Social Democrats, part of the ruling coalition, joined the WJC's call for the Cabinet to denounce Delamuraz and days later even demanded his resignation.

The Swiss government realized that it had to do something to placate the growing international hostility sparked in large part by Delamuraz's remarks. On January 7, the seven members of Switzerland's Cabinet issued a statement proposing that the 40 million Swiss francs, amounting to $29.5 million, which the banks acknowledged had been found in dormant accounts, should be "put to proper use." The Cabinet suggested that the money be used to set up "a fund in favor of Holocaust victims and their descendants."[21] This was precisely the type of fund Janner had suggested only a few weeks earlier. Finally, on January 14, Delamuraz apologized to Bronfman. "I am very sorry that I offended your feelings as well as those of many other people concerned," Delamuraz wrote, "particularly those of the Jewish community at large. I assure you this was not my intention. The information on which I had based my statement regarding the fund was inaccurate."[22] Bronfman replied, "I look forward to returning to constructive work together with the Swiss authorities and the Swiss banks."[23]

"The Swiss Did Not Care to Have History Brand Them as 'Thieves'"

On March 24, 1948, Swiss diplomat Walter Stucki, then negotiating the follow-up treaty to the 1946 Washington Accords, told his State Department hosts that "the Swiss did not care to have history brand them as 'thieves.'"[24] Nearly fifty years later, Rainer Gut, Chairman of Credit Suisse, made the same declaration. Both men were trying to salvage a bad situation for the Swiss banks. Stucki was thinking about history and perhaps a point of honor; Gut was much more interested in the bottom line: money. In an interview with the *Neue Zürcher Zeitung* on January 22, 1998, he said that Switzerland and its bankers had just about run out of time to defuse the public relations crisis in Switzerland.[25] He feared that the longer he waited, the more money his bank would lose.

Gut, a realist with the interests of his stockholders in mind, saw that the situation was only getting worse. Each day brought new revelations, and the press, Bronfman, D'Amato, and the growing army of critics at home and abroad were becoming too much for them to handle. Gut approached the other two big Swiss banks, Swiss Bank Corporation (SBC) and Union Bank of Switzerland (UBS), with a proposal to contribute, independent of the government, to a humanitarian fund to offer, in the words of the Swiss government's point person in this controversy, Ambassador Thomas Borer, "a gesture of goodwill." What Gut and the others were thinking would cost them little. A humanitarian fund comprising some $70 million was in essence a mere pittance; split by the three banks it amounted to a little more than $23 million each. In reality, a point missed by no one, the banks were buying a temporary peace. Within hours of the publication of Gut's proposal, SBC agreed to contribute funds. On February 6, Borer announced the creation of the fund. A year to the day after the SBA had enraged Bronfman by unilaterally announcing the results of its supposed survey into the Swiss banks' dormant accounts, the Swiss banks finally agreed to take a step, however small, however halting, in the right direction.

The Humanitarian Fund

Later that spring, the Humanitarian Fund was formally established. By the end of August, the Swiss Parliament's Legal Committee voted 12 to 5 to bypass parliamentary approval for a 100-million Swiss franc contribution to the Fund,[26] and the following month, the WJC was in the position to submit names of needy Holocaust survivors to the Swiss government and in turn to the Humanitarian Fund. On September 17, the WJC submitted the names of close to fourteen thousand survivors in Eastern Europe to the Swiss Consul General in New York. A day later, Hungary's Jewish community submitted a list of over sixteen thousand names to the Swiss embassy in Budapest. Together, the thirty thousand names would form the beginning tranche of payouts from the Humanitarian Fund. Each of the survivors would receive payments of $1,000. While not a great amount of money, the sum would equal perhaps a year's worth of pension for the recipients who had never before received compensation for their suffering.

On November 7, 1997, in a much-publicized ceremony in Riga, Latvia, Riva Sefere, a seventy-five-year-old Holocaust survivor, was the first to receive a check from the Fund. In December, twenty-three non-Jewish erstwhile victims of Nazi persecution and oppression in Albania, aged sixty-seven to eighty years, each received one-thousand-dollar payments from the Fund. This group was all that was left of five hundred Albanian Christian and Muslim survivors of the Mauthausen concentration camp in Austria. In January 1998, the Fund executive announced that within three to four months, needy survivors in the United States would begin receiving payments.

In due course, the Fund was divided into two sub-groups, with the first responsible for recommendations concerning applications on behalf of Jewish Holocaust survivors, and the second for applications for non-Jewish victims of Nazism. Swiss Jewish leader Rolf Bloch was president of the Fund executive, and the Jewish sub-group was chaired by Sam Bloch, Senior Vice President of the American Gathering of Holocaust Survivors.[27]

Other Players Join the Fight

In the meantime, other players had joined the fight. In 1996, lawsuits were brought against the banks by a number of high-powered and experienced class-action lawyers. These lawsuits were consolidated before US District Court Judge Edward R. Korman in Brooklyn. When the lawyers for the banks moved to have the cases dismissed on a variety of grounds, chief among them jurisdiction, they were joined by Alfred Defago, the Swiss ambassador to Washington. In an eight-page letter to Korman on June 3, 1997, Ambassador Defago wrote, "The Government of Switzerland believes that continuation of these lawsuits would be inconsistent with proper respect for Swiss sovereignty under internationally recognized legal principles."[28]

On June 20, D'Amato sent an *amicus curiae* (friend of the court) brief to Korman supporting the plaintiffs. D'Amato wrote that a hearing in a US court was essential to address the issue of "whether Swiss banks violated the laws of the United States or fundamental international human rights laws with regard to their banking activities between 1939 and 1945."[29] Following the hearing, Judge Korman did not hand down a decision, but he did not strike down the case either. The decision was left open, and so the issues remained unresolved for a long time. Month after month passed but without a word from the judge.

Simultaneously, Bronfman's coalition was further enlarged by a self-directed group of state and municipal officials willing to add their say and their power to the campaign directed against the Swiss. Alan Hevesi, then the comptroller of the City of New York, threatened investment boycotts of city funds in the New York branches of Swiss banks, and organized a December 1997 conference of public finance officers to publicly discuss the disinvestment option against Swiss banks. This conference would grow in the following year to a nationwide collaboration of more than eight hundred public finance officers who held the public investment portfolios of hundreds of millions of dollars in Swiss banks.

By December of 1997, the WJC concluded that a global settlement could be the way out of the stalemate. Bronfman, who as early as March had suggested that a method could be found to settle the issue out of court, now moved forward with his idea. Elan Steinberg, interviewed on Swiss television, said that the banks had approached the WJC in an effort to seek a settlement, and that if conditions were right, such a settlement might be possible.[30] Bronfman suggested that $1 billion would be a starting point. "If they want complete and honorable closure," he said, "then it's going to be a very expensive closure."[31]

August 12, 1998

Over the ensuing months, negotiations to settle the class-action lawsuits turned into full-scale negotiations toward a global settlement involving the Swiss and US governments, the WJC, and D'Amato, with Eizenstat acting on behalf of the Clinton administration. At 7:00 p.m. on August 12, 1998,

D'Amato walked onto the steps of the Brooklyn Court House. Surrounded by hordes of cameras, dozens of lawyers from both sides, representatives of the WJC, and others, D'Amato announced what thousands of survivors had waited a half-century to hear:

> I am tremendously pleased and gratified to announce that we've reached a historic agreement with the Swiss banks that will bring moral and material justice to those who have suffered for so long and bring closure on these issues around the world and in Switzerland.[32]

After more than fifty years of frustration, rejection, denial, and abhorrent treatment at the hands of the "gnomes of Zurich" as they had been called, Holocaust survivors around the world achieved a strategic and moral victory with this single statement. The banks agreed to settle all claims against them for a sum of $1.25 billion. After two and a half years of "political war" with the Swiss, the fighting was over. It was not perfect justice, but then again nothing like this really ever is. For Edgar Bronfman and the WJC, it was success on a grand scale. What began as a stubborn insistence to not take the Swiss at their word for their historic misdeeds became a historic campaign for justice that spanned the world and put a close to one of the last chapters of World War II.

Confronting Terror:
The Buenos Aires Bombings

Adela Cojab-Moadeb

On March 15, 2016, Ambassador Ronald S. Lauder, President of the World Jewish Congress, introduced the recently elected President of Argentina Mauricio Macri to more than four hundred delegates from Jewish communities around the world who had gathered in Buenos Aires for a special WJC plenary assembly. The timing of the event was symbolic. Twenty-four years earlier, almost to the day, a car filled with explosives had destroyed the Israeli embassy in Buenos Aires, killing twenty-nine people and wounding 242. Two years later, on July 18, 1994, in an even deadlier terrorist attack, eighty-five people were killed and hundreds injured when another car rammed into the Jewish Center of the Asociación Mutual Israelita Argentina (AMIA, the Argentine Israelite Mutual Association). More recently, on January 19, 2015, Alberto Nisman, the special prosecutor investigating the AMIA bombing, was found dead in his home, the victim of what is widely suspected to be a homicide, five days after issuing a report accusing Argentinean President Cristina Fernández de Kirchner and Foreign Minister Héctor Timerman of covering up Iranian responsibility for the 1994 terrorist act.

Adela Cojab-Moadeb is a student at New York University, studying International Relations.

"For more than twenty years," President Lauder said, "the terrorists of three great crimes still have not been brought to justice. . . . President Macri, you have promised that after all this time, Argentina will bring the perpetrators of these crimes to justice. We believe you. We believe you, we trust you, and the World Jewish Congress stands with you to help in any way we can."[1]

President Macri's response was unequivocal:

> As Ronald said, we do not forget that here we suffered the ravaging consequences of two bomb attacks, which brought a lot of pain, a lot of sadness and grief, and even today haunt us since we are still in the dark as to what actually happened or who was responsible for what happened. And on the other hand, a little over a year ago . . . a prosecutor died, a prosecutor who was trying to elucidate the truth about one of these attacks. And he had prepared a very important report as to why we were actually signing a memorandum of understanding with Iran, which he considered to be unconstitutional. Our government, only a few hours into office, decided to go ahead with what it had promised during the political campaign and make the memorandum unconstitutional. And we are fully committed to helping in anything that may depend on us in order for the investigations and inquiries to make headway, and I know that is a feeling shared by the highest authorities in the Argentine judiciary.[2]

The following day, President Lauder reiterated his position and that of the WJC in an article published in the Israeli newspaper *Haaretz*:

> Argentina owes it to the victims of both terror attacks, to the Jews of Argentina, and to the international community at large to pursue this matter to the end, and to ensure that justice is served, albeit belatedly. Impunity for the perpetrators of grave acts of international terrorism sends a dangerous signal to the world and encourages others to engage in such activities without jurisprudential concern.[3]

The WJC had been closely and deeply involved from the very beginning in the international campaign to bring to justice the perpetrators of the bombings of the Israeli embassy and AMIA. WJC Vice President Kalman Sultanik represented the WJC at the funeral of the victims of the Israeli embassy bombing, and within days of the AMIA bombing, WJC President Edgar M. Bronfman traveled to Buenos Aires as a demonstration of solidarity with the Argentine Jewish community. While he was there, it became known that Iranian officials were implicated in this terrorist attack. At a press conference, Bronfman said that Argentine President Carlos Saul Menem had promised to break off diplomatic ties with Iran if it were established that Iran had played a role in the bombing. Subsequently, Menem retreated somewhat from this position, telling reporters only that Argentina's diplomatic actions with regard to Iran would depend on the eventual evidence.[4]

Bronfman, accompanied by Ruben Beraja, President of the Delegación de Asociaciones Israelitas Argentinas (DAIA; Delegation of Argentine Jewish Associations) and a WJC Vice President; WJC Secretary-General Israel Singer; and Manuel Tenenbaum, director of the Latin American Jewish Congress (LAJC), a regional affiliate of the WJC, also met with Argentinean Foreign Minister Guido Di Tella, who said that his government would place the fight against international terrorism on the international agenda. Bronfman, Singer, and LAJC President Benno Milnitzky then participated in a special session of the DAIA. There, Beraja declared that "thanks to the WJC, no Jewish community in need is left alone but is supported by the entire Jewish world."[5] Subsequently, the WJC supported a resolution drafted by US Senator Howard Metzenbaum and adopted by the US Senate, which condemned "the worldwide targeting of Jewish communities by terrorists determined to disrupt the Middle East peace process." Beraja, accompanied by Israel Singer and WJC Washington Representative Douglas M. Bloomfield, also testified before the US House of Representatives Foreign Affairs Subcommittee on International Security, International Organizations, and Human Rights.[6]

In January 1995, Bronfman and Israel Singer met with United Nations Secretary-General Boutros Boutros-Ghali to discuss the rising threat of terrorism and the targeting of Jewish centers, specifically both Buenos Aires bombings and a terrorist attack in Tel Aviv.[7] On September 28, 1995, Beraja testified for a second time before the US House Foreign Affairs Committee. His testimony prompted the Argentine government, and later INTERPOL, to intensify the investigation and issue arrest warrants for suspects in the AMIA bombing case. In his testimony, Beraja said, "We criticize the fact that difficulties [in the AMIA case] were increased by the lack of cooperation between security and intelligence agencies."[8]

During the following decade, the WJC continued to take an active part in efforts to prod successive Argentine governments into taking more resolute steps in the investigations of the two Buenos Aires bombing attacks. In 2001, Bronfman led a WJC delegation that met in Buenos Aires with Argentine President Fernando de la Rua and the presidents of Argentina's Supreme Court and the upper and lower houses of Congress to discuss the lack of progress in the investigations. "I would like to say I was satisfied with what took place in our meetings," Bronfman told the media afterward, "but I cannot go that far. We made it clear that this was high on our priority list and not something on the back burner."[9] WJC Executive Director Elan Steinberg was blunter, saying that "[i]n the Western world, no investigation like this has progressed so little."[10]

In July 2006, Bronfman and other members of the WJC Executive met with Argentinean President Néstor Kirchner on the twelfth anniversary of the AMIA bombing.[11] In October of that year, after the Argentine state prosecutor investigating the AMIA bombing called for the arrest of former Iranian President Hashemi Rafsanjani, among others, for ordering and orchestrating the terrorist attack, WJC President Bronfman issued a strong statement of support:

> The official report of the state prosecutor confirms that the Iranian regime ordered and orchestrated the terrorist attack on a Jewish and civilian target. It specifically outlines that this was not the act of a radical group within Iran, but the work of the Iranian government and its terrorist proxies Hezbollah. . . . This makes clear yet again that Iran is a state sponsor of terrorism and shows for all the world the threat we now face. The entire international community has a moral responsibility to ensure that Iran is held accountable for its terrorist actions. It is time for the United Nations to take a strong stance against a sovereign state that violates the UN Charter by calling for the destruction of other nations and employing terrorist activity to murder civilians.[12]

In June 2008, one year after he was elected President of the WJC, Ambassador Ronald S. Lauder and WJC Secretary-General Michael Schneider visited Argentina to meet with newly elected Argentine President

Cristina Fernández de Kirchner. During this meeting, Ambassador Lauder also met family members of the victims of the two terrorist attacks, as well as Cardinal Jorge Bergoglio, the archbishop of Buenos Aires—today Pope Francis I—and the then mayor of Buenos Aires—today President of Argentina—Mauricio Macri.[13]

In 2009, on the fifteenth anniversary of the AMIA bombing, Alberto Nisman, the prosecutor on the case, announced his suspicion of Iranian involvement in the bombing, telling the public that Hezbollah infiltration ran deep in Argentina, as well as many other Latin American countries. He believed the terrorists had been stationed in mosques around the continent to find local individuals who could be easily radicalized and provide assistance for their operations.[14]

One year later, leaders of the Argentinean Jewish community were frustrated with the sluggishness of the justice system. In a statement released by WJC President Lauder at the time of the sixteenth anniversary commemoration, he declared:

> On this sad anniversary, we express our solidarity with the survivors, the families of the victims, and with the Argentine people. We applaud the remarkable efforts undertaken by the Argentine authorities and Prosecutor Alberto Nisman in recent years, to determine who committed this atrocity. However, yet another year has passed, and justice still hasn't been done. This is because the regime in Iran—a sponsor of terrorism worldwide—is refusing to cooperate."[15]

Ambassador Lauder continued to urge the United Nations to take action, not only in this case, but to combat state-sponsored terrorism throughout the world.

Beginning in 2007, the LAJC held its annual meeting with parliamentarians from across Latin America to mark the anniversary of the AMIA bombing. In 2011, on the seventeenth anniversary, the LAJC sought support from lawmakers for a petition that called for the acceleration of the investigation and cooperation with the Argentine government. In the weeks leading up to the meeting, LAJC Executive Director Claudio Epelman told reporters, "The masterminds of the attack have not been brought to justice yet, but only Iran is to blame since they refuse to cooperate with the Argentinean justice."[16]

In July 2012, on the eighteenth anniversary of the AMIA bombing, the LAJC hosted the sixth conference of regional parliamentarians focusing on the prevention of terrorism, with the participation of Argentinean Vice President Amado Boudou, former President of Uruguay Julio Sanguinetti, and lawmakers from nine South American countries. LAJC President Jack Terpins told the gathering, "It is lamentable that some nations, including in Latin America, are still fostering their relationship with Iran. We urge them: Think again! What happened in Buenos Aires can happen again, anywhere, and governments have a responsibility to protect all their citizens against such heinous crimes." [17] On this occasion, Ambassador Lauder reiterated his accusation against Iran:

> It is now almost five years that Interpol issued Red Notices, calling for the arrest of several Iranian suspects in the case, one of them being none other than Iran's current Defense Minister Ahmad Vahidi. Tehran has so far failed to hand them over to the Argentinean judiciary. The Iranian regime has blood on its hands, not only by suppressing dissent at home but also by sponsoring terrorism worldwide. [18]

The next development in connection with the AMIA bombing was not only controversial but was viewed by most Jewish leaders as negative in the extreme. As early as 2011, Argentinean Foreign Minister Héctor Timerman had suggested that due to the international nature of the AMIA allegations, a neutral committee should judge the citizens of Iran accused in the AMIA case. At first, Timerman's suggestion seemed to many people to be an acceptable and workable solution. Addressing the UN General Assembly on September 28, 2012, President Cristina de Kirchner put forward the same idea and assured the international community that she would not proceed with any possible Argentinean-Iranian deal without first discussing it with the families of the AMIA bombing victims. The families of the victims, Kirchner said, "have an obligation to voice an opinion publicly on a matter of this importance. . . . They are the ones who truly need answers; they need to understand what happened and who is responsible . . . this President will not take any decisions on any proposals put forward without first and foremost consulting them and the parliamentary representatives of my country." [19]

Kirchner's speech was generally well received. Indeed, there were expectations that the Kirchner government wanted to make progress in the investigation. The day before Kirchner's UN speech, following a meeting with Timerman, WJC President Lauder said, "The World Jewish Congress stands with the families of the victims. Justice cannot be delayed, and answers to the families and the Jewish community are long overdue."[20] As it turned out, such positive expectations proved to be unfounded. On January 27, 2013, the Kirchner government signed a memorandum of understanding (MOU) with Iran without the promised consultations with the families of the AMIA bombing victims. In the eyes of many Jews, both in Argentina and elsewhere, this was an act of ultimate betrayal. LAJC President Terpins said, "I don't understand how one can have relations with a country that is an enemy, a state which Argentina's own judiciary considers the mastermind of the bombings."[21]

The MOU provided for the establishment of a so-called Truth Commission made up of five supposedly nonaligned judges. In moving responsibility for the prosecution of accused Iranians from the Argentinean and Iranian governments to a third party, however, the MOU granted immunity to former Iranian diplomats from extradition to Argentina to stand trial. This Truth Commission, according to LAJC Director Epelman, was "an important step backward in the search [for] justice," with the accused nearly untouchable and the case's diligence compromised.[22]

It soon became clear that Iran had no intention of complying with the terms of the MOU under any circumstances. Evelyn Sommer, chairperson of the WJC's North American Section, said, "This Iranian refusal to abide by Argentinean jurisprudence is truly unacceptable."[23] Later that year, she added, "Iran is not concerned with the AMIA [bombing]; it is concerned with its larger economic issues."[24] Lead prosecutor Nisman offered to fly to Iran to record statements by the accused to comply with the MOU's premise that the Iranians were not to be extradited, but the Iranians refused to speak to him, and the trip never took place.[25] Ambassador Lauder called the MOU unconstitutional, and an agreement that was "flawed in its very conception."[26]

In February 2013, there were demonstrations in front of the Argentinean parliament and outside the Holocaust Museum in Buenos Aires to protest the MOU, while world leaders expressed outrage and disappointment in

Argentinean legislation.[27] In a joint statement Terpins and Lauder said, "This deal with Iran is an affront to justice. The Iranian government cannot be considered a neutral interlocutor in this affair because its leaders are involved in terrorist activities themselves."[28] On May 29, 2013, less than four months after the signing of the MOU, Nisman published and filed an indictment against Iran, accusing its government of infiltrating Latin American countries, setting up espionage bases, and coordinating the attack on the AMIA center.[29] After the report was published, Ambassador Lauder again urged governments to take the Iranian threat and accusation seriously, stating, "It is inconceivable that those who perpetrated heinous crimes against civilians and who continue to prepare acts of terrorism against people in Latin America oversee the legal investigation into these crimes. It is just like putting the fox in charge of the henhouse."[30]

On the nineteenth anniversary of the AMIA bombing, the LAJC hosted Nisman in Buenos Aires to present his case in front of Jewish leaders. Nisman had been invited, along with Matthew Levitt of the Washington Institute for Near East Policy and Ilan Berman of the American Foreign Policy Council, to testify before the US House of Representatives hearing on the Iranian threat to national security, but was denied funding for the trip by Argentine Attorney General Alejandra Gils Carbó.[31] Although he could not go to New York, he presented his case before the LAJC and the Argentine Jewish leadership, and later attended the official ceremony at the site of the bombing. It should be noted that President Cristina de Kirchner did not attend the briefing or the ceremony because of Jewish backlash against the signing of the MOU.[32]

In 2014, Pope Francis, former archbishop of Buenos Aires, recorded a video message to commemorate the twentieth anniversary of the AMIA bombing, in which he said that he stands "side-by-side with all those who have seen lives cut short, hopes destroyed, and ruined." He continued, "Terrorism is lunacy; its only purpose is to kill. It does not build anything; it only destroys." The video was recorded by LAJC Executive Director Epelman, a personal friend of the Pope for many years, and screened at the twentieth memorial ceremony in Buenos Aires. The Pope concluded his message with a cry for diligence in the AMIA bombing case: "Together with my solidarity and my prayers for all the victims, comes my desire for justice. May justice be done!" Ambassador Lauder thanked the Pope for making his opinion "known so forthrightly," adding that "the world needs to hear his message."[33]

On the occasion of the twentieth anniversary of the AMIA bombing, WJC CEO Robert Singer wrote in the New York *Jewish Week* of July 21, 2014: "We at the World Jewish Congress approach the AMIA anniversary, as we do each year, with a heavy heart. We grieve for our many friends lost and who are living with the aftermath of the atrocity." Singer said that the only way to right the wrong is to bring those responsible to justice, and for that to happen, the world must see Iran for what it is: a danger to the world at large. The AMIA tragedy, according to Singer, was an act against all Jewish people. "We've learned," he wrote, "that the world loves to forget. But as Jews, we must heed the commandment of *zakhor*—remember. . . . Some people say that 'justice delayed is justice denied,' but we will keep insisting until justice is done."[34]

On January 14, 2015, Special Prosecutor Nisman filed a criminal complaint against President Fernández de Kirchner and Foreign Minister Timerman, accusing them of having covered up the AMIA case and of signing the MOU with the intention of protecting the accused Iranian diplomats in exchange for enhanced trade with Iran. The case looked promising; a closed-door congressional hearing was scheduled for January 19, 2015 at which Nisman was to present evidence for the president's indictment. The AMIA case took a turn for the worse, however, when Nisman was found dead in his apartment in what the Argentinean authorities initially called a suicide on January 18, 2015—only one day before the scheduled congressional hearing. Nisman's death was a blow to the Jewish community of Argentina and sparked controversy among Argentinean and global audiences. Shortly after Nisman's death, Jewish neighborhoods in Argentina were vandalized with signs that read "A Good Jew is a Dead Jew; Nisman is a Good Jew." The Jewish community, with some support from the Argentinean society at large, reacted by holding signs that read "I am Nisman" in multiple languages, a display of solidarity among the Jewish community.[35]

On January 21, 2015, thousands gathered outside the AMIA center in a rally organized by the AMIA and the DAIA protesting Nisman's death. Julio Schlosser, president of the DAIA, and Leonardo Jmelnitzky, president of

AMIA, spoke to the audience and read a list of those killed by the bombings. The eighty-sixth and last name on the list was Alberto Nisman. Among those present, bowing his head in respect, was then-Buenos Aires mayor and current Argentinean president, Mauricio Macri.[36]

At a solemn commemoration in Buenos Aires marking the twenty-first anniversary of the AMIA bombing, WJC CEO Robert Singer, representing WJC President Lauder, sharply criticized the Argentinean government for having signed the MOU. "No matter how long it takes," he said, "we will not rest until justice has been done!"[37] Also on stage that day was Nisman's oldest daughter, fifteen-year-old Iara, who lit a candle for her father and the victims of the AMIA bombing. During the ceremony, Singer made special mention of Iara's father:

> After the tragic and mysterious death of Special Prosecutor Alberto Nisman last January, a man who did so much to advance this investigation and who is sadly missed, we are now faced with a crucial question: Will we ever see justice in the AMIA case? Will the Argentine government continue to have the worst terror attack in this country's history investigated, or will it try to close this chapter?[38]

Less than one year later Singer and Iara met again at the special WJC plenary assembly in Buenos Aires when the delegates honored her father's memory. This time, the atmosphere was more hopeful. Still, the perpetrators of the Israel Embassy and AMIA bombings had not been brought to justice, nor had those responsible for Alberto Nisman's death. The conclusion of this tragic chapter of both Jewish and Argentine history remains to be written, and it is a chapter in which the two histories have become intertwined.

As Ambassador Lauder emphasized, the two bombings were not just attacks on Jews, but attacks on Argentina, and "the killing of Alberto Nisman was not just an attack on a Jewish lawyer. This was an attack on Argentina's entire system of justice."[39] It is precisely because the Israeli embassy and AMIA bombings and the assassination of Alberto Nisman were not just attacks on Argentina but also, if not primarily, attacks on the Jewish community of Argentina that the WJC has stood shoulder to shoulder with the Jewish community of Argentina to demand that justice be done.

The World Jewish Congress Today

Robert R. Singer

The World Jewish Congress held its fourteenth plenary assembly in Budapest in May 2013, with six hundred delegates and guests in attendance, just a few days after I was confirmed as chief executive officer and executive vice president of the organization. Holding the plenary in that location for the first time was an extraordinary sign of Jewish strength in a country where right-wing extremism and anti-Semitism were on the rise; it was made all the more extraordinary by Prime Minister Viktor Orban's important declaration that anti-Semitism was never acceptable. Despite Orban's declaration, and against his government's orders, around seven hundred activists from the neo-Nazi Jobbik party staged a rally nearby, protesting against the WJC meeting.

Witnessing the grace and determination with which WJC President Ronald S. Lauder and the Executive Committee, management, staff, and delegates handled themselves during that week in Budapest filled me with a sense of nascent pride for the organization that I now would have the privilege of leading in a professional capacity. I knew that I had come to the right place.

Robert R. Singer is CEO and Executive Vice President of the World Jewish Congress.

I was no stranger to the Jewish world or its challenges. Before joining the WJC, I served for fourteen years as Director General and CEO of World ORT, the largest and oldest Jewish educational organization in the world. Prior to that, I spent twelve years in the Israeli Prime Minister's Office, instrumental in bringing more than a million Soviet Jews to Israel, and coordinating the activities of the Israeli government on these issues in North America.

With this experience, it was already immensely clear to me when I entered the position of WJC CEO that the Jewish people were facing difficult times and that there were still significantly more challenges ahead. Anti-Semitism was on the rise across Europe, global terrorism and the threat of a nuclear Iran had left Jewish communities feeling increasingly vulnerable, and the Boycott, Divestment, and Sanctions (BDS) movement and efforts to delegitimize the State of Israel within the United Nations and other international institutions were growing stronger every day.

It was also evident that the World Jewish Congress was not yet equipped to deal with these challenges, having only just begun its recovery following the difficult decade that had rocked the organization. Ronald S. Lauder has consistently shown incredible strength of character and resolve since being elected WJC president in 2007. He was undeterred by the challenge of rejuvenating the WJC and restoring its rightful title of most influential global Jewish advocacy organization.

Professionally, the groundwork for my tenure was laid out for me by Michael Schneider, a giant in the world of Jewish community work, who had served as WJC secretary-general in the years that followed the organization's inner turmoil, and who had executed admirable damage control in lifting the WJC back on its feet and straightening out the disarray that had been left for him. It is to all of our benefit that Michael agreed to return to the WJC as special adviser.

As a native of western Ukraine, I grew up with a strong sense of Jewish identity in a Communist world fraught with anti-Semitic overtures. It was clear to me from a young age that the only way to sustain a Jewish future for myself was by immigrating to Israel, which my family and I did when I was fifteen. In those days behind the Iron Curtain, our resources were scarce and our networks grass root. In today's world of mostly free and open borders, Jews no longer need to rely on underground efforts to embrace their identity.

Thanks to organizations like the World Jewish Congress, small communities even in difficult environments are able to send their children to Jewish camps and schools, to celebrate holidays and festivities, and to teach their young ones Hebrew, Jewish values, and Jewish history. They know that someone is advocating on their behalf. Thanks to organizations like the World Jewish Congress, the centralized organizations of communities of all sizes are represented on governmental levels and in the international playing field. Today, the sky is the limit for the Jewish world.

Priorities

What do we expect of a World Jewish Congress? We answer: "No miracles." The World Jewish Congress will not solve all, or most, or even many of the unsolved problems of the Jewish people. But a World Jewish Congress may perform these functions:

1. Bring Jews together of many different lands and many different views who do not meet together in any other way;
2. Bring Jews together on a new plane, not that of giving and receiving, but for an interchange of views touching every manner of Jewish problems with a view to their solution;
3. Jews of one land will face the problems of Jews of other lands, invite their counsel, and invoke their experience.[1]

These insightful words were spoken by World Jewish Congress co-founder Rabbi Stephen S. Wise in 1936 at the first plenary assembly in Geneva, and they ring true even today.

While many Jewish organizations convene every few years to redefine their mission, the WJC has always remained true to its original purpose: to deal with the core issues facing the Jewish people; to represent Jews in the international arena; to protect our communities against anti-Semitism and violence; to defend the right of the State of Israel to exist as a Jewish state; and to advocate the Jewish values of truth and justice.

When I took office as WJC CEO in 2013, I knew that the World Jewish Congress had to focus its priorities to maintain and promote itself as the preeminent global advocacy body for the Jewish people. To do so, the organization needed to consider its messaging and programming and to expand its connections to governments and international bodies around the world. Ambassador Lauder and Michael Schneider had already rescued the reputation of the World Jewish Congress. My job now was to put the WJC back on the map and get to work fulfilling our mandate. As such, a major priority when I joined the WJC was to instate a strong program department and completely restructure significant aspects of the organization's professional structure. I handpicked Sonia Gomes de Mesquita, my inimitable chief operating officer from World ORT, to run the program department, and the results have been astounding. In three years, working closely with Ambassador Lauder, we have reintegrated and greatly expanded the WJC's flagship Jewish Diplomatic Corps, established a successful International Yiddish Center in Vilnius, and reinvigorated the International Council of Jewish Parliamentarians. In Jerusalem, our Israel Council on Foreign Relations has become a critical center of dialogue, hosting some of the most important statesmen of our day. It was also our firm belief that the WJC could play a critical role in Jewish and international discourse by developing compelling original content for conventional and social media and providing a platform for academic experts—both tasks we have diligently and successfully taken upon ourselves.

It was also at the top of our priority list to establish closer relationships with international bodies and agencies, particularly the United Nations, and to develop close ties with states both large and small. In the years since I entered this position, Ambassador Lauder and I have visited more than sixty communities and have met with dozens of presidents, prime ministers, foreign ministers, as well as mayors and parliamentarians from around the world. I have been a member of delegations that met with powerful world players such as US President Barack Obama and Turkish President Recep Tayyip Erdogan, and have joined Ambassador Lauder for many other high-level meetings, including with Russian President Vladimir Putin. Pope Francis has welcomed delegations of WJC leaders and has given Ambassador Lauder a private audience several times. In September 2014, Ambassador Lauder and German Chancellor Angela Merkel stood side by side and addressed a rally of thousands gathered to protest the anti-Semitism exhibited in Germany during the summer war in Gaza.

Our relationship with the government of Israel is immeasurably strong. Together with senior WJC leaders, we have met on numerous occasions with Israeli Prime Minister Benjamin Netanyahu and President Reuven Rivlin. The WJC and the Israeli Missions partner consistently on matters of importance at UN headquarters in New York and Geneva, and we have forged deep friendships with cabinet ministers and members of Knesset across the political spectrum. Our relations with the US State Department and the White House have improved considerably in recent years due to Ambassador Lauder's extensive experience and connections, as well as to the successful efforts of the WJC American Section and of Special Adviser in Washington Mark Levin to establish and tighten ties with various elements within the US government and Congress.

Since expanding our executive headquarters in New York City, that office has gained the reputation of functioning as an international political salon. In addition to holding high-level meetings, we established an informal speakers' series in coordination with WJC North America, under the guidance of Executive Director Betty Ehrenberg, that meets regularly and features an impressive array of lecturers including analysts, ambassadors, and government officials.

Over the last couple of years, campaigns to delegitimize the State of Israel have gained steam at an alarming rate, from the BDS movement through resolutions drafted and approved in the United Nations. The WJC has taken an active role in the efforts to combat these campaigns recognizing our unique value as a well-connected political organization authorized to speak on behalf of more than one hundred Jewish communities worldwide. In partnership with the Israeli Mission to the United Nations, we held a well-attended conference on the issue in the General Assembly Hall in New York, and we have opened a special department dedicated to dealing with the matter in various forums.

Another of our priorities has been to strengthen the small Jewish communities whose centralized bodies lack the resources and connections of larger communities. Through visits to countries such as Peru, Uruguay, Panama, Costa Rica, Montenegro, Kazakhstan, Bulgaria, and Kyrgyzstan (to name but a few), and at meetings with community and local government leaders, I have witnessed the intensity with which these countries embrace their Jewish communities and I have pledged to assist them as much as possible.

In my first year as CEO, I also set up the National Community Directors' Forum (NCDF), an annual gathering of senior Jewish community professionals around the world, to enable one-on-one connections and roundtable brainstorming. The first meeting was held in Prague in November 2014, and the NCDF has reconvened each year since then—in Lisbon in 2015 and in Dublin in 2016. A sense of community shines strongly at forums such the NCDF and allows for a much stronger sense of cohesion among the various directors.

Our activities in smaller Jewish communities also manifest themselves in the security assistance we began providing in April 2016. Thanks to generous donations and the diligent efforts of our expert staff, we succeeded in assessing more than two dozen communities, began providing technical and professional services, as well as crisis management training, and have launched a process of reinforcing community infrastructures in the eventuality of an attack.

Programs

WJC—Jewish Diplomatic Corps

The WJC leadership strongly recognized the importance of energizing young Jewish leaders and restoring within them the same sense of Jewish pride that Ambassador Lauder experienced in his youth and continues to hold to this day. For this reason, he insisted on bringing the Jewish Diplomatic Corps (JDCorps), which had become an independent organization in 2009, back under the auspices of the WJC in 2013 as a flagship program.

By 2016, the JDCorps grew to include two hundred young Jewish professionals between the ages of twenty-seven and forty-five who engage in diplomacy and public policy on a volunteer basis. Our JDs, as they call themselves, have stood in the halls of the UN Human Rights Council and advocated for Israel in the face of hostile member states seeking resolutions against the Jewish state; they write letters to governmental and international officials against anti-Semitic and anti-Israel activities; they publish prolifically in newspapers on every continent and in many languages; and they intervene on municipal, national, and international levels in pursuit of justice. They are lawyers, policy analysts, journalists, and more. The JDs are not just the future leaders of tomorrow; they are already the young leaders of today.

INTERNATIONAL YIDDISH CENTER

The WJC views the revival of Yiddish as instrumental in regenerating Jewish culture in Eastern Europe after the tragedy of the Holocaust. In pursuit of this objective, the WJC formed its International Yiddish Center in Vilnius in 2014. The location was deliberately chosen because the Lithuanian capital was traditionally considered the major center of Jewish culture in Europe. In its heyday, Vilnius came to be known as *Yerushalayim de Lita* [the Jerusalem of Lithuania] or simply the Jerusalem of the North.

The Yiddish center organizes seminars and workshops for teachers engaged in formal and informal Jewish education around the world, providing them with the tools to successfully transmit the information to their own students. From Ukraine to Uruguay, the center has provided seminars to more than two thousand people of all ages—teaching them not just Yiddish words, but also about the vibrant folklore, literature, music, theater, film, and media produced in the pre-war heyday of Yiddish culture.

INTERNATIONAL COUNCIL OF JEWISH PARLIAMENTARIANS

The International Council of Jewish Parliamentarians (ICJP) is a global network of Jewish legislators, government ministers, and other elected officials. Its aim is to promote dialogue, the principles of democracy, the cause of human rights, and the rule of law, and to combat racism, anti-Semitism, xenophobia, terrorism, and Holocaust denial. The ICJP supports Israel and contributes to the creation of an enduring peace in the Middle East.

The ICJP provides a forum for the exchange of ideas and fosters greater knowledge and understanding of the challenges facing Jewish parliamentarians and communities in Israel and the Diaspora. The ICJP is currently chaired by US Congressman Eliot Engel.

Israel Council on Foreign Relations

The Israel Council on Foreign Relations (ICFR) is a strictly non-partisan forum for the study and debate of foreign policy. Established in 1989 by the late Dr. David Kimche and a group of prominent practitioners and scholars of international affairs, the Council aspires to stimulate public awareness of world events and insightful discussion of foreign policy issues, particularly regarding Israel, international Jewish affairs, and the Middle East, and is a favored platform for distinguished foreign visitors who wish to present their views in a non-governmental setting.

The ICFR operates under the auspices of the WJC and has, since its inception, hosted numerous heads of state, prime ministers, foreign ministers, and other outstanding guests from abroad, as well as prominent local scholars and politicians. Recent guest lecturers have included Lithuanian Prime Minister Algirdas Butkevičius, Bulgarian Prime Minister Plamen Oresharski, Dominican Republic President Leonel Fernández Reyna, former Dutch Foreign Minister Frans Timmermans (now first vice president of the European Commission), former Vice Chancellor and Minister of Foreign Affairs of Germany Joschka Fischer, Honduran President Juan Orlando Hernández, Paraguayan President Horacio Cartes, and the former mayor of Buenos Aires and now Argentinian President Mauricio Macri.

The Council publishes *The Israel Journal of Foreign Affairs*, which appears three times per annum, and is distributed to diplomats, academics, and influential think tanks. Over the years, the journal has developed a strong reputation, attracting the writings of many of the best-known practitioners and scholars in the field of foreign affairs from Israel and abroad. Many of the most important issues on the WJC agenda are addressed in the pages of the journal.

The ICFR also operates the Israeli-European Young Diplomats Forum, which enables young Israeli diplomats and their European counterparts currently posted in Israel to enhance their knowledge of, and exchange ideas on, issues of common interest. Through monthly policy talks on relevant topics, the European ambassadors of tomorrow are being imbued with both a substantive knowledge of Israel and a network of Israeli contacts, both of which will bear fruit in the evolution of European-Israeli relations. Similarly, the Israeli participants gain an invaluable understanding of Europe. The current ICFR president is Dan Meridor, and it is run by its director Dr. Laurence Weinbaum.

SACC World—Global Security Department

In March 2015, the World Jewish Congress Executive Committee decided to form a WJC global security department in response to an alarming increase in anti-Semitic violence in Europe and a series of fatal attacks against Jews. The department covers Europe, Eurasia, Latin America, and sub-Saharan Africa and coordinates all activity with WJC regional affiliates and individual member communities. In this capacity, the department provides professional and technical security services and intercedes with senior government and police officials to obtain necessary assistance. The WJC has focused its efforts in small Jewish communities with underdeveloped security operations and weaker relations with authorities.

Since it began operations in April 2016, the WJC's Security and Crisis Centre (SACC) has advised communities in twenty-eight countries on security measures, has begun reinforcing infrastructures in five communities, and is on track to work toward reinforcing fifteen to twenty communities each year for the next five years. It has conducted crisis management training courses in more than a dozen countries to enable community members to be prepared for any emergency, be it a natural disaster, security incident, or major accident.

Holocaust Commemoration

Since the end of World War II, the World Jewish Congress has played an integral role in combating anti-Semitism, sustaining the memory of the Holocaust, and fighting for the rights of survivors to restitution and dignity. The world marked the seventieth anniversary of the end of the war in 2015, and the World Jewish Congress was active in organizing and participating in a number of major commemorative events.

Auschwitz

On January 27, 2015, the eyes of the world turned to the largest German Nazi concentration and extermination camp, Auschwitz-Birkenau. On that day, the seventieth anniversary of its liberation was commemorated, with the World Jewish Congress playing a critical role in this momentous event. In front of the infamous Death Gate at Birkenau, Ambassador Lauder delivered an address to the more than three thousand people in attendance, reminding the world that Jews still find themselves under threat, even seventy years after the Shoah. In partnership with the USC Shoah Foundation, the WJC brought 101 Auschwitz survivors from twenty-three countries, together with members of their families, to Poland to participate in the commemoration.

Ambassador Lauder spoke of the growing anti-Semitism in Europe and the recent murders of Jews, simply because they were Jews, addressing his remarks to the leaders of the forty national delegations present—including Austrian President Fischer, Belgian King Philippe, French President François Hollande, German President Joachim Gauck, Dutch King Willem-Alexander, and Ukrainian President Petro Poroshenko. The ceremony was broadcast live to tens of millions of households globally, receiving unprecedented media coverage worldwide for any Holocaust commemoration.

Bergen-Belsen

Three months later, on April 26, 2015, Ambassador Lauder delivered a keynote address at the commemoration of the seventieth anniversary of the liberation of the Nazi concentration camp Bergen-Belsen in Germany. Bergen-Belsen is unique in that it is not only the site of a Nazi concentration camp where approximately fifty thousand inmates, the vast majority of them Jews, died. From 1945 until 1950, Bergen-Belsen was the largest Jewish Displaced Persons (DP) camp on German soil, where survivors of the Shoah were able to experience a physical, spiritual, cultural, and political rebirth, and where more than two thousand children were born in a spectacular affirmation of life. The WJC's British Section provided substantial political support to the DPs during those years.

THE INTERNATIONAL COMMITTEE OF THE RED CROSS

Two days later, in Geneva on April 28, 2015, the International Committee of the Red Cross (ICRC), the world's foremost humanitarian organization, and the WJC commemorated the seventieth anniversary of the liberation of the Nazi death camps. Ahead of the conference, an exhibition showcasing relevant material from the ICRC archives opened to the public at Geneva's Red Cross and Red Crescent Museum.

The conference, called Remembering the Shoah: The ICRC and the International Community's Efforts in Responding to Genocide and Protecting Civilians, reflected on how legal and political responses to mass killings have developed since the Holocaust. The event was attended by two hundred guests, including senior members of Geneva's diplomatic corps. It featured a panel discussion with the American Holocaust historian Deborah Lipstadt and the Canadian physician, writer, and humanitarian activist James Orbinski. In his keynote address at the event, ICRC President Peter Maurer said that the ICRC "failed to protect civilians and, most notably, the Jews persecuted and murdered by the Nazi regime. . . . It failed as a humanitarian organization because it had lost its moral compass."[2]

"World silence led to the Holocaust," said Ambassador Lauder, "World indifference led to the Holocaust. . . . The Red Cross chose silence as well. . . . The first lesson coming directly from the Holocaust is that in the face of a human catastrophe, silence is not a moral alternative. This is more important today than ever because of what we see throughout the Middle East, Africa, and even right here in Europe. . . . I believe the ICRC has an important obligation that goes beyond relief work."[3]

The proceedings of the April 28 program were published by the ICRC and WJC as a 36-page brochure that is available upon request.

BABI YAR

The WJC partnered with the Ukrainian Jewish Encounter, in cooperation with the Ukrainian government, in September 2016 to commemorate the seventy-fifth anniversary of the Babi Yar massacre. Hundreds of delegates, including more than two hundred young people, traveled to the Ukrainian capital of Kyiv (Kiev) from the United States, Canada, Israel, and other parts of Europe to participate in the commemorative events, which also included an academic symposium and a special concert.

Speaking at a commemorative dinner in Kyiv the night before the commemoration, Ambassador Lauder said: "Babi Yar is one of the most infamous pieces of ground in the entire world. Tens of thousands of our people were killed there for only one reason: because they were Jewish." He went on to highlight the fact that Ukrainians collaborated in the German effort to exterminate the Jews of Kyiv. "While Babi Yar was organized by the Nazis," he declared, "there were willing helpers in the Ukrainian militia. . . . In almost every occupied country, local people helped the Germans round up their Jews. In some cases, the locals were even more enthusiastic in their killing than the Nazis. And that is what happened at Babi Yar." At the same time, Ambassador Lauder praised those Ukrainians who "risked their lives to save their Jewish neighbors."

I was privileged to speak on behalf of our president, the WJC, and world Jewry at the public commemoration on September 29th, alongside Ukrainian President Petro Poroshenko, German President Joachim Gauck, and US Commerce Secretary Penny Pritzer. "Too many of those who did not help the Nazis conveniently looked the other way," I said on that occasion. "Too many ordinary people watched as their Jewish neighbors were taken away and pretended that they didn't see." I also reminded the audience that the world seems to have learned little since the Babi Yar massacre. "Today, after more than 500,000 Syrians have been slaughtered, the world still looks the other way. It was the same in Rwanda and Bosnia and Darfur. When whole populations of Christians disappear in the Middle East, we don't want to hear 'Never again,' because it is happening again."

Missions and Exhibitions

Israel

During the Israel Defense Forces' (IDF) Operation Protective Edge in the Gaza Strip in 2014, the WJC canceled a planned senior staff retreat in the United States and moved it to Jerusalem, in solidarity with Israelis as they came under rocket fire from Gaza. Our top professionals felt strongly that it was time to stand with the beleaguered Israelis and not spend time in the American mountains. The WJC also brought a solidarity mission to the south of Israel to meet with people hit by Hamas rocket attacks. Israeli President Shimon Peres and the seventy-eight-member WJC delegation paid a visit to Kibbutz Zikim near the Gaza Strip, close to where a terror attack had been narrowly thwarted a few days earlier by the IDF after a Hamas commando tried to land on Zikim Beach.

In 2015, the WJC engaged in a number of activities and initiatives in defense of Israel. Approximately one thousand participants from a dozen countries gathered in Geneva in June 2015 to express their support for the State of Israel as the UN Human Rights Council held another debate on Israel and on the Commission of Inquiry report into the Gaza conflict. Members and supporters of more than eighty non-governmental organizations (NGOs), including many Jews and Christians, traveled to the Swiss city to express their support for the Jewish state and to urge the United Nations to treat Israel fairly. In my speech to the crowd, I said: "The reason we are here today is to tell the United Nations that it needs to change. It needs to overcome its obsession with Israel. This obsession is destructive, and it stands in the way of an effective human rights policy that is so badly needed."

BELGIUM

A WJC mission comprising thirty-eight international Jewish leaders gathered in Brussels to express solidarity with Belgium's Jewish community immediately following the deadly attack on the Jewish Museum of Belgium in May 2014.

The delegation, led by Ambassador Lauder, paid homage to the three victims at the museum and met with Belgian Prime Minister Elio Di Rupo, Foreign Minister Didier Reynders, Interior Minister Joëlle Milquet, and Justice Minister Annemie Turtelboom. Both sides agreed on the necessity to strengthen cooperation on a European and worldwide level to prevent further deadly attacks. The prime minister also agreed to set up a joint commission of the government, the WJC, and the Belgian Jewish community tasked with identifying measures to improve security, fight growing hatred (including on the internet), strengthen Holocaust education in schools, and facilitate the exchange of information.

Speaking outside the Jewish Museum in central Brussels, Ambassador Lauder told reporters: "What we don't want is that a young generation of Jews grows up with fear."

EDUCATION WITHOUT BORDERS

The WJC was an integral partner in creating an exhibition showcasing the Israeli Education Without Borders program, an initiative co-organized by Israel's Ministry of Education, its SASA Setton Kav-Or initiative, and World ORT Kadima Mada, which provides activities and schooling in thirty-five hospitals across the country to children who are hospitalized for more than three days, as mandated by Israeli law.

Photographer Shahar Azran captured the daily activities of the children in many of these hospitals, who included Jews, Arabs and minorities, children of illegal immigrants, children from the Palestinian Authority coming to Israel for medical treatment, and children of Syrian refugees.

The exhibition was launched in Geneva in September 2015, in partnership with the Israeli Mission to the United Nations. It also has been exhibited at the United Nations Educational, Scientific, and Cultural Organization (UNESCO) headquarters in Paris, in partnership with the Israeli Mission to UNESCO and with the active participation of UNESCO Director General Irina Bokova, and at the Council of Europe in Strasbourg. The exhibition was scheduled for another run at the United Nations headquarters in New York.

Fighting the Delegitimization of Israel

BOYCOTT, DIVESTMENT, AND SANCTIONS (BDS)

The WJC has placed itself at the forefront of the fight against the BDS movement and other forms of delegitimization of Israel, coordinating closely with the Israeli Mission to the United Nations. Ambassador Lauder has committed himself to these efforts and to that effect, the WJC decided to open a department specifically dedicated to counter-delegitimization.

Over the course of 2014 and 2015, the WJC was active in campaigns to halt efforts by Fédération Internationale de Football Association (FIFA) members to boycott Israel, and intervened when the French cell phone giant Orange announced that it would be cutting ties with its Israeli counterpart, Partner Communications. In the summer of 2015, the WJC stepped in when it emerged that the Spanish Rototom music festival had disinvited the American Jewish musician Matisyahu after trying to coerce him to make a political statement in support of the Palestinians. In part thanks to the WJC's efforts, the festival directors recanted, and Matisyahu was re-invited to perform.

In May 2016, the WJC and the Israeli Mission partnered to host the first international conference on delegitimization in the General Assembly Hall at the United Nations headquarters. The conference, entitled Building Bridges, Not Boycotts, was attended by more than fifteen hundred people, a majority of them students. The audience heard addresses from dignitaries, including Israeli Ambassador to the United Nations Danny Danon, Ambassador Lauder, and Israeli Supreme Court Justice Elyakim Rubinstein and was treated to a special performance by Matisyahu. Three panel discussions featuring acclaimed experts followed, focused on the effects of the boycott movement in academia, the legal realm, and the public sphere.

UNESCO

In recent years UNESCO has become increasingly anti-Israel under the influence of countries hostile to Israel and other elements. In 2011, UNESCO was the first UN organization to accept Palestine as a member state. The WJC undertook proactive efforts to fight these wrong-headed attempts to politicize a cultural international agency, both in the media and by writing directly to Director General Irina Bokova and senior government officials of member states. Following a number of positive responses from Bokova, we established a close working relationship with her and have welcomed her professionalism and fairness in contending with highly sensitive and controversial issues. In February 2015, when we denounced the inclusion of

Palestinian-themed posters in UNESCO's list of world heritage objects on the grounds that the documents could fuel anti-Semitism, she concurred with a veto of her own: "It is my conviction that UNESCO should not associate itself with such documents whose inscription could fuel hatred and anti-Semitic perceptions."[4]

In 2016, the WJC leadership undertook an extensive advocacy campaign, including contacting representatives of UNESCO's World Heritage Committee and the ministers of foreign affairs of countries on the UNESCO Executive Board, urging them to vote against an egregious resolution that ignored the Jewish historical connection to Jerusalem and instead declared the Western Mount to be an exclusively Islamic site. Bokova herself publicly emphasized that, "The heritage of Jerusalem is indivisible. . . . To deny or conceal any of the Jewish, Christian, or Muslim traditions undermines the integrity of the site, and runs counter to the reasons that justified its inscription in 1981 as a World Heritage site."[5] Nonetheless, on October 13, 2016, the day after Yom Kippur, the UNESCO Executive Board adopted a resolution that declared the Temple Mount in Jerusalem to be exclusively "a Muslim Holy Site of worship,"[6] totally ignoring its millennia-old Jewish identity. Only six countries—the United States, Estonia, Germany, Lithuania, the Netherlands, and the United Kingdom—voted against this resolution.

On October 17, 2016, Ambassador Lauder in his capacity as president of the WJC denounced the UNESCO resolution in a full-page statement in *The New York Times*. "This outrageous vote," he wrote, "is an affront not just to the Jewish people, but to all those who value the vital role of historical truth in navigating current global issues. . . . For the UN to fulfill its potential and become a temple of peace, it must start by reversing its outrageous erasure of the Jewish people's ties to the Temple Mount."[7]

Other UN Bodies

The WJC has been an accredited NGO at the United Nations since 1947. In recent years, we have renewed and strengthened our positioning in the organization and have a strong connection with UN agencies, offices, and missions in New York, Geneva, and elsewhere. We advocate on all WJC core issues and promote programs on Holocaust education, combating anti-Semitism and racial discrimination, promoting religious tolerance and interfaith dialogue, as well as on countering resolutions that single out Israel.

Every year in September, at the high-level gathering opening the new session of the UN General Assembly, the WJC organizes a flurry of diplomatic meetings at the highest levels. In 2014, together with other organizations, we ensured that the unilateral bid by the Palestinians for statehood at the UN Security Council was defeated. We consistently stand up for Israel in Geneva, with regular statements at the UN Human Rights Council (UNHRC) and campaigns aimed at other UN bodies in both Geneva and New York, such as the United Nations Relief and Works Agency.

We also hold programs at the United Nations headquarters in New York to highlight the experience of Jews exiled from Arab lands, as well as coordinate with the Holocaust and United Nations Outreach Programme on regular programming for International Holocaust Remembrance Day each year on January 27.

The Iran Deal

The WJC closely followed the negotiations between the P5+1 powers to reach a deal with Iran over its contentious nuclear program. During this time, I took part in a small delegation of Jewish leaders that met with US President Barack Obama on the matter. When the final Joint Comprehensive Plan of Action was signed in Vienna in July 2015, Ambassador Lauder expressed appreciation for the intense efforts by the P5+1 group of nations, but said he remained deeply skeptical that the agreement's restrictions would ultimately prevent Iran from developing nuclear weapons. "I fear we may have entered into an agreement that revives the Iranian economy but won't stop this regime from developing nuclear arms in the long term, which would have disastrous consequences for the entire region and the world," said Ambassador Lauder. "As the famous proverb goes, 'the road to hell is often paved with good intentions.'"

INTERFAITH RELATIONS

The WJC has continued to take an active role in pursuing interfaith dialogue and relations, and has established a particularly close relationship over the past few years with the Catholic Church. On multiple occasions, Pope Francis has welcomed senior WJC delegations and held private audiences with Ambassador Lauder. On one such occasion, on the sidelines of our Governing Board meeting in Rome in October 2015, Pope Francis welcomed a delegation of WJC leadership and met privately with Ambassador Lauder to mark the fiftieth anniversary of *Nostra Aetate*, the breakthrough 1965 declaration that helped improve Jewish-Catholic relations. WJC delegates later took part in a public audience with Pope Francis in St. Peter's Square to commemorate the event.

The WJC has also met a number of times with leaders from the Evangelical Christian community, lauding their friendship to Israel, and works closely with a number of organizations representing those churches and denominations. The WJC Israel Branch also has close ties with the Knesset Christian Allies Caucus. Ambassador Lauder has spoken and written extensively on the plight of Christians persecuted in the Middle East.

Reaching Out to the World

MEDIA AND COMMUNICATIONS

Over the last few years, the presence of the WJC and, in particular, of Ambassador Lauder, in the media, both in print and online, has grown exponentially. When a major event pertaining to the Jewish world, global terrorism, Holocaust restitution, or anti-Semitism occurs, we are often the first address for a comment or remark. We issue regular statements on issues of concern; are quoted prominently in the international news wires and major European, Latin American, Israeli, and North American media outlets; and we are consistently interviewed about matters of concern to world Jewry and our affiliated communities across the globe. Our public relations efforts have resulted in reaching tens of millions of readers per topic or event. Opinion pieces by Ambassador Lauder, myself, Deputy CEO for Diplomacy Maram Stern, General Counsel Menachem Rosensaft, and members of the Jewish Diplomatic Corps have also become par for the course and a regular occurrence.

In addition, the WJC is working collaboratively with a cutting-edge, strategic marketing agency to enhance the organization's impact by developing innovative creative content and programs to address critical issues impacting the Jewish people and to combat anti-Semitism around the globe.

SOCIAL MEDIA

The WJC has also made enormous leaps in its social media profile in the last three years and has become an important and ever-present fixture on digital platforms, viewed and used by people of all ages, all over the world. Thanks to our growing presence on widely used platforms including Facebook, Twitter, YouTube, and Google+, the WJC maintains its relevance in the far reaches of the world for Jews and non-Jews alike. We are considered an important and well-respected source of news about Jewish communities and their activities everywhere; people turn to us for in-depth analyses and commentaries on a range of issues including anti-Semitism, Holocaust remembrance, Israel advocacy, Jewish traditions, and Judaism in general. Our upgraded website, www.worldjewishcongress.org, also hosts a wide selection of original content for social media distribution.

The WJC's Facebook pages—available in five languages—are among the most popular pages of all Jewish organizations and have more posts and engagements with users than any other Jewish organization. In total, the WJC speaks every day in multiple languages to more than two hundred thousand people who follow these pages. Over the last three years, we have managed to raise the weekly reach from three thousand to more than one million. The annual reach of the WJC's Facebook page in 2015 alone was close to ninety million, an increase from four million in 2013. We are constantly striving to produce compelling original content and hope to see even greater growth in the coming years.

FUNDRAISING AND CHARITY RATINGS

The World Jewish Congress has been able to operate so successfully in recent years thanks to the generous funding of our president, Ambassador

Lauder, and our thousands of donors committed to the Jewish cause. Randi Dubno, Acting Head of Development, and her team have worked diligently to reach out to our donor base and to update them on our activities and needs. As a charity, we depend on this funding and are enormously appreciative of each and every one of our donors.

Thanks to the professionalism of Chief Financial Officer Chaim Reiss, the WJC has been consistently cited by Charity Navigator—the largest and most utilized independent evaluator of more than eight thousand philanthropies in the United States—with its highest four-star rating for financial health, accountability, transparency, and efficiency. In a letter to the WJC's American Section, the president and CEO of Charity Navigator wrote: "We are proud to announce that the World Jewish Congress, American Section, has earned our 4-star rating. Receiving four out of a possible four stars indicates that your organization adheres to good governance and other best practices that minimize the chance of unethical activities and consistently executes its mission in a fiscally responsible way."

LAY LEADERSHIP

One of the main ingredients for a successful organization is the synergy between a president, a CEO, and its lay leaders. Ambassador Lauder and I work in constant symbiosis, and our relationship with our lay leaders is just as solid. The World Jewish Congress today is strong thanks to the dedication of Ambassador Lauder, Governing Board Chairman David de Rothschild, Treasurer Chella Safra, and the rest of the WJC Steering Committee: Eduardo Elsztain, Robert Goot, WJC-Israel Chairman Shai Hermesh, Yuri Kanner, European Jewish Congress President Moshe Kantor, Euro-Asian Jewish Congress President Julius Meinl, WJC North America Chairwoman Evelyn Sommer, and Latin American Jewish Congress President Jack Terpins.

PROFESSIONAL STAFF

Of course, an organization is only as good as its professional staff, and the World Jewish Congress is no exception. Our Latin American affiliate, run professionally under Claudio Epelman, has succeeded in becoming a preeminent organization in its region; under Executive Director Raya

Kalenova, the European Jewish Congress continues to be a major player across the continent; Natasha Schmidt, acting CEO of the Euro-Asian Jewish Congress, has immensely strengthened that region of smaller communities; and our North America Section, directed by Betty Ehrenberg, has strongly established itself as the global representative of world Jewry for the United States, Canada, and Mexico, which is no small feat in a playing field of dozens of influential Jewish organizations and lobby groups. The WJC Israel Branch, guided until August 2016 by Director-General Sam Grundwerg, together with its board of representatives from every Jewish party in the Knesset, has come to be seen as a colleague in Israel's political arena.

Our office in Brussels, led by Deputy CEO for Diplomacy Maram Stern and Chief Operations Officer John Malkinson for over twenty-five years, is our guiding force in operations and governance, and has become a beacon of light for the Jewish world in Europe. The WJC has remained fiscally sound and maintained best practices thanks to Chief Financial Officer Chaim Reiss. Under the guidance of Chief Program Officer Sonia Gomes de Mesquita, the WJC has become known for its extensive and intensive activities. Our fundraising efforts have successfully allowed us to grow and fulfill our mission, thanks to Acting Head of Development Randi Dubno. Our media relations activities are energetic and far reaching, ably conducted for almost twenty years by Director of Communications Michael Thaidigsmann. Our archivist Isabella Nespoli is the custodian of our institutional documentary memory. Lauren Rose, the WJC Representative to the United Nations in Geneva, has brought new life into our Geneva office and has solidified the WJC's place as a strong force there. My executive office in New York is run diligently and expertly under the guidance of Shira Copans. Our legal advice is always sound and robust, thanks to General Counsel Menachem Rosensaft, also the custodian of the WJC's historical memory, and without whom this eightieth anniversary volume would not have been possible.

Since joining the WJC as CEO and working together with my colleagues, I have completely changed the organizational structure, significantly expanded our executive headquarters in New York, reactivated our office in Geneva, and added more than a dozen new positions, while simultaneously securing our financial strength and dramatically increasing our professional and intellectual capabilities. In that time, we have more than doubled our staff, and in keeping with our vision for breathing new life into the WJC and focusing on the next generation, we sought out new hires in their twenties and thirties. Our young staff comes from a wealth of cultures and backgrounds, each endowed with professionalism and experience, and a hunger to help protect, defend, and empower the global Jewish community. The WJC is now filled with talented young people whom we have entrusted with taking leadership roles on the global political issues in which we engage each day, improving their expertise so as to someday take over the reins themselves. These young professionals are more than just the young faces of the World Jewish Congress—they are the core of the WJC today.

The World Jewish Congress is a vibrant and exciting place, with an incomparable staff and a bright future.

Conclusion

To reiterate the words of Rabbi Stephen S. Wise, we do not expect the World Jewish Congress to perform miracles. But we do expect a Jewish world that is protected, represented, and united as one Jewish community. The World Jewish Congress has succeeded in this mission for the last eighty years, and I have no doubt that it will continue to succeed for years to come. The WJC today is a remarkable organization, full of talented young professionals, and is constantly attracting new individuals capable of dealing with the most challenging issues and events.

I am very proud to lead the WJC professionally into its ninth decade of service to the Jewish people.

My Vision of the Jewish Future

Ambassador Ronald S. Lauder

Throughout the first half of my life, I was a three-day-a-year Jew. If you don't know the phrase, let me explain. There was no question in my mind that I was Jewish. I had a bar mitzvah like all of my Jewish friends and although the world knew Estée Lauder as a brilliant businesswoman, I knew her as a wonderful Jewish mother. Few people know this outside of our family, but Estée Lauder made the best matzah ball soup in New York. I was, in essence, someone who was socially Jewish; just not religiously. I only went to synagogue twice a year, on the High Holidays, and there was, of course, a seder in our home every Passover. Other than that, the Jewish part of my life was non-existent. I didn't understand the prayers because I didn't understand Hebrew. The service felt alien to me and if I had a choice, I would easily choose a Saturday morning at the Museum of Modern Art as opposed to the synagogue.

At the same time, I was always very proud of my connection to my faith. I felt a deep commitment to the State of Israel and to the Jewish people. I was constantly amazed by what this small fraction of humanity

Ambassador Ronald S. Lauder is President of the World Jewish Congress.

gave to the entire world, over and over again. I loved to hear the stories and accomplishments of this tiny and amazing country in the Middle East, small in size but huge in its achievement.

I will never forget my first trip to Israel, probably not unlike that of most Jews from the diaspora—I loved walking in the land of our fore-fathers. I loved seeing the actual places where the bible stories took place. And I loved seeing young Israelis walking with their heads held high.

So there was never any doubt in my mind whatsoever that I was Jewish. I just had many other things on my mind as well. As an adult, my interests in foreign policy led me first to the Pentagon in the Reagan administration, where I worked under Secretary of Defense Caspar Weinberger on NATO affairs. And then, in 1985, President Reagan appointed me as the United States ambassador to Austria.

This seemed like the perfect posting for my wife, Jo Carole, and myself. We loved Vienna. I had always been fascinated with the city, especially the artistic period around the turn-of-the-twentieth century. Some of the greatest works of expressionist art came from that period, in large part thanks to Jewish sponsors who dominated the artistic scene at the time. That period has always held a special place for me. So we eagerly embraced the new assignment and looked forward to it.

Needless to say, as we headed to Austria, I had no idea that this posting would be a major turning point in my life. It came about in a series of steps, and each one would move me closer to Judaism. The first step was a result of a sheer coincidence of timing. Just as I arrived in Vienna, Austria was thrown into what has become known as the Waldheim Affair. For readers who are too young to remember, Kurt Waldheim was an Austrian diplomat who became Secretary-General of the United Nations in the 1970s. I met Waldheim several times when he was in New York. I remember a tall man with impeccable manners. What I didn't know—what no one knew—was that he also had a dark past that he lied about and tried to hide. Waldheim served in the German Army during World War II as an intelligence officer, and his unit was involved in some particularly nasty reprisals against parti-sans in Yugoslavia and Greece. At first, Waldheim said he had no knowledge of these acts. But later, when he admitted that he did know about them, he said, "What could I do? I had to either continue to serve or be executed." That always seemed to be the standard line that I remembered hearing over the years, the same line that Eichmann used: "I was just following orders."

It was only after Waldheim had left the United Nations that his past came back to haunt him. Perhaps a wiser man would have gone quietly into retirement. That wasn't Waldheim's style. Instead, he doubled down and ran for president of Austria. When more details came out about his wartime past, many revealed by the World Jewish Congress, Waldheim denounced these as malicious lies. The Austrians, for their part, showed their true character by electing Waldheim as their president with full knowledge of who he really was. Some even put the blame on certain New York newspapers for dredging all of this up—one of the classic cases, in my mind, of blaming the victim.

As the newly arrived US ambassador to Austria, one of my first duties was to attend Waldheim's inauguration. I thought about it, I thought about my responsibility as a representative of the government of the United States, and I realized the message my not attending would send. I decided that I did not want to be there and notified the State Department. There were higher-ups at State who were not happy about my decision and told me I should attend. But there was one person who backed me up and that happened to be our boss, Secretary of State George Shultz. Years later, when asked why he supported me over the advice of others at State, Secretary Shultz answered in his characteristic, no nonsense way: "I thought Ronald Lauder was right." Period. End of story. The United States was absent for this event, and it was noticed.

For someone raised in the 1950s in New York, I have to say that I never encountered any anti-Semitism throughout my childhood. But for the first time in my life, I felt an undercurrent of animosity in Austria. It came out in direct ways and in ways that were more subtle. Throughout the Waldheim election campaign, Austrians made their feelings quite clear. Sometimes you would hear it from doormen and waiters and sometimes just on the street. One day I was enjoying one of my favorite pastimes, just walking in Vienna and admiring the architecture, when I came across something that made no sense to me. On one particular street of beautiful old buildings, there was an ugly garage in the middle that stood out. I know that could not have been the original building and as people walked by, I asked if they could tell me what had been there before. That question seemed to irk

people. They either pretended they didn't know or that they didn't hear me. This struck me as very strange. Finally, an old man with very clear eyes came up to me when he saw that we were alone. He had heard my questions and had heard the non-answers that I had been receiving. "The most beautiful synagogue in all of Europe once stood here," he told me. "It was burned down on Kristallnacht."

There we were again. I was reminding Austrians that they were not "the first victims of Nazism," the standard line they loved to use after the war. Instead, Austrians were, in too many cases, among the most vicious Nazis of all. Hitler was from Austria. So was Eichmann. When the two countries were united in the Anschluss in 1938, more than two million people came out to greet Hitler in wild celebrations. Almost immediately, Austrians set upon the Jewish community, forcing them into humiliating acts, like cleaning the streets with toothbrushes. Jews were beaten, and their property was soon confiscated. It was as if all of this pent-up hate had been building for years and as soon as there was an outlet, Austrians set upon their Jewish neighbors. They seemed to enjoy heaping abuse on people they had lived with in peace for decades if not centuries.

All of this is the background to one experience that truly and profoundly changed my life. My wife, Jo Carole, and I became friends with the Chabad rabbi in Vienna, Jacob Biderman, and his wife. There was something very special about this couple, and we enjoyed seeing them and going to their home for Shabbat. One day, Mrs. Biderman invited us to see a kindergarten they had started for Jewish children from the Soviet Union. At the time, Soviet Jews, who had not been allowed to practice their faith, were trying to leave for Israel. Many of these brave individuals, known as Refuseniks, were thrown in Soviet prisons, just for asking to be Jewish. But international pressure, especially from the Reagan Administration, was forcing the Soviets to allow some Jews to leave. Even though most wanted to go directly to Israel, the Soviets would not allow this, so they set up a procedure where the Jews who were allowed to leave would first go to Austria for a certain length of time and then from there they could travel to Israel.

I was interested to see this kindergarten and one afternoon, my wife and I went for a visit. As we walked into the school—it was really just a two-room apartment—we were confronted with something I still cannot explain. There were all of these bright, happy, young faces who were excited to see us. They sang Hebrew songs, something they had never been allowed to do in the Soviet Union, the walls were filled with children's drawings, and I was moved beyond words.

I just couldn't help thinking of the phrase: "There but for the grace of God, go I."

I was suddenly flooded with emotions and thoughts. I wondered to myself, how is it that these Jews hungered to be connected to a religion that was denied them and I, who was given the freedom to practice the same religion, just took it for granted? I also wondered what might have happened to me if my grandparents had not left Hungary for the United States. Since I was born in 1944, during one of the most horrific parts of the Holocaust that took place throughout Hungary, I knew the answer to my own question. I would not have survived. Neither would my parents, grandparents, and everyone around me.

That visit changed the focus of my entire life.

I started by buying the apartment and the apartment next to it, so the school could expand into the larger space that it needed to accommodate more children. Eventually, I bought an entire building for this school. But my mind was already moving ahead. I envisioned a much larger plan that would involve not just Vienna but all of Eastern Europe.

When I returned to the United States after my posting in Austria was over, I started a foundation that would build Jewish schools and sum-mer camps in that entire area. Some people involved in the Jewish world told me it was a silly idea. They said there were no Jews left in Eastern Europe—the Nazis had taken care of that forty years earlier, and then the Communists had driven out those who had survived. I ignored the criti-cism and moved ahead with my plan. One of the reasons was a fortuitous meeting with a Hasidic rabbi named Haskel Besser.

Rabbi Besser was one of the most extraordinary human beings I had ever met. He was born in Poland into one of the great Hasidic dynasties. He came to the United States shortly after World War II and lived on the Upper West Side of Manhattan. His knowledge of Judaism and Eastern Europe was tremendous. And his connections to the Jewish world were profound. But he was also someone completely at ease in the larger world around him. He had many friends in the Christian community, and his knowledge of literature, music, and history was formidable.

Rabbi Besser thought my idea had merit, and we began working together, starting schools in cities like Berlin, Budapest, and Warsaw. Eventually, we established Jewish schools throughout Central and Eastern Europe. All of the critics of my plan were silenced just two years later when the Soviet Union came to an end, and all of those countries that had been forced to live under Communism were suddenly free. What we saw almost immediately was that there were many, many more Jews than anyone had realized, and that these Jews soon came out of hiding and wanted to know more about their religion. The reasons were obvious—under the Communists, it was never in anyone's interest to be openly Jewish. But now they were free to learn.

Here was the problem that we encountered. All of us learn about our religion from our parents. But what happens when parents, because they were not allowed to learn about their religion, know nothing to pass on to their children? It represents a breakdown in the natural order of things. I think we found an answer to the dilemma. By starting Jewish schools in this area, the children learned the meaning of Judaism and then went home and taught their parents, who were eager to learn. Yes, it was a breakdown in the natural order, but it worked.

The Ronald S. Lauder Foundation was founded in 1987 and has been a pioneer in providing Jewish education to Jews in eastern and central Europe ever since. My goal from the start has been to underwrite the future of Jewish life in Europe, both communal and individual, by creating excellent Jewish schools. But what is an excellent Jewish school? I believe it must be one that prepares young Jews to be successful personally and professionally and one that inspires them to participate actively in Jewish life. Today, the Foundation operates or supports thirteen schools in eleven countries—Austria, Bulgaria, Croatia, the Czech Republic, Germany, Greece, Hungary, Poland, Romania, Russia, and Ukraine—with a total enrollment of twenty-five hundred students; thirteen kindergartens in nine countries, with a total enrollment of more than seven hundred children; nine youth centers and camps in six countries; as well as the Lauder Business School in Vienna and a Rabbinical Seminary—the Rabbinerseminar zu Berlin.

The foundation has helped build thriving Jewish communities in places where everything Jewish had disappeared. It has been successful beyond my wildest dreams.

I did not stop there. I became more active in the Jewish world.

I took over as head of the Conference of Presidents of Major American Jewish Organizations. I became the president of the Jewish National Fund and helped change its focus from planting trees, which was necessary when it was founded in 1901, to the problem of water today. I also became involved with the Claims Conference and established the Commission for Art Recovery. Then in 2007, when Edgar Bronfman stepped down as the head of the World Jewish Congress, I was asked to take his place. If ever there was a perfect match, I believe it was this organization at that moment.

The Future

As I write these words, I've been the head of the WJC for almost ten years. We have changed the organization in many ways and, I believe, it is now poised for the many problems that we face as a people. Sadly, the world is a much more dangerous place for Jews today than it was twenty or even ten years ago. In truth, it's a more dangerous place for all people, but Jews seem to be the targets for a particular hatred—one that we have seen before.

From the Middle East to Europe and around the globe, there is great danger, but there are also great opportunities. So it's time to ask the question, *eyfo anahnu?* "Where are we," and, more importantly, "where we are going?"

There is an old story from December 1899: a Jewish boy is sitting at home and calls out to his mother: "Great news, Mom! The twentieth century is coming next Thursday night!"The boy's mother looks up, probably over a pot of soup. "Whatever it is," she calls back, "it probably means more trouble for the Jews."There you have in a nutshell, the age-old Jewish dilemma. Tremendous optimism tempered by reality. As it turns out, they were *both* right. The twentieth century saw unbelievable miracles, including the return of the Jewish people to our eternal homeland after two thousand years in exile.

It also gave us Auschwitz.

So, seventy-two years after the liberation of the camps, sixty-nine years after the founding of Israel, and seventeen years into the twenty-first century, which way should we as a people turn: Should we be optimistic or pessimistic?

Let's begin with some numbers. We are just over fourteen million Jews worldwide. That's less than fifteen million in a world of over two billion Christians, 1.5 billion Muslims, and one billion Hindus. Fourteen million is not a lot. It's tiny. We're fewer than we were in 1933 when Hitler came to power. That's not exactly growth. In the United States, when I was born, Jews made up over 4 percent of the population. Today, we are less than half that—1.8 percent of all Americans are Jewish, and our numbers are decreasing. Except for the Orthodox, and the Jews in Israel, our birthrate is *below* the replacement level in North America and Europe. In the United States, the intermarriage rate remains stuck at 50 percent. We are decreasing in number, not increasing. Not enough Jewish children are being born, and too many of those who *are* born have no Jewish identity.

Although our demographics are deeply troubling, the challenges hardly stop there. Over the last twenty years, and for the first time since the Holocaust, anti-Semitism is out in the open again. It's become acceptable. Just after World War II, nobody said the kind of things we hear today in public because no sane person wanted to be associated with Nazis. But seventy-two years and three generations later, educated and sophisticated people, who should know better, say outrageous things about Jews. They say and write these things in newspapers, on television, and on the internet—things they would never dare say about other groups. Much of this hate speech comes from old sources like Europe and the Middle East. But unlike the anti-Semitism of the past, today it comes not just from the far right, but increasingly it comes from the so-called progressive left.

The new target for this hatred is not the "international Jew" as Henry Ford called us. Today it is the Jewish State of Israel, which is constantly vilified throughout the media, on the internet, at the United Nations, and on almost every college campus. Call it BDS—Boycott, Divestment, and Sanctions—or Justice for Palestine, or other hateful rhetoric one hears from major elements of the British Labour Party—it's still the same old hatred of Jews. Anti-Semites are not a very creative lot. They still blame all of the world's problems on us. Only now it's Israel that is behind everything from the 9/11 attacks to the Charlie Hebdo attack. Just like the old blood libels, they now make up preposterous lies, such as accusing Israel of killing children for body parts. Whatever is wrong in the world, according to today's anti-Semites, Israel is at fault. These are no longer just the ravings of a fringe element of society. Journalists, government officials, professors—even celebrities—blame Israel, and only Israel.

And, please, let's get one thing out of the way right now. When someone says he or she is not anti-Jewish, only anti-Israel, that is a lie. Because when you hold the only Jewish nation to a different standard, when you lie about the only Jewish nation, when you want the one Jewish nation to disappear from the face of the earth—that makes you an anti-Semite.

The threats hardly stop there. The much-heralded Iran deal of 2015 did not make the world safer. It only made Iran richer, stronger, and even more belligerent. In less than a decade Iran is likely to have nuclear weapons and the missiles to deliver them. Iran has not stopped calling for, and working toward, the destruction of the State of Israel. With the change in the US role in the Middle East, the entire region has become a much more dangerous place today. And Israel cannot count on any support from the United Nations. The world's only global body, the UN is a hotbed of anti-Israel anger and rhetoric, which is one of the world's great ironies. The UN was founded seventy-two years ago out of the carnage of World War II. It was founded on the broken bones of the Jewish people. It was founded on the belief that the human destruction forced on our people would never happen again. So it is completely unacceptable that the UN, of all places, would single out the only Jewish nation with lie, after lie, after lie.

Western democracies have been outnumbered by dictatorships and authoritarian regimes in the UN for a long, long time. Not too long ago, when Israeli civilians were randomly stabbed by Palestinians, UN Secretary-General Ban Ki-moon suggested it was human nature to react this way to occupation. This type of attitude doesn't stop terrorism; it only encourages terrorism. North Korea, Iran, Cuba, Sudan, and Syria, where five hundred thousand people have been slaughtered, are mostly overlooked, but Israel is condemned at the UN more than any other nation.

It is no coincidence that a Jewish boy wearing a yarmulke cannot walk safely down the streets of Paris, London, or Berlin. Jews have become the targets of terror throughout Europe. It has even been suggested, once again, that Jews should leave Europe. I can tell you this for sure: if every Jew left Europe today, this might be sad for Jews, but it would be a disaster for Europe. Jews create jobs, they heal disease, they educate, and they create. The biggest loser of a European Jewish exodus would be Europe.

The problems that we face as a people in 2016 are very real; they are not imagined. But there is something absolutely vital that we should remember: today, our destiny is in our own hands. It wasn't always that way. In the 1930s, the founders of the World Jewish Congress had to appeal to others for help. In 1936 a group of concerned Jewish leaders gathered in Switzerland to confront the growing threat coming from Nazi Germany and the anti-Semitism that prevailed in many European countries at that time. Six years later, in 1942, Gerhart Riegner, the WJC representative in Geneva, alerted the world to the fact that the Nazis had undertaken the annihilation of European Jewry. But that warning fell on mostly deaf ears. Today, the world's attitude toward us may not have changed enough, but one thing has definitely changed considerably. *We* have changed. The era of the quiet Jew, the timid Jew, the ghetto Jew, is long over. Those tough leaders of the early Zionist movement and those tough, outspoken Jews who founded the WJC in 1936 buried that quiet, timid, ghetto Jew three generations ago, and he's not coming back.

So, given everything we face as I write this, I want to tell you how the World Jewish Congress intends to deal with some of these problems. The World Jewish Congress does not have a military armed force to defend the Jewish people. It is not a global economic power like Israel. But the one thing that we do have is tremendous political clout, and we are not afraid to use it. Given our political access to governments and opinion shapers around the world, here is what we propose to do and what we are doing:

The World Jewish Congress will continue to stand side-by-side with Jewish communities across the globe, many of which face resurgent anti-Semitism and acts of terrorism. We will also defend Israel, and we will not stop defending Israel. I have visited over forty countries in just the past few years. I have met with world leaders, with popes, and with ordinary citizens. When they have opposed anti-Semitism, I thank them; and when they have not, I confront them publicly. I tell them about all of the great things that Israel has accomplished, and why it is in their interest to side with the Jewish state. I explain what Jerusalem means to every Jew in the world. We use our political clout wisely. There are fifty-four countries in Africa. Many of them would be willing to vote with Israel, but we have to give them a reason. That is exactly what the World Jewish Congress does.

At the same time, we are not afraid to use strong language, as we did in Hungary, to protect the Jewish community there from the growing threat of far-right neo-Nazis. The World Jewish Congress has created a Jewish Diplomatic Corps made up of young people ages twenty-seven to forty-five. We have trained them to act as emissaries for the Jewish people in their home countries. I have worked with these young people, the Jewish Diplomats. They are energetic, committed, and they will change things for the better. God knows, we have smart Jewish lawyers in abundance, and we will work with the brightest of them to fight the BDS movement in court because it is actually illegal in many countries to discriminate against any one people. These lawyers are going after BDS in courts around the world, and they are winning case after case.

We have created a global security department to advise and help protect Jewish communities worldwide. We will not rest until we are certain that governments and police around the world recognize the particular vulnerability of Jewish communities to the growing threats of terror and violence, and commit themselves to protecting our communities and their institutions. We will not rest until these communities are better prepared and equipped to protect and defend themselves against any and every threat.

We also want to expose the anti-Israel rhetoric that has become all too prevalent on many university and college campuses in the United States and in many other countries. Jewish alumni are among the biggest donors to their alma maters. We want to let them know when a professor spouts anti-Semitic views, or when a student group engages in anti-Israel bullying. If university and college administrators would never tolerate racist attacks against any other minority group, why is it acceptable to disparage Jews or Israelis?

I now return to my original question: Should we be optimistic or pessimistic? My answer comes in two photographs.

The first is this iconic photograph from the Holocaust. A frightened boy in short pants with a cap on his head walks out of the Warsaw Ghetto with his hands raised. Nazi storm troopers with automatic weapons stand nearby, smirking. We see this Jewish boy, who represents a million and a half other Jewish children who were murdered, six million Jews altogether. Our hearts break because we cannot help him; we cannot save him; we can do nothing for this frightened boy in short pants. But imagine this for a moment: What if an angel had come down at the moment the photo was taken and told this boy:

"Listen to me. In less than ten years, there will be a Jewish state in the homeland of our forefathers. And there will be a Jewish Army and a Jewish Air Force and a Jewish Navy to defend Jews. Jewish soldiers will fall from the sky and rescue Jews in far-off lands. And this country will open its doors to every Jew on earth who needs help."

Do you think that boy could have possibly believed this angel?

Would *you* have believed this angel at that time?

Here is my point: We must constantly remember what we have and what we have accomplished. Today, we can fly into Tel Aviv on a modern Jewish airline, with a bold, blue Star of David on the side, for the whole world to see. We must never, ever forget how far we have come, what we fought for, and what we have accomplished.

There is another photograph. It is also in black and white and, to my mind, it is the story not just of Israel. It is the story of the Jewish people.

© 1958 Micha Bar Am/Magnum Photos

This picture was taken by the great Israeli photographer Micha Bar Am. It was shot in the Kfar Saba refugee camp in 1958. A young female soldier is teaching one of the new immigrants how to count in his new language, Hebrew. Over a million new immigrants streamed into Israel in its first decade: concentration camp survivors, victims of pogroms, and over five hundred thousand Jews who were kicked out of Arab lands, losing all their property. Somehow we never hear about those refugees. That's because these Jews were not left in refugee camps for the rest of the world to feed and clothe. They were not fed lies and hate. They were not turned into political pawns. Instead, they were made full citizens in their new land. They were educated, taught skills, and welcomed with open arms. When they arrived in the first independent Jewish state in two thousand years, they were all told just one thing: Welcome home! That is what Jews do for other Jews. We help one another. We treat one another with respect. We welcome one another.

These two photographs take us from devastation to strength.

We must never forget that the State of Israel is an amazing achievement of our own making. It came from Jewish sacrifice, hard work, Jewish caring for one another, and our belief in God.

I saw a fascinating poll just a few weeks ago. No other nation has had to defend itself every minute of every day since its birth. But it turns out that Israelis are among the happiest and most satisfied people on earth. How can this be? I believe it comes from three things: a tremendous belief in freedom, an overabundance of courage, and from caring for one another.

We see it every single day. When a lone soldier fell in the 2014 Gaza conflict, more than ten thousand Israelis who had never even met him came to his funeral. Ten thousand! This lone soldier did not die alone.

That is what you see in a Jewish nation: freedom, courage, and a deep, deep caring for one another. We have faced darker times before, even within my lifetime. But today we face them with a Jewish state called Israel. We face them with tremendous resources around the world. And we must also remember that we have so much to be proud of. We belong to a people that disproportionally advanced civilization. Jews gave the world monotheism, Jews save lives—all lives. Jews make the world better with their ingenuity, their music, and their literature. We make up less than 1 percent of the world's population, yet we have won 20 percent of all the Nobel prizes. We may be only a little more than fourteen million people, but we have an incredible arsenal in those fourteen million. We have thousands of years of tradition. I would happily take our fourteen million creative minds over the billions elsewhere.

I have presented a long list of challenges that we face.

I have told you what I intend to do about those challenges.

But here's what I want you to remember: the Jewish people are not going to disappear. We have come too far, for too long, to just disappear. That is not part of God's plan. But we can't leave it completely in His hands. He expects us to do the work, but He has also amply supplied us with the means. And we will use that Jewish brilliance and Jewish creativity to solve our problems.

There is an old Hasidic tradition that inside every Jew there burns a flame. Sometimes that flame is obscured, and the person can't see it. But it is always there, it is always burning. All you have to do is dust off your heart and you will find it.

Thirty years ago, when I served as the US ambassador to Austria and I saw that group of Jewish children from the Soviet Union in a nursery school, something happened to me. Those children moved me in a way that I had never been moved before. Those children helped find the flame inside my heart. They helped me rediscover my Jewishness!

And this is the job before us now. We have to help our children and our grandchildren dust off their hearts. We have to help them rediscover that Jewish flame inside them. This isn't just important for Jews. It's important for everyone, Jews and non-Jews alike, because for over five thousand years, that flame has been lighting the entire world. We must never let that flame go out. We've come too far, and the stakes are too high. And that is the ultimate purpose of the World Jewish Congress—to make sure that flame continues to light the entire world.

Acknowledgments

Robert R. Singer

More than two years ago, when World Jewish Congress President Ronald S. Lauder and I first discussed the idea of producing a comprehensive historical record of the WJC's first eighty years, we both agreed that the ideal individual to spearhead such a daunting project was the WJC's general counsel, Menachem Rosensaft.

Menachem is in a very real sense our organization's institutional memory. His father, Josef Rosensaft, worked closely with many of the leaders of the WJC between 1945 and 1950 in his capacity as chairman of both the Central Committee of Liberated Jews in the British Zone of Germany and the Jewish Committee that administered the Bergen-Belsen Displaced Persons camp. During those years Menachem's father developed what proved to be life-long friendships with Nahum Goldmann, Gerhart M. Riegner, Noah Barou, and Alex Easterman, among others. As a result, Menachem grew up knowing many of the WJC personalities of the Goldmann era and became aware of our organization's activities in the international Jewish arena almost by osmosis.

Robert R. Singer is CEO and Executive Vice President of the World Jewish Congress.

It was Menachem who recommended to us that rather than commissioning a historian to write a chronological account, the book should be a collection of essays, each focusing on a specific theme or episode in the history of the WJC. He then proceeded to identify the most appropriate individuals to write these chapters, either themselves veterans of the events they described or scholars with unique insight and academic expertise. As a result, *The World Jewish Congress, 1936–2016* reflects the collective knowledge, perspectives, and in numerous cases, the personal experiences of its contributors. Each in his or her own way has brought the various episodes of the WJC's history to life with great sensitivity and an overarching respect for the subject matter. All of us at the WJC owe them a tremendous debt of gratitude.

I cannot overstate my personal and the WJC's appreciation to Menachem for the countless hours he devoted tirelessly to the compilation and editing of this book and, after the manuscript was complete, to turning it into a visually aesthetic volume. I also want to express my gratitude to Menachem's wife, Jeanie, and especially to his grandchildren Hallie and Jacob, for their patience and forbearance as the editing process repeatedly intruded on precious family time over the course of many nights, weekends, and holidays.

This book has been a collaborative endeavor by numerous members of the WJC family. WJC Chief Program Officer Sonia Gomes de Mesquita was the project's enthusiastic advocate from the outset, providing both encouragement and wise guidance at every step.

Laurence Weinbaum, director of the WJC's Israel Council on Jewish Relations, and Michael Thaidigsmann, the WJC's director of communications and media relations, in particular, were invaluable sounding boards throughout the planning and editing of the book, and read numerous chapters with a critical and constructive eye. Isabella Nespoli, the WJC's resident archivist, was an enthusiastic, efficient, and extremely helpful resource to Menachem as well as many of the contributors, providing them with documents and other historical sources, often at a moment's notice. Cory Weiss has been Menachem's capable, insightful, and always good natured administrative right hand during the entire editing process. I also want to thank Yfat Barak-Cheney, Betty Ehrenberg, Claudio Epelman, John Malkinson,

Yvette Shumacher, Aliyana Traison, Janice Wolpo, and WJC interns Adela Cojab-Moadeb and Abraham Silverstein for their assistance and their interest in the book.

Kevin Proffitt, Senior Archivist for Research and Collections at the American Jewish Archives, patiently, responsively, and repeatedly located and shared essential documents. Leslie Rubin is an extraordinarily gifted copy editor; her meticulous attention to detail immeasurably enhanced the present volume, as did her preparation of its index. Jim Harris and his team at G&H Soho skillfully shepherded the completed manuscript to the finished product. Judith Cohen, Chief Acquisitions Curator at the US Holocaust Memorial Museum, called our attention to the striking photograph of the second WJC plenary assembly, which graphic designer Semadar Megged creatively incorporated in the cover of this book. We are also most grateful to Michael W. Grunberger and Lenore Bell, respectively Director of Collections and Library Director at the US Holocaust Memorial Museum, for their kind advice, and to Jane Beirn for generously sharing her prodigious publishing expertise with Menachem.

There is no doubt in my mind that *The World Jewish Congress, 1936–2016* will become a permanent and essential resource for scholars, theologians, and all who are interested in the dramatic events, both tragic and glorious, of the past eighty years. In particular, however, it is my hope that this book will be read by many young people around the world, now and in the future, and that it will give them an understanding and appreciation of the WJC's pivotal role in modern Jewish history.

Endnotes

INTRODUCTION

PAGES 5—21

1. See, generally, Stephanie Strom, "Money-Shifting Uproar Shakes World Jewish Congress," *The New York Times*, November 30, 2004; Strom, "Spitzer Looking into World Jewish Congress," *The New York Times*, December 31, 2004; Strom, "World Jewish Congress Dismisses Leader," *The New York Times*, March 16, 2007; Strom, "New Accusations Are Raised after Firing in Jewish Group," *The New York Times*, April 6, 2007; Strom, "President of Jewish Congress Resigns after 3 Years' Turmoil," *The New York Times*, May 8, 2007; Strom, "Cosmetics Heir to Lead World Jewish Congress," *The New York Times*, June 11, 2007.

2. See, e.g., Craig Horowitz, "Machers in Meltdown," *New York Magazine*, February 28, 2005.

3. Marc Perelman, "Months after World Jewish Congress Breakup, Legal Battles Drag On," *Forward*, March 3, 2008.

4. *Unity in Dispersion: A History of the World Jewish Congress* (New York: Institute of Jewish Affairs of the World Jewish Congress, 1948), p. i. (A second edition of this book, also published in 1948, somewhat confusingly titled what had been Kubowitzki's "Preface" as "Foreword.")

5. "Jewish Aspects of Indemnification: A Statement of the World Jewish Congress," *Congress Weekly*, November 24, 1944, p. 6; "Declaration Adopted by Conference of the World Jewish Congress, November 30, 1944," *Congress Weekly*, December 15, 1944, p. 16.

6. Nehemiah Robinson, *Indemnification and Reparations: Jewish Aspects* (New York, 1944).

7. Henrik F. Infield, ed., *Essays in Jewish Sociology, Labour and Co-operation in Memory of Dr. Noah Barou, 1889–1955* (London, 1962), p. 10.

8. See, generally, Menachem Z. Rosensaft and Joana D. Rosensaft, "The Early History of German-Jewish Reparations," *Fordham International Law Journal*, Symposium (2001): pp. S-1–S-45.

9. Report dated May 10, 1919, *Comité des Délégations Juives auprès de la Conférence de la Paix*, Berman Jewish Policy Archives, http://www.bjpa.org/Publications/details.cfm ?PublicationID=16979.

10. Ibid. The principal British and French Jewish representative bodies, the Board of Deputies of British Jews, the Anglo-Jewish Association, and the Alliance Israélite Universelle, declined to join the *Comité des Délégations Juives. Unity in Dispersion*, p. 26.

11. See, e.g., "The revolutionary and anti-Semitic newspapers [in France] are starting a Jew-baiting campaign in view of Dreyfus's Semitic origins. La Libre Parole predicts that the Jews, by presuming to consider themselves the equals of Frenchmen, and competing with them, are preparing the most fearful disaster that ever marked the tragic history of the race" in "Irritation about Dreyfus," *The New York Times*, December 27, 1894; "Talk of the Parisians: Great Interest Manifested in the Guilt or Innocence of Former Captain Dreyfus," *The New York Times*, November 28, 1897; "Jews in Roumania and Poland Alarmed, Letters Show that Passion against Them Is Widespread," *The New York Times*, May 21, 1903; "Trying a Man for 'Ritual Murder,' and in 1913," *The New York Times*, September 7, 1913; "The second significant fact in the case is the nature of the accusation, the allegation of murder for Jewish ritual purposes. The crime does not and can not [*sic*] exist. . . . [I]t is a foolish, blind superstition bred of prejudice upon ignorance," "The Czar on Trial" (editorial), *The New York Times*, October 9, 1913; and "Reports Massacre of Jews in Ukraine," *The New York Times*, August 1, 1919.

12. "Tell of Jews' Part in Conduct of War," *The New York Times*, November 11, 1918.

13. "Marshall Praises Wilson and League," *The New York Times*, July 25, 1919.

14. See, e.g., "Plead for Jewish Rights, Draft to Be Presented to League—Want Safety in Hungary," *The New York Times*, December 10, 1920; "Jews Appeal to League, Ask Investigation of Condition of the Race in East Europe," *The New York Times*, December 12, 1920; "Report New Pogroms," *The New York Times*, August 1, 1921; "Attack Expulsion of Jews, Paris Delegates Appeal to League against Rumanian Order," *The New York Times*, September 28, 1923.

15. See, e.g., "Other Petitions to League," *The New York Times*, May 21, 1933; "Seek League Help for All Reich Jews," *The New York Times*, June 8, 1933; "See Reich Retreat on Silesian Jews," *The New York Times*, May 22, 1933; "Reich to End Curbs on Jews in Silesia," *The New York Times*, May 27, 1933. See also, *Unity in Dispersion*, pp. 34–35.

16. "Adopts Palestine as Jews' Homeland," *The New York Times*, December 18, 1918.

17. *Unity in Dispersion*, p. 28; "Jewish Congress to Meet on Oct. 14," *The New York Times*, May 14, 1923.

18. "Jewish Conference Meets in Zurich," *The New York Times*, August 18, 1927.

19. *Unity in Dispersion*, p. 30.

20. "Jewish Conference Meets in Zurich," *The New York Times*, August 18, 1927.

21. "Jews Pledge Efforts to End Discrimination," *The New York Times*, August 22, 1927; *Unity in Dispersion*, p. 30.

22. "Asks World Session on Rights of Jewry," *The New York Times*, October 19, 1931.

23. "World Conference of Jews Is Voted," *The New York Times*, April 25, 1932.

24. "World Parley Plan of Dr. Wise Scored," *The New York Times*, June 17, 1932.

25. "Dr. Adler Accused of Disrupting Jews," *The New York Times*, June 22, 1932.

26. *Unity in Dispersion*, p. 33.

27. See, generally, Jehuda Reinharz, "Nahum Goldmann and Chaim Weizmann: An Ambivalent 'Relationship,'" in *Nahum Goldmann: Statesman without a State,* ed. Mark A. Raider (Albany, NY, 2009), pp. 125–138.

28. "Weizmann Leaves Platform as Wise at Stormy Congress Session Indicts England for Failure with Mandate," *JTA*, July 6, 1931.

29. *Unity in Dispersion*, pp. 16–17.

30. *Protocole de la IIe Conférence Juive Mondiale, Genève, 5–8 Septembre 1933* (Genève: Comité Exécutif du Congrès Juif Mondial, 1933), p. 22.

31. *Protocole de la IIIme Conférence Juive Mondiale, Genève, 20–23 août 1934* (Genève: Comité Exécutif du Congrès Juif Mondial, 1934), p. 95.

32. "World Congress of Jews Opposed," *The New York Times*, January 7, 1935.

33. "Oppose Jewish Congress," *The New York Times*, June 7, 1936.

34. "Jewish Groups Vote for World Congress," *The New York Times*, June 8, 1936.

35. *Unity in Dispersion*, pp. 45–82.

36. *Protocole du Premier Congrès Juif Mondial, Genève, 8–15 août 1936* (Genève: Comité Exécutif du Congrès Juif Mondial, 1936), pp. 158–159.

37. "Statements from representatives at the Evian Conference in July 1938, discussing the Jewish refugee situation in Europe," *Facing History and Ourselves*, https://www.facinghistory.org/resource-library/text/statements-representatives-evian-conference-july-1938.

38. Memorandum of the World Jewish Congress submitted to Delegates to the Evian Conference, July 6, 1938, p. 3, AJA box A8, folder 2.

39. Yehuda Bauer, *My Brother's Keeper: A History of the American Jewish Joint Distribution Committee 1929–1939* (Philadelphia, 1974), pp. 235–236.

40. "Our Needy First, J. B. Wise Asserts," *The New York Times*, July 21, 1938.

41. Herbert Louis Samuel, 1st Viscount Samuel (1870–1963), first practicing Jew to serve as a British Cabinet minister. He was Home Secretary, 1916 and 1931–1932, and the first High Commissioner of Paleestine, 1920–1925

42. Selig Brodetsky (1888–1954), British Jewish leader and member of the World Zionist Executive. In 1940 he became president of the Board of Deputies of British Jews.

43. Nahum Goldmann, letter to Stephen S. Wise, July 16, 1938, AJA box A27, file 1.

THE WORLD JEWISH CONGRESS DURING WORLD WAR II
PAGES 25–39

1. "1,000,000 Jews Slain by Nazis, Report Says," *The New York Times*, June 30, 1942. This report described a variety of ways in which Jews had been killed, including by firing squad, disease, and starvation, but did not suggest the continent-wide, industrialized murder that was the Nazi's "Final Solution."

2. Gerhart M. Riegner, *Never Despair: Sixty Years in the Service of the Jewish People and The Cause of Human Rights* (Chicago, 2006), pp. 12–13, 18–22, 27–36, 38–39; Memorandum, Division of European Affairs, August 13, 1942, SD 862.4016/2235, reprinted in *America and the Holocaust: A Thirteen Volume Set,* ed. David Wyman (New York, 1990), 1:194, http://www.worldcat.org/titleamerica-and-the-holocaust-a-thirteen-volumset-documenting -the-editors-book-the-abandonment-of-the-jews-11-war-refugee-board-weekley-reports-1990-539-s/oclc/632304077?ht=edition&referer=di; see State Department to Bern Legation, August 17, 1942, SD 862.4016/2223, reprinted in *America and the Holocaust*, 1:188; Riegner, *Never Despair*, p. 43.

3. Riegner, *Never Despair*, pp. 42–43; David Wyman, *The Abandonment of the Jews: America and the Holocaust, 1941–45* (New York, 1984), p. 44.

4. Stephen Wise, *Challenging Years: The Autobiography of Stephen Wise* (New York, 1949), p. 275; Carl Hermann Voss, ed. *Stephen S. Wise: Servant of the People, Selected Letters* (Philadelphia, 1969), pp. 249, 251; Melvin I. Urofsky, *A Voice That Spoke for Justice: The Life and Times of Stephen S. Wise* (Albany, NY, 1982), p. 319; Riegner, *Never Despair*, p. 71.

5. Wyman, *Abandonment of the Jews*, pp. 45–46; Urofsky, *Voice That Spoke for Justice*, p. 321.

6. Riegner, *Never Despair*, pp. 44–51; Walter Lacqueur and Richard Breitman, *Breaking the Silence: The German Who Exposed the Final Solution* (Waltham, MA, 1994), p. 157.

7. Wise, *Challenging Years*, pp. 275–276; "Wise Says Hitler Has Ordered 4,000,000 Jews Slain in 1942," *New York Herald-Tribune*, November 25, 1942.

8. Wyman, *Abandonment of the Jews*, pp. 51–52, 70–71.

9. Notes of Adolph Held, December 8, 1942, http://www.jewishvirtuallibrary.org/jsource/Holocaust/fdrmeet.html; "11 Allies Condemn Nazi War on Jews," *The New York Times*, December 18, 1942; Wyman, *Abandonment of the Jews*, p. 76; "Memorandum Submitted to the President of the United States at the White House on Tuesday, December 8, 1942 by a Delegation of Representatives of Jewish Organizations," American Jewish Archives, box C89, folder 9 (courtesy Kevin Proffitt, Senior Archivist for Research and Collections).

10. *The Morgenthau Diaries, World War II and Postwar Planning, 1943–1945*, microfilm edition, vol. 688, pt. 2, pp. 223R–223S (American Legation (in Bern) to Welles, January 21, 1943 (paraphrase of cable 482)); see Wyman, *Abandonment of the Jews*, p. 80.

11. Wyman, *Abandonment of the Jews*, pp. 80–81; Welles to Wise, February 9, 1943, American Jewish Archives, World Jewish Congress Collection, Lillie Schultz/Stephen Wise Files, Central Files reprinted in *America and the Holocaust*, vol. 2, p. 150. By one account, when

Jewish groups received cable 482 on February 9, 1943, "they decided to call a mass meeting in Madison Square Garden, at which they would try to elicit public support and map out a program." *Morgenthau Diaries*, p. 245 (December 31, 1943, 11:45 a.m.), statement of Josiah DuBois, Jr. It is unclear whether the Division of European Affairs was actually aware that such a rally was imminent. But at least, the Division acted in the general belief that reports from Europe inevitably created pressure for rescue; *Morgenthau Diaries*, p. 223T; Hull to American Legation in Bern, February 10, 1943 (paraphrase of cable 354).

12. Stephen Walsh, *Stalingrad: The Infernal Cauldron, 1942–1943* (New York, 2000), pp. 165–166; C. L. Sulzberger, "Romania Proposes Transfer of Jews," *The New York Times*, February 13, 1943.

13. Wise to Welles, March 31, 1943, SD 862.4016/2266, reprinted in *America and the Holocaust*, vol. 6, p. 1; Welles to Atherton, April 5, 1943, SD 862.4016/2266; and Hull to American Legation, April 10, 1943, SD 862.4016/2266A, reprinted in *America and the Holocaust*, vol. 6, pp. 2–3.

14. Harrison to Secretary of State, April 20, 1943, SD 862.4016/2269 (sections 1 and 2), reprinted in *America and the Holocaust*, vol. 6, pp. 5–8.

15. Wise, *Challenging Years,* pp. 277–278.

16. The Consul General at Hamilton (Beck) to Secretary of State, April 8, 1943, SD 548G1/14, reprinted in *Foreign Relations of the United States*, vol. 1 (1943), p. 148; "Memorandum Submitted to the Bermuda Refugee Conference by the World Jewish Congress, April 14, 1943"; "Views of the Government of the United States Regarding Topics Included in the Agenda for Discussion with the British Government, March 1943" ("The refugee problem should not be considered as being confined to persons of any particular race or faith.").

17. "American Minutes of the Bermuda Conference Sessions, Morning Conference, April 20, 1943," http://www.jewishvirtuallibrary.org/jsource/Holocaust/bermudadiscuss.html; see Wyman, *Abandonment of the Jews,* pp. 114–115, 121; Gregory J. Wallance, *America's Soul in the Balance: The Holocaust, FDR's State Department and the Moral Disgrace of an American Aristocracy* (Austin, TX, 2012), pp. 166–169, 183–191.

18. "Program of General Measures of Relief and Rescue of the Jews Threatened with Extermination by the Enemy," submitted to the War Refugee Board by the World Jewish Congress; Wallance, *America's Soul*, pp. 250–264.

19. "Addresses and Resolutions," War Emergency Conference of the World Jewish Congress, Atlantic City, November 1944; Konrad Kwiet and Jurgen Matthaus, eds. *Contemporary Responses to the Holocaust* (Westport, CT, 2004), p. 179; "International Jewish Conference Opens in Atlantic City," Jewish Telegraphic Agency, November 27, 1944.

20. Clarence Schwab, "The circumstances of my father's survival and my grandfather's insistence on coming to the aid of others have always inspired me," quoted in *God, Faith & Identity from the Ashes: Reflections of Children and Grandchildren of Holocaust Survivors,* ed. Menachem Z. Rosensaft (Woodstock, VT, 2015), pp. 189–190; "Raoul Wallenberg and the Rescue of Jews In Budapest," United States Holocaust Memorial Museum,

https://www.ushmm.org/wlc/en/article.php?ModuleId=10005211; "Raoul Wallenberg," University of Minnesota, Center for Holocaust & Genocide Studies, http://chgs.umn .edu/histories/wallenberg/home.html.

21. Roger Manvell and Heinrich Fraenkel, *Heinrich Himmler: The Sinister Life of the Head of the SS and Gestapo* (New York, 2007), pp. 240–248; Norbert Masur, *My Meeting with Himmler, April 20/22, 1945: Report to the Swedish Section of the World Jewish Congress, Stockholm, Sweden,* http://harmonium.org/Annelies_MeetingWithHimmler.pdf; "History of Ravensbrueck Concentration Camp from 1939–1945" [in German], http://www.ravensbrueck.de/mgr/ index.html.

22. Zohar Segev, "The Untold Story: The World Jewish Congress Operation to Rescue Children in Portugal during the Holocaust," *The American Jewish Archives Journal* 66 (2014): pp. 35–58.

23. Letter from John J. McCloy dated August 14, 1944, to A. Leon Kubowitzki, American Jewish Archives, http://americanjewisharchives.org/exhibits/aje/details.php?id=584; see also, Rafael Medoff, *Blowing the Whistle on Genocide: Josiah E. Dubois, Jr., and the Struggle for a U.S. Response to the Holocaust* (Purdue, IN, 2009), p. 104.

24. Voss, *Stephen S. Wise*, pp. 282, 296–297 (Letter from Albert Einstein to James Waterman Wise and Justine Wise Polier, April 25, 1949); Riegner, *Never Despair*, p. 434; Glare Nullis, "Gerhart Riegner, warned of Holocaust," *Miami Herald*, December 5, 2001.

NUREMBERG AND BEYOND:
JACOB ROBINSON, A CHAMPION FOR JUSTICE
PAGES 46–60

1. Jacob Robinson's papers, including many of his brother Nehemiah's papers, are in the US Holocaust Memorial Museum, Washington, DC, Accession No. 2013.506.1, http:// collections.ushmm.org/findingaids/2013.506.1_01_fnd_en.pdf ("Robinson Papers"); the published records of the Institute of Jewish Affairs can be found in a number of places, including the American Jewish Historical Society, Center for Jewish History, New York, Accession No. I-371, http://digifindingaids.cjh.org/?pID=365637 ("IJA Papers"); and the papers of the relevant offices of the World Jewish Congress are in the Jacob Rader Marcus Center of the American Jewish Archives, in Cincinnati, OH, http://catalog.american-jewisharchives.org/cgi-bin/ajagw/chameleon ("WJC Papers"). I gratefully acknowledge the assistance of archivists at all three institutions. Shabtai Rosenne, "Jacob Robinson, 28 November 1889–24 October 1977," *An International Law Miscellany* (Dordrecht, NL, 1993), pp. 831–843, especially 842, originally published as "Jacob Robinson: In Memoriam," *Israel Law Review* 13, no. 3 (July 1978), pp. 287–297.

2. Works with significant discussions of Robinson include Shlomo Aronson, "Preparations for the Nuremberg Trial: The O.S.S., Charles Dwork, and the Holocaust," *Holocaust and Genocide Studies* 12 (1998): p. 257; Boaz Cohen, "Dr. Jacob Robinson, the Institute of Jewish

Affairs, and the Elusive Jewish Voice in Nuremberg," in *Holocaust and Justice: Representation and Historiography of the Holocaust in Post-War Trials*, ed. David Bankier and Dan Michman (Jerusalem, 2010), pp. 81–100; Laura Jockusch, "Justice at Nuremberg? Jewish Responses to Nazi War-Crimes Trials in Allied-Occupied Germany," *Jewish Social Studies* 19, no. 1 (Fall 2012): pp. 107, 111–117; Omry Kaplan-Feuereisen, "Im Dienste der jüdischen Nation: Jacob Robinson und das Völkerrecht," *Osteuropa* 8–10 (2008): pp. 279–294, translated as "At the Service of the Jewish Nation: Jacob Robinson and International Law," *Osteuropa 2008, Impulses for Europe* (2008): pp. 157–170, "Geschichtserfahrung und Völkerrecht: Jacob Robinson und die Gründung des Institute of Jewish Affairs," *Leipziger Beiträge zur jüdischen Geschichte und Kultur* 2 (2004): pp. 307–327, and "Jacob Robinson," *The YIVO Encyclopedia of Jews in Eastern Europe* (New Haven, 2008), pp. 1567–1568, http://www.yivoencyclopedia. org/article.aspx/robinson_jacob; Mark A. Lewis, "The World Jewish Congress and the Institute of Jewish Affairs at Nuremberg: Ideas, Strategies, and Political Goals, 1942–1946," *Yad Vashem Studies* 36, no. 1 (2008): pp. 181–210, adapted in *The Birth of the New Justice: The Internationalization of Crime and Punishment, 1919–1950* (Oxford, 2014), pp. 150–180; Michael R. Marrus, "Three Jewish Emigrés at Nuremberg: Hersch Lauterpacht, Jacob Robinson, and Raphael Lemkin," in *Against the Grain: Jewish Intellectuals in Hard Times*, ed. Ezra Mendelsohn, Steffani Hoffman, and Richard Cohen (New York, 2014), pp. 240–254, with a shorter version in "Three Roads to Nuremberg," *Tablet*, November 20, 2015; "A Jewish Lobby at Nuremberg: Jacob Robinson and the Institute of Jewish Affairs, 1945–46," *Cardozo Law Review* 27, no. 4 (2006): pp. 1651–1665, with a shorter version in *The Nuremberg Trials. International Criminal Law since 1945: 60th Anniversary Conference / Die Nürnberger Prozesse. Völkerstrafrecht seit 1945: Internationale Konferenz zum 60. Jahrestag*, ed. Herbert R. Reginbogin and Christoph J.M. Safferling (Munich, 2006), pp. 63–72; "The Holocaust at Nuremberg," *Yad Vashem Studies* 26 (1998): pp. 5–41; Maurice Perlzweig, s.v. "Robinson, Jacob," *Encyclopaedia Judaica*, vol. 14, col. 207 (Jerusalem and New York, 1971); Rosenne, "Jacob Robinson," pp. 831–843; Gil Rubin, "The End of Minority Rights: Jacob Robinson and the 'Jewish Question' in World War II," *Simon Dubnow Institute Yearbook* 11 (2012): pp. 55–71.

3. The recently published proceedings of the 2007 conference, "The Life, Times and Work of Jokūbas Robinzonas—Jacob Robinson," ed. Eglė Bendikaitė and Dirk Roland Haupt (Sankt Augustin, Germany, 2015) was not available to me for consultation at the time of this writing.

4. This and the following paragraph are drawn from various sketches by Kaplan-Feureisen.

5. *American Jewish Year Book 1933* (1934): pp. 74–101. Robinson and various Jewish organizations helped Bernheim bring an individual petition arguing that as an Upper Silesian, he was protected by the German–Polish Agreement on Upper Silesia (1922). Embarrassed by this legal scrutiny so soon after coming to power, the Nazis suspended certain racist laws in that territory until 1937. See A.W. B. Simpson, *Human Rights and the End of Empire* (Oxford, 2001), pp. 142–145; Carole Fink, *Defending the Rights of Others: The Great Powers,*

the Jews, and International Minority Protection, 1878–1938 (Cambridge, 2004), pp. 331–332; Rubin, "The End of Minority Rights," p. 57.

6. Formerly a part of the former Russian Empire, Memel was coveted by Poland and Germany but assigned to Lithuania under the five-power Allied oversight (1922). When German local officials made surreptitious visits to Nazi Germany, Lithuania removed them, prompting the five guarantors to seek a ruling about Memel's autonomy. The international court rejected Robinson's reasoning but largely accepted his conclusion that Lithuania as sovereign had a right to supervise its restive enclave, which it did until Hitler demanded and was ceded the territory in March 1939. *Interpretation of the Statute of the Memel Territory*, A/B 47 & 49 (1932), http://www.icj-cij.org/pcij/serie_AB/AB_49/01_Memel Arret.pdf. The case was Robinson's first appearance at the international court and became the occasion of his two-volume first book (1934). For Robinson's appearances at other international cases in this period, see Rosenne, "Jacob Robinson," p. 833.

7. During which time Robinson and his lobby group pressed Lithuania to receive Jewish refugees from Poland, as Kaplan-Feuereisen notes.

8. While in the town of Vichy, France, in autumn 1939, Robinson unsuccessfully used his contacts with diplomats and a US senator to try to obtain refugee status in the United States, France, Denmark, and probably elsewhere. Robinson Papers, box 1, folder 11.

9. Thus, it pre-dated other research and advocacy groups such as the American Jewish Committee's Institute on Peace and Postwar Problems and the Jewish Labor Committee's Research Institute for Jewish Postwar Problems.

10. Mark Lewis, *Birth of the New Justice*, pp. 162–163 (disagreement whether to press for a Jewish official prosecutor for war crimes).

11. The reparation clauses also were drafted by Jacob Robinson. Nana Sagi, *German Reparations: A History of the Negotiations*, trans. Dafna Alon (Jerusalem, 1980), pp. 24–26; Robinson Papers, box 4, folders 10 and 14.

12. Some of these agendas within the IJA are discussed in Rubin, "End of Minority Rights," pp. 58–61, 69–70; and Mark Mazower, *No Enchanted Palace: The End of Empire and the Ideological Origins of the United Nations* (Princeton, NJ, 2009), pp. 121–122.

13. Aronson, "Preparations for the Nuremberg Trial," p. 257.

14. "Minutes, Meeting of World Jewish Congress with Justice Robert H. Jackson in New York City, June 12, 1945," WJC Papers, http://www.trumanlibrary.org/whistlestop/study_collections/nuremberg/documents/index.php?documentdate=1945-06-12&documentid=C106-16-5&pagenumber=1. The IJA had by then accepted the British Section's proposal for a Jewish prosecutor though that section had had no luck in lobbying the UN War Crimes Commission in London to accept the view. Lewis, *Birth of the New Justice*, pp. 162–166.

15. Letter from Jacob Robinson to Robert H. Jackson, July 27, 1945, WJC Papers, http://www.trumanlibrary.org/whistlestop/study_collections/nuremberg/documents/index.php?documentdate=1945-07-27&documentid=C106-16-2&pagenumber=1.

16. Robinson's travels to London and Nuremberg are documented in IJA Papers, box 1, folder 3.

17. There are approximately a dozen memos between Robinson and other Jewish organizational leaders and the Nuremberg prosecutors, many of which are at http://www.trumanlibrary.org/whistlestop/study_collections/nuremberg/index.php?action=docs. But there is scant evidence that these Jewish organizational efforts were used by the four prosecution teams, even if we go beyond the familiar Robinson memos and OSS research and examine items such as the favorable references to Robinson's work in the diary of Seymour Krieger, a prosecutor working for Walsh on the Holocaust case or the participation at Nuremberg of a British WJC leader A. L. Easterman. On the contrary, there is evidence that Jewish groups felt frustrated by the way Nuremberg staffers were not following their advice. See the letter of Robinson to Dwork of June 23, 1945, WJC Papers, http://www.trumanlibrary.org/whistlestop/study_collections/nuremberg/documents/index.php?documentdate=1945-06-23&documentid=C106-18-22&pagenumber=1. Only occasionally is there direct evidence that IJA material reached top prosecutors, either directly or indirectly, through OSS staffers. See, e.g., Telford Taylor, "Progress Report No. 5" [minutes of planning Committee 2 and 3], 2, no. 12 (September 4, 1945) in Telford Taylor Papers, Columbia University ("Taylor Papers"), box 298.

18. See, e.g., the works by Aronson, Cohen, Jockusch, and Marrus cited above, as well as Donald Bloxham, "Jewish Witnesses in War Crimes Trials of the Postwar Era," *Holocaust Historiography in Context: Emergence, Challenges, Polemics and Achievements*, ed. David Bankier and Dan Michman (Jerusalem, 2008), pp. 539–553, especially 540; and *Genocide on Trial: War Crimes Trials and the Formation of Holocaust History and Memory* (Oxford, 2001), pp. 64–68, 101–115, 124; and Lawrence Douglas, *The Memory of Judgment: Making Law and History in the Trials of the Holocaust* (New Haven, 2005), pp. 60, 66, 72, 78–80.

19. See Jonathan A. Bush, "The Prehistory of Corporations and Conspiracy in International Criminal Law: What Nuremberg Really Said," *Columbia Law Review* 109, no. 5 (June 2009): pp. 1094, 1137–1138, 1140–1143; and "The Supreme . . . Crime' and Its Origins: The Lost Legislative History of the Crime of Aggressive War," *Columbia Law Review* 102, no. 8 (December 2002): pp. 2324, 2353–2370.

20. As an outsider to the process, Robinson could not have known that he had it upside down in attributing Jackson's theories to UN War Crimes Commission delegates Marcel de Baer and Bohuslav Ecer rather than Pentagon planners. Compare Robinson's report, "Minutes of the Office Committee Meeting . . . Dec. 10, 1945," WJC Papers, https://www.trumanlibrary.org/whistlestop/study_collections/nuremberg/documents/index.php?documentid=C14-16-2&pagenumber=1 with Bush, "Supreme Crime," pp. 2342–2343, 2346–2366.

21. Associate prosecutor Sidney Alderman recalled the early search for these experts in *Reminiscences of Sidney Sherrill Alderman: Oral History, 1953* (New York, 1953), pp. 854–870. Of the scholars, probably the most important was Harvard criminologist Sheldon Glueck, described in Bush, "Supreme Crime," pp. 2343–2369.

22. Telford Taylor, *The Anatomy of the Nuremberg Trials* (New York, 1992), p. 520; Letter from Benjamin Ferencz to Robert Kempner, Dec. 13, 1989, in Taylor Papers, box 270, 20-1-3-34.

23. Proposals for a Jewish co-chief prosecutor were spurned, as were similar requests by Czech, Polish, and Yugoslav leaders. Bloxham concludes that the refusals were based on different reasons in the case of the Jews and that the Robinson–Lauterpacht idea was rejected because of the Allies' inability to see Jewish identity as anything but a religious faith whose adherents were singled out, *Genocide on Trial*, p. 67, and there is something to that. This is supported by comparing the two different sets of notes kept for the same high-level meeting at which Allied delegates rejected the notion of an official Jewish prosecutor: the American team raised questions of policy, while the British team treated the idea with contempt and more than a whiff of anti-Semitism. Progress Report No. 4, Subcommittee 2 & 3, September 4, 1945, in Taylor Papers, box 298, unnumbered folder "International Indictment-drafting committees—minutes." As for an official Jewish witness, whether Weizmann or even Joseph Proskauer, president of the American Jewish Committee, the idea could easily have backfired at the hands of a defense counsel skillful at cross-examination.

24. Later research has shown that both Jackson and a senior associate, Executive Counsel Thomas Dodd, preferred to avoid having too many Jews on staff, especially on the Holocaust portion of the case. Jockusch, "Justice at Nuremberg?" pp. 117–118. Notwithstanding that, there were many Jewish lawyers on the US team, both on the Jewish portion of the case (Seymour Krieger, Isaac Stone) and throughout the higher echelons where strategy was made (Murray Bernays, Benjamin and Sidney Kaplan, and Murray Gurfein, who had been on the IJA board in 1941). Attempts to count Jews on staff, as some scholars do, are misleading because they exaggerate Jewish significance in counting junior and support staff or persons in titular authority only, or they omit staffers with Jewish family (Elwyn Jones) or otherwise wholeheartedly sympathetic to the Holocaust case. They also assume that a Jewish background signifies an agenda or single perspective. What matters is not the layered Jewish identities of the senior staff, but the support they broadly shared, as they seem to have, for the Jewish dimensions of the case.

25. This is not to deny that prosecutors, for various reasons, few of them defensible, seem to have avoided using Jewish survivor witnesses, for reasons that ranged from real or perceived courtroom advantage to anti-Semitism. Bloxham, *Genocide on Trial*, pp. 540, 548–549. Nevertheless, survivors were generally not needed for the case that the Allies, for better or worse, had ambitiously chosen to bring.

26. Telford Taylor was first liaison with the Polish and Soviet teams, and he brought Lemkin and Seymour Krieger to meet Polish historian Philip Friedman (with whom Robinson later published Holocaust documentation); other lawyers who later focused on the Holocaust included Brady Bryson and William Walsh and his team.

27. Bush, "Corporations and Conspiracy," describes narrow IMT rulings and contemporary reactions (pp. 1160–1163). More than most contemporary observers, Robinson

immediately saw and criticized these devastating jurisdictional rulings. "The Nuremberg Judgment," *Congress Weekly*, October 25, 1946, in Robinson Papers, box 4, folder 10.

28. "Minutes of the Office Committee Meeting . . ." Dec. 10, 1945, WJC Papers, https://www.trumanlibrary.org/whistlestop/study_collections/nuremberg/documents/index.php?documentid=C14-16-2&pagenumber=1.

29. One of the prosecutors he implicitly criticized on Walsh's team, Krieger, used Nuremberg evidence to publish the earliest Holocaust documentation in English (1947), and French prosecutor Henri Monneray published the first documentation in French (1947). Their pioneering work is discussed in Jonathan A. Bush, "Raul Hilberg (1926–2007): In Memoriam," *Jewish Quarterly Review* 100, no. 4 (2010): pp. 661, 669. Meanwhile, Raphael Lemkin used his new post in the Pentagon to assist in the later Nuremberg trials and to urge prosecutors to focus on the Holocaust and his genocide theory, especially in the Medical and Flick cases, the latter a case on which Robinson also helped.

30. Taylor to senior staff (Feb. 1947) and letters between Wise and Taylor, Secretary of the Army Kenneth Royall, General Daniel Noce, and Colonel Edward Young (November–December 1947), in Bush, "Corporations and Conspiracy," pp. 1187–1188, 1262; Bloxham, *Genocide on Trial*, pp. 73–75.

31. See, for example, Nehemiah Robinson's letters to Taylor throughout the 1950s, in Taylor Papers, box 188, folders 50 and 60, and box 190, folders 96–97; Jacob's letters to Taylor are all from the early 1950s and then the period of the Eichmann trial, and are scattered in a dozen boxes. Nehemiah Robinson's articles on prosecution and clemency over a ten-year span from the late 1940s are in IJA Papers, box 1, folders 1, 2, and 4; and box 2, folder 6.

32. "Jews in the USSR," *Jewish Affairs* 1, no. 3 (March 1, 1946) and "Unfinished Victory," *Jewish Affairs* 1, no. 8 (September 15, 1946), both in IJA Papers, box 2.

33. Abba Eban, *An Autobiography* (New York, 1977), p. 133; Rosenne, "Jacob Robinson," p. 836.

34. Robinson Papers, box 5, folder 13, and box 6, folder 1; IJA Papers, box 1, folder 5, and box 2, folder 6; Nicholas Balabkins, *West German Reparations to Israel* (New Brunswick, NJ, 1971), p. 136; Sagi, *German Reparations*, about Nehemiah on pp. 94–95, 189, and 206, and about Jacob on p. 90.

35. *International Court of Justice, Pleadings, Oral Arguments, Documents: Reservations to the Convention on the Prevention and Punishment of the Crime of Genocide Advisory Opinion of May 28, 1951: Part II, Public Sittings (from April 10 to 14 and on May 28th: Oral Statements* (The Hague, 1951): 328–357. For other international cases in which Robinson represented or prepared the case for Israel, see Rosenne, "Jacob Robinson," pp. 833–834.

36. The text of many of Jacob Robinson's presentations to UN committees are found in Robinson Papers, box 5, folders 9, 10, and 11; and box 6, folder 2, while others can be found in the negotiations that have been put online for some of these conventions. See, for example, http://www.unhcr.org/search?comid=3c07a8642&cid=49aea9390&scid=49aea9398 (1951 Refugee Convention). Nehemiah's pamphlets on the same topics are found in IJA Papers, box 2, folders 1 and 6. For details of Jacob Robinson's central role in

the Declaration of Death Convention, see Rosenne, "Jacob Robinson," p. 837; and in the Refugee Convention, see Gilad Ben-Nun, "The Israeli Roots of Article 3 and Article 6 of the 1951 Refugee Convention," *Journal of Refugee Studies* 27, no. 1 (2013), 101–125; and "The British–Jewish Roots of Non-Refoulement and Its True Meaning for the Drafters of the 1951 Refugee Convention," *Journal of Refugee Studies* 28, no. 1 (2015): pp. 93–117.

37. Eban, *Autobiography*, pp. 221–222.

38. E.g., "Are Eichmann's Memoirs Published in *Life* Magazine Authentic?" (December 5, 1960), IJA Papers, box 1, folder 3; "Eichmann's Confederates and the Third Reich Hierarchy" (May 1961), IJA Papers, box 1, folder 2.

39. Gideon Hausner, *Justice in Jerusalem* (New York, 1966), pp. 303, 313; Hanna Yablonka, *The State of Israel vs. Eichmann*, trans. Ora Cummings and David Herman (New York, 2004), pp. 98, 100–106, 147.

40. A typical assessment is given in Richard I. Cohen, "A Generation's Response to 'Eichmann in Jerusalem,'" in *Hannah Arendt in Jerusalem*, ed. Steven E. Ascheim (Berkeley, 2001), pp. 253–277, especially 266–267. Contrary to the stereotype, Robinson was not an automatic defender of the trial; all along, for instance, he questioned the death penalty, albeit on practical rather than legal grounds, Yablonka, *The State of Israel vs. Eichmann*, p. 147. Arendt's misuse of Hilberg's arguments to attack critics like Robinson is described in Bush, "Hilberg," pp. 673–675.

41. This and the next paragraphs are largely based on Robinson's correspondence, Robinson Papers, box 8 and box 9.

42. A dozen years earlier Robinson had helped bring Friedman to New York. Roni Stauber, "Philip Friedman and the Beginning of Holocaust Studies," in *Holocaust Historiography in Context*, pp. 83–102, esp., 91.

THE STATE OF WORLD JEWRY, 1948
PAGES 61–75

1. Leon (Lev) Pinsker (1821–1891) was an early pre-Herzl Zionist whose 1882 pamphlet, *Autoemancipation: Mahnruf an seine Stammesgenossen von eimem russischen Juden* (Autoemancipation: An appeal to his people by a Russian Jew) called for Jews to identify as a separate entity and for the establishment of a Jewish homeland.

GERHART M. RIEGNER: PIONEER FOR JEWISH–CATHOLIC RELATIONS
IN THE CONTEMPORARY WORLD
PAGES 76–87

1. Gerhart M. Riegner, *Never Despair: Sixty Years in the Service of the Jewish People and the Cause of Human Rights* (Chicago, 2006), p. 122.

2. Ibid., pp. 178–180.

3. Goldmann and Katz issued the memorandum in the name of the World Conference of Jewish Organizations (COJO), of which they were, respectively, the chairman and co-chairman. In addition to the WJC and B'nai Brith International, COJO consisted of the Board of Deputies of British Jews, the Canadian Jewish Congress, the Conseil Représentatif des Juifs de France (CRIF), the Executive Council of Australian Jewry, the South African Jewish Board of Deputies, the Delegación de Asociaciones Israelitas Argentinas (DAIA), the American Jewish Congress, and the Jewish Labor Committee.

4. Translated from the original [French] of the memorandum as sent to Cardinal Béa.

5. *Nostra Aetate* §1.

6. *Nostra Aetate* §5.

7. *Nostra Aetate* §4.

8. Riegner, *Never Despair*, p. 275.

9. "Memorandum of Understanding," International Catholic-Jewish Liaison Committee, initial meeting, Vatican City, December 1970, https://www.bc.edu/content/dam/files/research_sites/cjl/texts/cjrelations/resources/documents/interreligious/ILC_memo_understanding_1970.htm.

10. *The Church and Racism: Toward a More Fraternal Society*, Pontifical Commission for Justice and Peace, paragraph 15, signed November 3, 1988, https://www.ewtn.com/library/curia/pcjpraci.htm.

11. David Rosen, "Challenges Ahead in the Jewish Catholic Relationship," in *Gerhart M. Riegner,* ed. Isabella Nespoli (Brussels, 2001).

12. United States Conference of Catholic Bishops, "Cardinals Keeler and Kasper Pay Tribute to Jewish Official Who First Told the World of Hitler's Plan for the Holocaust," press release, December 5, 2001.

THE WORLD JEWISH CONGRESS AND THE STATE OF ISRAEL: A PERSONAL REMINISCENCE
PAGES 88–100

1. I have dealt with the issue of the nature of groups such as Jews, Arabs, Sikhs, and others in my *Group Rights and Discrimination in International Law* (The Hague, 2003).

2. As R. J. Zvi Werblowsky notes, Jews, despite their religious origin, consider themselves a people and a member of the "family of nations." See his "Religion and Peoplehood," in *The Jerusalem Colloquium on Religion, Peoplehood, Nation and Land* (Jerusalem, 1972), p. 17.

3. See Jacob Robinson, "The Problem of Minorities between the Two Wars," in *Fifty Years of Struggle for Jewish Rights* [in Hebrew] (Jerusalem, 1970).

4. See, "Resolution sur la Palestine" in *Protocole du Premier Congrès Juif Mondial Genève, 8–15 août, 1936* (Genève: Comité Exécutif du Congrès Juif Mondial, 1936), p. 361.

5. "Declaration on Israel," World Jewish Congress, Third Plenary Assembly (Geneva: Resolutions and Composition of Assembly, August 4–11, 1953), p. 11.

6. See in this volume, "The State of World Jewry, 1948," Nahum Goldmann's keynote address at the second WJC plenary assembly, Montreux, Switzerland, June 27, 1948.

7. *Proceedings of the Fourth Plenary Assembly of the World Jewish Congress* (Stockholm, 1959), p. 135.

8. Ibid., pp. 135–136.

9. "The 1950 Ben-Gurion-Blaustein Clarification Statements," in *Vigilant Brotherhood: The American Jewish Committee's Relationship to Palestine and Israel* (New York, 1964), pp. 54–56.

10. See *The Institute Anniversary Volume (1941–1961)* (New York, 1962), especially the articles by Nehemiah Robinson, Gerhard Jacoby, and Anatole Goldstein.

11. Arieh Tartakower, "Unity in Dispersion and the Jewish National Home," *World Jewry* (July/August 1961): p. 24.

12. See, e.g., *The Autobiography of Nahum Goldmann: Sixty Years of Jewish Life* (New York, 1969); Nahum Goldmann, *Le Paradoxe juif: Conversations en français avec Leon Abramowicz* (Paris, 1976); *Où va Israël?* (Paris, 1975); and other writings, including numerous articles and speeches.

13. See note 17 below.

14. "Nahum Goldmann Will Not Seek Re-election as President of World Zionist Organization," JTA, April 9, 1968.

15. See, generally, Meir Chazan, "Goldmann's Initiative to Meet with Nasser in 1970," in *Nahum Goldmann: Statesman without a State*, ed. Mark A. Raider (Albany, 2009), pp. 297–324.

16. Nahum Goldmann, "The Future of Israel," *Foreign Affairs* (April 1970): p. 453.

17. For a discussion of the WJC's approach to advocating on behalf of Soviet Jewry during the Goldmann years, see in this volume, "Soviet Jewry: Debates and Controversies," by Suzanne D. Rutland.

18. See in this volume, "Diplomatic Interventions: The World Jewish Congress and North African Jewry," by Isabella Nespoli and Menachem Z. Rosensaft.

19. See Nehemiah Robinson, "Spoliation and Remedial Action," *Institute Anniversary Volume*; also, Menachem Z. Rosensaft and Joana D. Rosensaft, "The Early History of German-Jewish Reparations," Symposium, *Fordham International Law Journal*, vol. 25 (2001): p. S-1.

20. See in this volume, "Gerhart M. Riegner: Pioneer for Jewish–Catholic Relations in the Contemporary World" by Monsignor Pier Francesco Fumagalli; also, e.g., Gerhart M. Riegner, "*Nostra Aetate*: Twenty Years After," in *Fifteen Years of Catholic Jewish Dialogue, 1970–1985: Selected Papers*, Libreria Editrice Vaticana (Vatican City, 1988). On the Holy See and Israel, see Chapter 13 of my *Religion, Secular Beliefs and Human Rights* (Leiden, 2012).

The World Jewish Congress, the League of Nations, and the United Nations
PAGES 101–114

1. See Natan Feinberg, "The Committee of Jewish Delegations 1919–1936" [in Hebrew], *Gesher* 63–64 (1970): pp. 15–16. See also Nahum Goldmann, "Fifty Years of Struggle for Jewish Rights," *Gesher* 63–64 (1970): pp. 7–12; A. Bein, "The Role of A. L. Motzkin in the Struggle for Jewish National Rights in the Diaspora and in the Founding of the Committee of Jewish Delegations," *Gesher* 63–64 (1970): pp. 30–38.

2. On Simon Dubnow (also spelled Shimon, Shimen, and Semyon; and Dubnov), see, e.g., Sophie Dubnov-Erlich, *The Life and Work of S. M. Dubnov: Diaspora Nationalism and Jewish History*, trans. Judith Vowles (Bloomington, IN, 1991), pp. 1–33.

3. Memorandum of the Executive Committee of the WJC, submitted to the League of Nations on December 16, 1936, American Jewish Archives (AJA), 361 A1/2.

4. Memorandum of the Directorate of the World Jewish Congress to the League of Nations, AJA, 361 A1/2.

5. Open letter from Wise to the Jews of America, March 1938 (no precise date given), AJA, 361 A9/4. For an address in a similar vein, see the public declaration by Louis Lipsky, May 9, 1938, AJA, 361 A9/4. See also the letter from Wise to Rabbi Joseph Rantz of Louisville, KY, December 1, 1941, AJA, 361 C68/13.

6. Wise, open letter; see note 5. Wise was chairman of the WJC's Executive Committee until 1943, when he was elected president.

7. Memorandum of the Executive Committee of the World Jewish Congress to the League of Nations committee dealing with the organization's charter, December 16, 1936, AJA, 361 A1/2. To impress upon the League's institutions the seriousness of the plight of the Jews in Germany and in Eastern Europe, WJC leaders made a point of passing on to them information on the deteriorating economic condition of Europe's Jews. See the memorandum of the WJC's Economic Committee submitted to the League of Nations, March 14, 1937, AJA, 361 A9/3.

8. *Report on the Activities of the Executive Committee of the WJC September–October 1938*, October 15, 1938, AJA 361 A1/1.

9. Natan Lerner, *The World Jewish Congress and Human Rights* (Geneva, 1978), p. 5.

10. *Unity in Dispersion: A History of the World Jewish Congress*, 2d. ed. (New York: World Jewish Congress, 1948), p. 313.

11. Ibid., p. 338.

12. Lerner, *World Jewish Congress and Human Rights*, p. 7, note 17.

13. *Report on Activities of the World Jewish Congress, January–May 1945*, World Jewish Congress (British Section), June 1945, p. 4.

14. Jacob Robinson, *Human Rights and Fundamental Freedoms in the Charter of the United Nations* (New York, 1946), p. 32.

15. Lerner, *World Jewish Congress and Human Rights*, p. 7, note 17.

16. Gerhart M. Riegner, *Never Despair: Sixty Years in the Service of the Jewish People and the Cause of Human Rights* (Chicago, 2006), pp. 366–368.

17. Ibid., p. 179.

18. Ibid., pp. 181–182.

19. Nehemiah Robinson, *The United Nations and the World Jewish Congress* (New York, 1955), hereafter Robinson, *UN*, p. 3.

20. UN Economic and Social Council, "The World Jewish Congress and the United Nations, 1953," box #134, folder #13, ms-361, World Jewish Congress Records, AJA, Cincinnati, OH.

21. On attempts to involve Jews and Congress activists in UNRRA activity, see Tartakower's report on his activity in London, AJA, 361 A1/4. Tartakower visited London as chairman of the WJC's Welfare and Relief Committee. Among his other efforts, he tried to convince the heads of UNRRA to hire Jews for their European activities.

22. WJC memorandum submitted to UNRRA, September 1944 (no precise date given), AJA, 361 C98/6.

23. "Political Aspects of Relief . . . Editorial," *Congress Weekly*, December 29, 1944, p. 5.

24. *Report on the WJC's Cultural and Educational Division*, March 20, 1946, AJA, 361 E10/14.

25. Ibid.

26. See a memorandum of the WJC's Paris office pertaining to future cultural activity, September 24, 1948, AJA, 361 E10/14. On the primacy and importance of the cultural aspect of processes of national crystallization, see John Hutchinson, "Cultural Nationalism and Moral Regeneration," in *Nationalism*, ed. John Hutchinson and Anthony D. Smith (Oxford, 1994), pp. 122–131.

27. See in this volume, "The State of World Jewry, 1948," Nahum Goldmann's keynote address at the second WJC plenary assembly in Montreux, Switzerland, June 27, 1948. See also *Congress Weekly*, August 20, 1948, p. 9.

28. Memorandum submitted by Dr. Robert Marcus, Chairman of the WJC Political Committee, to the UN Commission on Genocide, March 6, 1948, AJA, 361 B104/3.

29. On support for the United Nations, see memorandum to the WJC conference at Atlantic City, November 17, 1944, AJA, 361 A68/3. On the participation of WJC representatives in related activity in Washington and their support for the Bretton Woods agreements, the World Bank, and the International Monetary Fund, see the article written by Nehemiah Robinson in *Congress Weekly*, April 20, 1945, AJA, 361 B95/3. See also the memorandum by Robinson, undated, AJA, 361 B95/1 and the telegram from US Treasury Secretary Henry Morgenthau Jr. inviting the WJC to send a representative to the consultations in Washington regarding the Bretton Woods agreements, February 17, 1945, AJA, 361 B95/3. On the request to lobby members of Congress to support the Bretton Woods agreement, see the action guide of the WJC's Women's League, February 5, 1945, AJA, 361 C68/5. On the agreements and their significance, see John Maynard Keynes, *Activities 1941–1946: Shaping the Post War World: Bretton Woods and Reparations* (London, 1980).

30. See, generally, N. Robinson, *UN*.

31. N. Robinson, *UN*, pp. 116–126.

32. Professor John P. Humphrey, address at the opening of the WJC Third plenary assembly at Geneva, Switzerland, August 4, 1953, WJC Brussels office.

33. For more information regarding the WJC activities at the United Nations prior to 1955, see generally, N. Robinson, *UN*. See also the letter and memorandum signed by Nehemiah Robinson and Robert Marcus sent to the General Assembly of the United Nations, *World Jewry*, May/June 1967, and Nehemiah Robinson, *Convention Relating to the Status of Stateless Persons: Its History and Interpretation* (Institute of Jewish Affairs, Word Jewish Congress, 1955), reprinted by the Division of International Protection of the UN High Commissioner for Refugees.

From Pariah to Partner: The Jews of Postwar Germany and the World Jewish Congress
PAGES 115–127

1. Tyler Marshall, "New Germany Is Trustworthy, Kohl Tells Jews," *Los Angeles Times*, May 7, 1990.

2. *Jüdische Allgemeine,* September 17, 2014.

3. "Resolutions Adopted by the Second Plenary Assembly of the World Jewish Congress, Montreux, Switzerland, June 27th–July 6th, 1948" (hereafter "Montreux Resolutions") (London: World Jewish Congress, 1948), p. 7. Also in Tamara Anthony, *Ins Land der Väter oder der Täter? Israel und die Juden in Deutschland nach der Schoah* (Berlin, 2004), p. 123. For a discussion of the position of German and world Jewry, see also Shlomo Shafir, *Ambiguous Relations: The American Jewish Community and Germany Since 1945* (Detroit, 1999); and Anthony Kauders, *Unmögliche Heimat: Eine deutsch-jüdische Geschichte der Bundesrepublik* (Munich, 2007).

4. Wolfgang Jacobmeyer, "Jüdische Überlebende als Displaced Persons," *Geschichte und Gesellschaft* 9 (1983): pp. 429–444, here: p. 436. This number is of course not to be taken literally, as these counts overlooked a considerable number of non-officially registered displaced persons.

5. World Jewish Congress, *Survey of Policy and Action, 1948–1953*, p. 33.

6. Zohar Segev, *The World Jewish Congress during the Holocaust: Between Activism and Restraint* (Berlin, 2014), p. 169.

7. Josef Rosensaft, "Our Belsen," in *Belsen* (Tel Aviv, 1957), p. 32.

8. Segev, *World Jewish Congress during the Holocaust*, p. 175.

9. Ibid., p. 178.

10. "Montreux Resolutions," p. 8.

11. There is by now a long list of publications on Jews in the GDR, most recently Detlef Joseph, *Die DDR und die Juden* (Berlin, 2010), with a bibliography by Renate Kirchner. In

English, see Robin Ostow, *Jews in Contemporary East Germany: The Children of Moses in the Land of Marx* (New York, 1989).

12. Quoted in: Anthony, *Ins Land der Väter*, p. 61.

13. The previous quotations all appear in Michael Brenner, *After the Holocaust: Rebuilding Jewish Lives in Postwar Germany* (Princeton, 1997), p. 66.

14. Letter from Livneh to the Western European Division of the Foreign Ministry, February 12, 1951, quoted in Anthony, *Ins Land der Väter*, p. 173. Letter from Gershon Avner to Livneh, May 16, 1951, ibid., p. 174.

15. Anthony, *Ins Land der Väter*, pp. 125–126.

16. *Report by the Institute of Jewish Affairs,* vol. 2, no. 1 (July 1949), published by the World Jewish Congress. RG-68.059M WJC London, reel 233.

17. *The Jewish Chronicle,* August 24, 1962, in RG-68.059M WJC London, reel 351.

18. "Short Minutes of the Meeting of the London Members of the WJC Executive Committee, October 28, 1948," p. 10. RG-68.059M WJC London, reel 62.

19. "European Executive Meeting, Feb. 13–14, 1949," RG-68.059M WJC London, reel 62.

20. "Enlarged Meeting of the European Members of the World Executive, August 25–28, 1949," RG-68.059M WJC London, reel 62.

21. "Short Minutes of the Meeting of the London Members of the WJC Executive Committee, July 14, 1950," RG-68.059M WJC London, reel 62.

22. "Meeting of the London Members of the European Executive, September 16, 1954," RG-68.059M WJC London, reel 62.

23. "Meeting of the London Members of the European Committee, July 4, 1951," RG-68.059M WJC London, reel 62.

24. Memorandum from S. Sokal to A. L. Easterman, May 27, 1952, RG-68.059M WJC London, reel 164. Relations between the WJC and the Central Council remained tense for over a decade. Much of the tension around this time was based on the WJC's accusation that the Central Council belittled the anti-Semitic incidents starting with the swastika graffiti at the Cologne synagogue in 1959. See also the letter of Dr. Hans Lamm to WJC, London, January 19, 1960, RG-68.059M WJC London, reel 165.

25. *Allgemeine Jüdische Wochenzeitung,* July 20, 1951, p. 1.

26. *Proceedings of WJC Plenary Session 1953,* RG-68.059M, reel 130.

27. See, e.g., the reports of Dr. Jacoby, who directed the WJC Frankfurt office. See minutes of the meeting of the London members of the WJC Executive Committee, May 14, 1950, RG-68.059M WJC London, reel 62.

28. "Special Discussion: Germans and Jews—A Problem Unresolved" (hereafter "Special Discussion: Germans and Jews"), in *Proceedings of the Fifth Plenary Assembly of the World Jewish Congress, Brussels July 31–August 9, 1966* (Geneva: World Jewish Congress, 1974), pp. 197–199.

29. Ibid., pp. 199–200.

30. *Deutsche und Juden: Ein unlösbares Problem. Reden zum Jüdischen Weltkongress,* n.p.: Verlag Kontakte, 1966, pp. 5–6. The accounts were also published by the better-known Suhrkamp Verlag (Frankfurt am Main, 1967) in a different translation but without the transcript of the protocol, and without the contribution of Hendrik George van Dam.

31. RG-68.059M WJC London, reel 132, letter by Bergman, dated August 2, 1966.

32. JTA, July 29, 1966, http://www.jta.org/1966/07/29/archive/world-jewish-congress-opens-10-day-assembly-in-brussels-on-sunday.

33. "Special Discussion: Germans and Jews," p. 203.

34. Ibid.

35. Ibid., p. 201; see also *Proceedings of the Conference,* p. 24, RG-68.059M WJC London, reel 132.

36. "Special Discussion: Germans and Jews," pp. 240–241. See also, *Deutsche und Juden,* p. 97.

37. "Zentralarchiv zur Erforschung der Geschichte der Juden in Deutschland Heidelberg," B.1/7. 818, S. 1966-04-30, *Protokoll über die Sitzung des Verwaltungsrats des Direktoriums des Zentralrats der Juden in Deutschland* am 30 April 1966 in München.

38. "Special Discussion: Germans and Jews," pp. 254. See also, *Deutsche und Juden,* p. 56.

39. Joachim Prinz, *Rebellious Rabbi: An Autobiography—The German and American Years,* ed. Michael A. Meyer (Bloomington, IN, 2008), p. 160.

40. "Special Discussion: Germans and Jews," p. 249.

41. "Bericht des Verwaltungsrates des Direktoriums des Zentralrates der Juden in Deutschland." Referiert von Generalsekretär Dr. H. G. van Dam, 22.3.1964. In RG-68.045 WJC Geneva, reel 127.

42. See in this volume, Maram Stern, "The Communist Years: A Jewish Perspective." For a critical view, see Michael Wolffsohn, *The World Jewish Congress and the End of the German Democratic Republic* (Washington DC, 1991).

Diplomatic Interventions: The World Jewish Congress and North African Jewry
pages 128–141

1. Gerhart M. Riegner, *Never Despair: Sixty Years in the Service of the Jewish People and the Cause of Human Rights* (Chicago, 2006), p. 354.

2. *Protocole du Premier Congrès Juif Mondial, Genève, 9–12 août 1936* (Genève: Comité Exécutif du Congrès Juif Mondial, 1936), p. IX.

3. Isaac I. Schwarzbart—*25 Years in the Service of the Jewish People* (New York: World Jewish Congress, 1957), p. 15.

4. "The Abrogation of the Cremieux Decree," *Congress Weekly* (May 28, 1943): pp. 15, 20.

5. *Unity in Dispersion: A History of the World Jewish Congress* (New York: World Jewish Congress, 1948), p. 211.

6. Ibid., p. 218.

7. Ibid., p. 219; "Algiers French Thanked; Jewish Committee Praises Cremieux Decree Restoration," *The New York Times*, October 24, 1943.

8. Stephen S. Wise, "Address of Welcome to Delegates," WJC British Section January 1945—War Emergency Conference of the WJC (Atlantic City, NJ, November 1944), pp. 4–8.

9. Nahum Goldmann, *The Jewish Paradox: A Personal Memoir of Historic Encounters That Shaped the Drama of Modern Jewry,* trans. Steve Cox (New York, 1978), pp. 48–49.

10. Riegner, *Never Despair*, p. 354.

11. Ibid., p. 356.

12. Goldmann, *Jewish Paradox*, p. 49.

13. Ibid.

14. Michael M. Laskier, *North African Jewry in the Twentieth Century: The Jews of Morocco, Tunisia, and Algeria* (New York, 1994), p. 102.

15. *Report of the World Jewish Congress Organization Department, August 1949–August 1951*, p. 52.

16. Laskier, *North African Jewry*, p. 102.

17. Ibid., p. 105.

18. Ibid., pp. 106–108.

19. Ibid., p. 109.

20. Ibid., p. 111.

21. Ibid., p. 169.

22. Ibid.

23. Yigal Bin-Nun, "The Contribution of World Jewish Organizations to the Establishment of Rights for Jews in Morocco (1956–1961)," *Journal of Modern Jewish Studies* 9, no. 2 (2010): pp. 255–256.

24. Laskier, *North African Jewry*, pp. 170–171.

25. Ibid., p. 171.

26. Ibid., pp. 171–172.

27. Ibid., p. 172.

28. Bin-Nun, "Contribution of World Jewish Organizations," p. 257.

29. Ibid.

30. Ibid., p. 259.

31. Ibid., p. 260.

32. Laskier, *North African Jewry*, p. 177.

33. Bin-Nun, "Contribution of World Jewish Organizations," p. 260.

34. Much of what follows from here can be found in: Yigal Bin-Nun, "The Disputes Regarding the Jewish Emigration from Morocco 1956–1961," in *Jews and Muslims in the Islamic World,* ed. Bernard Dov Cooperman and Tsevi Zohar (Bethesda, MD, 2013), pp. 67–77.

35. Bin-Nun, "Contribution of World Jewish Organizations," p. 72.

36. Ibid., p. 74.

37. "Morocco Accused of Breaking Promises on Jewish Emigration," *The New York Times*, June 14, 1956.

38. Laskier, *North African Jewry*, p. 184.

39. Ibid., p. 185.

40. Riegner, *Never Despair*, p. 363.

41. Laskier, *North African Jewry*, p. 258.

42. Riegner, *Never Despair*, p. 357. For a more comprehensive account of the Easterman-Bourguiba relationship, see in this volume, "Bourguiba's Jewish Friend" by S. J. Goldsmith.

43. Laskier, *North African Jewry*, pp. 262–263.

44. Riegner, *Never Despair*, p. 358.

45. Michael James, "Tunisia Is Found Unbiased on Jews," *The New York Times*, July 20, 1958.

46. Riegner, *Never Despair*, p. 358.

47. Ibid., pp. 363–364.

48. Laskier, *North African Jewry*, pp. 332–333.

49. Quoted in Maud S. Mandel, *Muslims and Jews in France: History of a Conflict* (Princeton, 2014), p. 47.

50. Tom Segev, "The Joe Golan Affair," *Haaretz*, December 29, 2005, http://www.haaretz.com/the-joe-golan-affair-1.177773.

51. Laskier, *North African Jewry*, p. 333.

52. Goldmann, *Jewish Paradox*, p. 49.

53. Letter from A. Leon Kubowitzki, WJC Secretary-General, and Robert S. Marcus, Acting Director of WJC Political Department, to Jan Papanek, Acting President of the Economic and Social Council of the United Nations, January 19, 1948, submitting Memorandum on the Situation in Arab Countries submitted to the Economic and Social Council by the World Jewish Congress, January 19, 1948, AJA, The World Jewish Congress Collection, C137, file 18; see also, Mallory Browne, "Jews in Grave Danger in All Moslem Lands," *The New York Times*, May 16, 1948.

54. "Congress Asks U.N. Action," *The New York Times*, February 7, 1950.

55. Nehemiah Robinson, *The Arab Countries of the Near East and Their Jewish Communities* (New York: Institute of Jewish Affairs, World Jewish Congress, 1951).

56. http://www.worldjewishcongress.org/en/news/peace-only-possible-if-plight-of-jewish-refugees-from-arab-countries-is-addressed-lauder-tells-un.

57. Riegner, *Never Despair*, p. 356.

Soviet Jewry: Debates and Controversies
pages 145–159

1. "Executive Council of Australian Jewry (ECAJ) Minutes," May 17, 1967.

2. "WJC General Assembly, 1953," official communique no. 1, August 4, 1953, Z6/751, CZA.

3. See *The Autobiography of Nahum Goldmann: Sixty Years of Jewish Life*, trans. Helen Sebba (New York, 1969), p. 334.

4. "WJC General Assembly, 1953," official communique no. 1, August 4, 1953, Z6/751, CZA.

5. Telephone interview by author with Meir Rosenne, Jerusalem, January 14, 2004.

6. Goldmann to Stephen Pollack, "WJC-Great Britain 1956," WJC London, August 9, 1956, Z6/1127, CZA.

7. "Speeches on Jews, 1957," opening address, WJC Executive meeting, London, April 29 to May 2, 1957, Z6/2060, CZA.

8. "The Jews of the USSR and Eastern Europe: A Major Problem of Our Day and Proposals for Its Solution," press release by Dr. Nahum Goldmann, May 1957, "Speeches on Jews, 1957," Z6/2060, CZA.

9. Letters of Rabbi Judah Leib Levin, Moscow, July 16, and Rabbi Dimant, Odessa, July 18, 1959, translated from Russian, "WJC 1959," Z6/1961, CZA.

10. This letter was published on November 27, 1959, with signatures from Lord Pakenham, Dr. Donald Soper, Anthony Wedgewood, MP Bertrand Russell, Lord Boothby, and Philip Toynbee, "WJC-Great Britain, April–Dec 1959," Z6/1973, CZA.

11. Letter from Goldmann to Easterman, December 2, 1959, "WJC-Great Britain, April–Dec 1959," Z6/1973, CZA.

12. Interview with Rosenne, January 14, 2004.

13. Harry Schwartz, "Soviet Restricts Matzot Output," *The New York Times*, March 20, 1960, "Conference on Soviet Jewry—Dr. Goldmann Dossier 1960," Z6/1339, CZA.

14. Letter from Goldmann to Jayaprakash Narayan, India, March 15, 1960, "Conference on Soviet Jewry, 1960," Z6/1337, CZA.

15. See envelope of press cuttings compiled by Meir Rosenne, "1960 Paris Conference," Z6/1337, CZA.

16. Statement, September 15, 1960, "1960 Paris Conference," Z6/1337, CZA.

17. "First Interim Report," July 1961, "Soviet Jews 1961," Z6/1882, CZA.

18. See correspondence May 14, 1962, "Russia 1961–1962,", Z6/2180, CZA.

19. Yaacov Ro'i, *The Struggle for Soviet Jewish Emigration, 1948–1967* (Cambridge, 1991), p. 197.

20. Petrus Buwalda, *They Did Not Dwell Alone: Jewish Emigration from the Soviet Union, 1967–1990* (Baltimore, 1997), p. 39.

21. Statement by Dr. Nahum Goldmann, President of WZO, press conference, June 10, 1965, "Press Statements by Goldmann, 1964–1965," Z6/2079, CZA. See also Gal Beckerman, *When They Come for Us, We'll Be Gone: The Epic Struggle to Save Soviet Jewry* (Boston, 2010), p. 139.

22. "Goldmann on Soviet Jewry: Press Cuttings, 1964–1965," *The Times* of London, July 30, 1965, Z6/1250, CZA.

23. Perlzweig to Goldmann, "J. Prinz on Conference on Jews, 1964–1965," October 22, 1965, p. 3, Z6/1168, CZA.

24. As quoted in Wendy Eisen, *Count Us In: The Struggle to Free Soviet Jews: A Canadian Perspective.* (Toronto, 1995), p. 22.

25. As quoted in Buwalda, *"They Did Not Dwell Alone,"* p. 39.

26. Easterman to Hausmann, February 21, 1967, "Jewry 1966," Z6/1176, CZA.

27. Hausmann and Michael Hunter to Easterman, February 28, 1967, "Jewry 1966," Z6/1176, CZA.

28. Easterman to Hausmann and Hunter, March 7, 1967, "Jewry 1966," Z6/1176, CZA.

29. Jack Winocow, "Highlights of the WJC Executive," June 1965, Leibler Archive, Jerusalem.

30. Leibler's handwritten notes on the meeting, July 13, 1965, Leibler Archive, Jerusalem.

31. Ibid.

32. *Australian Jewish News*, July 23, 1965.

33. Handwritten notes, WJC Plenary Session, July 31–August 9, 1966, Brussels, Leibler Archive, Jerusalem.

34. *The Jewish Chronicle*, August 12, 1966.

35. "Activities of the WJC, January 1970–June 1973," *Report of the Secretary-General of the World Executive of the WJC* (Israel, June 27–July 4, 1973), p. 8.

36. Lionel Kochan, ed., *The Jews in the Soviet Union Since 1917* (London, 1970).

37. "USSR—Political Nationalities—Jews, 1 Jan 1971–16 Feb 1971: The Leningrad Trial," National Archives of Australia (NAA): Department of Foreign Affairs, A1838, file no. 69/2/5/7, part 6, memo (January 1971), p. 1.

38. "Activities of the WJC, January 1970–June 1973," *Report of the Secretary-General of the World Executive of the WJC* (Israel, June 27–July 4, 1973), p. 9.

39. Ibid.

40. Ro'i, *Struggle for Soviet Jewish Emigration*, p. 59.

41. Inward cable from the Australian Embassy (Moscow, October 21, 1972), NAA: A1838, file no. 69/2/5/7, part 11.

42. *Riegner Report* (January 1970–June 1970), p. 12.

43. "WJC Minutes, Meeting of the World Executive Committee" (Jerusalem, June 27–July 4, 1973).

44. "Policy and Action of the World Jewish Congress, 1966–1974," p. 37.

45. For a detailed account of the development, see Sam Lipski and Suzanne D. Rutland, *Let My People Go: The Untold Story of Australia and Soviet Jews, 1959–89* (Jerusalem, 2015), pp. 222–229.

46. Beckerman, *When They Come for Us*, p. 457.

THE STRUGGLE FOR HISTORICAL INTEGRITY
AT AUSCHWITZ-BIRKENAU
PAGES 164–175

1. "Speech of World Jewish Congress President Ronald S. Lauder at the ceremony in Auschwitz," January 27, 2015, http://www.worldjewishcongress.org/en/news/speech-of-world-jewish-congress-president-ronald-s-lauder-at-the-ceremony-in-auschwitz.

2. Ronald Lauder's involvement in the restoration of Auschwitz preceded his involvement in the WJC. He first visited the camp in June 1987 while still US ambassador to Austria. "I

went there and was shocked ... you could see the entire place deteriorating before your very eyes—the shoes, the suitcases, the wooden barracks. ... I realized that in another few years the place would be gone forever. Something had to be done." The following year, Lauder enlisted conservationists from New York's Metropolitan Museum with which he had long been associated and to which he had made many contributions. After a thorough onsite inspection, they determined that $42 million would have to be raised to ensure the long-term preservation of the camp and its artifacts. Lauder strongly believed that the governments of the countries whose citizens had perished should be asked to help underwrite the preservation effort. To advance the work of fundraising, which was authorized by the Polish government, Lauder established the International Auschwitz-Birkenau Preservation Committee. The Committee went on to secure $17 million from Germany and millions more from other countries across Europe. According to Bohdan Rymaszewski, a renowned Polish expert on conservation affiliated with the Polish ministry of culture and a member of the International Auschwitz Council, "People have been telling us for years that we should do something about preserving Auschwitz. But Ron Lauder went ahead and did something. The world owes him a great deal of thanks." Lauder was aided in those efforts by the WJC's Kalman Sultanik. See Timothy W. Ryback, "Evidence of Evil," *The New Yorker,* November 15, 1993, pp. 68–81.

3. Irena Zarecka, *Neutralizing Memory* (New Brunswick, NJ, 1989), p. 156.

4. Alex L. Easterman, "Auschwitz Martyrs Remembered," *Jewish Chronicle* (London), April 21, 1967, p. 20. Goldmann had purportedly declined to attend because of the failure of the organizers to include a single identifiably Jewish speaker in the program.

5. Over the years, that memorial was altered to reflect the changing realities of memory. In 1990, the plaques were removed to eventually be replaced with texts stating the more accurate figure of "one and a half million."

6. Easterman, "Auschwitz Martyrs Remembered," p. 20. Exceptionally, Robert Waitz, President of the Internatonal Auschwitz Committee, however, declared in his speech "Among the four million victims, the overwhelming majority were Jews. Auschwitz was, among other camps, the largest center for their extermination. This extermination took on a special character. It dealt the entire Jewish population—men, women, and children—a decisive blow ... The Nazis intended to prepare a similar fate for other peoples." Jonathan Huener, *Auschwitz, Poland, and the Politics of Commemoration, 1945–1979* (Athens, OH, 2003), pp. 166–167. In photographs of that event, the Israeli flag is seen flying together with the flags of other nations.

7. This had not been the case in Treblinka, Bełżec, Sobibór, or Chełmno, to which Jews had also been deported and were murdered upon arrival. There, the Germans had dismantled the camps so as to conceal evidence of their crimes. Those camps were murder factories from which only a handful of Jews survived.

8. *Unity in Dispersion: A History of the World Jewish Congress* (New York: Institute of Jewish Affairs of the World Jewish Congress, 1948), p. 239.

9. To be sure, many Jewish-born Communists vociferously echoed this sentiment. Describing his meeting in the summer of 1963 with Hersz Smolar, editor of the Yiddish language *Folsztymme* in Warsaw, Rabbi Israel Goldstein recounted: "Smolar, an ardent Communist, strongly opposed the idea of a special Jewish exhibit at Auschwitz, asserting that the Jewish tragedy could be represented adequately in each of the scheduled European pavilions." Goldstein also recounted his conversation with Bernard Mark, who headed the Jewish Historical Institute (ŻIH). Mark accused the Communist-dominated Jewish Social Cultural Organization (TSKŻ) of opposing any distinct Jewish memorialization at Auschwitz. Many of the early Jewish accounts also stressed such an "internationalist" view and actually reinforced it. See Israel Goldstein, *My World as a Jew* (New York, 1984) p. 136. Nahum Goldmann, on successive visits to Poland in 1964 and 1978, perhaps in an effort to win over the Poles, also stressed Polish suffering: "The Poles suffered no less than we did. Proportionally we suffered more, but the Poles have been also horribly affected by extermination," he declared.

10. Paul Lendavi, *Antisemitism without Jews: Communist Eastern Europe* (Garden City, NY, 1971).

11. Piotr Osęka, *Rytuały stalinizmu: oficjalne święta i uroczystości rocznicowe w Polsce 1944—1956* (Warsaw 2006), pp. 56—57 as quoted by Sławomir Kapralski, "The Role Played by the Auschwitz State Musuem," in *Jewish Presence in Absence—The Aftermath of the Holocaust in Poland, 1944—2010*, ed. Feliks Tych and Monika Adamczyk-Garbowska (Jerusalem, 2014), p. 606.

12. Over the course of the 1970s and 1980s, these countries were joined by Yugoslavia, Austria, France, the Netherlands, and Italy. Even Denmark and Bulgaria, whose citizens were not deported to Auschwitz, were accorded space in what amounted to a world's fair of suffering and martyrdom. According to some accounts, the exhibition in the Bulgarian Pavilion, opened in 1977, was devoted to a history of that country's Communist Party.

13. Shortly after the museum opened in 1947, a hall in one of the barracks had, in fact, been devoted to the story of the Jews who had perished at Auschwitz, but this seems to have been closed at the end of 1948.

14. Marcos Silber, "Foreigners or co-nationals? Israel, Poland and Polish Jewry (1948—1967)," *The Journal of Israeli History* 29, no. 2 (2010): pp.221—222.

15. Ibid., p. 223. Easterman subsequently wrote in a 1968 internal WJC report that "it was on [Winiewicz's] initiative, in response to my representations, that the Polish Government withdrew its objections" to a Jewish pavillion at Auschwitz. A. L. Easterman, "Poland," London, October 4, 1968, WJC Archives, Brussels.

16. "World Jewish Conference in Geneva Assails Soviet Policy on Jews in USSR," JTA, August 3, 1964, http://www.jta.org/1964/08/03/archive/world-jewish-conference-in-geneva-assails-soviet-policy-on-jews-in-ussr. Elsewhere, in correspondence that was published contemporaneously in the press, Goldmann maintained that "[t]he Polish government insists on financing the whole project and will not accept gifts from outside organizations

nor will it allow non-Polish Jewish groups to supervise the project, etc." Contents of letter to Herb Brinn as published in *The Jewish Post & Opinion*, May 12, 1967.

17. Huener, *Auschwitz, Poland, and the Politics of Commemoration*, p. 180.

18. *Activities of the World Jewish Congress, 1975–1980: Report to the Seventh Plenary Assembly*, p. 67. Article 4 of the Convention Concerning the Protection of World Culture and National Heritage bound the Poles to uphold the "protection, conservation, preservation and transmission to future generations of the cultural and national heritage of the site."

19. In fact, the inspiration for this was derived from John Paul II, who in June 1979 had staged a mass at Birkenau attended by some 500,000 Catholic faithful.

20. "WJC Urges Pope to Use Authority to Remove Convent from Auschwitz," JTA, May 11, 1989.

21. Edgar M. Bronfman, *The Making of a Jew* (New York, 1996), p. 132.

22. Riegner, of course, in his wartime capacity as Geneva representative of the WJC had himself played an important role in making known the terrible news of the German plans to annhilate European Jewry. The dispatch of the so-called Riegner telegram in August 1942 was an important milestone in revealing the magnitude of the catastrophe engulfing the Jews of Europe.

23. Gerhart M. Riegner, *Never Despair: Sixty Years in the Service of the Jewish People and Human Rights* (New York, 2006), p. 294.

24. Emma Klein, *Battle for Auschwitz: Catholic-Jewish Relations under Strain* (London, 2001), p. 6.

25. Rabbi Weiss and his group later demonstrated in Kraków in front of the landmark Marian Church and at the Archbishop's curia. That same day they returned to Auschwitz, again climbed over the fence and held a six-hour vigil, but this time were left unmolested.

26. In *Newsweek* (July 31, 1989) the event was characterized as "one of the worst cases of antisemitism in Poland since the Communist Party forced thousands of Jews to leave the country in 1968."

27. Telephone interview with Rabbi Avi Weiss, February 2016.

28. Nahum Goldmann, *The Jewish Paradox* (New York, 1978), p. 47.

29. Avi Beker, "Sixty Years of World Jewish Congress Diplomacy," in *Jewish Centers & Peripheries—Europe between America and Israel Fifty Years after World War II*, ed. S. Ilan Troen (New Brunswick, NJ, 1999), p. 382.

30. Even the distinguished voice of Polish-Jewish reconciliation, the late Prof. Władysław Bartoszewski, a Righteous among the Nations and an honorary citizen of Israel, called the chapter in his book *The Convent at Auschwitz* (New York, 1991) on Rabbi Weiss's actions "Invasion," and began with the subtitle "Rabbi Weiss Invades the Convent" (p. 86). Bartoszewski was himself a survivor of Auschwitz.

31. The so-called Papal Cross, erected in 1989 near Block 11 in Auschwitz I, remains despite protests.

32. Laurence Weinbaum, "The struggle for Memory in Poland: Auschwitz, Jedwabne and Beyond," Institute of the World Jewish Congress Policy Study No. 22 (Jerusalem, 2001).

New Directions and Priorities, 1985
pages 176—180

1. Walter Reder (1915–1991), Waffen-SS officer sentenced to life imprisonment in 1951 by an Italian court for war crimes, but released in January 1985. Upon his return to his native Austria, he was welcomed by Austrian Defense Minister Friedhelm Frischenschlager, causing international outrage.

Fighting Delegitimization: The United Nation's
"Zionism Is Racism" Resolution, a Case Study
pages 181—190

1. Resolution 3379 (XXX), November 10, 1975; *The New York Times*, November 11, 1975.
2. Resolution 3151 (XXVIII), December 14, 1973.
3. *Proceedings of the Sixth Plenary Assembly of the World Jewish Congress* (Jerusalem 1975), pp. 277–278.
4. Ibid., pp. 369–370.
5. "Declaration of Mexico on the Equality of Women and Their Contribution to Development and Peace," World Conference of the International Women's Year Mexico City, July 2, 1975, UN Documents, E/CONF.66/34.
6. Gil Troy, *Moynihan's Moment: America's Fight against Zionism as Racism* (New York, 2012), p. 120.
7. "U.S. Denounces U.N. Resolution Equating Zionism with Racism," statement of Leonard Garment, *The Department of State Bulletin* 73, no. 1901 (December 1, 1975): pp. 789–790.
8. Gerhart M. Riegner, *Never Despair: Sixty Years in the Service of the Jewish People and of Human Rights* (Chicago, 2006), p. 396.
9. Ibid., pp. 396–397.
10. Paul Hofmann, "U.N. Votes, 72–35 to Term Zionism Form of Racism," *The New York Times*, November 11, 1975.
11. Chaim Herzog, "Speech to the General Assembly on the Anti-Zionist Resolution November 10, 1975," in *Israel in the Middle East, Documents and Readings on Society, Politics and Foreign Relations, Pre-1948 to the Present*, 2nd ed., ed. Itamar Rabinovich and Jehuda Reinharz (Waltham, MA, 2008), pp. 351–352.
12. "U.S. Denounces U.N. Resolution Equating Zionism with Racism," *The Department of State Bulletin* 73, no. 1901 (December 1, 1975): pp. 790–791 (statement of Ambassador Moynihan).
13. Ibid., p. 397.
14. "Issues in Focus Abuse of Zionism Spreading," JTA, Feb. 10, 1982.
15. "WJC Boycott Confab to Combat Racism," JTA, August 11, 1978.
16. "Bronfman Says World Peace Can't Allow Denial of Israel's Legitimacy," JTA, June 28, 1982.

17. *News & Views* (November–December 1982): p. 12.

18. *News & Views* (September–October 1984): p. 4.

19. *News & Views* (January 1985): p. 1.

20. JTA, July 12, 1985.

21. Elaine Sciolino, "Reagan Backs Effort to Repeal U.N. Vote Attacking Zionism," *The New York Times*, November 11, 1985.

22. "World Council of Churches Tells WJC It Rejects UN Resolution Equating Zionism with Racism," JTA, Aug. 7, 1985.

23. "World Jewry Mobilizing in Effort to Repeal UN Zionism-Racism Resolution," JTA, November 5, 1985.

24. Thomas L. Friedman, "Baker, in a Middle East Blueprint, Asks Israel to Reach Out to Arabs," *The New York Times*, May 23, 1989.

25. "New Brazilian Leader Promises to Rethink Zionism-Racism Vote," JTA, January 29, 1990.

26. "New Leader of Uruguay to Spur Drive to Repeal U.N. Resolution," JTA, February 13, 1990.

27. "WJC Lobbies Leaders to Repeal Zionism Is Racism Resolution," JTA, July 10, 1991.

28. Ibid., p. 3.

29. *News & Views* (September–October 1991): p. 3.

30. Stanley Meisler and Douglas Jehl, "Bush Urges U.N. to Repeal Zionism-Racism Resolution," *Los Angeles Times*, September 24, 1991.

31. "Soviets, at U.N., Back Bush's Call for Repeal of '75 Zionism Edict," *The New York Times*, September 25, 1991.

32. "Jewish Leaders Hail Soviet Call to Repeal U.N. Zionism Resolution," JTA, September 26, 1991.

33. Troy, *Moynihan's Moment*, pp. 248–249.

34. Paul Lewis, "U.N. Repeals Its '75 Resolution Equating Zionism with Racism," *The New York Times*, December 17, 1991.

35. *The WJC Report* (February–March 1992): p. 2.

NAVIGATING THE COMMUNIST YEARS: A JEWISH PERSPECTIVE
PAGES 191–203

1. See, in this volume, Suzanne D. Rutland, "Soviet Jewry: Debates and Controversies."

2. Isaac I. Schwarzbart, *25 Years in the Service of the Jewish People: A Chronicle of the Activities of the World Jewish Congress, August 1932–February 1957* (New York: World Jewish Congress Organization Department, 1957), p. 6.

3. *Protocole du Premier Congrès Juif Mondial, Genève, 8–15 août, 1936,* (Genève: Comité Exécutif du Congrès Juif Mondial, 1936), *Liste de présence des délégués*, pp. VII–XI.

4. Jacob Lestschinsky (1876–1966) was a Jewish statistician and sociologist who wrote in Yiddish, German, and English. He specialized in Jewish demography and economic history.

In 1938 he moved to New York, and he worked with the Institute of Jewish Affairs of the WJC, for which he prepared surveys of post–World War II Jewish communities.

5. *Protocole du Premier Congrès Juif Mondial*, pp. 57–66.

6. On July 4, 1946, "a mob of Polish soldiers, police officers, and civilians" in the city of Kielce "murdered at least 42 Jews and injured over 40 in the worst outburst of anti-Jewish violence in postwar Poland." "The Kielce Pogrom: A Blood Libel Massacre of Holocaust Survivors," *Holocaust Encyclopedia*, U.S. Holocaust Memorial Museum, https://www.ushmm.org/wlc/en/article.php?ModuleId=10007941.

7. *WJC 1936–1986—50th Jubilee Anniversary* (Jerusalem: WJC, 1986), p. 61.

8. Stephen S. Wise, "Jewish Unity for Survival" (address at WJC assembly), *Congress Weekly*, August 20, 1948, p. 3.

9. See, in this volume, Nahum Goldmann, "The State of World Jewry, 1948." See also *Congress Weekly*, August 20, 1948, p. 8.

10. See I. Schwarzbart, *Report of the World Jewish Congress Organizational Department August 1949–August 1951* (New York: World Jewish Congress, 1951), pp. 4, 14, 47.

11. World Jewish Congress, third plenary assembly, Geneva, 4–11 August 1953, Resolutions and Composition of Assembly, pp. 15-16.

12. Nahum Goldmann, "Jewish Life in Freedom," *World Jewry*, June 1967, p. 14.

13. *WJC in Action—August 1966–December 1969: Report of the Secretary-General to the World Executive of the WJC at its meeting in Israel, 7–14 January 1970* (Geneva: Office of the Secretary-General, December 1969), pp. 9–11.

14. Nahum Goldmann, "Jewish Life in Freedom" (statement at a press conference in Geneva, April 17, 1967); *World Jewry*, May/June 1967, p. 14.

15. *WJC in Action—August 1966–December 1969: Report of the Secretary-General to the World Executive of the WJC at its Meeting in Israel, 7–14 January 1970* (Geneva: Office of the Secretary-General, December 1969), pp. 9–11.

16. See, e.g., "Paris Daily Discloses Meeting between Marshal Tito and Nahum Goldmann," JTA, November 28, 1967, http://www.jta.org/1967/11/28/archive/paris-daily-discloses-meeting-between-marshal-tito-and-nahum-goldmann; Raphael Patai, *Nahum Goldmann: His Mission to the Gentiles* (Tuscaloosa, AL, 1987), pp. 221–223; Mark A. Raider, ed., *Nahum Goldmann, Statesman without a State* (Albany, NY, 2009), pp. 49, 301–316.

17. *WJC—Activities of the WJC 1975–1980: Report to the Seventh Plenary Assembly* (Geneva: Office of the Secretary-General, 1980), p. 28.

18. *WJC News & Views* (Summer 1983): pp. 1, 4–6.

19. The Nansen passports were internationally recognized as refugee travel documents, first issued by the League of Nations to stateless refugees. The Nansen International Office for Refugees, as an internal office of the League of Nations, handled the issuing of the passports, and they were issued in the name of the League. The office was closed in 1938; passports were thereafter issued by a new agency: the Office of the High Commissioner for Refugees in London.

20. *WJC News & Views* (December/January 1986): pp. 1, 4.

21. *WJC News & Views* (September 1987): pp. 1, 4.

22. *WJC News & Views* (December 1988): pp. 1, 7–8.

23. Ari L. Goldman, "Upheaval in the East: East Germany; East Germany Agrees to Pay Reparations to the Jewish Victims of the Nazis," *The New York Times*, February 9, 1990, http://www.nytimes.com/1990/02/09/world/upheaval-east-east-germany-east-germany -agrees-pay-reparations-jewish-victims.html.

24. *WJC News & Views* (September/October 1990): p. 3.

25. Ronald Lauder, "All of us, Jews and non-Jews, stand together as one people," September 14, 2014, http://www.worldjewishcongress.org/en/news/ronald-lauder -all-of-us- jews-and-non-jews-stand-together-as-one-people.

THE KURT WALDHEIM AFFAIR

PAGES 204–217

1. Officially, Steinberg was Executive Director of the WJC's American Section, but the "American Section" part of the title was essentially a formality.

2. Stuart Taylor, "Emigres Criticize U.S. Nazi-Hunters," *The New York Times*, April 21, 1985.

3. Regarding Robinson, see, in this volume, Jonathan Bush, "Nuremberg and Beyond: Jacob Robinson, a Champion for Justice."

4. With the public backing of the WJC, Menachem Rosensaft, the founding chairman of the International Network of Children of Jewish Holocaust Survivors, who is today my successor as the WJC's general counsel, organized an important demonstration at the site of the former Nazi concentration camp of Bergen-Belsen to confront Reagan and Kohl there on their way to Bitburg.

5. The account that follows of the Kurt Waldheim affair is adapted principally from my book (co-authored with William Hoffer) *Betrayal: The Untold Story of the Kurt Waldheim Investigation and Cover-Up* (New York, 1993).

6. In 1991, the SPÖ was renamed the *Sozialdemokratische Partei Österreichs*, which remains its name to this day.

7. Yehuda Blum quoted in Jane Rosen, "The U.N.'s Man in the Middle," *The New York Times Magazine*, September 13, 1981, p. 70.

8. Karl Schuller is a pseudonym.

9. Eli M. Rosenbaum, *Kurt Waldheim's Hidden Past: A Report to the President of the World Jewish Congress* (New York, 1986).

10. US Department of Justice, "Waldheim Report Released by Justice Department," press release, March 14, 1994. Full 232-page report available (as of August 27, 2016), https://www .justice.gov/sites/default/files/criminal-hrsp/legacy/2011/02/04/04-09-87waldheim-rpt.pdf.

11. "Like a Beggar," *Der Spiegel*, October 8, 1986.

12. The closest Waldheim would ever come to an official reception in a major foreign country was a visit he made to Bavaria in March 1992. Invited to Germany by the conservative Peutinger Collegium Foundation to receive an award for his "contributions to world peace and freedom," Waldheim was met at a red-carpet ceremony at Munich's airport by an old friend, German Chancellor Helmut Kohl. Although the visit was technically "unofficial," Kohl's involvement—which marked the first (and, ultimately, only) time a Western leader met Waldheim outside Austria—was widely viewed as a calculated move specifically intended to bring at least a symbolic end to Waldheim's pariah status while there was still time; just twenty-nine days remained before elections in Austria to choose a successor to Waldheim.

13. See, in this volume, Gregg Rickman, "In Search of Justice: The World Jewish Congress and the Swiss Banks."

In Search of Justice:
The World Jewish Congress and the Swiss Banks
pages 218–233

1. *Swiss Banks and the Status of Assets of Holocaust Survivors or Heirs*, p. 9, Hearing Before the US Senate Committee on Banking, Housing, and Urban Affairs (April 23, 1996) (opening statement of Edgar M. Bronfman).

2. Jacques Picard, *Switzerland and the Assets of the Missing Victims of the Nazis: Assets in Switzerland Belonging to Victims of Political Persecution and Their Disposition between 1946 and 1973* (Zurich, 1993).

3. Itamar Levin, *The Last Deposit: Swiss Banks and Holocaust Victims' Accounts*, trans. Natasha Dornberg (Westport, CT, 1999), p. xiii.

4. Itamar Levin, *The Last Chapter of the Holocaust? The Struggle over the Restitution of Jewish Property in Europe*, trans. Miriam Shimoni (Jerusalem, 1997), p. 22.

5. Ron Kampeas, "54 Leaders Join in WWII Observance," Associated Press, May 8, 1995.

6. Letter from Maram Stern to the SBA, Brussels, February 6, 1996.

7. Bronfman, *Swiss Banks and the Status of Assets*, pp. 9–11.

8. Ibid., p. 9.

9. *Swiss Banks and the Status of Assets of Holocaust Survivors or Heirs*, p. 27, Hearing before the U.S. Senate Committee on Banking, Housing, and Urban Affairs (April 23, 1996) (opening statement of Hans J. Baer).

10. Ibid., p. 26.

11. William Drozdiak, "Lost Assets Found in Swiss Accounts," *The Washington Post*, November 13, 1996.

12. David E. Sanger, "Swiss Funds That May Belong to Nazi Victims," *The New York Times*, June 11, 1997.

13. Stuart E. Eizenstat, *Imperfect Justice: Looted Assets, Slave Labor, and the Unfinished Business of World War II* (New York, 2004), pp. 90–91.

14. *U.S. and Allied Efforts To Recover and Restore Gold and Other Assets Stolen or Hidden by Germany during World War II—Preliminary Study*, coordinated by Stuart E. Eizenstat, Undersecretary of Commerce for International Trade, Special Envoy of the Department of State on Property Restitution in Central and Eastern Europe; prepared by William Z. Slany, the Historian, Department of State, May 1997, p. v.

15. Hearing on the *Eizenstat Report Regarding Holocaust Assets*, Senate Banking, Housing, and Urban Affairs Committee (May 15, 1997), http://www.banking.senate.gov/97_05hrg/051597/witness/eizenst.htm (prepared testimony of Ambassador Stuart E. Eizenstat, Undersecretary for International Trade, United States Department of Commerce).

16. "D'Amato Insists on Gesture," *Tages-Anzeiger*, December 12, 1996, trans. Brian Hufker.

17. "Swiss President Says Pleas for a Holocaust Fund Are 'Blackmail'," *The New York Times*, January 1, 1997.

18. "Spat with Switzerland Persists: Letter Reveals Nazi Collaboration," JTA, January 13, 1997.

19. Clare Nullis, "Swiss Jews 'deeply hurt' by government response to compensation fund," Associated Press, January 2, 1997.

20. Nicholas Burns, US State Department briefing, Reuters, January 3, 1997.

21. Alan Cowell, "Swiss Offer to Set Up Fund for Victims of Holocaust," *The New York Times*, January 8, 1997.

22. Letter of Jean-Pascal Delamuraz to Edgar Bronfman, January 14, 1997.

23. Letter of Edgar Bronfman to Jean-Pascal Delamuraz, January 14, 1997.

24. "Meeting with Mr. Walter Stucki, Swiss Foreign Office," memorandum of conversation, p.1. RG 59, entry 1945–49, box 4243, records of the US Department of State, NARA.

25. William Hall, "Divided by Goodwill," *The Financial Times*, January 25, 1997.

26. Fredy Rom, "Swiss Legislators Remove Hurdle to Central Bank's Donation to Fund," *MetroWest Jewish News*, September 11, 1997.

27. *Swiss Fund for Needy Victims of the Holocaust / Shoah*, final report (Bern, 2002), pp. 13, 21.

28. Letter of Swiss Ambassador to the United States Alfred Defago to Judge Edward R. Korman, June 3, 1997.

29. Senator Alfonse M. D'Amato, *Swiss Banks Settlement: In Re Holocaust Victim Assets Litigation*, amicus curiae brief (June 20, 1997), p. 7.

30. "Estimation of the Cost of the Crisis," *L'Hebdo*, Switzerland, October 30, 1997.

31. "Historians Say Swiss Moved Most Nazi Gold," *San Antonio Express-News*, December 2, 1997; William Hall, "Swiss Banks Inching to Holocaust Settlement," *New York Jewish Week*, December 12, 1997.

32. Transcript of *Morning Edition*, National Public Radio, August 13, 1998.

CONFRONTING TERROR:
THE BUENOS AIRES BOMBINGS
PAGES 234—243

1. Opening session transcript, World Jewish Congress, special plenary assembly, Buenos Aires, March 15, 2016.

2. Ibid.

3. Ronald S. Lauder, "Argentina, Don't Let the Terrorists Win," *Haaretz*, March 16, 2016, http://www.haaretz.com/opinion/.premium-1.709218.

4. Tracy Wilkinson, "Iran Officials May Be Linked to Jewish Center Bombing, Argentina Says," *Los Angeles Times*, July 29, 1994, http://articles.latimes.com/1994-07-29/news/mn-21192_1_jewish-community-center.

5. *The WJC Report* (October/November, 1994): pp. 1, 4.

6. *The WJC Report* (October/November, 1994): p. 6.

7. *The WJC Report* (January/February 1995): p. 1.

8. *The WJC Report* (January/February 1996): p. 4.

9. *The WJC Report* (July/August 2001): p. 1.

10. Ibid., p. 2.

11. "El Presidente recibió a los miembros del Congreso Judío Mundial," *Infobae*, July 18, 2006, http://www.infobae.com/2006/07/18/266354-el-presidente-recibio-los-miembros-del-congreso-judio-mundial/.

12. PR newswire, WJC press release, October 25, 2006, http://www.newswest9.com/story/5590128/wjc-supports-argentine-prosecutors-call-for-arrest-of-former-iranian-president-rafsanjani-urges-international-community-to-assist-arrest.

13. "Ronald S. Lauder begins first official visit to Argentina," WJC website, June 25, 2008, http://www.worldjewishcongress.org/en/news/ronald-s-lauder-begins-first-official-visit-to-argentina?printable=true.

14. "Argentinean prosecutor warns of growing Iranian influence in Latin America," WJC website, December 3, 2009, http://www.worldjewishcongress.org/en/news/argentinean-prosecutor-warns-of-growing-iranian-influence-in-latin-america.

15. "New calls for justice 16 years after devastating terrorist attack against Jewish center in Buenos Aires," WJC website, July 19, 2010, http://www.worldjewishcongress.org/en/news / new-calls-for-justice-16-years-after-devastating-terrorist-attack-against-jewish-center-in-buenos-aires.

16. Diego Melamed, "Petition Calls for Justice in AMIA Attack," JTA, July 3, 2011, http://www.jta.org/2011/07/03/news-opinion/world/petition-calls-for-justice-in-amia-attack.

17. "Ronald S. Lauder says world must hold Iran accountable for 1994 AMIA bombing," WJC website, July 17, 2012, http://www.worldjewishcongress.org/en/news/ronald-s-lauder-says-world-must-hold-iran-accountable-for-1994-amia-bombing.

18. Ibid.

19. "Address by Cristina de Kirchner at UN General Assembly, 2012," September 25, 2012, http://www.cfkargentina.com/address-by-cristina-kirchner-at-un-general-assembly-2012/.

20. http://www.worldjewishcongress.org/en/news/argentinean-and-iranian-ministers-meet-in-new-york-to-discuss-1990s-terrorist-attacks.

21. "Argentinean and Iranian ministers meet in New York to discuss 1990s terrorist attacks," WJC website, September 28, 2013, http://www.worldjewishcongress.org/en/news/argentinean-and-iranian-ministers-meet-in-new-york-to-discuss-1990s-terrorist-attacks.

22. Sam Sokol and Herb Keinon, "Argentina Okays Pact with Iran to Probe AMIA Bombing," *The Jerusalem Post*, February 1, 2013, http://www.jpost.com/International/Argentina-okays-pact-with-Iran-to-probe-AMIA-bombing.

23. "Para el Congreso Judío Mundial, el acuerdo Argentina—Irán 'coloca a los victimarios en el mismo nivel que las víctimas,'" trans. Adela Cojab Moadeb, Agencia Judia de Noticias (AJN), February 12, 2013, http://www.prensajudia.com/shop/detallenot.asp?notid=32376.

24. "AMIA Para el Congreso Judio Estadosuniense a Cristina de Kirchner: 'Esta Mezclando las Cosas,'" trans. Adela Cojab Moadeb, Agencia Judia de Noticias (AJN), October 1, 2013, http://www.agenciajudiadenoticias.com/shop/detallenot.asp?notid=35200.

25. "Iran rejects grilling of officials in Argentina bomb probe," WJC website, February 12, 2013, http://www.worldjewishcongress.org/en/news/iran-rejects-grilling-of-officials-in-argentina-bomb-probe.

26. "Argentine court says agreement with Iran to probe AMIA bombing is unconstitutional," WJC website, May 16, 2014, http://www.worldjewishcongress.org/en/news/argentine-court-says-agreement-with-iran-to-probe-amia-bombing-is-unconstitutional.

27. "Hundreds Protest Iran-Argentina Pact," *Canadian Jewish News*, February 19, 2013, http://www.cjnews.com/news/international/hundreds-protest-iran-argentina-pact.

28. See note 25 above.

29. Julie R. Butler, "Timeline: AMIA Bombing, Buenos Aires—Special Prosecutor Alberto Nisman's Death," February 21, 2015, https://medium.com/@julierbutler/timeline-amia-bombing-buenos-aires-special-prosecutor-alberto-nisman-s-death-1a29b5aa42ac#.u2jh0y43t.

30. "World Jewish Congress urges Latin American nations to take Iranian threat seriously," WJC website, May 30, 2013, http://www.worldjewishcongress.org/en/news/world-jewish-congress-urges-latin-american-nations-to-take-iranian-threat-seriously?printable=true.

31. See note 29 above.

32. "AMIA bombing anniversary: Nisman presents Iran report to Latin American Jewish Congress," WJC website, July 17, 2013, http://www.worldjewishcongress.org/en/news/amia-bombing-anniversary-nisman-presents-iran-report-to-latin-american-jewish-congress.

33. "Video message: Pope Francis urges justice for victims of AMIA bombing," WJC website, July 18, 2014, http://www.worldjewishcongress.org/en/news/video-message-pope-francis-urges-justice-for-victims-of-amia-bombing.

34. Robert Singer, "Hold Iran to Account on AMIA Bombing," *The Jewish Week*, July 21, 2014, http://www.thejewishweek.com/editorial-opinion/opinion/hold-iran-account-amia-bombing.

35. Isi Leibler, "Cry for me, Argentina," *The Jerusalem Post*, February 10, 2015, http://www.jpost.com/Opinion/Candidly-speaking-Cry-for-me-Argentina-390621.

36. "Argentina: Thousands gather outside Amia to protest Nisman's death," Courcy's Intelligence, January 2015, http://www.courcyint.com/component/k2/item/63494-argentina-thousands-gather-outside-amia-to-protest-nismans-death.html.

37. "Jewish Congress criticizes 'lack of progress' in investigation of 1994 AMIA bombing," *Merco Press*, July 18, 2015, http://en.mercopress.com/2015/07/18/jewish-congress-criticizes-lack-of-progress-in-investigation-of-1994-amia-bombing.

38. "Late Argentine prosecutor remembered at commemoration of Jewish center bombing," JTA, July 17, 2015, http://www.jta.org/2015/07/17/news-opinion/world/auto-draft-122.

39. Opening session transcript, World Jewish Congress, special plenary assembly, Buenos Aires, March 15, 2016.

The World Jewish Congress Today
PAGES 244–265

1. *Protocole du Premier Congrès Juif Mondial, Genève, 8–15 aout 1936*, edité par le Comité Exécutif du Congrès Juif Mondial (Genève, 1936), p. 10.

2. Menachem Z. Rosensaft, ed., *Remembering the Shoah: The ICRC and the International Community's Efforts in Responding to Genocide and Protecting Civilians* (New York and Geneva: International Committee of the Red Cross and the World Jewish Congress, 2015), p. 5.

3. Ibid., pp. 8–9.

4. "At meeting with WJC leader, UNESCO chief condemns Iranian Holocaust cartoon contest," March 3, 2015, https://www.worldjewishcongress.org/en/news/at-meeting-with-wjc-leader-unesco-chief-condemns-iranian-holocaust-cartoon-contest?printable=true.

5. "Statement by the Director-General of UNESCO on the Old City of Jerusalem and its Walls on the occasion of the 40th session of the World Heritage Committee of UNESCO in Istanbul," July 15, 2016, http://www.unesco.org/new/en/media-service/single-view/news/statement_by_the_director_general_of_unesco_on_the_old_city/#.WAolotiXCUk.

6. "Full Text of UNESCO's Contentious Resolution on Jerusalem and the Countries That Voted," *Haaretz*, October 18, 2016, http://www.haaretz.com/israel-news/1.747982.

7. Ronald S. Lauder, "The United Nations Cannot Erase Jewish History," *The New York Times*, October 17, 2016, p. A5.

Contributors

MICHAEL BRENNER is the Seymour and Lillian Abensohn Chair in Israel Studies at American University in Washington, DC, and a professor of Jewish history and culture at Ludwig Maximilian University in Munich. He is the international president of the Leo Baeck Institute and an elected member of the Bavarian Academy of Science. His latest publication is *Israel: From a State of the Jews to a Jewish State*. Brenner's previous books include *A Short History of the Jews; Prophets of the Past: Interpreters of Jewish History; Zionism: A Brief History; The Renaissance of Jewish Culture in Weimar Germany;* and *After the Holocaust: Rebuilding Jewish Lives in Postwar Germany*.

EDGAR M. BRONFMAN (1929–2013) was president of the World Jewish Congress from 1981 until 2007 after serving as acting president for two years while his predecessor Phillip M. Klutznick was on leave as US Secretary of Commerce. He was the founding chairman of the International Board of Governors of Hillel: The Foundation for Jewish Campus Life, a worldwide organization uniting Jewish students on college and university campuses. Bronfman also served as president of the World Jewish Restitution Organization. In 1998, President Bill Clinton appointed him as chairman of the Presidential Advisory Commission on Holocaust Assets. The following year, President Clinton awarded him the Presidential Medal of Freedom. Bronfman was the author of numerous books including *The Making of a Jew*, *The Bronfman Haggadah* (with Jan Aronson), and the posthumously published *Why Be Jewish? A Testament*.

JONATHAN A. BUSH is a lawyer and legal historian. After earning degrees from Princeton, Oxford, and Yale, he clerked for Judge William Timbers of the US Second Circuit Court of Appeals. He was a trial attorney with the US Justice Department's Office of Special Investigations and founding general counsel of the US Holocaust Memorial Museum. Bush has taught criminal and international law including seminars on the law of war, war crimes trials, reparations and restitution, and cultural property at Brooklyn, Cardozo, Santa Clara, University of Texas, and Columbia law schools, co-teaching in 1993–1994 and 1997–1998 with the chief Nuremberg prosecutor Telford Taylor. He has published approximately sixty books, articles, reviews, essays, and speeches.

ADELA COJAB-MOADEB was born in Mexico City, Mexico, and raised in Deal, New Jersey. She is a sophomore at New York University (NYU), studying international relations with a concentration on the Middle Eastern conflict and Latin America. She is vice president of Realize Israel, a student-run activism group that celebrates Israel's vibrant culture. At NYU she has co-hosted the weekly radio talk show *NYView* on WNYU Radio. She joined the Alpha Epsilon Phi sorority and sits on the Panhellenic and the Inter-Greek Councils. She was an intern in the WJC's New York office, 2015–2016.

MONSIGNOR PIER FRANCESCO FUMAGALLI is Vice Prefect of the Biblioteca Ambrosiana in Milan and director of the classes of Far Eastern Studies and Near Eastern Studies at the Ambrosiana Academy. From 1986 to 1993, he was secretary of the Commission of the Holy See for Religious Relations with the Jews. He has taught at the Catholic University of Milan in Brescia and at the Institute of Christianity and Cross-Cultural Studies at Zhejiang University, Hangzhou, China. Fumagalli is the author of *Ecumenismo: I movimenti e le idee* (Ecumenism: The movements and the ideas) and *Roma e Gerusalemme: La Chiesa cattolica e il popolo d'Israele* (Rome and Jerusalem: The Catholic Church and the people of Israel).

NAHUM GOLDMANN (1895–1982) was the most prominent Jewish political personality of the twentieth century, simultaneously occupying for more than three decades leadership positions on behalf of world Jewry and the Zionist movement. Born in the Lithuanian town of Visznevo (today in Belarus), he was raised in Germany from the age of five and received his doctorate in law from the University of Heidelberg in the tumultuous years after World War I. He was also one of the publishers of a Jewish encyclopedia in German, ten volumes of which appeared before the enterprise came to a halt with the coming to power of the Nazi Party in 1933. That same year, Goldmann left Germany, and in 1935 he became the representative of the Jewish Agency at the League of Nations in Geneva. Together with Rabbi Stephen S. Wise, he was one of the principal founders of the WJC. He became the organization's acting president in 1949, and was its president from 1953 until 1977. He was also president of the World Zionist Organization from 1956 until 1968. Starting in 1951, Goldmann was one of the architects of German reparations for both Israel and for Jewish survivors of the Holocaust, serving as chairman of the Conference on Jewish Material Claims Against Germany for more than thirty years.

S. J. GOLDSMITH (1910–1995) was a Lithuanian-born journalist, author, and editor. As a British war correspondent, he was the first journalist to enter the Bergen-Belsen concentration camp after liberation and among the first journalists to enter the camp in Dachau. He covered the Belsen trial in Lüneburg and the Nuremberg trials. Goldsmith served as European editor of the Jewish Telegraphic Agency (JTA) from 1958 to 1975 and was a founding member and chairman of the London branch of the World Hebrew Union. He was the author of *Twenty 20th Century Jews, Jews in Transition, In the Passage of Time, The Slaughter of Sacred Cows,* and *On the Edge of the Conflagration.*

PHILIP MORRIS KLUTZNICK (1907–1999) succeeded Nahum Goldmann as president of the World Jewish Congress in 1977 but took a leave of absence after President Jimmy Carter appointed him as Secretary of Commerce in November 1979. Klutznick was the international president of B'nai B'rith from 1953 to 1959. In 1957, President Dwight D. Eisenhower appointed him to the US delegation to the United Nations, and he served as US representative to the UN Economic and Social Council with the rank of ambassador from 1961 to 1963. Klutznick also served as the general chairman of the United Jewish Appeal and as the president of the Memorial Foundation for Jewish Culture.

RONALD S. LAUDER was born in New York City on February 26, 1944. He received his BA in International Business from the Wharton School of the University of Pennsylvania. From 1983 to 1986, he served as US Deputy Assistant Secretary of Defense for European and NATO Affairs, and in 1986, he was appointed by President Reagan as US Ambassador to Austria. In 1987 he established the Ronald S. Lauder Foundation, which has revitalized Jewish life in Eastern and Central Europe through a network of Jewish schools, kindergartens, camps, and community centers. He is a past chairman of the Conference of Presidents of Major American Jewish Organizations, former president of the Jewish National Fund, and serves on many Jewish institutional boards. He is also a former chairman of the Board of Trustees of the Museum of Modern Art, and in 1997 he created the Commission for Art Recovery that helps retrieve artworks looted by the Nazis during World War II and return them to the heirs of their rightful owners. In 2001 he opened the Neue Galerie in New York, a museum dedicated to art from Germany and Austria from the early twentieth century. He has served as president of the World Jewish Congress since June 2007. Ambassador Lauder is married to the former Jo Carole Knopf and the father of two daughters.

NATAN LERNER was born in Poland in 1925 and received his law degree and his doctorate in law and social sciences from Buenos Aires University. He is Professor Emeritus of international law at the Radzyner Law School of the Interdisciplinary Center (IDC) Herzliya, and he previously taught at Tel Aviv University. From 1963 to 1966 Lerner was in charge of the Latin American Desk of the World Jewish Congress in New York and was director of the Israel Branch of the WJC from 1966 until 1984. He is the author of numerous books, including *Religion, Secular Beliefs and Human Rights* and *The UN Convention on the Elimination of All Forms of Racial Discrimination*.

JULIAN WILLIAM MACK (1887–1943) was an American jurist and Jewish leader. In 1910, President William Howard Taft appointed him to serve on the US Court of Appeals for the Seventh Circuit and the US Commerce Court. Mack was one of the founders of the American Jewish Committee in 1906 and, together with Rabbi Stephen S. Wise, of the American Jewish Congress in 1918. He was chairman of the *Comité des Délégations Juives* (Committee of Jewish Delegations) at the Versailles Peace Conference in 1919 and served as honorary president of the World Jewish Congress from August 1936 until his death on September 5, 1943.

ISABELLA NESPOLI is the archivist of the World Jewish Congress, based in the organization's Brussels office, and was previously the WJC's director for interfaith relations. Before joining the WJC in 1991, she was European Secretary-General of the International Movement of Catholic Students (IMCS). Nespoli edited a collection of tributes in honor of former WJC Secretary-General Gerhart M. Riegner, published on the occasion of his ninetieth birthday in 2001.

GREGG J. RICKMAN was on the staff of US Senator Alfonse M. D'Amato from 1991 to 1998; and from 1995 to 1998, he led the US Senate Banking Committee's examination of the Swiss banks and their treatment of Holocaust-era assets during and after World War II. He is the author of three books and dozens of articles on international relations and current events. One of his books, *Swiss Banks and Jewish Souls*, chronicles the Swiss banks investigation. Rickman received his BA and MA in Russian and Middle Eastern history from John Carroll University in Cleveland and his PhD in international relations from the University of Miami.

ELI M. ROSENBAUM is the world's longest-serving prosecutor and investigator of Nazi criminals and other perpetrators of human rights violations, having worked on these cases at the US Department of Justice for over thirty years, including fifteen years as the director of the former Office of Special Investigations. He has also been a corporate litigator in Manhattan with the law firm of Simpson Thacher & Bartlett, and from 1985 to 1987 he was the general counsel of the World Jewish Congress. Rosenbaum holds degrees from the Wharton School of the University of Pennsylvania (BS and MBA, finance) and Harvard Law School (JD).

MENACHEM Z. ROSENSAFT is general counsel of the World Jewish Congress, adjunct professor of law at Cornell Law School, and lecturer in law at Columbia Law School. He received MA degrees in creative writing from Johns Hopkins University and in modern European history from Columbia University, and his JD from Columbia Law School. He is the founding chairman of the International Network of Children of Jewish Holocaust Survivors, and past president of Park Avenue Synagogue in New York City. He was appointed to the US Holocaust Memorial Council by Presidents Bill Clinton and Barack Obama. Rosensaft is the editor of *God, Faith & Identity from the Ashes: Reflections of Children and Grandchildren of Holocaust Survivors.*

SUZANNE D. RUTLAND (OAM, MA (Hons), PhD, Dip Ed), Professor Emerita, Department of Hebrew, Biblical and Jewish Studies, University of Sydney, has published widely on Australian Jewish history, the Holocaust, Israel, and Jewish education, including *The Jews in Australia*. She received a government grant from the Australian Prime Minister's Centre to research Australia and the campaign for Soviet Jewry, and in 2015 she published *Let My People Go: The Untold Story of Australia and Soviet Jews, 1959–1989* with co-author Sam Lipski. In 2008 Rutland received the Medal of the Order of Australia for services to higher Jewish education and interfaith dialogue.

ZOHAR SEGEV is a professor of Jewish history and the head of the Wolfson Chair in Jewish Religious Thought and Heritage at the University of Haifa. He is the author of *The World Jewish Congress during the Holocaust: Between Activism and Restraint* and *From Ethnic Politicians to National Leaders: American Zionist Leadership, the Holocaust and the Establishment of Israel*. Segev is co-editor (with Danny Ben-Moshe) of *Israel, the Diaspora and Jewish Identity*. He received his PhD from the University of Haifa and teaches courses on American Jewish history and Zionist history.

ROBERT R. SINGER has been the CEO and executive vice president of the World Jewish Congress since May 2013. Born in Ukraine in 1956, he immigrated to Israel at the age of fifteen and graduated from Tel Aviv University with a degree in political science and history. He served in the Israel Defense Forces for eleven years and left the army with the rank of Lieutenant Colonel and then spent twelve years with the Office of the

Prime Minister in Israel in a number of senior posts. Prior to joining the WJC, Singer served for fourteen years as the CEO of World ORT, one of the world's largest non-governmental education and training providers. In 1996, he received a Masters degree in management engineering from the University of Bridgeport.

EVELYN SOMMER was born in Parana, Argentina, and is the founding president of WIZO USA. She is the representative of WIZO at the Economic and Social Council of the United Nations (ECOSOC), its commission on the Status of Women, and UNICEF. Her role as representative of a Zionist organization with consultative status at the United Nations has placed her in the forefront of the struggle against anti-Semitism in the international arena. Sommer is chair of the North American Section of the WJC, a member of the WJC's Steering Committee, and a past chair of the WJC American Section.

MARAM STERN has been deputy CEO for diplomacy of the World Jewish Congress since May 2013. Prior to assuming that position, he served as deputy secretary-general from 1996 to 2013. Based in Brussels, he is also responsible for the WJC's participation in inter-religious dialogue and consultations with Christian churches and other faiths. From 1983 to 1988, Stern was president of the European Union of Jewish Students. In 2004 he was awarded the Golden Laurel Medal of the Republic of Bulgaria and in September of that year, he was appointed as Honorary Consul of Bulgaria in Belgium (Province de Liège).

GREGORY J. WALLANCE is a lawyer in New York City, author, human rights activist, and former federal prosecutor. His most recent book is *America's Soul in the Balance: The Holocaust, FDR's State Department, and the Moral Disgrace of an American Aristocracy.* He is also the author of *Papa's Game*, about the theft of the French Connection heroin from the New York City Police Department, and the historical novel, *Two Men Before the Storm: Arba Crane's Recollection of Dred Scott and the Supreme Court Case That Started the Civil War.* Wallance is currently working on a book about Sarah Aaronsohn and the NILI (ניל״י — נצח ישראל לא ישקר netzaḥ yisra'el lo yeshakker [the Eternal One of Israel does not deceive], 1 Samuel 15:29) spy ring in World War I Palestine.

LAURENCE WEINBAUM has been with the WJC since 1994. He is director of the Israel Council on Foreign Relations (ICFR) and is the founding chief editor of *The Israel Journal of Foreign Affairs*. Weinbaum is a graduate of the School of Foreign Service of Georgetown University where he served as assistant to Jan Karski. He earned his PhD in history from Warsaw University and was the recipient of a Fulbright scholarship. Among his publications is his most recent book (in Polish), co-authored with historian Dariusz Libionka and published by the Polish Academy of Sciences, *Bohaterowie, Hochsztaplerzy, Opisywacze, Wokol Żydowskiego Związku Wojskowego* (Heroes, hucksters and story-tellers: On the Jewish military union in the Warsaw ghetto).

RABBI STEPHEN S. WISE (1874–1949) was one of the foremost American Jewish and Zionist leaders of the first half of the twentieth century. He received his rabbinic ordination from Rabbi Adolf Jellinek in Vienna in 1893, and in 1907 he established what today is called the Stephen Wise Free Synagogue, where he officiated until his death. In 1898, Wise was a delegate at the Second Zionist Congress in Basel where he met Theodor Herzl who appointed him American Secretary of the World Zionist movement. In 1918 he was one of the driving forces behind the formation of the American Jewish Congress, and in 1922 he founded the Jewish Institute of Religion, which merged in 1950 with Hebrew Union College. Beginning in the 1920s Wise advocated the creation of an international Jewish organization that would represent the interests of Jews across the globe. After Hitler's rise to power in 1933, he led the movement to boycott Nazi Germany because of its anti-Semitic policies. He was elected chairman of the Executive Committee of the World Jewish Congress at the WJC's first plenary assembly in Geneva and became the organization's president in 1944.

Photograph Credits

Index